"The Book of Revelation's Hidden Warning for America"

THE
TRUMPET
I

THE **ANCIENT PROPHECY** THAT
REVEALS **AMERICA'S FINAL HOUR**

LORI ANN MOESZINGER

THE RIDGE

PUBLISHING GROUP

THE RIDGE PUBLISHING GROUP
COUER D'ALENE, IDAHO

THE RIDGE

PUBLISHING GROUP

The Ridge Publishing Group
Visit us at https://www.RidgePublishingGroup.com

The Ridge Publishing Group is headquartered in Coeur d'Alene, Idaho, 83814 USA.

The name, house mark, logo, and all associated trademarks—including *Guardians of Biblical Truth* and *New Narrated Study Bible (NNSB)*—are trademarks or service marks of The Ridge Publishing Group.

All Scripture quotations are taken from the Holy Bible, King James Version (KJV), translated out of the original tongues and published in 1611, with the former translations diligently compared and revised.

Cover design by Eric Moeszinger
Interior design and images by Guardians of Biblical Truth

ABOUT THE NEW NARRATED STUDY BIBLE (NNSB)

Guardians of Biblical Truth Publishing Group, an imprint of The Ridge Publishing Group, proudly presents the NEW NARRATED STUDY BIBLE (NNSB)—a bold, immersive translation of Scripture arranged in chronological order and enriched with vivid fictional narrative. Unlike any Bible you've encountered, the NNSB preserves the full integrity of God's Word while illuminating biblical events, people, and prophetic themes through engaging storytelling. This creative approach makes Scripture more accessible to every generation, helping readers experience the redemptive story from beginning to end.

Library of Congress Cataloging-in-Publication Data

Names: Moeszinger, Lori Ann, author
Title: *The Trumpet I: The Ancient Prophecy That Reveals America's Final Hour*

Description: The Book of Revelation NNSB edition. | Idaho : The Ridge Publishing Group, 2025. | Includes biblical text reference.

Identifiers: LCCN 2025909981 | ISBN 978-1-956905-58-8 (hardcover) | ISBN 978-1-956905-59-5 (softcover) | 978-1-956905-60-1 (e-book)

Subjects: Religion, Biblical Studies, Prophecy | Religion, Eschatology | Religion, Christian Theology, Apocalyptic and Eschatology | Fiction, Christian, Futuristic

Printed in the United States of America

To the watchmen on the wall, the seekers of truth, and those who refuse to slumber in this late hour. May this book awaken what the Spirit is still whispering—before the trumpet sounds.

Contents

AUTHOR'S NOTE

What you are about to read is presented in the form of a story, but at its core, it is a deep and reverent exploration of the Book of Revelation.

All Scripture quotations are taken from the 1611 Authorized King James Version (KJV), with slight revisions for clarity—similar to the approach used in modern translations such as the NLT, NIV, NKJV, NASB, ESV, and NEB. Indented sections contain direct Scripture, while the surrounding narrative includes interpretation, explanation, and storytelling—drawn from my vision, my research, my spiritual insight, and my voice.

One of the most profound discoveries I made while writing *The Trumpet* is the remarkable interconnectedness between the Book of Revelation and the Old Testament. Nearly every verse echoes earlier prophecies, divine patterns, and foreshadows of what is to come—together painting a unified picture of God's redemptive plan and prophetic timeline. For this reason, I have included select Old Testament references throughout, to highlight the inseparable bond between the Testaments.

As we examine America's prophetic role in the end times, it's important to understand that this book is only the beginning. *The Vanishing: The Day Will Begin Like Any Other—Until the Rapture Silences the World* will further explore biblical cycles, Shemitah years, and our current place in prophetic history.

It is my prayer that *The Trumpet I: The Ancient Prophecy That Reveals America's Final Hour* (covering Revelation 1–11) and *The Trumpet II: The Prophecy Continues—America's Final Hour Unveiled* (covering Revelation 12–22) will bring biblical prophecy to life—awakening insight, stirring conviction, and equipping readers with wisdom for what is coming and how to prepare.

Preface

For centuries, the Book of Revelation has both captivated and confounded scholars, theologians, and truth-seekers alike. It is a book of mystery, prophecy, and divine unveiling. Yet one question remains largely unexamined.

IS AMERICA IN THE BIBLE?

To many, the idea seems implausible. After all, the United States was founded long after the last words of Scripture were written. But what if the Bible is more than a historical record? What if it is our pre-written story—past, present, and future—divinely authored and recorded long before nations like America even existed?

If Scripture is God's revelation to humanity, then it stands to reason that no major world power—especially one as influential as the United States—would be excluded from its prophetic timeline. The real question isn't *whether* America is in the Bible, but rather, *where*?

The Bible is filled with harbingers—divine warnings and prophetic patterns meant to guide, correct, and forewarn nations and people of impending judgment or redemption. From the fall of Babylon to the rise of Rome, Scripture offers a prophetic blueprint for how God moves through history. This shows us that history is not chaotic or random, but unfolding according to a sovereign plan.

If God, in His infinite wisdom, foretold the rise and fall of ancient empires, then we must ask: Does America have a place in the biblical narrative? Are there clues within the pages of prophecy that reveal America's destiny—either as a nation blessed by divine purpose or one standing at the threshold of judgment?

WHAT THIS BOOK REVEALS

The Trumpet I: The Ancient Prophecy That Reveals America's Final Hour is the result of years of study in Bible prophecy, eschatology, and scriptural patterns. It walks readers through the Book of Revelation—uncovering two key chapters that offer undeniable evidence of America's presence in the prophetic timeline.

But the trail of truth doesn't end there. Both the Old and New Testaments confirm this revelation—revealing that America's role in the end times is not speculation, but a biblically grounded reality.

In these pages, you will discover:

- The two chapters in Revelation that unveil America's prophetic destiny.
- How ancient harbingers mirror America's modern trajectory.
- Why Scripture has always spoken of the fate of great nations.
- How present-day events align with long-foretold prophecy.
- What the Bible says about America's future—and what is coming next.

This is not just another end times book. It is a wake-up call—a challenge to read the Bible with new eyes and recognize that the truth about America's prophetic role has been hidden in plain sight.

But this is only the beginning.

The Trumpet I explores Revelation chapters 1 through 11, laying the foundation for understanding God's message to the Church, the seals and trumpet judgments to come, and America's unique position in this divine timeline.

To complete the journey, *The Trumpet II: The Prophecy Continues—America's Final Hour Unveiled* takes readers through Revelation 12 to 22, unveiling the rise of the Antichrist and the False Prophet, the battle for Israel, the return of the King, and the climactic hour of judgment and glory.

Together, these two volumes form a complete prophetic blueprint—one message, one warning, one hope. So, are we in the final days?

- Is America part of God's divine plan—or nearing judgment?
- Will we recognize the signs—or ignore the harbingers before us?
- The answers have been there all along, hidden in prophecy, waiting for those willing to seek and find.

The journey begins now.

Chapter 1

An Ancient Mystery

THE HARBINGER—The cafe was quiet, the scent of fresh coffee lingering in the air as I slid the manuscript across the small table. Irene, my publisher, adjusted her reading glasses and picked it up, her fingers tracing the title on the first page. She looked at me, curious but cautious.

"You always bring me something interesting, Ann, but this—" she taps the title "—feels different. '*The Trumpet I: The Ancient Prophecy That Reveals America's Final Hour.*' You really think you've uncovered something that scholars, theologians, and prophecy experts have missed?"

I leaned back, clasping my hands together. "Not just think, Irene. I know. The world is changing too fast for this to be coincidence. We are watching Bible prophecy unfold in real-time. The Book of Daniel. The Book of Revelation. Everything they wrote is happening right now."

She raised an eyebrow, flipping through the pages. "Ann, you know I love prophecy books, but people have been saying 'we're in the last days' for centuries. How is your book any different?"

I leaned forward; voice steady. "Because for centuries, people assumed the prophecies of the Bible were either symbolic or meant for some distant future. But what if that future is now? What if the signs we've been warned about—the harbingers—are happening at this very moment?"

Irene sipped her coffee, contemplating my words. I knew she was skeptical, but I also knew the weight of what I was about to tell her.

"Look around. The world is spiraling—faster than ever before. The moral decay, the economic instability, the push for global governance, digital control, religious compromise—it's all part of a preordained script written thousands of years ago. The Bible is not just a collection of ancient stories. It's a prophetic timeline, and we are at the final countdown."

She sighed, setting the manuscript down. "Okay, let's say I'm intrigued. What's the evidence? What makes you so certain we're living in the final moments before the end of the age?"

I exhaled, knowing this was where it all began. "Because the signs are all around us. Daniel and John saw things they couldn't fully understand in their time, but we—living in this age—can now see them unfolding exactly as they described."

I reached for my bag, pulling out my worn Bible. I flipped through its pages, landing on Daniel's vision.

"Take Daniel's prophecy, for example. He saw a time when knowledge would increase, when people would run to and fro. Doesn't that sound like the explosion of technology, AI, digital surveillance, and globalization? Or what about John's vision in Revelation? He saw a future where a world leader would rise, where people would be controlled by an economic system that determines who can buy or sell—doesn't that sound eerily like the digital currencies and biometric tracking systems being developed today?"

She stared at me, her fingers tapping the manuscript thoughtfully. "You're saying the signs aren't coming. They're already here."

Nodding. "Exactly. And they aren't just vague signs. They're harbingers—divine warnings—telling us we're at the final countdown before the world enters its most chaotic era."

She leaned back in her chair, staring out the cafe window. "Alright. I'll bite. But here's my question, Ann—where does America fit into all this?"

I smiled. That was the very question that led me to write this book. And it was the question I knew would change everything.

"That's where things get even more shocking. America isn't missing from the Bible—it's hidden in plain sight. And by the time we're done, you won't just believe it . . . you'll see it."

Irene sat forward, flipping to the first section of my manuscript. I had her attention now—and this was only the beginning.

THE UNMISTAKABLE SIGNS OF THE END TIMES

Irene adjusted her glasses and leaned forward, flipping to the next section of my manuscript. Her expression had shifted—from curiosity to concern.

"Alright, Ann. You've got my attention. You're saying we're in the final countdown, that prophecy is unfolding right now. But let's get specific. What exactly are the signs we should be looking for?"

I tapped my finger on the manuscript, nodding.

"I thought you'd ask that. The Bible doesn't leave us guessing—it gives us clear prophetic markers, and they're all manifesting now. Let me break it down for you."

The Rise of Globalist Elites

"First, let's talk about power—real power. Not the politicians you see on TV, but the ones behind the scenes. There's a group of ultra-powerful individuals, corporations, and institutions working to collapse national sovereignty, personal freedoms, and economic stability."

Irene frowned, flipping through some of my notes.

"You mean the whole 'New World Order' thing?"

"Call it whatever you want, but it's not a conspiracy—it's their stated agenda. Just look at the World Economic Forum (WEF), the United Nations (UN), and global banking institutions. They're pushing for a 'Great Reset'—a total reimagining of how the world operates. And their vision eerily matches what the Bible describes as the rise of a One World Government."

I pulled out my phone and scrolled through bookmarked articles: WEF's 2016 article about the future of global economies, discussing a shift toward renting over ownership.

"Klaus Schwab, head of the WEF, openly says, 'You will own nothing, and you will be happy.' They want to eliminate private property, redefine capitalism, and centralize power under a global authority. Sound familiar?"

Irene's brows knitted together as she skimmed that page.

"Yeah . . . Revelation talks about that, doesn't it? A system where people are totally controlled?"

"Exactly. And they're using fear—economic collapse, pandemics, climate change—to push the world toward surrendering their freedoms in exchange for 'safety and stability.' It's happening faster than people realize."

The Formation of a One World System in Finance, Technology, and Governance

Irene tapped her pen on the table.

"Okay, but the world's always had powerful people pulling strings. What makes this different?"

"Because this time, the infrastructure for a One World System is already being built. It's not theoretical anymore—it's here."

I flipped open my Bible and pointed to Revelation 13.

> And that no man might buy or sell, except he that had the mark, or the name of the beast, or the number of his name. (Revelation 13:17)

"The Bible predicts an economic system where total financial control is enforced. Look at what's happening now—Central Bank Digital Currencies (CBDCs) are being rolled out across the world. Cash is disappearing. Everything is going digital, which means total surveillance and control."

Irene sat back, processing.

"And with digital currency, the government—or whoever's in charge—could freeze your money if you don't comply."

"Exactly! And it's not just finance. AI-driven surveillance, biometric tracking, social credit scores—all of it is designed to monitor and control populations. The lines between nations are blurring, and governments are destabilizing. The world is being prepped to accept a centralized system of governance. And people will welcome it because they'll be desperate."

Irene let out a slow breath, shaking her head.

"It's terrifying how fast things are moving."

"And it gets worse."

The Corruption of Religious Institutions

I watched Irene brace herself, flipping the page.

"One of the biggest signs of the end times is what's happening in the Church," I continued. "Christianity was once the moral foundation of Western civilization. But look at it now."

Irene sighed, rubbing her temples.

"Yeah. Churches today barely sound like churches anymore."

"Because many have abandoned the authority of Scripture. They've traded truth for social agendas, cultural trends, and universalism. It's exactly what Bible prophecy said would happen—a One World Religion that dilutes the gospel and welcomes a false messiah."

I pointed to another verse.

> For the time will come when they will not endure sound doctrine; but after their own lusts shall they heap to themselves teachers, having itching ears. (2 Timothy 4:3)

"The Bible warns that in the last days, people will reject sound doctrine and embrace deception. We're seeing it now—churches promoting moral compromise, replacing the gospel with feel-good messages, and even merging with other religions in the name of 'unity.'"

"And that paves the way for the One World Religion."

"Exactly. A faith system that removes Christ as the only way to God and promotes tolerance over truth."

Irene shook her head, crossing her arms.

"It's all coming together, isn't it?"

The Increase in Natural Disasters and Geopolitical Conflicts

"And let's not forget the chaos happening in nature and geopolitics. Jesus warned that before the end, there would be an increase in wars, famines, pestilences, and earthquakes."

> For nation shall rise against nation, and kingdom against kingdom: and there shall be famines, and pestilences, and earthquakes, in diverse places. All these are the beginning of sorrows. (Matthew 24:7–8)

"Look at the world right now—earthquakes, wildfires, record-breaking storms. Wars and rumors of wars. Food shortages, supply chain collapses, disease outbreaks. It's all happening at once, just as Jesus predicted."

"And you're saying these aren't just random events?"

"No. They're contractions. Birth pains. Warnings that the world is heading toward something final."

Irene drummed her fingers on the table, her mind visibly racing.

"I never thought I'd live to see this."

"Most people didn't. That's why they're not paying attention. But it's all unfolding just as the Scripture said it would."

Irene exhaled, sitting back in her chair. She stared at my manuscript, then at me.

"Alright. You've convinced me that we're in the middle of something big. But here's what I still don't understand."

She looked me directly in the eye.

"Where is America in all of this?"

I smiled. That was the question—the one that changes everything.

"That's exactly what this book is about. America is in the Bible. It's been there all along. And once you see it, you'll never be able to unsee it."

Irene picked up her coffee, staring into it as if trying to process everything. She nodded, flipping to the next section. Now, she was hooked.

AMERICA—THE MISSING PIECE OF THE PROPHETIC PUZZLE?

Irene sat back in her chair, arms crossed, a skeptical expression on her face. I could tell she was processing everything we had discussed so far, but there was still hesitation.

"Alright, Ann. You've laid out the signs—the rise of globalism, financial control, religious deception, and increasing disasters. It's all compelling, and honestly, a little unsettling."

She tapped her pen against the manuscript, eyes narrowing.

"But what I don't understand is America's role in all of this. You're telling me the Bible has predicted everything, from Babylon to Rome, and it didn't just skip over the most powerful nation in modern history? That doesn't add up."

I smiled. This was the moment—the question I had spent years wrestling with myself.

"I thought the same thing. For generations, prophecy teachers have insisted that America isn't in the Bible. But what if we've been looking at it the wrong way? What if America's prophetic destiny has been hidden in plain sight?"

Irene's skepticism deepened, but I could see the curiosity flickering in her eyes.

"Alright, I'll bite. If America is in the Bible, why hasn't anyone figured it out before?"

I leaned forward, lowering my voice slightly, as if revealing a long-guarded secret.

"Because prophecy is revealed in its appointed time. Daniel himself was told to 'seal up the vision' until the end. The pieces didn't make sense until history unfolded."

I flipped open my Bible to Daniel.

But you, Daniel, shut up the words and seal the book, even to the time of the end: many shall run to and fro, and knowledge shall increase. (Daniel 12:4)

"God's timeline has always been exact. Babylon, Medo-Persia, Greece, and Rome—each empire was named in Scripture long before they rose to power. And each one played a critical role in fulfilling God's divine plan."

Irene nodded slowly, thinking.

"Okay. But why wouldn't America be mentioned explicitly? If it's as important as you say, why not name it like the others?"

"Two reasons. First, the Bible often uses symbolic language to describe future nations. Think about how John described the final empire in Revelation—he didn't call it by a modern name because the name didn't exist yet. Instead, he gave us characteristics that we could recognize when the time was right."

And I stood upon the sand of the sea, and saw a beast rise up out of the sea, having seven heads and ten horns, and upon his horns ten crowns, and upon his heads the name of blasphemy. And the beast which I saw was like unto a leopard, and his feet were as the feet of a bear, and his mouth of a lion: and the dragon gave him his power, and his seat, and great authority. (Revelation 13:1–2)

I watched as Irene jotted down notes, her interest growing.

"Second, there are two major viewpoints about America's prophetic role. Some believe that America isn't mentioned because it will be destroyed or become irrelevant before the final prophecies unfold."

Frowning. "Destroyed? As in, wiped off the map?"

"Not necessarily in a single moment, but look at history—every great nation that turned away from God eventually collapsed. And America is following that same pattern. Moral decay, political corruption, economic instability—these are the signs of a nation under judgment."

Irene exhaled, tapping her fingers against the table, as if weighing the idea.

"And the other viewpoint?"

"That America is in the Bible, but it's been hidden in symbolic language—waiting for the right time to be revealed."

I reached for my manuscript and turned to the section I had marked earlier.

"Think about it, Irene. The Bible describes a final global empire that will dominate the world before the return of Christ. It also warns of judgment upon nations that turn away from God and embrace wickedness. And throughout history, God has always used nations for His purposes—raising them up and bringing them down according to His plan."

The Most High rules in the kingdom of men, and gives it to whomsoever He will. (Daniel 4:17)

"The question isn't whether America is in the Bible. The question is—have we failed to recognize it?"

Irene's expression shifted—concern flickering in her eyes.

"So you're saying America's fate is already sealed?"

"Not necessarily. But prophecy warns that nations who reject God don't last. America, once a beacon of Christianity and freedom, is now at a crossroads. The real question is—will we see the truth before it's too late?"

Irene closed my manuscript and sat back, arms crossed, deep in thought. She looked at me, and for the first time since we started, her voice was quieter.

"I need to read more."

I smiled. She was beginning to see it. And this was only the beginning.

AMERICA'S ROLE IN THE END TIMES

Irene tapped her pen against the manuscript, her brows furrowed in thought. The cafe had grown quieter, the morning rush fading into a lull. She looked up at me, her expression skeptical, but no longer dismissive.

"Ann, you're saying America is in the Bible—hidden in prophecy. But what about its role in the end times? Are you telling me the United States isn't just another nation in history but an actual player in biblical prophecy?"

I leaned forward; my voice steady.

"I'm saying exactly that. America isn't just mentioned—it has a critical role in the final events. And that role isn't one of salvation or revival—it's one of judgment."

Irene exhaled, flipping to the next page in my manuscript.

"Okay . . . explain."

"Look at history. Nations rise and fall based on their spiritual condition. When they honor God, they thrive. When they turn away, judgment follows. It happened to Israel. It happened to Babylon. It happened to Rome. And now . . ." I tapped the table for emphasis. ". . . it's happening to America."

Irene studied me, waiting for more.

"America was founded on biblical principles—its very structure was built on God's moral law. But look where we are now: the moral collapse, the rebellion against God, the open celebration of sin. It's not just cultural decay, Irene—it's spiritual warfare."

The Spiritual Forces Behind America's Decline

Irene glanced at her notes, then back at me.

"So, you're saying the decline isn't just political or social—it's spiritual?"

"Absolutely. The same demonic forces that corrupted Babylon, Rome, and every other fallen empire are at work in America today. And they're using deception as their greatest weapon."

I pointed to my manuscript, where I had outlined key areas of deception:

- Technology and Transhumanism—The rapid advancement of artificial intelligence, genetic modification, and human-machine integration is moving toward something beyond human control. The Bible warns that in the last days, man will seek to become like God—but it will lead to destruction.
- The Redefining of Morality—What was once considered evil is now celebrated. What was once sacred is now mocked. Gender, family, life,

truth—everything that God established is under attack. And it's happening at an unprecedented speed.

- The Suppression of Biblical Truth—Christians who stand for truth are labeled as intolerant, dangerous, even criminal. The world isn't just rejecting God—it's criminalizing His followers. And that's exactly what prophecy foretells.

Irene leaned back; arms crossed.

"I can't argue with that. But deception has always existed. Why is this different?"

"Because Jesus said the deception in the last days would be unlike anything before—so powerful that even the elect could be led astray."

For false Christs and false prophets shall rise, and shall show signs and wonders, to seduce, if it were possible, even the elect. (Mark 13:22)

A Nation on the Edge of Judgment

Irene's fingers traced the rim of her coffee cup as she stared at the page. I could see the weight of it settling in.

"So . . . where does that leave us? Is America doomed?"

"The trajectory isn't good. Every nation that defied God eventually fell. America is following the same pattern. And just like with Israel and Babylon, the warnings have already been given—but few are listening."

And the LORD says, Because they have forsaken My law which I set before them, and have not obeyed My voice, neither walked therein; But have walked after the imagination of their own heart, and after Baalim, which their fathers taught them: Thus says the LORD of hosts, the God of Israel; Behold, I will feed them, even this people, with wormwood (bitter substance or plant), and give them water of gall to drink. I will scatter them also among the nations, whom neither they nor their fathers have known: and I will send a sword after them, till I have consumed them. (Jeremiah 9:13–16)

"This is why we can't afford to be passive. The deception is already here. The judgment is coming. And many Christians won't be ready."

Irene let out a slow breath, shaking her head.

"So what do we do?"

I met her gaze, my voice unwavering.

"We prepare. We open our eyes. We wake up the Church. Because whether people realize it or not . . . the clock is almost at midnight."

She didn't argue this time. She just nodded, flipping to the next page. And I knew . . . she was starting to see it.

IS AMERICA IN THE BIBLE?

Irene adjusted her glasses and flipped to the next section of my manuscript. She looked up at me, skeptical as ever, but something in her expression told me she was starting to wonder.

"Okay, Ann. I'll admit, the signs are there. The world is heading toward something big. But this is the part I still don't get—if America is so important, why isn't it clearly named in the Bible? Why not just say 'the United States' like it does Babylon, Greece, or Rome?"

I smiled. I knew this question was coming—it was another one of those questions I had wrestled with for years.

"Because prophecy doesn't work that way. Again, the Bible wasn't written to give us modern names; it was written to give us patterns and characteristics so we would recognize things when the time was right."

I tapped my manuscript, then flipped open my Bible to Daniel.

"Look at Daniel's visions. When he described the rise of empires, he didn't call them by their modern names—he used symbols. A lion for Babylon. A bear for Medo-Persia. A leopard for Greece. A terrifying beast for Rome. Each nation was described by its attributes and influence, not by its name."

Irene nodded slowly, considering.

"So what you're saying is . . . just because the Bible doesn't say 'America' outright doesn't mean it isn't there."

"Exactly. And if we believe the Bible is the inspired, infallible, and prophetic Word of God, then we have to accept that it's fully capable of foretelling not just ancient history, but the rise and fall of modern nations too—including America."

America's Global Influence: Too Big to Ignore

Irene leaned back, crossing her arms.

"But how do you know for sure? Couldn't America just be another nation, one that fades into history before the final prophecies unfold?"

"That's exactly what some people argue. There are two common views on this: either America isn't in the Bible at all because it will collapse before the end times, or it is there, but hidden in prophetic language. But let's think about this logically for a second—"

I glanced around the cafe, then looked back at her, lowering my voice.

"If the Bible has foretold the rise of Babylon, Medo-Persia, Greece, and Rome—four of the most powerful empires in world history—how could it possibly skip over America? A nation that has shaped global economics, military strategy, culture, and morality more than any other in the modern era?"

Irene tilted her head, thinking.

"That's a fair point. The U.S. has been the dominant world power for the last century. You'd think something that significant would be mentioned somewhere."

"Exactly! And that's where people get it wrong. They assume because 'America' isn't spelled out in black and white, it must not exist in prophecy. But the Bible doesn't work like that. It uses symbols and foreshadowing, waiting for the appointed time for those things to be revealed."

A Nation Hidden in Plain Sight

Irene drummed her fingers on the table, flipping back through some of the earlier pages. I could see her skepticism softening.

"Okay, Ann. I'll admit, that makes sense. But you still haven't told me where exactly America is in prophecy."

I smiled, pushing my coffee cup aside.

"That part I can't just tell you—I have to show you. Because like I said, once you see it, you'll never be able to unsee it."

Irene smirked.

"That sounds like something a prophet would say."

Grinning. "Then maybe it's time we hear from one."

I turned the page to the next section, where John the Apostle—writer of the Book of Revelation—would begin to reveal America's role in the final days.

AMERICA'S FATE IN BIBLE PROPHECY: THE SHOCKING TRUTH

Irene set down her coffee cup and folded her arms, staring at me like she was trying to solve a puzzle.

"Alright, Ann, let's say I accept that the Bible speaks in symbols. Let's say I even accept that America's role has been hidden, waiting for the right time to be revealed. But how do you know for sure? How do you connect modern America to biblical prophecy?"

I reached for my Bible and flipped to the Book of Daniel, running my finger over the well-worn pages.

"Because history follows patterns. And the Bible is filled with them. Every major world empire—Babylon, Medo-Persia, Greece, and Rome—was foretold in prophecy. Each played a critical role in shaping world events. And each was judged for its rebellion against God."

I paused, letting that sink in before I continued.

"America is no different. It has followed the same trajectory—rising to power, influencing the world, shaping economies, militaries, and even morality. And now? It's following the same pattern of decline that doomed the great empires before it."

Irene frowned, flipping through my manuscript.

"But doesn't Revelation describe the final world power as a global system? A kind of empire that dominates before the last judgment? How do you know that's not just some future government instead of America?"

I leaned in, lowering my voice slightly, knowing this was where it got even more interesting.

"Because the Bible doesn't just speak in broad terms—it gives characteristics of this final power. It describes a nation that is wealthy, influential, morally corrupt, and deeply entangled in global affairs. It describes a nation that will lead the world into deception, one that started strong but turned away from God. Sound familiar?"

Irene's jaw tightened. She didn't answer right away, and I knew why.

"It does sound familiar."

The Biblical Pattern of Judgment

I tapped my Bible, continuing.

"This isn't just my opinion, Irene. The Bible has a clear pattern when it comes to nations. It blesses those who follow God and judges those who rebel against Him. Babylon, Egypt, Rome—each of them had their moment of warning before destruction came."

> For the nation and kingdom that will not serve You shall perish; yea, those nations shall be utterly wasted. (Isaiah 60:12)

"And now, look at America. It was founded on Christian principles, dedicated to freedom and righteousness. But today? It's leading the charge in moral corruption, rebellion against God, and the normalization of sin."

Irene sighed, rubbing her temple.

"So, you're saying that America isn't missing from prophecy—it's just been misinterpreted?"

"Exactly. People have overlooked it because they didn't want to believe that a nation once dedicated to God could become the very thing prophecy warns about."

Irene exhaled sharply, tapping her fingers on the table.

"Alright. I can't deny that America has changed. But are you saying we're past the point of no return? Is there no hope?"

I held her gaze, my voice firm but not without hope.

"That depends. If history teaches us anything, it's that God always gives a warning before judgment. The question is . . . will we listen before it's too late?"

Irene stared at me, silent. Then, slowly, she nodded and turned the page. She was beginning to see it. And deep down, I knew she felt what I felt—something was coming. And America's place in prophecy was clearer than ever before.

THE TWO CHAPTERS THAT REVEAL AMERICA'S PROPHECY

Irene flipped the page, then stopped. She looked up at me, curiosity flickering in her eyes.

"Wait—you're telling me that America's prophecy isn't just hinted at in Scripture—it's actually laid out in two specific chapters of Revelation?"

I nodded, watching her reaction.

"Yes. Two chapters that, once you read them with fresh eyes, makes it unmistakably clear. They describe America's role, its rise, and ultimately, its fate."

Leaning forward, intrigued. "Which two chapters?"

I shook my head, smiling.

"Not yet. You have to see it unfold step by step. If I just told you, you'd read them the way you always have—without realizing what's hidden in plain sight."

She exhaled, but I could tell she was hooked now.

"Alright, fine. But tell me this—why haven't prophecy teachers figured this out before?"

I pointed to her Bible, open beside her coffee cup. "Because prophecy is revealed in its appointed time. Even John, who wrote Revelation, didn't understand everything he saw. That's why Jesus told him—"

He who has ears to hear, let him hear what the Spirit says to the churches. (Revelation 2:7)

"People couldn't see it before because the pieces hadn't fallen into place. But now? The signs are all around us. The timing is right. And once you see what's written in these two chapters, you'll never look at prophecy the same way again."

Irene sat back, arms crossed, studying me. Finally, she nodded.

"Fine. Show me."

I reached for the next section of my manuscript, flipping to the beginning of the chapter. This was where everything would change.

THE HARBINGER OF JUDGMENT

Irene rubbed her temples and leaned back in her chair. She had been skeptical at first, but now I could see the concern settling in. She let out a slow breath and looked up at me.

"Ann, this keeps getting heavier. First, you show me that America is in prophecy. Then, you explain how it's been building the system for a One World Order. And now, you're telling me it's also following the exact pattern of nations that were judged in the Bible?"

I nodded; my voice steady.

"That's right. And not just any pattern—the harbinger of judgment."

Irene sat forward, flipping to the next page in my manuscript.

"Okay, walk me through this. You're saying that God warns nations before He judges them?"

I opened my Bible and pointed to a verse:

The LORD does nothing without revealing His plan to His servants the prophets. (Amos 3:7)

"God is merciful, Irene. He never brings judgment without first sending a warning. Look at history—Babylon, Assyria, Rome—all were given divine warnings before their destruction. The prophets warned them, but they refused to listen. And what happened? Their downfall was swift."

Irene nodded, flipping back and forth between pages.

"Okay . . . but what makes you think America is at that point?"

I leaned forward, voice firm.

"Because the warning signs are here. And they match exactly what happened before those empires collapsed."

America's Warning Signs of Judgment

- A Moral and Spiritual Decline—America's rapid descent into moral chaos mirrors ancient Rome before its fall. Sin is not only accepted but celebrated. Biblical values are mocked. The nation that once stood as a beacon of faith now leads the world in rebellion against God.
- Political Corruption and National Division—The Bible warns that a nation divided against itself cannot stand. America is more divided now than ever—politically, socially, and spiritually. Corruption runs deep, and instead of working to unite, leaders are tearing the country apart from within.

Every kingdom divided against itself is brought to desolation; and every city or house divided against itself shall not stand. (Matthew 12:25)

- Economic Instability and Growing Global Debt—Babylon was wealthy before its collapse. Rome was powerful before it crumbled. America is following the same path. The debt is unsustainable, inflation is rising, and the financial system is unraveling—just as prophesied in the Bible.

- Natural Disasters and Global Conflicts—Jesus warned in Matthew 24 that before the end, there would be "wars and rumors of wars," earthquakes, famines, and pestilences. We're seeing these "birth pains" increase, just as prophecy foretold.

And you shall hear of wars and rumors of wars: see that you be not troubled: for all these things must come to pass, but the end is not yet. (Matthew 24:6)

"Ann . . . this is overwhelming. If all of this is true, then what you're saying is . . . we're on the edge of prophetic fulfillment?"

Quietly. "Yes. If history repeats itself—and it always does—America is standing on the very edge."

Irene exhaled, staring at my manuscript in front of her. She tapped her fingers on the table, then looked up at me with a seriousness I hadn't seen before.

"So the real question is . . . will we listen to the warning, or will we follow the same path as every fallen empire before us?"

I nodded, and we both knew the answer was coming. The only question now was—would the world be ready for it?

THE FINAL EMPIRE: UNVEILING THE ONE WORLD SYSTEM

Irene leaned forward, her fingers tapping against my manuscript as she scanned the next section. Her usual skepticism was shifting into something else—unease.

"Ann," she said, lifting her gaze, "this is starting to sound less like speculation and more like reality. You're telling me the Bible didn't just predict the rise and fall of individual nations—it actually lays out a blueprint for a final global empire?"

I nodded, flipping my Bible open to Revelation.

"That's exactly what it says. The Bible isn't just a collection of ancient stories—it's a prophetic timeline. And one of its biggest warnings is about the emergence of a final, dominant world empire that will rise in the last days."

Irene crossed her arms. "A global empire? Sounds like something out of a dystopian movie."

I smiled grimly. "That's what people used to think. For centuries, the idea of a One World System seemed impossible—just a wild conspiracy. But now? It's happening in real-time."

She raised an eyebrow. "Alright. Show me."

I pointed to Revelation 13 and began reading:

And he causes all, both small and great, rich and poor, free and bond, to receive a mark on their right hand, or on their foreheads: And that no man might buy or sell, except he that had the mark. (Revelation 13:16–17)

"This prophecy describes total global control—economic, political, religious, and military—under one ruling system. And that system? It's already forming."

The Blueprint for the Final Empire

Irene flipped to the next page in my notes. "Okay, let's break this down. You're saying this One World System will control more than just politics?"

"Yes. It's a five-part system, and every piece is already being built."

1.   One World Government

"World leaders and global organizations are openly calling for the end of national sovereignty. The push for a 'Great Reset' is just the beginning—global governance is the goal."

2.   One World Economy

"Digital currencies, AI-driven banking, and the elimination of cash are moving us toward complete financial surveillance. The infrastructure of the 'mark of the beast' system is already in place."

Irene frowned. "You mean, like the Central Bank Digital Currencies (CBDCs)?"

I nodded. "Exactly. Once cash is eliminated, every financial transaction will be tracked, monitored, and—if necessary—restricted."

3.   One World Military

"International military coalitions like NATO and the UN have more power than ever. The idea of a global security force enforcing world laws isn't science fiction—it's a reality waiting for the right crisis to activate it."

4.   One World Religion

"Traditional Christianity is being compromised in favor of a unified, inclusive global faith. Many religious leaders are abandoning biblical doctrine in favor of a system that will ultimately pave the way for the Antichrist's rule."

5.   One World Leader

"And finally, this system is waiting for one man to rise—the Antichrist. He will unite the world under a false banner of peace."

Irene leaned back, rubbing her temples. "Okay. I'll admit, that's . . . a lot. But doesn't every generation think their time is the end? What makes this different?"

I exhaled, meeting her gaze. "Because, Irene, for the first time in history, all of these things are happening at the same time. Every piece is in place. The infrastructure for this global system isn't just being built—it's being openly promoted."

I read from Luke 21:28:

When these things begin to come to pass, then look up, and lift up your heads; for your redemption draws near. (Luke 21:28)

Irene exhaled, shaking her head. "So you're telling me . . . the system is already here, waiting for the right crisis to make it official?"

Quietly, I responded. "That's exactly what I'm telling you."

For the first time since we started, Irene was silent. She wasn't arguing. She wasn't debating. She was just staring at the pages in front of her, realizing—maybe for the first time—that everything she thought she knew about the future was about to change.

The Road to a One World System

After a long pause, Irene turned the page, still shaking her head as she read through the next section.

"Ann, you keep talking about a final world system, but I have to admit—I didn't think it would be this obvious. You're saying the infrastructure for the Antichrist's empire is already being built? Right now?"

I nodded, flipping back to Revelation 13:16–17.

"It's not just being built—it's being actively promoted. And the scary part? Most people don't even see it happening."

Irene exhaled sharply. "Alright. Let's breaks this down. What are the clear signs that we're on this road?"

I laid out the facts.

1.   Digital Currencies Are Replacing Cash

"Governments and financial institutions are aggressively pushing Central Bank Digital Currencies (CBDCs). Once cash is gone, every transaction will be tracked, monitored, and—if necessary—restricted."

2.   AI Surveillance and Social Credit Systems

"China already has a social credit system that determines whether people can travel, get loans, or even buy groceries based on their compliance with government mandates."

Irene's brow furrowed. "You're telling me they want to control everything about people's lives?"

I nodded. "It's not a theory, Irene. It's happening. AI-driven surveillance, digital IDs, and facial recognition technology are already being used worldwide. It's just a matter of time before they become mandatory."

3. The UN, WEF, and global organizations are pushing for the 'Great Reset'

I pulled up a quote on my phone and slid it toward her.

> "The COVID-19 pandemic represents a rare but narrow
> window of opportunity to reflect, reimagine, and reset our
> world."—Klaus Schwab, Founder and Executive Chairman of
> the World Economic Forum (WEF)

Irene read the words, then exhaled sharply. "Okay . . . that's unsettling."

"It should be. The UN, the WEF, and other globalists are actively working to dismantle the old world order and replace it with a centralized global government. They're using climate change, economic instability, and social justice as the justification for total control."

Everything the Bible Predicted Is Happening Now

Irene put down my manuscript and looked at me, her eyes filled with a mix of unease and realization.

"Ann . . . I don't even know what to say. I always thought of prophecy as something distant. But you're telling me it's happening right now?"

Softly, I answered. "Yes. And it's moving fast. The final empire isn't coming—it's already here. The pieces are in place. All that's missing is the leader who will bring them together."

Irene leaned forward, her voice quieter now.

"And when that leader comes . . . what happens to America?"

I met her gaze, flipping to the next section of my manuscript.

"That's what we're about to find out."

She turned the page, and we both knew—there was no turning back now.

AMERICA—THE FINAL PIECE OF THE PUZZLE

Irene sat still, gripping the edges of my manuscript as if steadying herself. Her eyes flickered with something between curiosity and hesitation.

"Ann . . . I don't know if I'm ready for this next part. You're saying America—our country—might not be the defender of freedom we think it is, but instead, a key player in the rise of this final world system?"

I took a deep breath and nodded.

"That's exactly what I'm saying. And Irene, I know it's a tough pill to swallow. America has long been seen as a beacon of democracy, religious freedom, and economic opportunity. But the real question is—has that influence been used to restrain global tyranny, or has it actually been paving the way for it?"

Irene frowned, flipping through my notes.

"Alright, let's start from the beginning. What makes you think America is even involved in this at all?"

I reached for my Bible and turned to Daniel 7, running my finger over the passage.

> After that, in my vision at night I looked, and there before me was a fourth beast—terrifying and frightening and very powerful. (Daniel 7:7)

"The Bible tells us that before the Antichrist takes control, nations will be weakened, their sovereignty will be eroded, and global power will be consolidated. And if we look at America today, what do we see?"

America's Role in the Coming Global System

- Spreading Democracy—or Laying the Groundwork for a One World Government?

Reading aloud. "America has led the way in spreading democracy, but has it also laid the foundation for a One World Government?"

"Think about it. America has promoted democratic systems around the world, but in doing so, it has also encouraged the centralization of power—whether through global alliances, trade agreements, or military interventions. Every major global institution—the UN, NATO, the World Economic Forum—has relied on America's influence. But what happens when those institutions merge into one single governing body?"

Irene exhaled, her brows knitting together.

"You're saying that by pushing democracy worldwide, we've actually been creating the infrastructure for a global government?"

"Exactly. And that's a government the Bible warns us not to trust."

- Championing Capitalism—or Enabling Global Financial Control?

Irene pointed to the next section, narrowing her eyes.

"America has championed capitalism and free markets, but has it also enabled the rise of global financial control?"

"Look at how our economy has evolved. The U.S. dollar has been the world's reserve currency for decades, but now we're moving toward digital finance—

Central Bank Digital Currencies (CBDCs), crypto regulation, and biometric payment systems. These are the very tools that will allow total financial surveillance and control."

Shaking her head. "You mean the ability to block transactions? To decide who can buy and sell?"

Firmly. "Yes. And what does Revelation warn us about?"

That no man might buy or sell, except he that had the mark. (Revelation 13:17)

- Defending Religious Freedom—or Promoting a Counterfeit Universal Faith?

"This one really gets me. America was founded on religious freedom. How could it possibly be leading us into a One World Religion?"

"Because modern 'religious freedom' has morphed into something else— religious compromise. Today, biblical truth is being rewritten in the name of tolerance and inclusivity. Leaders are promoting interfaith unity, blending beliefs into a single, counterfeit faith that rejects Jesus as the only way."

For that day shall not come, except there comes a falling away first. (2 Thessalonians 2:3)

"The push for interfaith harmony sounds noble, but it's exactly what the Bible warned would happen—a deception that prepares the world for a leader who will unite all religions under one system."

The Ultimate Question: What Is America's True Role?

Irene put the pages down, rubbing her forehead. She was silent for a moment, then finally spoke.

"So what are you saying? That America is part of this final kingdom? That we're not actually stopping it, but helping build it?"

I looked at her, knowing the weight of my words.

"That's the question we need to ask. Is America a restraining force holding back the rise of the Antichrist's empire? Or has it unknowingly—or even willingly—become the driving force behind it?"

- Is America delaying the final kingdom by standing for truth and righteousness?
- Or is it facilitating its rise by leading the world toward global unity, economic control, and religious deception?

Quietly. "Which one do you think it is?"

I didn't answer right away. I let the silence settle between us. Then I turned to the next page, looking her in the eyes.

"That's what this book is going to uncover."

Irene nodded slowly, then turned the page. We both knew—the answer was coming.

THE COMING GREAT DECEPTION

Irene rubbed her temples, her voice quieter now as she read through the next section. She had gone from skeptical to concerned—and now, I could tell, something else was setting in. A realization.

"Ann, this part is unsettling. You're saying that America—our country—once stood under God's blessing, but now it's leading the world into spiritual deception?"

I folded my hands on the table, meeting her gaze.

"That's exactly what I'm saying. And it's not just America—it's the entire world. But because America has been a leading influence for centuries, its moral collapse is having a global impact. And that collapse? It isn't accidental."

Irene leaned back, exhaling sharply.

"Alright, let's start at the beginning. America was founded on biblical principles. We've all heard that. But how does that connect to what's happening now?"

I turned to a passage in my Bible, reading aloud.

Blessed is the nation whose God is the LORD. (Psalm 33:12)

"America flourished because it once honored God. It wasn't perfect, but its foundation was built on biblical truth. Religious freedom, justice, morality—these were the pillars of our nation. That's why America prospered and became a beacon of hope to the world."

Nodding slowly. "Okay . . . but what changed?"

America's Spiritual Decline: A Nation Turning Away from God

"Like every great empire before it, America is following the same pattern—turning away from God and embracing corruption."

- The Normalization of Sin—What was once unthinkable is now celebrated. What was once immoral is now law. The very foundation of biblical morality is being dismantled.
- The Corruption of the Church—Many churches no longer preach repentance or righteousness. Instead, they cater to culture, embracing progressive ideologies over biblical truth.

For the time will come when they will not endure sound doctrine; but after their own lusts shall they heap to themselves teachers, having itching ears. And they shall turn away their ears from the truth, and shall be turned unto fables. (2 Timothy 4:3–4)

- The Rise of Idolatry—Money, entertainment, technology, and self-worship have replaced God. Just like in ancient Rome and Babylon. America is obsessed with pleasure and power.
- The Rejection of Absolute Truth—The idea that "truth is relative" has infiltrated every institution. Morality is now defined by personal feelings, not by God's Word.

Irene shook her head, setting the manuscript down.

"I see it. I mean, we're living in it. But Ann, here's what I don't get—why now? Why is this happening so fast?"

I turned another page in my Bible and looked up at her.

"Because we're being prepared for the greatest deception the world has ever seen."

The Spiritual Forces Behind the Great Deception

Frowning. "You mean Satan?"

Nodding. "Yes. The same forces that led to the downfall of Babylon, Rome, and Sodom and Gomorrah are at work today. But this time, the deception isn't just targeting one nation—it's global."

And for this cause God shall send them strong delusion, that they should believe a lie. (2 Thessalonians 2:11)

- Satan is corrupting every level of society. Government, entertainment, education, even churches—all are being used to spread lies, distort truth, and lead people away from God.
- False teachings are preparing the world for a counterfeit religion. Many churches have replaced the gospel with self-help messages, prosperity teachings, and universalism.
- Technology is being used as a tool of deception. AI, digital surveillance, and the merging of man and machine (transhumanism) are all part of the enemy's plan to reshape what it means to be human.
- A counterfeit "Messiah" is coming. The world is being conditioned to accept a global leader who will promise peace, prosperity, and unity—but will ultimately lead humanity into darkness.

Irene was silent, her fingers resting on the pages. She finally looked up; her expression unreadable.

"Ann . . . what if people don't believe this? What if they think it's just conspiracy or paranoia?"

I leaned in, lowering my voice.

"That's part of the deception, Irene. The greatest trick the enemy ever pulled was convincing the world God doesn't exist. And when the real deception comes, it's going to be so powerful, so convincing, that even believers will be at risk."

Irene swallowed hard, nodding slowly.

What's Coming Next?

Quietly. "So what happens now?"

I closed my Bible and took a deep breath.

"The deception is already here, but it's going to get worse. The Bible tells us a time is coming when people will trade truth for lies, morality for lawlessness, and faith for deception. And when that happens, the final world system—the one we've been talking about—will rise."

Irene exhaled, rubbing her temples.

"Ann . . . if what you're saying is true, we're running out of time, aren't we?"

Meeting her eyes. "Yes. And that's why this book needs to be written."

She nodded; her expression grim but determined. We both knew—there was no stopping now.

THE MECHANISMS OF DECEPTION

Irene flipped through the pages; her brow furrowed. She had been skeptical before, hesitant. But now? Now, she was disturbed. And I could tell she didn't know whether to challenge me or admit that everything I was saying made a chilling kind of sense.

"Ann . . . I keep thinking about what you said earlier—that the greatest deception the world has ever seen is already happening. But how? How could something so massive, so dangerous, unfold right in front of us, and no one seems to notice?"

I leaned forward; hands clasped together.

"Because Satan is the master of deception. Jesus called him 'the father of lies.' He doesn't just lie—he distorts truth so convincingly that people embrace the lie willingly."

> You are of your father the devil, and the lusts of your father you will do. He was a murderer from the beginning, and does not stand in the truth, because there is no truth in him. When he speaks a lie, he speaks of his own: for he is a liar, and the father of it. (John 8:44)

Crossing her arms. "Alright, but what exactly is his strategy? How does he convince an entire world to turn from God?"

I reached for my notes, flipping to the section I knew would make her pause.

- The Carefully Orchestrated Deception
  - The Corruption of Morality

"The first step? Redefining morality. Satan takes what is good and calls it evil. He takes what is evil and calls it good."

Woe unto them that call evil good, and good evil; that put darkness for light, and light for darkness. (Isaiah 5:20)

Skeptical. "Like what?"

"Look around you. Abortion—once unthinkable—is now celebrated as a 'human right.' Gender confusion is being pushed on children, and anyone who speaks against it is silenced. Traditional family values? Mocked. Righteousness? Labeled as tolerance. Christianity? Branded as hate speech."

Rubbing her temples. "And people don't even realize they're being manipulated."

"Exactly. When you control morality, you control the direction of an entire civilization."

  - The Attack on God's Created Order

Reading from my notes. "The biological reality of male and female is being erased, replaced by fluid, subjective identities based on personal feelings rather than God's truth."

Looking up. "You really believe this is intentional?"

"It's not just social change—it's rebellion against God's design. Satan's goal is to corrupt what God created. Marriage, gender, even human life itself—it's all being redefined to strip away God's authority."

Flatly. "But why does it matter?"

Holding up my Bible. "Because it's not just about social trends. It's spiritual warfare. The Bible tells us that in the last days, people will reject truth entirely."

  - The Rise of Artificial intelligence and Transhumanism

Irene squinted at this section, re-reading it twice.

"Transhumanism? Merging humans with machines? That sounds . . . out there."

"Really? Because right now, we're seeing major tech companies and governments invest billions into AI-driven enhancements, genetic modifications, and human-computer integration. Elon Musk's Neuralink is testing brain chips.

AI is replacing human decision-making. Scientists are even discussing ways to 'upload' consciousness into machines."

Shaking her head. "Wait—you think the Antichrist will use this kind of technology?"

"Absolutely. The Bible tells us he will perform 'miraculous' signs that will deceive the masses. What if some of those 'miracles' are advanced technology that people mistake for divine power?"

Irene sat back, exhaling slowly.

- The Suppression of Biblical Truth
  o Truth Is Now Labeled as Hate Speech

"The Bible is clear—truth will be rejected in the last days. We're already seeing it."

Reading aloud. "The Bible is being removed from schools, government, and public discourse. Persecution against Christians is increasing, and freedom of religion is being systematically attacked in the name of 'tolerance.'"

Looking up. "You think this is all connected?"

"Without a doubt. Jesus warned that believers would be hated for His name's sake. But here's what's terrifying—many Christians won't even realize they're being deceived."

  o Christianity Is Being Rewritten

"Have you noticed that many churches no longer preach about sin? Repentance? The Second Coming of Christ?"

Frowning. "Yeah . . . now it's all about love, acceptance, and personal fulfillment."

"Exactly. It's not Christianity—it's a counterfeit gospel. One that makes people feel good while leading them straight into deception."

Irene put my manuscript down, running her hands through her hair.

"Ann . . . this is a lot. And it's terrifying."

I nodded, understanding the weight of what we were discussing.

"I know. But Irene, people need to wake up. Satan's deception isn't just about changing laws or social values—it's about preparing the world to accept a new reality that directly contradicts God's Word."

Irene was silent for a long moment. Then she picked up her pen and tapped it against the table.

"So what do we do?"

I exhaled, flipping to the next section of my manuscript.

"We prepare. And we make sure that when the deception comes in full force, we aren't the ones who fall for it."

Irene gave a slow nod, then turned the page. She was starting to see. And once she saw—there was no going back.

EVEN THE ELECT WILL BE DECEIVED

Irene sat back, shaking her head, her expression a mix of disbelief and growing concern. She tapped her pen against the table, staring at the passage in front of her.

"Ann, this . . . this part is terrifying."

I nodded. I knew this was going to be one of the hardest truths to accept.

"I know. And that's why it has to be said."

She pointed at the verse from Matthew 24:24, her eyes scanning it over and over, as if trying to find a loophole.

> For there shall arise false Christs, and false prophets, and shall show great signs and wonders; insomuch that, if it were possible, they shall deceive the very elect. (Matthew 24:24)

"I don't think people really grasp what Jesus is saying here. This isn't just some minor deception. This is something so convincing, so powerful, that even people who have dedicated their lives to God might fall for it."

Quietly. "Exactly. This is a warning that no one should take lightly."

Irene leaned forward, lowering her voice like she was afraid someone might overhear us.

"But Ann, we're talking about believers. People who pray, study the Bible, go to church. How could they possibly be deceived?"

The Danger of False Security

I sighed, knowing this was the part most Christians don't want to hear.

"Because many of them have built their faith on comfort rather than conviction."

> Because straight is the gate, and narrow is the way, which leads unto life, and few there be that find it. (Matthew 7:14)

"Too many Western Christians assume that they will be raptured out of here before things get bad. They've been told that they won't have to suffer, won't have to endure persecution, won't have to make hard choices. But that's not what Scripture teaches."

Sitting up. "Wait—you're saying the Rapture might not happen before all of this?"

"I'm saying we need to be prepared for anything. What if we have to endure part of the Tribulation? What if we're called to stand firm while the world crumbles around us? If our faith is based on the idea that we'll be gone before trouble comes, what happens when we're still here?"

Irene exhaled sharply, rubbing her temples.

"But that's not what most churches teach."

Nodding. "I know. But Jesus warned us that most people wouldn't be ready."

When the Son of Man comes, will He find faith on the earth? (Luke 18:8)

A Faith Built on Convenience

Irene was quiet now, flipping through my manuscript with a newfound intensity.

"I can't stop thinking about that last verse. Jesus is literally questioning if faith will even exist when He returns."

"Because He knew what was coming. He knew that in the last days, many would abandon their faith—not because they stopped believing in God, but because they never really knew Him in the first place."

Looking up. "What do you mean?"

"There a lot of people sitting in church pews today who have never truly surrendered their lives to Christ. Their faith is cultural—it's based on tradition, routine, or even social acceptance. They believe in Jesus, but they don't follow Him. And when the time comes to take a stand, they'll be the first to fall away."

Not everyone who says to Me, 'Lord, Lord,' will enter the Kingdom of Heaven, but only the one who does the will of My Father who is in heaven. (Matthew 7:21)

Irene swallowed hard, nodding slowly.

"So what you're saying is . . . a lot of people think they're saved, but they're not?"

Looking her in the eye. "I'm saying the Bible is clear—many people will assume they are following Christ, but when the testing comes, their faith won't stand."

Irene leaned back in her chair, staring at the ceiling for a moment. When she finally spoke, her voice was softer, almost shaken.

"Ann, this book . . . this book isn't just about prophecy, is it?"

I smiled sadly.

"No, Irene. This book is about waking people up before it's too late."

She nodded slowly, then turned the page. The pieces were falling into place, and there was no unseeing the truth.

A TIME TO PREPARE

Irene sat back, arms crossed, her face unreadable. She had listened to everything, taken it all in. And now, I could see the weight of it pressing down on her.

"Ann . . . I need to ask you something. What do we do with all of this? I mean, okay—we're being deceived, the world is shifting toward the final system, faith is weakening—but what now? How do we respond?"

I leaned forward, resting my hands on the table.

"We prepare. Because this is not a time for passivity, Irene. This is not a time for complacency."

She watched me carefully, waiting for more.

"The deception is here, and it's growing stronger every day. The world is changing at a rate we've never seen before. And everything—everything—is being aligned for the arrival of the Antichrist."

Irene inhaled deeply, as if steadying herself.

"So what must we do?"

I pulled out my notes, flipping to the section I had written just for this.

- The Call to Action: What Must Believers Do?
  o Ground Yourself in Scripture

"The first thing? Know God's Word so well that deception can't take root. The Bible isn't just a history book—it's our survival guide for the days ahead."

My people are destroyed for lack of knowledge. (Hosea 4:6)

Nodding slowly. "If you don't know truth, you won't recognize a lie."

"Exactly. If the enemy can twist Scripture—like he did when tempting Jesus in the wilderness—he can twist it against us too. We need to be so anchored in truth that we cannot be shaken."

  o Strengthen Your Prayer Life

"Second, prayer isn't optional anymore. It's our direct line to God's wisdom, discernment, and protection."

Pray without ceasing. (1 Thessalonians 5:17)

Frowning. "You're saying we have to pray like our lives depend on it."
Meeting her eyes. "Because they do."

  o Separate from False Teachings

"Irene, the hard truth is that many churches today are embracing compromise, humanism, and worldliness. Just because something calls itself Christian doesn't mean it's of Christ."

Exhaling. "I've seen it. Churches that avoid talking about sin, repentance, or the Second Coming. Instead, they focus on self-help messages and feel-good sermons."

"Exactly. And that's why believers need to find Bible-believing, Spirit-filled communities. If a church isn't preaching the full gospel, it's time to walk away."

o   Prepare Spiritually and Practically

"Difficult days are ahead, Irene. Faith will be tested, and courage will be required. We have to prepare, both spiritually and practically."

Be sober, be vigilant; because your adversary the devil walks about like a roaring lion, seeking whom he may devour. (1 Peter 5:8)

Tilting her head. "Practically? You mean physically preparing too?"

"Absolutely. The early church knew persecution. They were ready to endure hardship, to stand strong when things got hard. Today's believers? Most aren't ready for any kind of suffering. But we need to be. We need to be prepared in every way."

o   Share the Truth Boldly

"We are called to be watchmen, Irene. We don't just prepare for ourselves— we warn others."

Son of man, I have made you a watchman for the people of Israel; so hear the word I speak and give them warning from Me. (Ezekiel 3:17)

Her voice softer now. "That's what you're doing with this book, isn't it?"

Looking at her. "Yes. But Irene—it can't just be me. Every believer is called to share this truth. Every believer is responsible for standing in the gap."

Irene was silent, gripping her pen so tightly her knuckles turned white. When she finally spoke, her voice was laced with urgency.

"Ann . . . people aren't ready."

I nodded; my expression solemn.

"No, they're not. But God has given us His Word. He has warned us of what's to come."

Irene took a deep breath, staring at the words on the page.

"So the real question is—will we listen?"

I met her gaze, my voice steady.

"That's exactly the question."

She slowly turned the next page, her face set in determination. The veil was lifting, revealing a reality she could no longer ignore.

WHY THIS BOOK?

Irene closed my manuscript and set it down, staring at the cover for a long moment. I could see the gears turning in her head. When she finally spoke, her voice was measured, thoughtful.

"Ann . . . I have to ask. Why did you write this book? What is it that you want people to walk away with?"

I exhaled, leaning back in my chair. It was a question I had asked myself a thousand times as I wrote these pages. And the answer had never been clearer than it was now.

"Because people are asleep, Irene. They're walking through life, completely unaware of what's happening around them. They see the chaos, they see the changes in society, they feel the weight of it all—but they don't realize that it was all foretold."

Nodding slowly. "You mean prophecy."

"Exactly. The Bible has been warning us about these times for thousands of years. The prophetic books of Daniel and Revelation have laid it all out in stunning detail. But for so long, people have either misunderstood them, dismissed them as metaphor, or pushed them into some distant, irrelevant future."

Flipping through the pages. "So you're saying . . . those prophecies aren't just about some far-off future. They're happening now."

Pointing to the manuscript. "Irene, everything the Bible said would happen in the last days—it's unfolding before our eyes. We aren't waiting for prophecy to be fulfilled. We're living in it."

A Wake-Up Call, Not Fear-Mongering

Tilting her head. "Some people are going to say this book is fear-mongering."

Shaking my head. "That's the thing, Irene. This book isn't about fear. It's about truth. And truth isn't always comfortable."

Eyebrows raised. "But you're talking about things like the Antichrist, the rise of a One World Order, America's possible judgment . . ."

"I am. And people need to hear it."

I picked up my Bible, flipping to a familiar passage.

When it is evening, you say, 'It will be fair weather, for the sky is red.' And in the morning, 'Today it will be stormy, for the sky is red and overcast.' You know how to interpret the appearance of the sky, but you cannot interpret the signs of the times. (Matthew 16:2–3)

"Jesus Himself rebuked the people for understanding the weather better than they understood the signs of the times. It's no different today. People are watching world events unfold, but they don't see what's really happening."

Muttering. "They don't connect it to prophecy."

"Exactly. And that's why I wrote this book. To wake people up before it's too late."

The Choice We Must Make

Irene drummed her fingers on the table, deep in thought.

"Okay, let's say people read this book. Let's say they start to see it. What then?"

"Then they have a choice."

Leaning forward. "What choice?"

I met her gaze, unwavering.

"To accept what God has already revealed, or to ignore it and remain unprepared."

Irene sucked in a breath. She was starting to understand the weight of this book now.

"God doesn't leave His people in the dark, Irene. He has already shown us what's coming. He has already given us the signs. The question is—will we listen?"

Irene exhaled, nodding slowly.

"So this book is a roadmap."

"A roadmap through the last days. A guide to help people understand where we are in prophecy, where we're headed next, and what they need to do to prepare."

America's Role in Prophecy

Pausing. "And you really believe America is in the Bible?"

"Not just in the Bible, Irene. Central to it."

Leaning back in her chair, processing. "Ann . . . this is a big claim."

"I know. And that's why I don't ask anyone to take my word for it. This book will walk them through it verse by verse—the evidence is there. Once they see it, they'll never look at prophecy the same way again."

She nodded slowly, then flipped through the pages. The weight of it all settled in, but this time, there was something else—resolve. This wasn't just a story. It was a message the world needed to hear.

A FINAL WARNING

Her hands rested on the manuscript; her expression unreadable. She looked up at me, her voice quieter now.

"Ann, this . . . this is serious. You're saying we're the watchmen now?"

I met her gaze, nodding slowly.

"That's exactly what I'm saying."

She exhaled, looking away for a moment, then back at me.

"But what if people don't listen? What if they don't want to hear it?"

Leaning forward, resting my hands on the table. "That's not our job, Irene. Our job is to warn—not to decide who listens."

Watchmen On the Wall

"God has always sent watchmen to warn His people. In ancient Israel, He sent Isaiah, Jeremiah, and Ezekiel—each one standing alone, pleading with the people to turn back."

"And most of them weren't exactly . . . well-received."

Smiling grimly. "That's putting it lightly. They were mocked, rejected, imprisoned. Some were even killed. But that didn't change their mission."

Leaning back, arms crossed. "So you think we're in the same position now?"

"Look at history. When Nineveh was heading toward destruction, God sent Jonah. When Babylon was about to conquer Israel, God sent warning after warning. God has never judged a nation without first sending a messenger."

Slowly, realization dawning. "And now, in the last days, the warnings are still coming."

The Message is Clear

She picked up my manuscript again, reading aloud.

"The world will be shaken. Nations will fall. A final empire will rise."

She set it down, meeting my gaze.

"That sounds . . . final."

"Because it is. We're not talking about another cycle of history here. We're talking about the final act."

She rubbed her temples, processing everything.

"You really believe the time is that close?"

I didn't hesitate.

"I don't just believe it, Irene. I know it. And deep down . . . I think you do too."

She didn't say anything. She didn't have to. The weight of truth had already settled in.

Irene closed my manuscript and set it down, staring at me for a long moment. The weight of it all was settling in. I could see it in her eyes—the realization that this wasn't just another book. It was a warning. A message that, once heard, couldn't be ignored.

Softly. "Ann . . . what happens to those who don't listen?"

I let the question linger for a moment before answering.

"History answers that question for us."

She looked up, waiting for me to continue.

"There have always been two types of people in moments like these—when God sends a warning."

Leaning forward. "Go on."

"First, there are the ones who listen, take it seriously, and prepare."

Nodding slowly. "And the second?"

Exhaling. "The ones who ignore it. Who dismiss it. Who laugh at it—right up until it's too late."

She frowned, flipping through the pages, then looking up at me.

"Like in Noah's day?"

"Exactly. He warned them for 120 years. They laughed at him, mocked him—until the rain started falling. By then, the door was shut."

They knew nothing about what would happen until the flood came and took them all away. That is how it will be at the coming of the Son of Man. (Matthew 24:39)

"Same with Lot. The people of Sodom mocked the idea that their city would be destroyed. But when the fire fell, only a handful escaped."

The same day that Lot went out of Sodom, it rained fire and brimstone from heaven and destroyed them all. (Luke 17:29)

Irene ran a hand through her hair, shaking her head.

"And then there's Jerusalem. Jeremiah warned them for years . . . but they didn't listen."

"They refused to believe Babylon would conquer them. They thought their city was invincible. But when judgment came? Jerusalem fell. The temple was destroyed. Thousands were taken into captivity."

A heavy silence filled the space. We both knew what came next.

Almost whispering. "And now . . . it's happening again."

I nodded.

The thing that has been, it is that which shall be; and that which is done is that which shall be done: and there is no new thing under the sun. (Ecclesiastes 1:9)

"Today's world is no different. People are ignoring the warnings. They're choosing comfort over conviction, distraction over discernment."

Shaking her head. "It's like people think if they just ignore prophecy, it won't happen."

"But prophecy isn't dependent on whether people believe it or not. It will happen. Exactly as God has spoken."

Irene was silent for a long moment, absorbing everything.

Finally. "Ann, this is . . . terrifying."

Shaking my head. "It's not about fear, Irene. It's about discernment."

Meeting my gaze. "So what now? What do we do?"

I leaned in, voice steady.

"We watch. We prepare. And we warn."

She picked up her notes, reading aloud.

"The warnings have been delivered. The signs are clear. The time is short."

She exhaled, gripping my manuscript tightly.

"Then let's make sure people hear this before it's too late."

————◆◆◆————

Chapter 2

Revelation 1:
The Prologue—
Christ Appears to John

THE FORBIDDEN PROPHECY—Irene settled into her chair, flipping through the fresh pages of my manuscript with a deliberateness that told me she was weighing every word. It had been months since our last meeting—months since she'd first given me the green light. And now, here we were, poised at the threshold of something altogether different.

She glanced up at me, her expression unreadable. "Alright, Ann. We've covered the warnings, the deception, the rise of the final world order . . . and now, we're stepping into the Book of Revelation itself."

She said it carefully, as though she were testing the weight of the words before setting them down between us.

I nodded, already feeling the gravity of where we were headed. Everything up until this point had been a foundation—necessary, urgent—but now we were moving beyond speculation, beyond theory. Now, we were stepping into the very pages of Scripture that most people fear to tread.

Leaning forward slightly. "Yes. This is where everything shifts. Up until now, we've been laying the groundwork, examining the signs and patterns, tracing the path that history has taken. But now . . . we are stepping straight into the vision God gave to John. We are no longer just discussing prophecy; we are witnessing it unfold through his eyes."

Irene exhaled, tapping a finger against my manuscript. I could sense her hesitation—not out of doubt, but out of the awareness that we were about to cross a threshold most people never dared to approach.

Raising an eyebrow. "And that's exactly where people start to hesitate. The Book of Revelation is one of the most avoided books of the Bible. People either don't understand it, or they're afraid of what it means. I can't tell you how many people have told me they've started reading it and then stopped, overwhelmed."

I had heard the same thing countless times before. For so many, Revelation was an uncharted wilderness—an unfamiliar, mysterious landscape where dragons, beasts, seals, and trumpets blurred together in what seemed like an impenetrable maze of symbols and warnings. And yet, the irony was that the book's very purpose was to illuminate, not to confuse.

Smiling slightly. "And that's exactly why we're here, Irene. The purpose of this book isn't to obscure the truth—it's to reveal it. The very name 'Revelation' means an unveiling. It's not meant to be hidden or sealed up. God is pulling back the curtain and showing us what has been, what is, and what will be."

I could see Irene processing that, her eyes narrowing slightly as she considered my words. I continued before she could voice her next thought.

Leaning back. "Think about it—would God really give us a book, make it the final word of His divine revelation, and then make it impossible to understand? That wouldn't make any sense. The problem isn't Revelation itself—the problem is how we've approached it. We've been conditioned to see it as a puzzle instead of a prophecy. But Revelation isn't a cryptic riddle that only a handful of scholars can decode. It's a message for God's people, written for us to read, to hear, and to understand."

Tilting her head, skeptical but intrigued. "Okay, but if that's true, why do so many people struggle with it? Why is it that whenever the Book of Revelation is mentioned, people either shrug it off or panic?"

Pausing, then speaking deliberately. "Because it's not just another book of the Bible, Irene. It's the conclusion of everything. It is the final chapter of God's plan—the fulfillment of all that was prophesied throughout Scripture. It is the revealing of Jesus Christ in His full glory, as King and Judge. And, let's be honest, that's not always a comfortable thing for people to confront."

Nodding slowly. "So, in other words, people avoid Revelation not just because they find it difficult, but because deep down, they know it demands a response."

I pointed at her with a knowing smile.

"Exactly. Revelation isn't just about what's coming—it's about what we do with what's coming. It requires us to make a choice. And that's why the enemy has done everything he can to keep people away from it."

Leaning forward, her voice lower. "You think there's an actual strategy behind that? A reason why this book, above all others, has been sidelined, dismissed, or misinterpreted?"

Without hesitation. "Absolutely. Look at what's happening in the world right now. We are watching biblical prophecy unfold in real-time. And yet, how many Christians are truly prepared? How many are even aware? The enemy knows that if people understood Revelation, they would wake up. They would recognize the deception, they would see through the lies, and they would know how to stand firm in the days ahead. But if he can keep them confused, fearful, or uninterested, then they remain blind to what's coming."

Irene tapped her fingers on my manuscript, her eyes narrowing. "But if that's true, why is Revelation the one book in the Bible that so many churches and pastors ignore?"

I leaned forward, locking eyes with her. "Because it's the forbidden prophecy, Irene."

She blinked. "The forbidden prophecy?"

Nodding. "Think about it. This is the one book that exposes Satan's final plan. It lays out his defeat in detail. If there's one book the enemy would want people to ignore, it's this one."

Irene considered that for a moment, her skepticism giving way to curiosity. "Okay, but it's not just fear, is it? I mean, even theologically trained people struggle with this book."

Leaning back slightly. "That's the brilliance of the deception. The enemy doesn't just want people to be afraid of Revelation—he wants them to misunderstand it, dismiss it, or even twist it into something unrecognizable. He's made it seem too complicated, too symbolic, or irrelevant for today. And he's done it so well that even the Church has fallen for it."

Irene exhaled. "So you're saying people avoid Revelation not because it's impossible to understand, but because they've been conditioned to believe they can't understand it?"

"Exactly. Would God really give us a book, make it the final word of His divine revelation, and then make it impossible to interpret? That wouldn't make any sense. Revelation isn't a puzzle for elite scholars—it's a prophecy for the Church. But if people never read it, they'll never see what's coming."

Irene drummed her fingers against my manuscript, absorbing my words. "And if they don't see what's coming . . . they won't be prepared."

I nodded. "Which is exactly why we're diving into this book. The enemy wants people to stay in the dark—but Revelation is the book that turns the lights on."

She exhaled deeply, shaking her head. "Alright, Ann. I get it now. This book isn't just a prophecy—it's a battle plan. So . . . where do we start?"

Opening my Bible, I turned to the very first words of Revelation. "We start at the beginning. With the unveiling."

She leaned in, flipping the page. "Then let's unveil it."

THE PROLOGUE

The Prologue of the Book of Revelation is a threefold literary structure. As we walk through Revelation 1:1–8, we see that the Book of Revelation is unique in its structure, blending three distinct types of literature into one:

1. **Apocalypse (Revelation 1:1)**—The book begins as an unveiling or revelation—a divine disclosure of things hidden, revealing Jesus Christ in His full glory and the unfolding of God's final plan for humanity.

2. **Prophecy (Revelation 1:3)**—Revelation is not just historical or symbolic; it is a prophetic book that declares what is to come. It provides a roadmap of God's ultimate judgment, the triumph of Christ, and the establishment of His eternal Kingdom.

3. **Letter (Revelation 1:4)**—This book was also written as a letter addressed to real churches in Asia Minor (modern-day Turkey), offering encouragement, warning, and instruction. It carries the personal tone of an epistle while maintaining its apocalyptic and prophetic nature.

Through this threefold structure, Jesus Christ is fully revealed:

- He is our Redeemer—washing us clean with His blood.
- He is our Intercessor—standing as our advocate in heaven.
- He is our coming King—returning *with* His Church and the armies of heaven to establish His reign.

God's grace not only forgives our past but transforms our present, making us more like Christ each day. No matter the struggle, He is with us—guiding, strengthening, and preparing us for His return. Revelation is not merely a book of end-time events; it is a book of hope, victory, and the ultimate fulfillment of God's promises.

THE REVELATION OF JESUS CHRIST REVEALS:

[1:1] The Revelation of Jesus Christ, which God gave unto Him, to show unto His servants things which must shortly come to pass; and He sent and signified it by His angel unto His servant John.

The opening verse of the Book of Revelation establishes a divine chain of communication, illustrating how God's final message to humanity has been revealed. It begins in the heart of God the Father, who entrusts this revelation to Jesus Christ, His Son. Jesus, in turn, delivers it through a heavenly messenger, an angel, who then passes it to John the Apostle on the island of Patmos. John, acting as a faithful servant, records this vision under divine inspiration, ensuring that future generations—including us today—would have access to this prophetic unveiling.

This divine order of revelation highlights both the authority and urgency of the message. The phrase "things which must shortly come to pass" does not necessarily mean immediate fulfillment but rather events that will unfold rapidly and with certainty once they begin. The emphasis here is on their imminence and divine appointment, warning us that these events will happen without delay when their time comes.

The word "signified" (Greek: *semaino*) means to communicate through symbols, signs, and visions. This is a key theme in Revelation, as much of its message is conveyed through symbolic imagery—not to obscure the truth but to make it known in a way that carries deeper meaning. This method of divine communication is not unique to Revelation; throughout Scripture, God has used dreams, visions, and angelic messengers to reveal His will.

Angels play a crucial role in this book as divine messengers, delivering God's decrees, announcing judgments, and guiding John through his visions. Their presence throughout Revelation underscores the supernatural nature of the events being revealed. However, these angels are not acting on their own authority—they are representatives of the eternal, sovereign God, carrying His words and executing His commands.

Thus, Revelation 1:1 serves as the foundation for the entire book, emphasizing that what follows is not a human interpretation or speculation, but a direct, divine revelation from God Himself. It is a prophetic message meant not to instill fear, but to prepare and awaken those who have ears to hear.

OLD TESTAMENT FORESHADOWS REVELATION:

But there is a God in heaven that reveals secrets, and makes known to the King Nebuchadnezzar what shall be in the latter days. Your dream, and the visions of your head upon your bed, are these; As for you, O king, your thoughts came into your mind upon your bed, what should come to pass hereafter: and He that reveals secrets makes known to you what shall come to pass. (Daniel 2:28–29)

The very first verse of Revelation establishes its purpose: to reveal. This is not a book of hidden mysteries meant to confound, but a prophecy given by God to Jesus Christ, then delivered through an angel to John—so that His servants (us) might understand what must shortly come to pass.

This concept of divine revelation is not new. In Daniel 2:28–29, God revealed the future to King Nebuchadnezzar through a dream, foretelling the rise and fall of kingdoms and the ultimate establishment of God's eternal reign. Just as Daniel interpreted that vision, unveiling what was to come, so too does Revelation lift the veil on the final chapters of history.

From the Old Testament to the New Testament, God has always revealed His plans to those who seek Him. The Old Testament is the account of a nation—God's chosen people, Israel. The New Testament is the account of a Man—Jesus Christ, the Creator who became flesh. His appearance is the central event of all history. He died to purchase us with His blood and now lives forever. Revelation is the final and ultimate unveiling—the prophecy that completes the divine narrative, preparing God's people for the days ahead. The most exalted privilege in all of Scripture is not just to understand prophecy—but to know Him. That's what the Bible is truly about.

THE REVELATION OF JESUS CHRIST REVEALS:

[1:2] Who bear record of the Word of God, and of the testimony of Jesus Christ, and of all things that he saw.

This verse establishes John's role as the chosen witness of the Revelation. He is not merely writing a personal account; he is bearing record—testifying—to three things:

1. **The Word of God**—John affirms that the message of Revelation is not from man, but directly from God. Just as the prophets of the Old Testament recorded divine revelations, John is given the responsibility of documenting God's final prophetic word to humanity.

2. **The Testimony of Jesus Christ**—Jesus Himself is the central figure of Revelation. His testimony is the fulfillment of prophecy, the revelation of His divine authority, and the declaration of His coming Kingdom. John is recording the vision exactly as he receives it—nothing altered, nothing omitted.

3. **All That He Saw**—The phrase "all things that he saw" emphasizes that John's testimony is visual as well as verbal. Revelation is unique among

biblical books in that it is primarily a prophetic vision, filled with imagery, symbols, and apocalyptic scenes. John is not giving philosophical ideas or abstract theology—he is reporting actual, supernatural events as they were revealed to him.

This verse reassures us that the Book of Revelation is not speculation or human interpretation. It is a firsthand account of divine truth, a vision given to John by God Himself. John is not the author of this prophecy—he is the faithful scribe, ensuring that God's message is recorded and preserved for all generations.

OLD TESTAMENT FORESHADOWS REVELATION:

And the LORD answered me, and said, Write the vision, and make it plain upon tablets, that he may run that reads it. For the vision is yet for an appointed time, but at the end it shall speak, and not lie: though it tarry, wait for it; because it will surely come, it will not tarry. (Habakkuk 2:2–3)

In this passage, the LORD instructs the prophet to write the vision plainly, emphasizing that it is for an appointed time and will surely come to pass. Like John, Habakkuk was called to faithfully record what he saw, ensuring the message would be clear and enduring. Both were entrusted with divine revelation and were to serve as faithful witnesses of what God has shown them. These passages highlight the prophetic calling to preserve God's Word, bear testimony to His truth, and make known what is yet to come.

Irene leaned forward, tapping her pen against her notebook as she glanced up at me. "Alright, Ann, I've got a question for you—why John? Out of all the disciples, why did Jesus choose him to receive this incredible vision?"

I smiled, flipping through my Bible slowly. "That's a great question, Irene. The answer isn't just found in one place—it's in the whole story of who John was. He wasn't just one of the *twelve*. He had a relationship with Jesus that was personal, deep, and unwavering. He was part of the inner circle with Peter and James—the three who were present for moments no one else witnessed. Like the Mount of Transfiguration in Matthew 17, the raising of Jairus' daughter, and the intimate night in Gethsemane."

Irene nodded; eyes thoughtful. "And wasn't he also there when Jesus gave the Olivet Discourse in Matthew 24?"

"Exactly," I said. "But what sets John apart even more is how the Bible refers to him—not just as a disciple, but as *the disciple whom Jesus loved*. John 13:23 even tells us he leaned on Jesus' chest during the Last Supper. That's spiritual and emotional closeness—not just proximity."

"Doesn't that verse almost sound poetic?" she mused. "'Now there was leaning on Jesus' bosom one of His disciples, whom Jesus loved.'"

"It is poetic," I agreed. "But it's also revealing. John's devotion ran deep. He was the only one who stayed at the foot of the Cross when the others fled. And Jesus didn't ignore that loyalty. He entrusted His own mother, Mary, into John's care."

Irene flipped to the passage quickly, John 19:26–27, reading:

> When Jesus therefore saw His mother, and the disciple standing by, whom He loved, He says unto His mother, Woman, behold your son! Then says He to the disciple, Behold your mother! And from that hour that disciple took her unto his own home. (John 19:26–27)

She looked up, her voice soft. "That's powerful."

"It really is," I nodded. "John was faithful. And Jesus honored that faithfulness. Remember, after the crucifixion and resurrection, John didn't fade into the background. He went on to write the Gospel of John, three epistles—1 John, which is like a sermon on love; 2 John, a personal letter likely to Mary; and 3 John, a note to a man named Gaius."

"And Revelation," Irene added.

I nodded. "Yes—what the Greeks called the *Apokalypsis*. The final unveiling. But before that? John had been a Galilean fisherman from Bethsaida, son of Zebedee and Salome. He partnered with Peter and Andrew in the fishing business and had surprising connections—he knew the High Priest, Nicodemus . . . He wasn't some random outsider. He had influence."

"And didn't he live a long life compared to the other apostles?" Irene asked.

"He did," I confirmed. "After being exiled by Emperor Domitian to the island of Patmos—a small, rock island just 40 miles off the coast of Turkey—he received the vision of Revelation. Church historians like Irenaeus and Eusebius say that after Domitian died, John was released, returned to Ephesus, and appointed leaders in the churches, setting things in order before retiring there."

Leaning back in her chair, Irene looked thoughtful. "So Jesus didn't just choose him because of proximity. He chose him because John knew Him. Really *knew* Him. Loved Him. Stayed with Him. And could be trusted to write down the final chapter of the divine story."

"Exactly," I said with a smile. "The Lamb entrusted the vision of the end to the one who leaned on His heart. And because of that, we now hold in our hands the Book of Revelation—a message not just of judgment, but of victory, restoration, and eternal hope."

———◆◆◆———

THE REVELATION OF JESUS CHRIST REVEALS:

[1:3] Blessed is he that reads, and they that hear the words of this prophecy, and keep those things which are written therein: for the time is at hand.

Revelation 1:3 opens with an extraordinary promise—one that sets the tone for the entire book. This is the first of seven "beatitudes" or *spiritual blessings* found in the Book of Revelation, echoing the structure of Jesus' famous Beatitudes at the beginning of His Sermon on the Mount in Matthew 5:3–12. The Greek word for beatitudes (*makarioi*) conveys the values and characteristics of the Kingdom of Heaven. Each one begins with "Blessed is/are."

This verse is not a warning to avoid the book, but an invitation to embrace it. It assures the reader that Revelation is not meant to intimidate, but to bless those who approach it with faith, humility, and obedience.

A threefold responsibility:

1. **Read**—In the early church, Scripture was read aloud to the congregation. This blessing begins with the one who boldly proclaims the words of this prophecy in a public setting.

2. **Hear**—The blessing then extends to those who listen with spiritual discernment. In Revelation, Jesus repeatedly says, "He that has an ear, let him hear." It is a call to receive and respond.

3. **Keep**—Finally, the blessing is for those who obey. Revelation is not just a book to study—it is a divine message meant to shape our behavior, worldview, and urgency for Christ's return.

John reminds us that "the time is at hand." This phrase suggests that the prophetic events described are poised and ready to unfold. God's timetable is already in motion, and the return of Christ could come at any moment.

Again, Revelation 1:3 is the first of seven blessings Jesus speaks in this book. Together, they form a pattern of encouragement and promise to those who endure, believe, and obey:

1. Blessed is he that reads, and they that hear and keep those things which are written therein (Revelation 1:3).
2. Blessed are the dead who die in the Lord (Revelation 14:13).
3. Blessed is he that watches and keeps his garments (Revelation 16:15).
4. Blessed are they who are called unto the marriage supper of the Lamb (Revelation 19:9).
5. Blessed and holy is he that has part in the first resurrection (Revelation 20:6).

6. Blessed is he that keeps the words of the prophecy of this book (Revelation 22:7).
7. Blessed are they that wash their robes (Revelation 22:14).

Each of these blessings mirrors the heart of the beatitudes Jesus gave in the gospels—honoring humility, purity, perseverance, and longing for righteousness. But here in Revelation, they also speak to readiness, endurance, and victorious faith in the midst of tribulation.

This opening beatitude is a call to action—a promise that those who read, hear, and keep the words of this prophecy will not only be informed . . . they will be blessed.

OLD TESTAMENT FORESHADOWS REVELATION:

This book of the law shall not depart out of your mouth; but you shalt meditate therein day and night, that you may observe to do according to all that is written therein: for then you shalt make your way prosperous, and then you shalt have good success. (Joshua 1:8)

From the Old Testament to Revelation, God emphasizes the power of His Word—not just in reading it, but in meditating on it, obeying it, and allowing it to shape our lives. Joshua 1:8 declares that success and prosperity come from keeping God's law, just as Revelation 1:3 promises a blessing to those who read, hear, and obey the words of prophecy.

This divine pattern reveals an eternal truth: God's Word is not merely to be studied—it is to be lived. Those who treat it as a living guide will find both wisdom and the assurance that they are prepared for what is to come. The time is at hand, and the call to be spiritually awake has never been more urgent.

THE REVELATION OF JESUS CHRIST REVEALS:

[1:4] John to the seven churches which are in Asia: Grace be unto you, and peace, from Him who is, and who was, and who is to come; and from the sevenfold Spirits which are before His throne.

John addresses his letter to seven specific churches in Asia Minor, which were real, historical congregations in cities including Ephesus, Smyrna, Pergamum, Thyatira, Sardis, Philadelphia, and Laodicea. These churches represent both literal congregations in the first century and symbolic stages of church history, offering timeless messages relevant to believers throughout the ages.

John opens with the traditional greeting of grace and peace, but with divine significance. This is not just a polite salutation—it is a proclamation of God's unchanging nature and sovereignty over time. The phrase "Him who is, and who was, and who is to come" reflects God's eternal existence, echoing Exodus 3:14, where He declares, "I AM THAT I AM." This title establishes Christ's supremacy over past, present, and future, reassuring believers that He is in control of all history and eternity.

- "Who was"—Christ is the eternal Creator, existing before time began. He was with the Father in the garden of Eden, the active agent in creation (John 1:1–3). He appeared throughout the Old Testament in pre-incarnate form, preparing the world for His First Coming.
- "Who is"—Christ is alive today, seated at the right hand of the Father (Hebrews 1:3). His tomb is empty, and He reigns as our High Priest, interceding for His people (Romans 8:34).
- "Who is to come"—Christ's Second Coming is certain. As Matthew 24:27 states: "For as the lightning comes out of the east, and shines even unto the west; so shall also the coming of the Son of Man be."

One day, the earth will tremble, nations will fall, and Christ will return in power and glory. Every prophecy in Revelation points to this climatic event—the day when the King of kings returns to establish His Kingdom.

"And from the sevenfold Spirits which are before His throne" is a reference to the Holy Spirit in His fullness. This imagery aligns with Isaiah 11:2, which describes the sevenfold nature of the Spirit of God:

1. The Spirit of the Lord
2. The Spirit of Wisdom
3. The Spirit of Understanding
4. The Spirit of Counsel
5. The Spirit of Might
6. The Spirit of Knowledge
7. The Spirit of the Fear of the Lord

This signifies the completeness and perfection of the Holy Spirit's work in the church and the world. The Holy Spirit stands before the throne of God, actively preparing, guiding, and empowering the church for what is to come.

OLD TESTAMENT FORESHADOWS REVELATION:

And God said unto Moses, I AM THAT I AM: and He said, thus shalt you say unto the children of Israel, I AM has sent me unto you. (Exodus 3:14)

And the Spirit of the LORD shall rest upon Him, the Spirit of wisdom and understanding, the Spirit of counsel and might, the Spirit of knowledge and of the fear of the LORD. (Isaiah 11:2)

Exodus 3:14 parallels Revelation 1:4 because both declare the eternal nature of God—past, present, and future. In Exodus, God reveals Himself as "I AM," signifying His unchanging, self-existent nature. In Revelation, John describes Him as "who is, who was, and who is to come," reinforcing that God's presence spans all of time, from eternity past to eternity future.

Additionally, the sevenfold Spirit in Revelation 1:4 is reflected in Isaiah 11:2, where the Spirit of the LORD is described in seven aspects, symbolizing His completeness and divine perfection.

Irene leaned forward, flipping through her notes with a puzzled expression. She tapped her pen against the page and looked up at me.

"Alright, Ann, I need some clarity here. In Revelation, it talks about the 'sevenfold Spirits of God' before the throne. But then, in 1 Corinthians, Paul talks about the nine gifts of the Holy Spirit. Are these the same thing? Or are they completely different?"

I smiled, knowing this was a common question.

"Great question, Irene. And I'm glad you asked because this can be confusing at first. Let's start with the most important foundation—there is only one Holy Spirit."

"So the 'sevenfold Spirits' doesn't mean there are seven Holy Spirits?"

"Exactly. The Bible is clear—there is one Holy Spirit. Paul affirms this in Ephesians 4:4 when he says:"

There is one body, and one Spirit, even as you are called in one hope of your calling. (Ephesians 4:4).

And in 1 Corinthians 12:11, he says:"

But all these works that one and the selfsame Spirit, dividing to every man severally as He will. (1 Corinthians 12:11)

Nodding. "Okay, that makes sense. But then why does Revelation refer to the 'sevenfold Spirits of God?'"

"Great observation. The phrase 'sevenfold Spirits of God' appears multiple times in Revelation—Revelation 1:4, 3:1, 4:5, and 5:6. But this is not referring to seven separate Spirits. Instead, it's referring to the sevenfold nature of the Holy Spirit—seven ways in which He expresses Himself in His fullness and perfection."

"Sevenfold nature? Where do we find that in Scripture?"

"We see it clearly in Isaiah 11:1–2. It describes seven aspects of the Holy Spirit that rest upon the Messiah, Jesus Christ."

And there shall come forth a rod out of the stem of Jesse, and a Branch shall grow out of His roots: And the Spirit of the LORD shall rest upon Him, the Spirit of wisdom and understanding, the Spirit of counsel and might, the Spirit of knowledge and of the fear of the LORD. (Isaiah 11:1–2)

Flipping through her Bible. "I see it now! So, when Revelation talks about the 'sevenfold Spirits of God,' it's referring to these seven attributes of the Holy Spirit, not separate spirits."

"That's exactly right. The number seven in the Bible represents completion and perfection. The Holy Spirit is completely perfect in His nature, wisdom, power, and work. So, the sevenfold Spirits of God are a picture of the fullness of the Holy Spirit's ministry."

"Okay, that clears up a lot! But where do the nine gifts of the Holy Spirit fit in?"

"Great question! The nine gifts of the Holy Spirit, found in 1 Corinthians 12:7–11, are different. These are spiritual abilities that the Holy Spirit distributes to believers as He sees fit. Here they are . . ."

1. The Word of Wisdom
2. The Word of Knowledge
3. The Gift of Faith
4. The Gift of Healing
5. The Working of Miracles
6. Prophecy
7. The Discerning of Spirits
8. The Gift of Tongues
9. The Interpretation of Tongues

"So, the sevenfold Spirits of God are about the Holy Spirit's nature and fullness, while the nine gifts of the Holy Spirit are about how He operates through believers?"

"Exactly! The sevenfold Spirits describe who He is, and the nine gifts describe how He works. Two different but equally important truths."

"Wow. That makes so much sense now! The Holy Spirit is so much more than just a *force*—He's powerful, complete, and actively working in us today."

"Yes! And that's why understanding both the sevenfold Spirits and the nine gifts of the Spirit is so important. The Holy Spirit is not distant or impersonal—He is fully involved in our lives, guiding, empowering, and perfecting us."

Smiling. "I love it. Alright, I'm ready—let's dive deeper into Revelation!"

I grinned, flipping the page. We were just getting started.

◆ ◆ ◆

THE REVELATION OF JESUS CHRIST REVEALS:

^{1:5} And from Jesus Christ, who is the faithful witness, and the first begotten of the dead, and the prince of the kings of the earth. Unto Him that loved us; and washed us from our sins in His own blood.

Jesus is called the faithful witness, meaning He testifies to the truth of God's Word without fail. He is the embodiment of truth (John 14:6), the ultimate revelation of God to mankind (Hebrews 1:1–2), and the fulfillment of prophecy. His earthly ministry, sacrificial death, and resurrection serve as the perfect testimony to God's redemptive plan.

The phrase "first begotten of the dead" does not mean Jesus was the first person to be resurrected, as others like Lazarus were raised before Him. Instead, it means He is the preeminent one over all who will rise. His resurrection was unique—it was a permanent victory over death (Romans 6:9), and He is the firstfruit or prototype of the resurrection that all believers will experience (1 Corinthians 15:20–23).

Jesus is not just a spiritual leader—He is the ruler of all earthly kings. Though earthly powers may claim sovereignty, all authority ultimately belongs to Him (Matthew 28:18). This foreshadows His coming reign as the King of kings (Revelation 19:16), when He will overthrow all human kingdoms and establish His eternal rule.

The phrase "loved us" is in the past tense, pointing to the definitive act of His love—His sacrifice on the Cross. Romans 5:8 echoes this truth: "But God commends His love toward us, in that, while we were yet sinners, Christ died for us." His love is not just a feeling but an action that secured our redemption.

Sin is an unpayable debt, but Jesus paid it in full through His own blood. The word "washed" conveys a complete cleansing, not just covering sin but removing it entirely. Unlike the Old Testament sacrifices, which only temporarily atoned for sin, Christ's blood fully redeems and restores us (Hebrews 9:12–14).

OLD TESTAMENT FORESHADOWS REVELATION:

But He was wounded for our transgressions, He was bruised for our iniquities: the chastisement of our peace was upon Him; and with His stripes we are healed. (Isaiah 53:5)

Revelation 1:5 declares Jesus as the faithful witness, the firstborn from the dead, and the ruler of kings, emphasizing His love and the cleansing power of His blood. This echoes Isaiah 53:5, where the suffering of the Messiah is foretold—His wounds would bring healing, and His sacrifice would remove sin. The Old Testament foreshadowed the atonement, and Revelation confirms its fulfillment.

Christ's blood is not just a covering—it is complete redemption, washing us clean in the blood forever.

THE REVELATION OF JESUS CHRIST REVEALS:

1:6 And has made us kings and priests unto God and His Father; to Him be glory and dominion forever and ever. Amen.

This verse reveals the incredible transformation that Christ has accomplished for believers. Through His sacrifice, we are not merely forgiven—we are elevated to the status of kings and priests in His Kingdom. This echoes Exodus 19:6, where God declared to Israel: "And you shall be unto Me a kingdom of priests, and a holy nation. These are the words which you shalt speak unto the children of Israel." What was once a promise to Israel is now fulfilled in Christ's Church.

Being made kings signifies the authority believers have in Christ. As members of His Kingdom, we are called to walk in spiritual authority, ruling over sin, darkness, and the enemy through the power of the Holy Spirit. Though we may not see this kingship fully realized now, Revelation 5:10 affirms that we "shall reign on the earth." This points to the coming Millennial Kingdom, where believers will rule with Christ.

Being made priests speaks of direct access to God, something previously reserved only for Israel's high priests. Now, through Jesus—our ultimate High Priest (Hebrews 4:14)—we can boldly approach God's throne. As priests, we are called to intercede, worship, and offer spiritual sacrifices (Romans 12:1, 1 Peter 2:5).

This passage ends with a declaration of eternal praise: "to Him be glory and dominion forever and ever. Amen." Christ is not only the one who saves but the eternal King who reigns forever. Every act of redemption and transformation ultimately points back to His glory, and one day, all creation will recognize His dominion (Philippians 2:10–11).

OLD TESTAMENT FORESHADOWS REVELATION:

But you shall be named the priests of the LORD: men shall call you the ministers of our God: you shall eat the riches of the Gentiles (non-Jews), and in their glory shall you boast yourselves. (Isaiah 61:6)

Isaiah 61:6 prophesies that God's people will be priests of the LORD, ministering on His behalf. This verse finds its ultimate fulfillment in Revelation 1:6, where Jesus, through His redemptive work, elevates His followers to kings and priests in His eternal Kingdom.

In the Old Testament, the priesthood was limited to the Levites, but through Christ, all believers now share in this royal priesthood (1 Peter 2:9). As priests, we have direct access to God, and as kings, we are given spiritual authority under Christ's dominion.

Isaiah's prophecy also points to a time when God's people will experience abundance and honor, reflecting Revelation's promise that Christ's redeemed will reign with Him forever.

THE REVELATION OF JESUS CHRIST REVEALS:

1:7 Behold, He comes with clouds; and every eye shall see Him, and they also which pierced Him: and all nations of the earth shall wail because of Him. Even so, Amen.

This verse is one of the most powerful declarations of Jesus Christ's visible, triumphant return. Unlike His First Coming in humility, His Second Coming will be with clouds—a symbol of divine presence, majesty, and judgment. This imagery echoes Daniel 7:13, where the Son of Man is seen coming with the clouds of heaven to receive dominion over all nations.

"Every eye shall see Him." This is a clear statement that Christ's return will be undeniable and universal. His coming will not be hidden, symbolic, or spiritualized—it will be a literal, global event witnessed by every human being. This stands in contrast to the Rapture, which happens in the twinkling of an eye (1 Corinthians 15:52) and is only for the redeemed. The Second Coming, however, will be a public, unmistakable event that no one can ignore.

The phrase "they also which pierced Him" refers directly to those responsible for Christ's crucifixion, which includes the Jewish leaders and the Roman authorities of His day, but extends to all who reject Him throughout history. This prophecy echoes Zechariah 12:10, which foretells a day when Israel will look upon the One they have pierced and mourn. It signifies the moment of national repentance when many in Israel will finally recognize Jesus as their Messiah.

"And all nations of the earth shall wail because of Him." The entire world will react to Christ's return with fear, sorrow, and dread—not because of uncertainty, but because they know judgment has come. The "wailing" (*kopsontai* in Greek) refers to deep mourning and despair as people realize they have rejected the true King. This reflects Matthew 24:30, where the tribes of the earth mourn at His appearing.

For believers, His return is a glorious hope (Titus 2:13), but for the rebellious world, it will be a day of reckoning. In other words, for 6,000 years, the world has suffered under the rule of sin, corruption, and Satan's dominion. But when Jesus returns, He comes to redeem, to restore, and to reign. This is not a moment of retreat—it is a moment of victory.

Jesus is not returning as a Suffering Servant, but as a victorious King.

- The First Coming was marked by humility—a manger in Bethlehem.
- The Second Coming will be marked by glory—lightning, clouds, and angelic armies.
- The First Coming led Him to a Cross.
- The Second Coming will lead Him to a throne.
- The First Coming He came to save.
- The Second Coming He will come to judge and rule.

John wastes no time in Revelation—from the very beginning, he proclaims the central truth of prophecy: Jesus is coming again. Every eye will see Him. Every nation will mourn. Every knee will bow. And He will reign forever and ever.

OLD TESTAMENT FORESHADOWS REVELATION:

And I will pour upon the house of David, and upon the inhabitants of Jerusalem, the spirit of grace and of supplications: and they shall look upon Me whom they have pierced, and they shall mourn for Him, as one mourns for his only son, and shall be in bitterness for Him, as one that is in bitterness for his firstborn. In that day shall there be a great mourning in Jerusalem, as the mourning of Hadad Rimmon in the valley of Megiddo (Armageddon). And the land shall mourn, every family apart; the family of the house of David apart, and their wives apart; the family of the house of Nathan apart, and their wives apart; The family of the house of Levi apart, and their wives apart; the family of Shimei apart, and their wives apart. All the families that remain, every family apart, and their wives apart. (Zechariah 12:10–14)

This passage in Zechariah is a direct prophetic parallel to Revelation 1:7, foretelling the moment when Israel and the world will recognize Jesus as the pierced Messiah. The mourning described in Zechariah aligns with the global wailing in Revelation when Christ returns in power and glory.

Leaning forward, confused. "Wait a second. I thought Jesus was coming like a thief in the night? But now you're saying every eye will see Him?"

Smiling knowingly. "You're right—He does come as a thief . . . but that's at the Rapture."

Raising an eyebrow. "So, there are two comings?"

Nodding. "Yes. The Bible presents a paradox. One coming is secret, like a thief—the Rapture. The other is open and visible—the Second Coming of Christ. They are separate events."

Crossing her arms. "That's a pretty big distinction."

Chuckling softly. "I know—it's a lot to take in. But think of it this way: the Rapture is like a midnight evacuation, sudden and unseen, while the Second Coming is a full-scale invasion, undeniable and glorious. When we get to chapter 4: The Rapture of the Church—Revelation 4:1, we'll unpack the two distinct future comings of Christ. I promise, it'll all come together."

Sighing. "Alright, but I'm holding you to that."

"Deal." Turning back to the text. "Now, where were we?"

THE REVELATION OF JESUS CHRIST REVEALS:

^{1:8} I am the Alpha and Omega, the Beginning and the Ending, says the Lord, which is, and which was, and which is to come, the Almighty.

Jesus proclaims Himself as Alpha and Omega, the first and last letters of the Greek alphabet, signifying that He is both the origin (beginning) and the completion (ending) of all things. This declaration affirms His eternal nature— before anything existed, He was; when all things come to an end, He remains.

"Which is, and which was, and which is to come" echoes Exodus 3:14, where God revealed Himself to Moses as "I AM THAT I AM." This phrase encapsulates Christ's sovereignty over past, present, and future, reinforcing His unchanging nature (Hebrews 13:8).

Jesus concludes with the title "the Almighty" (Greek: *Pantokrator*), meaning the all-powerful One, who reigns over all creation with absolute authority. This is both a warning to His enemies and a comfort to His followers—no matter how chaotic the world becomes, Christ holds dominion over history, eternity, and the unfolding events of Revelation. His victory is certain, and He alone governs the destiny of all things.

OLD TESTAMENT FORESHADOWS REVELATION:

Who has performed and done it, calling the generations from the beginning? I the LORD, the First, and with the Last; I am He. (Isaiah 41:4)

Thus says the LORD the King of Israel, and his Redeemer the LORD of hosts; I am the First, and I am the Last; and beside Me there is no God. (Isaiah 44:6)

Listen unto Me, O Jacob and Israel, My called; I am He; I am the First, I also am the Last. (Isaiah 48:12)

Revelation 1:8 declares Jesus Christ as the Alpha and Omega, the Beginning and the End, affirming His eternal nature and sovereignty over time, history, and all creation. This powerful statement echoes the words of Isaiah 41:4, 44:6, and

48:12, where God alone declares Himself as the First and the Last, emphasizing that there is no other God beside Him.

These Old Testament passages foreshadow Christ's divine identity, revealing that the same eternal, unchanging God of Israel is the Lord of Revelation, reigning over the past, present, and future. His supremacy is not just in creation but also in redemption and ultimate victory, securing the hope of all who trust in Him.

CHRIST APPEARS TO JOHN

With the Prologue complete, the Book of Revelation transports us nearly 2,000 years back to a desolate island in the Aegean Sea—Patmos. This barren, rocky prison was a place of exile and suffering, yet it became the setting for one of the most extraordinary revelations in human history.

By the end of the first century, Christianity had spread throughout the Roman Empire, igniting fierce persecution. Seen as a growing threat to imperial rule, believers were hunted, imprisoned, and executed. Among them was John, the last living apostle of Jesus Christ. For refusing to renounce his faith, he was banished to Patmos, a remote island where Rome sent political and religious dissidents to silence them. Isolated from the churches he once shepherded, John was physically bound—but spiritually, he was about to receive a vision unlike any before.

In his darkest exile, heaven opened. The silence of Patmos was shattered by the voice of the Almighty, revealing Christ in His full glory. The once-veiled mysteries of the end times would now be unveiled. From that place of suffering came the final, triumphant prophecy of Scripture—a revelation of judgment, redemption, and ultimate victory.

Revelation is not merely a book of warning; it is a declaration of Christ's return, the final defeat of evil, and the fulfillment of God's eternal plan. It unmasks the enemy's schemes, affirms the certainty of God's Kingdom, and offers hope to all who long for His appearing.

Now, we step into the vision. The veil is lifted. Heaven speaks. The Revelation of Jesus Christ begins.

THE REVELATION OF JESUS CHRIST REVEALS:

[1:9] I John, who also am your brother, and companion in tribulation, and in the kingdom and patience of Jesus Christ, was in the isle that is called Patmos, for the Word of God, and for the testimony of Jesus Christ.

At the close of the first century, the Roman Empire was at the height of its power. While it tolerated many religions, it demanded absolute loyalty to the emperor. Worshiping Roman gods was not optional—it was expected. And one of the most common practices was to burn incense in honor of the emperor, acknowledging his divinity.

But John refused. He stood for the truth of the gospel, refusing to bow to the false gods of Rome or acknowledge Domitian—the reigning emperor—as divine. His unwavering testimony of Jesus Christ as the only true King led to severe persecution. According to early Christian accounts, Domitian first attempted to execute John by immersing him in a vat of boiling oil. Yet, miraculously, John survived unharmed, leaving even his enemies astonished.

Unable to kill him, Domitian resorted to another form of punishment—exile. John was sent to Patmos, a small, rocky island in the Aegean Sea, about nine miles long and five miles wide, located near modern-day Turkey and Greece. This exile was intended to silence him, to remove his influence from the rapidly growing Christian movement. But what Domitian meant for isolation; God used for revelation.

It was on Patmos, during this time of persecution, that John received the most extraordinary vision ever given to man—a revelation of Jesus Christ in His full glory, the future of the Church, the final judgment of evil, and the ultimate triumph of God's Kingdom.

John describes himself not as an exalted apostle, but as a "brother and companion in tribulation," standing in solidarity with all believers who endure hardship for the sake of Christ. His testimony reminds us that faithfulness to God often comes at a cost, but no trial—no exile—is beyond the reach of God's purpose and power. The Book of Revelation is living proof that, even in our darkest moments, God is still speaking, still revealing, and still in control.

OLD TESTAMENT FORESHADOWS REVELATION:

Shadrach, Meshach, and Abednego answered and said to the king, O Nebuchadnezzar, we are not careful to answer you in this matter. If it be so, our God whom we serve is able to deliver us from the burning fiery furnace, and He will deliver us out of your hand, O king. But if not, be it known unto you, O king, that we will not serve your gods, nor worship the golden image which you have set up. (Daniel 3:16–18)

Just as John refused to bow to the emperor and suffered exile for his faith, Shadrach, Meshach, and Abednego refused to worship Nebuchadnezzar's image, knowing their stand for God could lead to death. Both accounts highlight faithfulness in the face of persecution, the refusal to compromise with worldly powers, and God's sovereignty over those who endure suffering for His name.

Like John on Patmos, the three Hebrew men were exiled—cast into the fiery furnace—yet their suffering became a stage for God's power to be revealed. John's exile led to the unveiling of Christ's ultimate victory in Revelation, just as

Shadrach, Meshach, and Abednego's trial resulted in a miraculous deliverance that demonstrated God's supreme authority over kings and empires.

THE REVELATION OF JESUS CHRIST REVEALS:

[1:10] I was in the Spirit on the Lord's Day, and heard behind me a great voice, as of a trumpet.

Revelation 1:10 captures a pivotal moment in biblical history—the beginning of John's supernatural vision that unveils the final chapter of God's redemptive plan. John opens with the striking declaration that he was "in the Spirit on the Lord's Day." This was no ordinary prayer experience. He was spiritually transported into a divine realm, where earthly boundaries faded and heaven itself broke into his consciousness. In this Spirit-empowered state, John became the vessel through which Jesus Christ would reveal the apocalyptic vision.

The phrase "the Lord's Day" is unique—appearing only once in all of Scripture—and yet it bears immense theological significance. The early church universally recognized this as Sunday, the first day of the week, marking the resurrection of Jesus Christ and establishing it as the appointed day of Christian worship. Though the Jewish Sabbath (the seventh day) was divinely instituted in Eden (Genesis 2:1–3) and practiced even before the giving of the Mosaic Law (Exodus 16:23–30), the resurrection shifted the worship focus from Sabbath to Sunday. This wasn't a rejection of the Sabbath's sanctity but a fulfillment of its deeper prophetic meaning. The empty tomb on the first day of the week declared that a new covenant had been sealed in Christ's blood.

This shift, however, wasn't without controversy. The early church, especially Jewish believers, wrestled with how much of the Law Gentile converts were to observe. Acts 15 recounts the Jerusalem Council's resolution–not to bind Gentile believers to the ceremonial laws of Moses, but to emphasize a life of holiness centered on Christ. Worshiping on Sunday became an expression of New Covenant life—joyfully proclaiming the risen Lord.

Still, the Sabbath's prophetic thread weaves throughout Scripture. Passages such as Ezekiel 46:1 reveal that in the Millennial Kingdom, the temple will be open only on the Sabbath and on the new moon. This indicates that God's appointed times still hold significance in His eternal plan. Moreover, Daniel 7:25 prophesies that the Antichrist will "think to change times and laws," suggesting an end-time distortion of God's established rhythms. Proverbs 22:28 solemnly warns, "Do not move the ancient landmarks," underscoring that God's timing and order are not to be tampered with.

John's experience, then, takes place within this tension of fulfilled prophecy and enduring sacred order. While Sunday commemorates resurrection, the seventh day remains a marker of divine rhythm, still pointing forward to the coming reign of Christ—the true Sabbath rest for God's people.

And then comes the sound—a voice "as of a trumpet." In Scripture, trumpets are never random. They announce divine intervention, summon God's people, initiate battle, and declare royal decrees. From Sinai's thunderous trumpet blast to the final trumpet in Paul's epistles, these sounds mark God's movements. So too here—John hears a heavenly blast, not from an instrument, but from the very voice of Jesus Christ. It signifies that something extraordinary is about to be revealed: the unfolding of the final era of human history.

Revelation 1:10 is far more than a timestamp. It's a convergence of old and new—a moment where prophetic time, covenantal fulfillment, and divine revelation collide. The Lord's Day, the Spirit's presence, and the trumpet voice together launch the greatest unveiling in all of Scripture: *the Revelation of Jesus Christ*.

OLD TESTAMENT FORESHADOWS REVELATION:

And it came to pass on the third day in the morning, that there were thunders and lightnings, and a thick cloud upon the mount, and the voice of the trumpet exceeding loud; so that all the people that were in the camp trembled. (Exodus 19:16)

Just as John heard a voice like a trumpet announcing the revelation of Christ, the Israelites at Mount Sinai heard the divine trumpet blast announcing God's presence and the giving of the Law. Both events mark a pivotal moment of divine revelation—one at the foundation of the Old Covenant and the other at the unveiling of the New Covenant's final fulfillment.

Additionally, both involve a chosen servant in a place of separation—Moses on Mount Sinai, and John on Patmos—receiving a message directly from God that would shape the future of His people. This connection emphasizes that God's voice like a trumpet is a symbol of divine authority, revelation, and a call to attention for His people, whether at Sinai, in Revelation, or at the return of Christ.

THE REVELATION OF JESUS CHRIST REVEALS:

1:11 Saying, I am Alpha and Omega, the First and the Last; and, What you see, write in a book, and send it unto the seven churches which are in Asia; unto Ephesus, and unto Smyrna, and unto Pergamos, and unto Thyatira, and unto Sardis, and unto Philadelphia, and unto Laodicea.

Jesus reaffirms His divine authority by declaring Himself as the Alpha and Omega, the First and the Last—a title emphasizing His eternal nature and sovereignty over all creation. As Alpha (the beginning), He is the source of all things; as Omega (the end), He is the fulfillment of all things. Again, this echoes

Isaiah 44:6, where God declares, "I am the First, and I am the Last, and beside Me there is no God." It reinforces Christ's deity and His role as the ultimate authority over history and eternity.

John is given a clear command: to document the vision he is about to receive and distribute it to the seven specific churches in Asia Minor. These churches were real congregations, but their inclusion also symbolizes the complete Church Age throughout history. The number seven represents perfection and completeness in biblical numerology, indicating that this message is for all believers across time.

"Unto Ephesus, and unto Smyrna, and unto Pergamos, and unto Thyatira, and unto Sardis, and unto Philadelphia, and unto Laodicea." Each of the seven churches represents different spiritual conditions found in both the early church and churches throughout history.

1. **Ephesus**—The church that had forsaken its first love.
2. **Smyrna**—The persecuted church that remained faithful.
3. **Pergamos**—The compromising church that tolerated false teaching.
4. **Thyatira**—The corrupt church that allowed immorality.
5. **Sardis**—The spiritually dead church that needed revival.
6. **Philadelphia**—The faithful church with an open door.
7. **Laodicea**—The lukewarm church, spiritually indifferent and self-sufficient.

These churches were real, historical churches that existed in the first century, in Asia Minor. However, their significance goes far beyond their physical locations. They represent prophetic messages applicable to different periods of church history, illustrating the spiritual condition of the Church throughout the ages. They also carry personal applications—every believer can find warnings, encouragements, and calls to repentance in these messages.

The Book of Acts covers about 30 years of early church history, while the Book of Revelation unveils nearly 2,000 years of church history—Revelation 2–3. Jesus is declaring in this verse that He is not only the beginning of the Church Age but also the One who will sustain it until the very end.

By commanding John to write these messages in a book and send them to the churches, Christ affirmed that He is the God over the entire Church Age—from the first church in Ephesus to the final church in Laodicea. As Alpha and Omega, the First and the Last, He alone holds authority over the destiny of the Church. He birthed the church, and He will see it through to its final victory in the New Jerusalem.

This passage is a powerful reminder that Jesus Christ is sovereign over history, guiding His Church through every trial, every victory, every failure, and every moment of revival—until the day He returns in glory.

OLD TESTAMENT FORESHADOWS REVELATION:

Who has performed and done it, calling the generations from the beginning? I, the LORD, am the First; and with the Last, I am He. (Isaiah 41:4)

Then the LORD said to Moses, Write this for a memorial in the book and recount it in the hearing of Joshua. (Exodus 17:14)

Again, Isaiah 41:4, spoken by God, establishes His sovereignty over all time—past, present, and future. Similarly, in Revelation 1:11, Jesus declares Himself as Alpha and Omega, the First and Last, reinforcing His eternal nature and divine authority.

Additionally, Exodus 17:14 provides a connection to the command to write in a book. Just as Moses was instructed to record God's revelation, John is commanded to write down what he sees and send it to the churches. This shows that God has always used written revelation to instruct, warn, and guide His people.

THE REVELATION OF JESUS CHRIST REVEALS:

$^{1:12}$ And I turned to see the voice that spoke with me. And being turned, I saw seven golden candlesticks (menorah).

As John hears the majestic voice speaking to him, he instinctively turns to see who is speaking. But instead of seeing a single figure at first, his eyes fall upon seven golden candlesticks—a profound and symbolic image.

The seven candlesticks represent the seven churches in Asia Minor (Revelation 1:11, 20). In ancient times, a candlestick or lampstand was not the source of light itself—it was merely a vessel that held the flame. Likewise, the Church does not produce its own light but is called to hold and reflect the light of Christ to the world.

These candlesticks are not made of common material, but gold—symbolizing their great value and divine purpose. Though churches may face persecution, trials, and spiritual battles, they remain precious in the sight of God. They are meant to shine His truth, His love, and His righteousness in a world of darkness.

The most significant truth in this verse is where Jesus is—He is standing among the candlesticks (Revelation 1:13). This is a powerful assurance that Christ is not distant from His Church but present, watching, guiding, and protecting. He is actively involved in the life of His people, offering strength, correction, and encouragement.

OLD TESTAMENT FORESHADOWS REVELATION:

And (the angel) said unto me, What do you see? And I said, I have looked, and behold a candlestick all of gold, with a bowl upon the top of it, and is seven lamps thereon, and seven pipes to the seven lamps, which are upon the top thereof. (Zechariah 4:2)

A strong Old Testament parallel to Revelation 1:12 is found in Zechariah 4:2. This vision given to Zechariah closely resembles John's vision of the seven golden candlesticks in Revelation. In Zechariah's prophecy, the lampstand represents Israel as God's chosen people, shining His light in the world. The vision emphasizes that the power to shine does not come from human strength but from God's Spirit (Zechariah 4:6).

Similarly, in Revelation, the seven candlesticks symbolize the Church, which is called to be a light in a dark world. Just as the menorah in the tabernacle and temple stood as a symbol of God's presence among His people, the candlesticks in John's vision represent Christ's presence among the churches.

THE REVELATION OF JESUS CHRIST REVEALS:

$^{1:13}$ And in the midst of the seven candlesticks One like unto the Son of Man, clothed with a garment down to the foot, with a gold sash across His chest.

In Revelation 1:13, John sees "One like unto the Son of Man" standing in the midst of the seven golden candlesticks. This is none other than Jesus Christ, a title He often used for Himself throughout the gospels, emphasizing both His humanity and His divine authority as the prophesied Messiah (Daniel 7:13).

Additionally, His golden sash (Revelation 1:13) reveals His role as the High Priest, interceding on behalf of believers before the throne of God. As the all-knowing, all-seeing, and all-powerful Son of God, Jesus is both the merciful intercessor and the righteous judge, ensuring that evil will not go unpunished, and righteousness will be upheld.

John immediately recognizes Jesus—not only as the teacher and friend he walked with for three and a half years but also as the glorified Son of God, whom he had glimpsed at the Transfiguration (Matthew 17:1–2). Now, standing among the churches, Jesus is clothed in a long robe with a golden sash, a clear symbol of His high priestly role (Exodus 28:4; Hebrews 4:14), interceding for His people.

This vision reassures believers that Christ is not distant—He walks among His churches, watching over them with authority, power, and an enduring love that will never fade.

OLD TESTAMENT FORESHADOWS REVELATION:

I saw in the night visions, and, behold, One like the Son of Man came with the clouds of heaven, and came to the Ancient of Days, and they brought Him near before Him. (Daniel 7:13)

The vision of One like the Son of Man in Revelation 1:13 directly connects to Daniel 7:13, where the Messianic ruler approaches the Ancient of Days in heavenly glory. In both passages, Jesus is revealed as the exalted Son of Man, standing in divine authority. His long robe and golden sash signify His role as High Priest and King, while His presence among the seven candlesticks (churches) affirms His continued leadership, intercession, and protection over His people. This imagery confirms that the same Christ who ascended in Daniel's vision is now revealed in Revelation as the triumphant Lord over His Church and all creation.

THE REVELATION OF JESUS CHRIST REVEALS:

[1:14] His head and His hairs were white like wool, as white as snow; and His eyes were as a flame of fire.

In this vision, Jesus appears in His divine glory, displaying characteristics that emphasize His wisdom, purity, and righteous judgment. The white hair is a powerful symbol of His eternal nature and infinite wisdom, echoing Daniel 7:9, where the Ancient of Days is described with hair as pure wool. This imagery ties Jesus directly to God the Father, reinforcing His deity.

His eyes like a flame of fire signify His penetrating gaze, He sees all things and judges with perfect righteousness. Fire in Scripture often represents purification and judgment (Malachi 3:2; Hebrews 12:29). Jesus' fiery eyes indicate that nothing is hidden from Him—He sees into the hearts of men and discerns truth from deception.

This verse sets the stage for His coming judgment and the unveiling of His authority over all things, reminding us that Jesus is not just the suffering Lamb, but also the sovereign Lord and King of kings.

OLD TESTAMENT FORESHADOWS REVELATION:

I beheld till the thrones were cast down, and the Ancient of Days did sit, whose garment was white as snow, and the hair of head like the pure wool: His throne was like the fiery flame, and His wheels as burning fire. (Daniel 7:9)

A strong Old Testament parallel to Revelation 1:14 is found in Daniel 7:9. This passage in Daniel describes God the Father—the Ancient of Days—clothed in white with hair like pure wool, emphasizing His eternity, wisdom, and holiness.

In Revelation, Jesus appears with the same attributes, signifying His divine nature and unity with the Father (John 10:30).

THE REVELATION OF JESUS CHRIST REVEALS:

[1:15] And His feet like unto fine brass, as if they burned in a furnace, and His voice as the sound of many waters.

In Revelation 1:15, John describes Jesus with feet like fine brass, as if burned in a furnace, and a voice like the sound of many waters. These powerful images symbolize both judgment and authority.

Brass in the Bible often represents purity through judgment and refining fire. In the Old Testament, the brazen altar (Exodus 27:1–2) was where sacrifices were offered for sin, pointing to Jesus as the ultimate sacrifice. His feet of burnished brass signify that He has walked through the fire of suffering and emerged victorious, standing firm in righteousness and justice.

His voice like the sound of many waters conveys power, majesty, and divine authority. Just as the roar of the ocean is overwhelming and undeniable, so is the voice of Christ—commanding, unstoppable, and filled with sovereign might. This imagery connects with Ezekiel 43:2, where the glory of God is described with a voice like rushing waters, underscoring that Jesus is fully divine and reigns as King and Judge.

This verse reminds us that Christ's judgment is pure, His authority is unshakable, and His voice carries the very word of life and power.

OLD TESTAMENT FORESHADOWS REVELATION:

His body also was like the beryl, and His face as the appearance of lightning, and His eyes as lamps of fire, and His arms and His feet like in color to polished brass, and the voice of His words like the voice of a multitude. (Daniel 10:6)

And, behold, the glory of the God of Israel came from the way of the east: and His voice was like a noise of many waters: and the earth shined with His glory. (Ezekiel 43:2)

A strong Old Testament parallel to Revelation 1:15 is found in Daniel 10:6. This vision of a heavenly figure, likely a pre-incarnate appearance of Christ or an angelic being reflecting His majesty, closely mirrors John's description—particularly the burnished brass feet and the thunderous voice, representing divine power, judgment, and purity.

Another parallel is found in Ezekiel 43:2. This passage emphasizes the majestic and overwhelming nature of God's voice, just as John describes Jesus' voice as the sound of many waters—a voice that commands, shakes the heavens, and establishes divine authority.

———◆◆◆———

Leaning forward, intrigued. "Ann, I've heard people say, 'passing through the refiner's fire.' What exactly does that mean? And does it have anything to do with John's vision of the Son of Man?"

Smiling knowingly. "That's a great question, Irene. The phrase 'passing through the refiner's fire' comes from the process of purifying precious metals like gold and silver. The metal is heated in a furnace until the impurities rise to the surface, where they can be removed. It's a biblical metaphor for how God purifies His people through trials, refining their faith, and making them spiritually stronger."

Nodding slowly. "So, it's about testing and purification . . . but how does that connect to John's vision?"

"In Revelation 1:15, John describes Jesus' feet as 'like fine brass, as if they burned in a furnace.' Brass, or bronze, in the Bible represents judgment and purification. The fact that Jesus' feet appear this way means that He has been through the ultimate refining process—He endured suffering, was tested beyond measure, and emerged victorious. His very presence speaks of holiness and justice."

Eyes widening. "Wow, so when people say they're 'going through the refiner's fire,' it means they're being tested and purified, just like Christ was. But unlike us, He came through it completely pure, without sin."

I smiled. "Exactly! Christ went through the fire, not for His own purification, but so that He could purify us. And when we go through trials, God is refining us, making us more like Him. John's vision isn't just about what Jesus looks like—it's a declaration of who He is: the holy, victorious, and reigning King who has overcome the fire of judgment on our behalf."

Sitting back in thought. "That makes so much sense. And it means that no trial we go through is wasted—God is using it to refine us."

"Exactly. Just like the refiner watches over the gold in the fire, making sure it isn't destroyed, God is watching over us in our trials. And when we emerge, we reflect His glory even more."

"I love that. Passing through the fire isn't easy, but knowing that it's making me more like Jesus? That's worth it."

———◆◆◆———

THE REVELATION OF JESUS CHRIST REVEALS:

1:16 And He had in His right hand seven stars: and out of His mouth went a sharp two-edged sword: and His countenance was as the sun shines in its strength.

In Revelation 1:16, we see a striking depiction of Jesus Christ in His glorified state. He holds seven stars in His right hand, symbolizing His authority and protection over the seven churches (as later explained in Revelation 1:20). The right hand in Scripture often represents power, security, and control. This imagery reassures us that Christ upholds His Church, ensuring that His people remain in His grasp, no matter the trials they face.

The sharp two-edged sword proceeding from Jesus' mouth symbolizes the power and authority of His Word. This echoes Hebrews 4:12, which describes the Word of God as "living and active, sharper than any two-edged sword." The Word of Christ has the power to judge, correct, divide truth from error, and bring both salvation and destruction. In the gospels, Jesus spoke with authority, silencing demons, calming storms, and declaring eternal truths. Here, in Revelation, His words carry divine judgment and sovereign decree, showing that His speech is not merely persuasive but decisive—bringing either redemption or wrath.

Additionally, John describes Christ's countenance as shining like the sun in its full strength. This glorious radiance signifies His divine majesty and holiness. In the Old Testament, Moses' face glowed after encountering God's presence (Exodus 34:29–35), and at the Transfiguration, Jesus' face shone like the sun (Matthew 17:2), giving a glimpse of His divine nature. Now, in this heavenly vision, John sees the fullness of Christ's glory as the exalted King of kings.

This verse encapsulates Christ's supreme authority—He holds the Church, speaks with divine power, and radiates His unmatched holiness. It is a powerful reminder that Jesus is not only the gentle Lamb of God but also the righteous Judge who will execute justice upon the earth.

OLD TESTAMENT FORESHADOWS REVELATION:

And He has made My mouth like a sharp sword; in the shadow of His hand has He hid Me, and made Me a polished shaft; in His quiver has He hid Me. (Isaiah 49:2)

Isaiah 49:2 prophesies the coming of the Messianic Servant, describing His mouth as a sharp sword, hidden in the hand of God, prepared for a divine purpose. This directly parallels Revelation 1:16, where Jesus, in His glorified state, speaks with the authority of a two-edged sword—a symbol of His Word's power to judge, refine, and pierce the hearts of mankind. Just as Isaiah's prophecy foretells a Savior whose words would cut through deception and establish righteousness, Revelation unveils Christ as the ultimate fulfillment of this prophecy, wielding divine truth and executing righteous judgment.

———◆◆◆———

Leaning forward, raising an eyebrow. "Okay, Ann, that's the second time you've referenced the Transfiguration. What is that all about? I feel like I should know, but I don't think I really get it."

Nodding. "I'm glad you asked, Irene. The Transfiguration is one of the most incredible moments in Jesus's ministry. It's recorded in Matthew 17, Mark 9, and Luke 9—and it's basically a glimpse of Jesus in His glorified state before His resurrection."

Curious. "Glorified? You mean like how John describes Him in Revelation?"

"Exactly! Picture this: Jesus takes Peter, James, and John—yes, the same John who wrote Revelation—up a high mountain. While they're there, something incredible happens. Right in front of them, Jesus' face begins to shine like the sun, and His clothes become dazzling white—brighter than anything on earth."

Eyes widening. "Whoa. That sounds like something straight out of Revelation."

"It is! And get this—Moses and Elijah appear beside Him, talking with Him. Then, a bright cloud overshadows them, and God's voice thunders from heaven, saying, 'This is My beloved Son, in whom I am well pleased. Listen to Him!'"

"Wait—Moses and Elijah? Why them?"

"Great question! Moses represents the Law, and Elijah represents the Prophets—and both are fulfilled in Jesus. This moment confirmed to Peter, James, and John that Jesus wasn't just a teacher or prophet—He was the Son of God, the fulfillment of everything the Old Testament pointed to."

Processing. "So, this was like . . . a preview of Jesus' full glory before He died and rose again?"

"Exactly! And it mirrors how John sees Him in Revelation—not as the Suffering Servant, but as the King of Glory. The Transfiguration gave those three disciples a brief but powerful revelation of who Jesus really is—the same Christ who will return in glory."

Leaning back, shaking her head in amazement. "Okay, that's incredible. And John saw both—the Transfiguration on earth and Jesus in full glory in heaven. No wonder he was the one chosen to write Revelation."

Smiling. "Now you're getting it! John had already seen a glimpse of Jesus in His glory, so when he encountered Him again on Patmos, he recognized Him immediately. The Jesus he walked with was the same Jesus who reigns in glory—and the same Jesus who is coming back."

"Wow. That gives me chills."

"It should! And this is why Revelation isn't just about prophecy—it's about Jesus, the Kings of Kings, revealed."

THE REVELATION OF JESUS CHRIST REVEALS:

1:17 And when I saw Him, I fell at His feet as dead. And He laid His right hand upon me, saying unto me, Fear not; I am the First and the Last.

John, the beloved disciple, had seen Jesus in His earthly ministry, had leaned on His chest at the Last Supper, and had even witnessed His resurrection and ascension. Yet, when he encountered Christ in His unveiled glory on the island of Patmos, he was utterly overwhelmed. The mere sight of Jesus—His eyes burning like fire, His face shining like the sun, His feet glowing like fine brass—was too much for John to bear. In that moment, he collapsed at Christ's feet, as though dead.

This reaction wasn't unique to John. The Bible records similar experiences from men of God who, when confronted with the divine, became painfully aware of their unworthiness. Daniel was left with no strength when he saw the vision of the LORD (Daniel 10:8). Isaiah cried out, "Woe is me! For I am undone," upon seeing the LORD's glory (Isaiah 6:5). Even Moses and the Israelites trembled at God's voice at Mount Sinai (Exodus 20:19). Abraham, despite being a friend of God, acknowledged his own insignificance, calling himself "dust and ashes" (Genesis 18:27).

John's overwhelming reaction stemmed from two key realities. First, he was witnessing unveiled deity. During Jesus' earthly ministry, His divine glory was veiled in human flesh. Even at the Transfiguration, when Jesus' glory shone before Peter, James, and John, it was only a glimpse. But here in Revelation, John saw Christ in the fullness of His divine majesty—the Ancient of Days in all His splendor. The sight was so overwhelming that he had no strength left; he could do nothing but collapse before the glory of the risen King.

Secondly, he was overcome by his own nothingness. In the presence of pure holiness, human frailty becomes painfully evident. Even a disciple as close to Jesus as John was reduced to complete helplessness. This moment reminds us that before the Almighty, every knee must bow—not out of obligation, but out of sheer awe and reverence.

Yet, in this moment of fear and reverence, Jesus did not leave John trembling on the ground. Instead, He laid His right hand upon him and spoke words of reassurance and love: "Fear not; I am the First and the Last." What a powerful contrast! The same hand that had healed the sick, touched blind eyes, and blessed children now rested upon John. The same voice that calmed storms and spoke life into the dead now comforted His beloved disciple.

Though John now saw Jesus in radiant glory, His tender heart remained unchanged. The eyes of fire were the same eyes that had wept over Jerusalem and at Lazarus' tomb. The feet of brass were the same feet that had walked through Galilee, bringing the message of salvation. Jesus had not changed—only the way John saw Him had.

OLD TESTAMENT FORESHADOWS REVELATION:

So He came near where I stood: and when He came, I was afraid, and fell upon my face: but He said unto me, Understand, O son of man: for at the time of the end shall be the vision. Now as He was speaking with me, I was in a deep sleep on my face toward the ground: but He touched me, and set me up rightly. (Daniel 8:17–18)

Encounters with God throughout Scripture evoke awe and fear. Daniel fell on his face until God's touch lifted him. Similarly, in Revelation 1:17, John falls dead before Christ's unveiled glory. But Jesus, in divine tenderness, lays His right hand on John and says, "Fear not; I am the First and the Last." God's power is overwhelming, yet His touch is always comforting and reassuring.

THE REVELATION OF JESUS CHRIST REVEALS:

1:18 I am He who lives, and was dead; and behold, I am alive forevermore, Amen; and have the keys of hell and of death.

This powerful statement affirms Christ's deity, His resurrection, and His dominion over life and death.

"I am He who lives, and was dead." This phrase underscores both Christ's divinity and humanity. Jesus, the eternal Son of God, took on flesh and died for the sins of the world. But death could not hold Him. His resurrection is the cornerstone of Christian faith, proving that He is the source of eternal life (John 11:25–26).

Jesus said unto her, I am the resurrection, and the life: he that believes in Me, though he were dead, yet shall he live. And whosoever lives and believes in Me shall never die. Believe you this? (John 11:25–26)

The contrast between "was dead" and "lives" also emphasizes the uniqueness of Christ. No other religious leader has claimed to have died and risen to eternal life. Jesus alone has conquered death permanently, not temporarily like those whom He resurrected during His earthly ministry (for example, Lazarus in John 11:43–44).

"And behold, I am alive forevermore, Amen." Jesus' resurrection is not temporary but eternal. He did not rise only to die again—He rose never to die again. This is the guarantee of victory for all who believe in Him. Romans 6:9 affirms this truth: "Knowing that Christ being raised from the dead dies no more; death has no more dominion over Him."

The word "Amen" serves as a solemn confirmation—a divine affirmation of His unchanging, eternal existence.

"And have the keys of hell and of death." The *keys* symbolize authority and control. In biblical times, keys were signs of power—the one who held the keys had access, ownership, and the right to admit or deny entry.

- Jesus rules over the unseen world—He has authority over Hades (the realm of the dead) and death itself.
- Jesus ensures eternal security—Just as God shut the door of Noah's Ark to protect those inside, Jesus secures the eternal safety of those who trust in Him.
- Jesus guarantees victory over death—For believers, death is not the end, but a doorway to eternal life in His presence.

This verse stands as one of the most triumphant declarations of Christ's eternal reign, His sovereignty over the grave, and the unshakable hope for all who trust in Him.

OLD TESTAMENT FORESHADOWS REVELATION:

He that is our God is the God of salvation; and unto God the LORD belong the issues from death. (Psalm 68:20)

He will swallow up death in victory; and the Lord GOD will wipe away tears from off all faces. (Isaiah 25:8)

I will ransom them from the power of the grave; I will redeem them from death: O death, I will be your plagues; O grave, I will be your destruction: repentance shall be hid from My eyes. (Hosea 13:14)

Psalm 68:20 affirms that ultimate power over life and death belongs to God alone, just as Jesus declares His victory over the grave in Revelation 1:18. Isaiah's prophecy further aligns with Christ's triumph, revealing that He, having died and risen, now holds the keys to hell and death, ensuring that death itself will one day be completely defeated. Hosea's prophecy foreshadows this truth, proclaiming that God will ransom His people from the power of the grave, and through Christ's authority, death is conquered, securing eternal life for all who believe Him.

THE REVELATION OF JESUS CHRIST REVEALS:

[1:19] Write the things which you have seen, and the things which are, and the things which will be hereafter.

This verse serves as the divine outline of the entire Book of Revelation. It is the only book in the Bible that provides its own structured breakdown at the very beginning, guiding readers through past, present, and future events. Jesus Himself commands John to document what he has witnessed and what is yet to come, providing a progressive, systematic revelation of end-time prophecy.

To help visualize the divine outline of Revelation (Revelation 1:19), I've created an infographic that breaks down the book into its three main sections: the things John has seen (chapter 1), the things which are (chapters 2–3), and the things which will be hereafter (chapters 4–22). This structured timeline highlights the progression of prophecy, the role of the Church, and the unfolding of end-time events. Use this as a quick reference guide to understand the flow and sequence of Revelation as revealed by Jesus Christ!

THE BOOK OF REVELATION

OUTLINE OF THE BOOK OF REVELATION

Revelation 1	Revelation 2-3		Revelation 4-19		Revelation 20		Revelation 21-22
Have Seen	Are Now		Will Happen		Will Happen		Will Happen
Vision	Church Age	Rapture of the Church	Tribulation Age	Second Coming of Jesus Christ	Millennial Age	Great White Throne Judgment	Eternal Age
AD 95	2000 Years		7 Years (3-1/2 + 3-1/2)		1000 Years		New Heaven, New Earth, New Jerusalem
	Rebirth of Israel 1948		7 Seals 7 Trumpets 7 Bowls				

In addition to the structured outline found in Revelation 1:19, the Book of Revelation also contains seven interludes—pauses in the narrative that provide insight, encouragement, and a moment of reflection amidst the unfolding judgments. These interludes do not advance the chronology but instead serve as parenthetical sections, offering important details and spiritual perspective to the events taking place.

The interludes often occur between the judgments, providing a break between the intensity of the seals, trumpets, and bowls. They remind the reader of God's sovereignty, mercy, and redemptive plan, even in the midst of divine wrath. These pauses serve as opportunities for those experiencing the judgments to reflect, repent, and recognize the unfolding plan of God.

Interludes and parentheticals in the Book of Revelation:

1. **Revelation 7**—A divine pause between the sixth and seventh seal judgments, reveals the sealing of 144,000 Israelites, and a great multitude from every nation worshiping before the throne.

2. **Revelation 10–11**—The longest interlude, taking place between the sixth and seventh trumpet judgments, features the mighty angel with the little book and the powerful ministry of the Two Witnesses.

3. **Revelation 12**—A parenthetical chapter presenting a symbolic vision of Israel (the woman), Christ (the Man-child), and the cosmic conflict with Satan, highlighting the spiritual battle behind end-time events.

4. **Revelation 13**—A parenthetical chapter that introduces two beasts—the Antichrist and the False Prophet—revealing their rise to power, global influence, and role in deceiving the world during the Tribulation.

5. **Revelation 14**—A prophetic preview and prelude to the bowl (vial) judgments, featuring the Lamb on Mount Zion, three angelic proclamations, and the final harvest of the earth.

6. **Revelation 17**—The fall of Mystery Babylon (America), portrayed as the great harlot, symbolizing the corrupt religious and political systems of the world under divine judgment.

7. **Revelation 18**—The destruction of Mystery Babylon (America), representing the global economic and commercial system, as God brings swift judgment on its materialistic empire.

The most significant interlude in Revelation occurs between the sixth and seventh trumpet judgments, spanning Revelation 10:1 to 11:14. This extended pause includes the appearance of a mighty angel with a little book, John's renewed call to prophesy, the measuring of the temple, and the ministry, death, and resurrection of the Two Witnesses. Rather than being a simple break in action, this interlude serves as a divine reassurance that even during the darkest times, God's plan continues to unfold with purpose and grace.

Revelation 1:19 provides the divine structure for the entire book, revealing its prophetic timeline—past, present, and future. This key verse assures believers that Jesus Christ, who holds the keys of death and hell (Revelation 1:18), also holds authority over history and eternity. The interludes scattered throughout Revelation serve to remind believers that while judgment is certain, God's mercy and redemption remain central to His plan.

Even in the midst of judgment, God offers hope, instruction, and a call to faithfulness. These interludes reinforce the faithfulness of God's promises and the certainty of Christ's final victory.

OLD TESTAMENT FORESHADOWS REVELATION:

Remember the former things of old: for I am God, and there is none else; I am God; and there is none like Me. Declaring the end from the beginning, and from ancient times the things that are not yet done, saying, My counsel shall stand, and I will do all My pleasure. (Isaiah 46:9–10)

Isaiah 46:9–10 serves as a powerful Old Testament parallel to Revelation 1:19, as both passages affirm God's sovereign control over all of time—past, present, and future. In Isaiah, God declares the "former things of old" and reveals "the end from the beginning," demonstrating His unique authority and omniscient perspective. Similarly, in Revelation 1:19, John is commanded to write the things he has seen, the things which are, and the things which will be hereafter. Both scriptures highlight the prophetic and revelatory nature of God's Word, where divine insight into future events confirms that history is not random but is orchestrated according to God's unchanging counsel and eternal purpose.

THE REVELATION OF JESUS CHRIST REVEALS:

[1:20] The mystery of the seven stars which you saw in My right hand, and the seven golden candlesticks. The seven stars are the angels of the seven churches: and the seven candlesticks which you saw are the seven churches.

Revelation 1:20 serves as a divine key, unlocking the symbolic meaning of the seven stars and seven candlesticks (lampstands). Jesus Himself explains their significance—removing the mystery and reinforcing the importance of His presence among His churches.

The "seven stars" represent the angels (messengers) of the seven churches. The Greek word *angelos* and the Hebrew word *malak* both mean "messenger." While *angelos* often refers to celestial beings, in this context, it is widely understood to mean earthly messengers—leaders of the churches, likely the pastors or elders entrusted with the spiritual oversight of each congregation.

In the Old Testament, the term "messenger" (*malak*) is used for God's chosen representatives: See Haggai 1:13 and Malachi 2:7, next. Since angels are never assigned to the leadership of a church in Scripture, the stars symbolize human messengers—pastors, priests, bishops, or spiritual overseers—entrusted with divine communication from Jesus Christ to guide their churches.

The "seven candlesticks" (lampstands) are the seven churches. A lampstand holds a light, but it is not the source of light—it merely carries and reflects the light of Christ. This imagery shows that the church is meant to illuminate the world with the truth of the gospel (Matthew 5:14–16).

Revelation 1:20 reassures us that Jesus is actively involved in His Church. He is walking among His people, strengthening them, guiding their leaders and upholding His Church through every age. This passage is a powerful reminder that no matter what the Church faces—persecution, trials, or tribulation—Christ remains the light in the darkness, present and sovereign over His people.

OLD TESTAMENT FORESHADOWS REVELATION:

Then spoke Haggai, the LORD's messenger in the LORD's message unto the people, saying, I am with you, says the LORD. (Haggai 1:13)

For the priest's lips should keep knowledge, and they should seek the law at his mouth: for he is the messenger of the LORD of hosts. (Malachi 2:7)

Haggai 1:13 and Malachi 2:7 highlight God's messengers as His appointed spokesmen. In Revelation 1:20, Jesus unveils the mystery of the seven stars (church leaders) and seven candlesticks (churches), affirming His presence among them. Just as God guided Israel through His messengers, Christ now leads and sustains His Church through His appointed servants.

SUMMARY OF REVELATION 1

Revelation chapter 1 serves as both the introduction and foundation of the entire book. It reveals Jesus Christ in His full glory, establishes the divine authorship of the prophecy, and sets the stage for the messages to the seven churches.

John opens with a profound declaration: *This is the Revelation of Jesus Christ*, given by God to His servant to show what must soon take place. A blessing is pronounced upon those who read, hear, and keep the words of this prophecy (Revelation 1:1–3).

John greets the seven churches with grace and peace, acknowledging Jesus as the faithful witness, the firstborn from the dead, and the ruler of the kings of the earth. He praises Christ's redemptive work—how He washed us from our sins with His blood and made us kings and priests to God. Then comes a powerful proclamation: Behold, He is coming with clouds, and every eye will see Him (Revelation 1:4–8).

John then describes his vision of the glorified Christ while exiled on the island of Patmos. On the Lord's Day, he hears a voice like a trumpet commanding him to write to the seven churches (Revelation 1:9–11).

Overwhelmed by this vision, John falls at Jesus' feet as though dead. But Jesus comforts him, saying, Fear not; I am the First and the Last. I am He who lives and was dead, and behold, I am alive forevermore, and I have the keys of Hell and of Death (Revelation 1:17–18).

Finally, Jesus commands John to write the things he has seen, the things which are, and the things which shall be hereafter—outlining the entire structure of the Book of Revelation (Revelation 1:19). Jesus then reveals the mystery of the seven stars and seven golden lampstands, explaining that the stars represent the church leaders (messengers) of the seven churches, and the lampstands symbolize the churches themselves (Revelation 1:20).

KEY TAKEAWAYS

- Jesus is revealed in His full divine glory—not as the Suffering Servant, but as the exalted King and Judge.
- The Book of Revelation is a prophetic message—a divine unveiling of things past, present, and future.
- The Church belongs to Christ—He walks among the lampstands, upholding His people through every age.
- Jesus holds all authority—He is the Alpha and Omega, the First and the Last, and He alone has the power over death and the grave.

With this powerful introduction, the stage is set for the next chapters (Revelation 2 and 3) in the Book of Revelation—where Jesus will address the seven churches, providing encouragement, correction, and prophetic insight into the Church Age and the events to come.

Chapter 3

Revelation 2–3:
The Church Age: 2,000 Years

THE FIRST AND THE LAST—"Ann, before we dive into Revelation chapters 2 and 3, I have to ask—how did Christianity grow from a handful of followers in the first century to what we know as the Church Age? I mean, it started with Jesus and the disciples, but what happened after that?"

"Great question, Irene! The growth of Christianity is nothing short of miraculous. It all began in AD 30 with about 120 disciples in the Upper Room in Jerusalem (Acts 1:15). But Jesus' command to 'Go and make disciples of all nations' (Matthew 28:19) set everything in motion."

"Right, but how fast did it grow? I mean, it's one thing to spread a message, but Christianity reached every continent."

"That's the amazing part, Irene. The Church Age, which spans from Pentecost (Acts 2) to present, has seen incredible growth. Here's an overview."

1. **Early Explosive Growth (AD 30–AD 300)**

   - By AD 100, Christianity had around 7,500–10,000 followers.
   - By AD 200, it grew to 200,000–250,000 believers.
   - By AD 300, estimates suggest 6–7 million Christians.
   - That's an annual growth rate of 3–4 percent, despite persecution.

2. **Imperial Recognition and Medieval Expansion (AD 300–AD 1500)**

- Emperor Constantine's conversion in AD 312 changed everything. By AD 500, there were 30–40 million Christians.
- Growth slowed during the Middle Ages, reaching 80–100 million by AD 1500.
- The growth rate was 0.5–1 percent per year during this time.

3. **Global Expansion (AD 1500–AD 1900)**

- Christianity spread to the Americas, Africa, and Asia during the Age of Exploration.
- By AD 1800, about 200–250 million Christians.
- By AD 1900, it surged to 500–600 million.
- The growth rate was 1.2–1.5 percent per year.

4. **Modern Explosion (AD 1900–Present)**

- By AD 1950, about 850 million Christians.
- By AD 2000, 2 billion Christians.
- By AD 2025, 2.5–2.6 billion Christians worldwide.
- In the 20th century, Christianity grew 1.8–2 percent yearly, especially in the Global South (Africa, Asia, and Latin America). In the 21st century, growth has continued steadily, with the majority of new believers still emerging from these same regions.

"Wow, that's incredible! From 120 people in AD 30 to 2.5 billion today?"

"Yes. In the last 1,995 years (AD 30–AD 2025), Christianity has grown to over 2.5 billion people today. And if you calculate the overall average growth rate since AD 30, it's about 0.46 percent per year. But that rate fluctuated—early Christianity grew exponentially, the Middle Ages saw slower growth, and modern missionary movements reignited expansion."

"So, Christianity isn't just a Western religion?"

"Not at all. Today, the fastest-growing Christian populations are in Africa, Asia, and Latin America. Europe and North America have slowed, but Christianity continues to expand globally."

Irene nodded. "That's a perfect setup for Revelation chapters 2 and 3, where Jesus addresses the seven churches—each representing different phases of church history spanning nearly 2,000 years!"

"Exactly! The seven churches aren't just historical—they show the evolution of the Church Age from its birth to today. And with that, let's dive in!"

———◆◆◆———

THE CHURCH AGE: A PROPHESIED MYSTERY REVEALED

Before we examine Revelation 2 and 3, it's crucial to understand the Church Age—a period that began with Christ and will continue until the Rapture of the Church. Jesus first prophesied its coming in Matthew 16:18, declaring:

> And I say also unto you, that you are Peter, and upon this rock I will build my church; and the gates of hell shall not prevail against it. (Matthew 16:18)

This was a groundbreaking revelation—before this, the concept of the Church did not exist. The Old Testament speaks of Israel and synagogues, but not the Church. Why? Because the Church was a mystery—hidden between the 69th and 70th week of Daniel's prophecy, a divine "pause" in God's timeline. (I explain Daniel's 70th Week herein chapter 7.)

Paul later confirmed this hidden truth:

> How that by revelation He made known unto me the mystery (as I wrote afore in few words, Whereby, when you read, you may understand my knowledge in the mystery of Christ). (Ephesians 3:3–4)

The Church Age officially began on the Day of Pentecost, as recorded in Acts 2:1–4, when the Holy Spirit descended upon the apostles and the 120 believers in the Upper Room. This monumental event occurred ten days after Jesus' ascension into heaven and fifty days after His resurrection—hence, Pentecost is always celebrated 50 days after Resurrection Sunday. The outpouring of the Holy Spirit fulfilled Old Testament prophecy and marked the birth of the Church, inaugurating its global mission to proclaim the gospel to all nations.

> And they were all filled with the Holy Ghost, and began to speak with other tongues, as the Spirit gave them utterance. (Acts 2:4)

Many say the Book of Acts is the history of the Church, but it covers only 30 years—the remaining years of Church history are revealed prophetically in the seven letters to the seven churches in Revelation chapters 2 and 3.

Why the Seven Letters Matter

God wrote 21 letters—also called epistles—to the Church through the apostles in the New Testament. Yet many believers overlook the seven personal letters from Jesus Himself in the Book of Revelation. These letters reveal His direct message to His Church—historically, prophetically, and personally.

The seven letters to the churches, representing the Church Age, will culminate with the Rapture—an event that will usher in the Tribulation, a time of global judgment. While the Rapture will be a profound blessing for believers who are ready, it will also signal a worldwide reckoning for Israel, unbelievers, and all who are left behind. (I explore the Rapture in the next chapter.)

How Close Are We?

This question has stirred the hearts of scholars, pastors, and watchmen for generations. While no one knows the exact hour, the Bible gives us prophetic patterns and divine appointments that serve as clear warnings to those who are watching. God's prophetic timeline moves in cycles—marked by the signs in the heavens, the biblical feast days, and the seven-year Shemitah cycle. These are not random spiritual rhythms; they are divine countdowns.

In *The Vanishing: The Day Will Begin Like Any Other—Until the Rapture Silences the World*, I explore how God's prophetic calendar reveals patterns and harbingers that have echoed throughout history, each one pointing more urgently to the return of Christ *for* His Church. This leads to a compelling question: could the current Shemitah cycle (2022/2023 to 2028/2029) mark the end of the Church Age, with the Rapture as the next major event on God's timeline? The timing is especially provocative, as God's calendar appears to highlight 2028/2029, while the globalist World Order simultaneously targets the year 2030 as a milestone for their so-called "Great Reset"—a convergence too significant to dismiss.

If we are indeed living in the final Laodicean age—the lukewarm era foretold in the Book of Revelation—then understanding these patterns is not just a matter of curiosity. It's a matter of urgency. The signs are converging. The hour is late. And the next sound we may hear could be the blast of a trumpet.

Irene leaned forward, tapping her pen against her notebook. "Okay, Ann, let's talk about the Upper Room. Where exactly was it? And why was it so important?"

I smiled, recognizing the curiosity in her voice. "Yes, the Upper Room was in Jerusalem. It's traditionally believed to be the same place where several major events in biblical history happened."

Raising an eyebrow, she tilted her head. "Such as?"

I held up a finger. "First, it's where Jesus observed the Last Supper with His disciples before His crucifixion—Luke 22:12–20."

She nodded, scribbling a note. "Right, where He broke the bread and established communion."

"Exactly. But it didn't end there. After Jesus' death, the disciples gathered in that very same room, hiding in fear from the Jewish leaders—John 20:19."

Irene frowned. "I can't imagine what they were feeling at that moment—grief, fear, confusion."

"Exactly. But then," I continued, "Jesus appeared to them after His resurrection—John 20:26."

Her eyes widened. "Wait—in the Upper Room?"

I nodded. "Yes! That's where He showed them His wounds, where Thomas doubted and then believed, saying, 'My Lord and my God.'"

Irene let out a low whistle. "So this place isn't just a random meeting room—it's a sacred spot where their faith was shaken and restored."

I smiled. "And there's more. Pentecost happened in the Upper Room too—Acts 2:1–4. That's where the Holy Spirit descended on the disciples, and they began speaking in tongues."

She leaned back in her chair, her expression shifting from curiosity to amazement. "So, in one place, the Last Supper, the resurrected Jesus, and the birth of the Church all took place?"

I nodded. "That's why it's so significant. It was a large, furnished upstairs room in a private home, prepared ahead of time for the Passover meal (Mark 14:15). Scripture doesn't name the homeowner, but early Christian tradition suggests it may have belonged to John Mark's family—specifically his mother, Mary (Acts 12:12). This house was a known gathering place for early Christians. Many scholars associate it with Mount Zion, an important part of Jerusalem's history. Today, there's a site called the Cenacle—which means 'dining room' in Latin—that is traditionally recognized as the Upper Room."

Irene tapped her chin. "But the original building—does it still exist?"

I sighed. "Not exactly. The current structure was built during the medieval period, but it's still considered sacred as the possible site of these incredible events."

She exhaled, shaking her head. "I never realized how pivotal one room could be in biblical history. First, Jesus breaks bread, then His followers mourn Him there, then He returns to them there, and finally, the Holy Spirit arrives, launching the Church Age. That's . . . incredible."

I grinned. "It really is. The Upper Room wasn't just a place—it was a turning point. It marked both the Last Supper and the First Church gathering."

Irene chuckled, closing her notebook. "Well, that changes how I picture Pentecost."

I nodded. "And now, as we step into the letters to the seven churches, we'll see how that moment in the Upper Room led to a global movement—one that spans nearly 2,000 years and brings us right to today."

She smirked, flipping to the next page of my manuscript. "Alright, Ann. Let's keep going."

———◆◆◆———

THE SEVEN LETTERS: A COUNTDOWN TO THE END

The Book of Revelation stands apart as the only book where Jesus Himself directly addresses His Church. Unlike messages given through prophets or apostles, these seven letters were dictated by Christ alone and sent to seven real churches in Asia Minor. Yet their significance extends far beyond the first century. Their sequence forms a prophetic timeline, tracing the entire Church Age and leading us to today—11:59 on God's prophetic clock, standing on the threshold of the final era.

These seven churches were not the largest or most influential of their time, but they were strategically placed along a major trade and communication route in Asia Minor. Their circular path was no coincidence. Beginning with Ephesus on the Aegean coast, the route moved inland through Smyrna, Pergamos, Thyatira, Sardis, Philadelphia, and finally Laodicea, before looping back toward Ephesus. This geographic pattern mirrors a prophetic cycle, showing how Revelation's message was meant to be passed down—from church to church, generation to generation. Just as a courier would have physically delivered these letters in sequence, history itself has unfolded in the same pattern, with each church symbolizing a distinct era in the Church Age.

A Prophetic Timeline of the Church Age

Each of the seven churches corresponds to a phase in Church history. The first three churches (Revelation 2:1–17) are typically seen as sequential and complete—distinct eras that rose, peaked, and faded before the next began. In contrast, the last four churches (Revelation 2:18–3:22) are viewed as coexisting until Christ's return, representing the ongoing spiritual conditions of the Church today. Both the remnant (Philadelphia) and the apostate (Laodicea) remain present right up to the Rapture—making them types of both churches and believers today.

1. **Ephesus (Apostolic Church)**—The first century church, grounded in sound doctrine but gradually losing its first love for Christ (AD 30–100).

2. **Smyrna (Persecuted Church)**—The era of intense Roman persecution, when believers endured suffering and martyrdom (AD 100–313).

3. **Pergamos (Compromising Church)**—The church after Constantine, when Christianity was married to the state, leading to compromise with worldly power (AD 313–600).

4. **Thyatira (Corrupt Church/Papal Church)**—Marked by the rise of Roman Catholicism, this period saw growing tradition, spiritual corruption, and centralized religious authority (AD 600–1517).

5. **Sardis (Dead Church/Protestant Church)**—Representing the Reformation churches—doctrinally reformed but spiritually incomplete and lacking vitality (AD 1517–1700).

6. **Philadelphia (Faithful Church/Missionary Church)**—A time of spiritual revival, missions, and open doors for evangelism worldwide (AD 1700–1900).

7. **Laodicea (Lukewarm/Apostate Church)**—Symbolic of the modern Church Age, marked by lukewarm faith, materialism, and self-sufficiency (AD 1900–present).

While the seven churches of Revelation 2–3 reflect distinct historical phases of the Church Age, they also represent spiritual conditions present in every generation. Ephesus's loss of love, Smyrna's suffering, Pergamos's compromise, Thyatira's corruption, Sardis's dead religion, Philadelphia's faithfulness, and Laodicea's lukewarmness all still echo in church today.

Prophetically, many see the final four churches—Thyatira, Sardis, Philadelphia, and Laodicea—as continuing into the last days. Of these, Philadelphia is promised deliverance from the coming trial (Revelation 3:10), while Laodicea stands as a sobering picture of end times complacency.

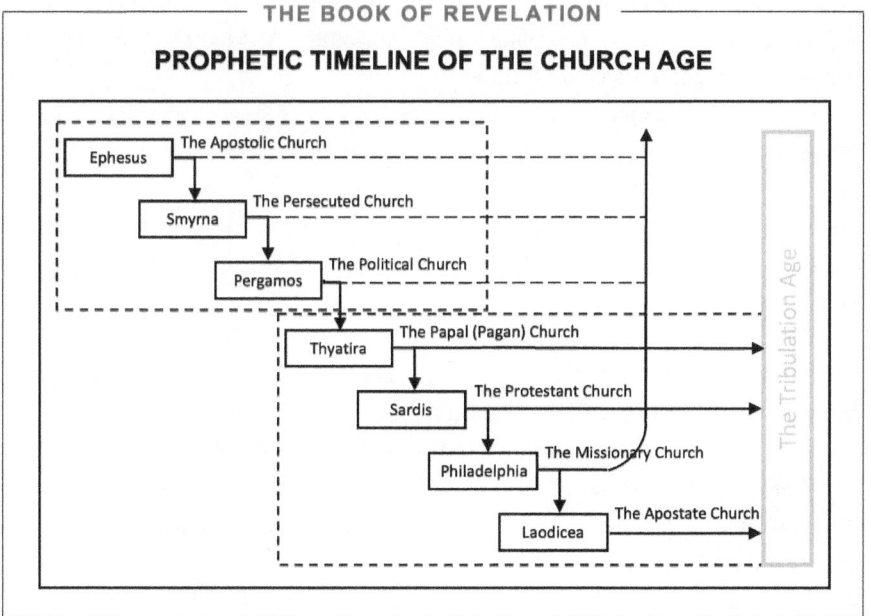

The Sevenfold Design Hidden in the Seven Letters

Revelation follows a heptadic (sevenfold) structure, signifying completion and divine perfection. Each letter follows a seven-point pattern:

1. **Greeting**—Addressing the church.
2. **Jesus' Title**—Christ reveals Himself uniquely to each.
3. **Recognition**—Commending strengths.
4. **Reprimand**—Exposing spiritual failure.
5. **Recommendation**—Calling to repentance.
6. **Closing Remarks**—Encouraging individuals.
7. **Reward**—A promise to the overcomers.

These letters are more than ancient messages—they form a divine countdown and a wake-up call to the Church. Christ is speaking not only to history, but to His Bride today—and to each of us personally. Through them, He warns and invites. He calls us to wake up, repent, and prepare. The time is short, and the voice of Jesus still echoes through the ages to those willing to listen.

Irene frowned, flipping through her notes, then abruptly set her pen down. "Alright, Ann, before we go any further, I have to ask—what's with all these different time markers? BC, AD, CE, BCE, AM—it's like a secret code!"

I smirked, already sensing where this was going. "Ah yes. The great calendar confusion. Alright, let's break it down."

Irene held up a hand. "Wait—before you start, I thought BC meant 'Before Christ' and AD meant 'After Death' . . . but if that's true, where do those missing thirty-some years of His life fit in?"

I chuckled. "Common misconception. BC does mean 'Before Christ,' but AD stands for 'Anno Domini'—Latin for 'In the Year of Our Lord.' It doesn't start after Jesus' death; it starts at His birth."

She squinted. "So, Jesus was born in AD 1?"

I shook my head. "Not exactly. Most scholars place His birth around 4 BC due to historical records of King Herod's reign."

Irene groaned. "That's already confusing. So what about CE and BCE?"

I leaned back. "CE and BCE are the secular versions. CE stands for 'Common Era,' and BCE is 'Before Common Era.' They follow the same dating system but remove the explicit reference to Christ."

She raised an eyebrow. "So, it's basically BC and AD, just without Jesus?"

"Pretty much," I said with a shrug. "They're used in academic and secular contexts to avoid religious connotations, but the actual dates don't change."

Irene sighed. "Okay, that makes sense. But now I've got another one—AM? That's totally different."

I nodded. "AM stands for 'Anno Mundi,' which means 'Year of the World.' It's the biblical dating system based on Jewish chronology, counting years from Creation."

She blinked. "Wait—so, how old is the world according to that?"

I smiled. "According to the traditional Jewish calendar, we're currently in the year 5785 AM—which spans from fall 2024 through fall 2025 on our calendar."

Irene's mouth fell open. "Five thousand seven hundred eighty-five years since Adam and Eve? That's what the Jewish calendar says?"

"Yep," I said. "It's based on a timeline from Genesis and early biblical genealogies."

She shook her head, rubbing her temples. "So, to summarize: BC and AD are the original system, CE and BCE are just secular versions of the same thing, and AM is the biblical clock?"

I nodded. "You got it."

Irene exhaled, sitting back. "Okay. I think my brain just aged a few decades. But at least now, when I see these terms, I won't feel like I'm decoding ancient hieroglyphs."

I chuckled. "Well, now that we've got our timelines straight, how about one more stop before Revelation 2:1?"

She tilted her head, intrigued. "Oh?"

I nodded. "The Kingdom Parables—Jesus' hidden prophecies of the Church Age. They're too important to skip."

She smiled, flipping back a few pages. "Alright, one more detour. Let's uncover what He was really saying."

———◆◆◆———

THE KINGDOM PARABLES: PROPHECIES OF THE CHURCH AGE

Matthew 13 contains a series of seven parables that Jesus used to reveal the hidden mysteries of the Kingdom of Heaven. These parables, often misunderstood or dismissed as mere illustrations, actually unfold a prophetic overview of the Church Age. From the very beginning, Jesus made it clear that these parables were not meant for everyone. In Matthew 13:10–12, Jesus explained that the parables were given to those who are spiritually enlightened so they could understand the mysteries of the kingdom—insights hidden from the foundation of the world (Matthew 25:34; Luke 11:50; Hebrews 4:3; Revelation 13:8).

1. **The Four Soils (Matthew 13:3–9, 18–23)**—God is the Sower, and the seed is His Word. The parable outlines four types of soil, representing the conditions of human hearts. The birds in verse 19 represent the evil one who snatches away the Word—birds are consistently portrayed negatively in these parables. The second type of soil is shallow; it symbolizes those who receive the Word but fall away under pressure or persecution. The third group is entangled in the cares and riches of the world. The fourth soil is fertile, producing a fruitful spiritual harvest. This parable correlates with the church of Ephesus.

2. **The Tares and the Wheat (Matthew 13:24–30, 36–43)**—Here, the enemy sows tares—a weed called *zizania* that looks identical to wheat until maturity. As it ripens, it turns black and must be separated because it is poisonous. Jesus explains that this separation will occur at the end of the age, when the angels will gather the tares to be burned and the wheat brought into His barn. This parallels the church of Smyrna.

3. **The Mustard Seed (Matthew 13:31–32)**—Mustard seeds typically grow into shrubs, not towering trees. In this parable, the mustard seed becomes an unnaturally large structure, large enough for birds (ministers of Satan, from the first parable) to lodge in its branches. This symbolizes the external growth and corruption of the Church—a system that grows beyond its intended design. This relates to the church of Pergamos.

4. **The Woman and the Leaven (Matthew 13:33)**—Leaven in Scripture consistently symbolizes sin and corruption. This parable portrays a woman hiding leaven in three measures of meal—a reference to the fellowship offering from Genesis 18. Leaven represents pride, the root of all sin, stemming from Satan (Isaiah 14). This illustrates the infiltration of sin and false doctrine into the Church, aligning with the church of Thyatira.

5. **The Treasure in the Field (Matthew 13:44)**—The field is the world. The treasure is not Christ, but the believer. Jesus bought the entire field to obtain the hidden treasure. This speaks of Christ's sacrificial death for the world, but especially for those who would become His redeemed possession (Exodus 19:5; Psalm 135). This reflects the church of Sardis.

6. **The Pearl of Great Price (Matthew 13:45–46)**—Unlike other jewels, pearls are formed by a living organism as a response to irritation, symbolizing the Gentile Church. Pearls were not valued by Jews and considered unclean, but they were prized by Gentiles. This parable

speaks to the Church—a single, unified body brought forth through suffering. This correlates with the church of Philadelphia.

7. **The Dragnet (Matthew 13:47–50)**—The dragnet gathers all kinds of fish, both good and bad. At the end of the age, the bad will be separated and cast into the furnace of fire. This final parable represents the judgment to come and connects with the church of Laodicea.

These parables aren't just moral stories; they are divine prophecies detailing the spiritual journey and corruption of the Church Age—a prophetic blueprint. They follow the pattern of the seven churches in Revelation 2–3, each revealing a layer of spiritual history, doctrinal deviation, and ultimate destiny. From the pure beginnings to institutional corruption, and finally to judgment, Jesus' Kingdom Parables offer a sweeping overview of the Church's unfolding narrative through the ages.

CHRIST'S LETTER TO THE CHURCH OF EPHESUS

The first letter in Revelation is addressed to the church in Ephesus, a pivotal center for early Christianity. Prophetically Ephesus represents the Apostolic Church era (AD 30–100)—the foundational period when the original apostles and their disciples spread the gospel across the known world.

Ephesus holds a unique place in the New Testament, having been planted by Paul, pastored by Timothy, and, according to tradition, later led by John before his exile to Patmos. It's very name, *Ephesus*, meaning "desired one," reflects the early Church's devotion and purity, rooted in firsthand encounters with Christ.

Yet, despite their strong doctrine and tireless work, Jesus warns that the Ephesians had begun to lose their first love. Their passion for Christ had dimmed, replaced by routine obedience rather than heartfelt devotion.

This letter is both a commendation and a caution—a call to remember, repent, and return to the love that once defined them. As we step into Revelation 2:1, Christ's words to Ephesus still echo today, urging His Church to remain faithful and reignite the fire of true devotion.

THE REVELATION OF JESUS CHRIST REVEALS:

2:1 To the angel of the church of Ephesus write these things says He that holds the seven stars in His right hand, who walks in the midst of the seven golden candlesticks.

In Revelation 2:1, Jesus addresses the church of Ephesus, the first of the seven churches, representing the Apostolic Church era (AD 30–100). The "angel of the church" refers to the messenger or pastor responsible for delivering and safeguarding Christ's message.

Jesus identifies Himself as "He that holds the seven stars in His right hand," emphasizing His sovereign authority and control over the church's leaders. The seven stars, as explained in Revelation 1:20, represent the leaders (or angels) of the seven churches, symbolizing Christ's divine protection, guidance, and oversight. His right hand signifies power, favor, and security, ensuring that no leader or believer is beyond His grasp.

Furthermore, Jesus is described as "walking in the midst of the seven golden candlesticks," reinforcing His active presence among His churches. The golden candlesticks symbolize the churches themselves, which are called to shine His light in the world (Matthew 5:14–16). This image serves as a reminder that Jesus is not distant from His people—He is present, watching, and intimately involved in their spiritual condition.

This verse sets the tone for the commendation and correction that follows. While Ephesus was a strong, doctrinally sound church, it had begun to lose its first love (Revelation 2:4). The message is clear: no church or believer can thrive on past faithfulness alone—true devotion requires an ongoing, intimate relationship with Christ.

OLD TESTAMENT FORESHADOWS REVELATION:

And he said unto me, What do you see? And I said, I have looked, and behold a candlestick all of gold, with a bowl upon the top of it, and his seven lamps thereon, and seven pipes to the seven lamps, which are upon the top thereof . . . Not by might, nor by power, but by My Spirit, says the LORD of hosts. (Zechariah 4:2, 6)

Revelation 2:1 closely parallels Zechariah 4:2, 6, where the prophet Zechariah sees a golden lampstand with seven lamps, symbolizing God's presence and the empowering of His people by the Holy Spirit.

This passage highlights God's presence and sustaining power among His people, just as Jesus walks among the seven golden candlesticks (churches) in Revelation 2:1. Both passages emphasize that the light of God's people—Israel (Old Testament) and the Church (New Testament)—comes not from their own strength but from His Spirit.

THE REVELATION OF JESUS CHRIST REVEALS:

2:2 I know your works, and your labor, and your patience, and how you cannot bear them which are evil: and you have tried them which say they are apostles, and are not, and have found them liars.

In this verse, Jesus commends the church of Ephesus for its diligent works, perseverance, and commitment to truth. The Ephesian believers were not passive in their faith; they actively labored for the gospel and displayed steadfast patience in the face of opposition. Their endurance reflects a church that refuses to grow weary despite trials and hardships.

Additionally, they upheld doctrinal purity, refusing to tolerate false apostles—those who claimed spiritual authority but were exposed as frauds. This highlights the importance of discernment in the Church. The Ephesian believers tested teachings against the truth of God's Word, setting a powerful example for believers today.

However, zeal for truth must be accompanied by love (Revelation 2:4). While commendable in their discernment, the Ephesians would later be warned not to let their devotion to sound doctrine overshadow their passion for Christ. This verse reminds us to uphold truth while keeping our love for God and others at the center of our faith.

OLD TESTAMENT FORESHADOWS REVELATION:

Thus says the LORD of hosts, Listen not unto the words of the prophets that prophesy unto you: they make you vain; they speak a vision of their own heart, and not out of the mouth of the LORD. (Jeremiah 23:16)

This verse parallels Revelation 2:2 because both passages emphasize the importance of discernment in identifying false teachers. Just as the church in Ephesus tested those who claimed to be apostles and found them false, God warned Israel against listening to false prophets who spoke from their own imagination rather than divine revelation.

THE REVELATION OF JESUS CHRIST REVEALS:

2:3 And has borne, and has patience, and for My name's sake has labored, and has not fainted.

In this verse, Jesus commends the church of Ephesus for their perseverance and dedication. The word "borne" suggests that they have endured hardships and carried burdens for the sake of Christ. Their "patience" reflects their steadfastness in the face of trials, refusing to abandon their faith despite opposition.

"And for My name's sake" signifies that their labor was not for personal gain or recognition but out of devotion to Jesus Christ. This highlights their commitment to upholding His truth, even in a culture that opposed them.

The phrase "has labored, and has not fainted" acknowledges their tireless efforts in ministry. Though they may have grown weary, they did not give up.

Their endurance serves as a model for believers today, reminding us that faithful service to Christ requires perseverance, even when faced with difficulties.

However, while their endurance is commendable, the following verses reveal that something was lacking in their spiritual walk—their first love. This serves as a reminder that diligent labor must be accompanied by heartfelt devotion to Christ.

OLD TESTAMENT FORESHADOWS REVELATION:

But they that wait upon the LORD shall renew their strength; they shall mount up with wings as eagles; they shall run, and not be weary; and they shall walk, and not faint. (Isaiah 40:31)

This verse mirrors the endurance, patience, and perseverance described in Revelation 2:3. Just as the church of Ephesus labored and did not faint in their devotion to Christ, Isaiah reminds us that those who trust in the LORD will be strengthened, sustained, and empowered to continue their journey without growing weary. Both verses emphasize that faithfulness in serving God requires endurance and that He provides the strength needed to remain steadfast.

THE REVELATION OF JESUS CHRIST REVEALS:

2:4 Nevertheless I have somewhat against you, because you have left your first love.

In Revelation 2:4, Jesus commends the Ephesian church for their works, patience, and discernment, yet He issues a serious rebuke: "Nevertheless, I have somewhat against you, because you have left your first love."

This is a sobering reminder that spiritual activity is not a substitute for intimacy with Christ. The Ephesians were doctrinally sound, hardworking, and persevering, yet their devotion to Christ had grown cold. They had maintained the structure of faith but lost the passion that once fueled it.

"First love" refers to the deep, personal, and fervent love believers have when they first come to Christ—a love that is marked by joy, intimacy, and unwavering devotion. Over time, religious duty can replace relational closeness, and faith can become mechanical rather than passionate.

Jesus' rebuke here warns all believers against allowing routine faithfulness to replace a heart deeply in love with Him. True Christianity is not just about right doctrine or good works—it is about a love relationship with Jesus. He calls His people to return to the love they once had, rekindling the fire of devotion that once burned brightly.

This verse serves as a call to examine our hearts: Are we still in love with Jesus, or have we become distant, even while remaining active in religious life?

OLD TESTAMENT FORESHADOWS REVELATION:

Go and cry in the ears of Jerusalem, saying, Thus says the LORD; I remember you, the kindness of your youth, the love of your espousals, when you went after Me in the wilderness, in a land that was not sown. (Jeremiah 2:2)

In this passage, God recalls the early devotion of Israel, comparing it to a bride's first love for her husband. The imagery reflects the intimacy, passion, and faithfulness of the early days of Israel's covenant relationship with God. However, just as Israel later turned away, the church in Ephesus had also drifted from its initial zeal and affection for Christ. This parallel highlights the pattern of spiritual drift—a warning that religious activity and doctrinal soundness must always be accompanied by a heartfelt love for God.

THE REVELATION OF JESUS CHRIST REVEALS:

2:5 Remember therefore from where you have fallen, and repent, and do the first works; or else I will come unto you quickly, and will remove your candlestick out of its place, except you repent.

In Revelation 2:5, Jesus gives the Ephesian church a clear call to action—a threefold command:

1. **Remember**—They are urged to reflect on their former devotion, recalling the passion and love they once had for Christ. Spiritual decline often happens gradually, and remembering the past can rekindle a desire for renewal.

2. **Repent**—Recognizing their drift from their "first love," they must turn away from their spiritual complacency and return to God with sincerity and humility. Repentance isn't just feeling remorseful—it's a change in direction.

3. **Do the first works**—Jesus calls them to return to their early acts of love, service, and devotion. Their faith should be marked by a genuine relationship with Christ, not just rigid doctrine and works.

If they fail to repent, Jesus warns of a severe consequence: He will remove their candlestick (lampstand) from its place. This symbolizes the removal of their influence, effectiveness, and possibly even the church itself. History confirms this judgment—Ephesus eventually lost its spiritual vitality and ceased to exist as a church.

This verse serves as a warning to all believers: It's not enough to be theologically sound and active in ministry—we must guard against losing our love and passion for Christ. If we neglect our relationship with Him, we risk becoming spiritually ineffective.

OLD TESTAMENT FORESHADOWS REVELATION:

Come, and let us return unto the LORD: for He has torn, and He will heal us; He has smitten, and He will bind us up. (Hosea 6:1)

This verse reflects God's call for His people to return to Him, much like Jesus' plea to the Ephesian church to repent and rekindle their first love. The Ephesians had not fully turned away, but they had lost their devotion, and Jesus is calling them back—just as God called Israel back in Hosea's time.

THE REVELATION OF JESUS CHRIST REVEALS:

[2:6] But this you have, that you hate the deeds of the Nicolaitans, which I also hate.

In Revelation 2:6, Jesus commends the church of Ephesus for their hatred of the deeds of the Nicolaitans, affirming that He also hates their practices. This is a rare instance in Scripture where Christ explicitly states His hatred toward a particular group's actions, emphasizing the severity of their corruption.

The Nicolaitans are believed to have promoted a form of compromise and moral laxity within the church, possibly blending pagan customs with Christian faith. Some scholars link them to Nicolas, one of the seven deacons chosen in Acts 6:5, suggesting that His followers distorted grace into license for sin, embracing idolatry and sexual immorality (similar to the doctrine of Balaam mentioned in Revelation 2:14–15).

The Ephesian church, while having lost its first love (Revelation 2:4), was still doctrinally sound, refusing to tolerate false teachings and corrupt practices. Christ praises them for their spiritual discernment, showing that while love is crucial, truth and holiness must also be upheld.

This verse serves as a reminder that God not only loves righteousness but also hates sin. Believers are called to reject false teachings and stand firm in the truth, resisting anything that compromises the purity of the gospel.

OLD TESTAMENT FORESHADOWS REVELATION:

You that love the LORD, hate evil: He preserves the souls of His saints; He delivers them out of the hand of the wicked. (Psalm 97:10)

This verse aligns with Jesus' commendation of the Ephesian church for hating the deeds of the Nicolaitans, which He also hates. It reinforces the biblical principle that those who love God must also reject evil and falsehood. Just as the Ephesians refused to tolerate corrupt teachings, Psalm 97:10 commands believers to actively stand against sin and deception, trusting in God's protection.

THE REVELATION OF JESUS CHRIST REVEALS:

2:7 He that has an ear, let him hear what the Spirit says to the churches; To him that overcomes will I give to eat of the Tree of Life, which is in the midst of the paradise of God.

In Revelation 2:7, Jesus concludes His message to the church in Ephesus with a call to spiritual attentiveness and a promise to those who overcome.

"He that has an ear, let him hear what the Spirit says to the churches." This phrase appears throughout the letters to the seven churches, urging believers to listen carefully and discern the message of the Holy Spirit. This is not just about physical hearing but about spiritual receptivity—understanding and applying God's truth. The plural "churches" suggests that these messages are not just for Ephesus but for all believers throughout history.

"To him that overcomes." The promise is directed to the overcomer, a recurring theme in Revelation. The Greek word *nikao* means to conquer, prevail, or be victorious. Overcoming refers to remaining faithful in the midst of trials, temptations, and spiritual warfare. In the context of Ephesus, it means restoring their first love for Christ and persevering in faith.

"Will I give to eat of the Tree of Life." The Tree of Life first appeared in Genesis 2:9, located in the garden of Eden, representing eternal life and fellowship with God. However, after the fall of Adam and Eve, humanity was barred from it (Genesis 3:22–24). Now, Jesus promises that those who remain faithful will regain access to what was lost—eternal life in God's presence.

"Which is in the midst of the paradise of God." The word paradise (Greek: *paradeisos*) refers to a garden or enclosed place of bliss. It is used in Luke 23:43, where Jesus tells the repentant thief on the cross, "Today you will be with Me in paradise." This paradise is the restored Eden, the eternal dwelling place of the redeemed in the New Jerusalem (Revelation 22:1–2), where God's presence is fully realized.

OLD TESTAMENT FORESHADOWS REVELATION:

And out of the ground made the Lord GOD to grow every tree that is pleasant to the sight, and good for food; the Tree of Life also in the midst of the garden, and the tree of knowledge of good and evil. (Genesis 2:9)

This verse directly connects to Revelation 2:7, as the Tree of Life first appears in Eden, symbolizing eternal life and perfect communion with God. Adam and Eve had access to it before the Fall, but sin severed that privilege. In Revelation, Jesus promises that the overcomers—those who remain faithful—will regain what was lost in Eden, restoring perfect fellowship with God in the eternal paradise.

CHRIST'S LETTER TO THE CHURCH OF SMYRNA

The second letter in Revelation is addressed to Smyrna, a church that prophetically represents the Persecuted Church era (AD 100–312)—a time when the Roman Empire sought to crush Christianity through brutal oppression.

The very name *Smyrna* carries profound meaning. It is derived from *myrrh*, a fragrant spice used for burial and anointing the dead. This connection sets the tone for the church's story—one of suffering, sacrifice, and unwavering faith in the face of death.

If you recall, *myrrh* was one of the gifts brought to Jesus by the Magi when they visited him in a house, likely when He was around two years old (Matthew 2:11), symbolizing His future suffering and sacrificial death on the Cross. Yet, in the Millennial Kingdom (Isaiah 60:6), Scripture speaks of gifts presented to Christ—gold for His kingship and frankincense for His priesthood—but no mention of myrrh. Why? Because His suffering is finished. The death He endured is now behind Him.

Smyrna, then, is a metaphor for the persecuted believer—pressed and crushed like myrrh, yet releasing a fragrance that is precious in the sight of God. Christ's message is clear: Stay faithful, even in suffering. Do not fear. Through Christ, the resurrected and victorious King, you can overcome.

THE REVELATION OF JESUS CHRIST REVEALS:

2:8 And to the angel of the church in Smyrna write these things says the First and the Last, which was dead, and is alive.

In Revelation 2:8, Jesus addresses the church in Smyrna, a congregation experiencing intense persecution. He identifies Himself as "the First and the Last, which was dead, and is alive." This introduction is deeply significant, offering hope and encouragement to a church facing suffering and even martyrdom.

"The First and the Last." This is a title of divinity, echoing Isaiah 44:6, where God declares, "I am the First, and I am the Last; and beside Me there is no God." By using this title, Jesus asserts His eternal existence, sovereignty over time, and His authority over all things—including life and death.

"Which was dead, and is alive." This directly references Christ's death and resurrection, a powerful reminder that He has conquered death itself. To the persecuted believers in Smyrna, this would have been a profound reassurance—even if they faced death for their faith, they served a risen Savior who had already defeated the grave.

Smyrna was a city where Christians were heavily persecuted under Roman rule. Many were executed for refusing to worship the emperor. Jesus, knowing their suffering, reminds them that He also suffered, died, and rose again. His words encourage them to remain faithful, assuring them that eternal life awaits those who persevere.

This verse sets the tone for the message to Smyrna—a call to endurance and faithfulness in the face of suffering, with the promise that just as Christ overcame death, so too will those who remain steadfast in Him.

OLD TESTAMENT FORESHADOWS REVELATION:

He will swallow up death in victory; and the Lord GOD will wipe away tears from off all faces; and the rebuke of His people shall He take away from off all the earth: for the LORD has spoken it. (Isaiah 25:8)

This verse foretells God's victory over death, which Jesus fulfilled through His death and resurrection. The connection reinforces the promise that believers in Smyrna, though facing persecution and even death, will share in Christ's resurrection and eternal life.

THE REVELATION OF JESUS CHRIST REVEALS:

$^{2:9}$ I know your works, and tribulation, and poverty, (but you are rich) and I know the blasphemy of them which say they are Jews, and are not, but are the assembly of Satan.

Jesus' words to the church in Smyrna reflect His deep awareness of their struggles, suffering, and perseverance. Smyrna, a persecuted church, endured hardship, oppression, and extreme poverty, yet Christ declares them spiritually rich—a contrast between earthly deprivation and eternal wealth in Him.

"I know your works, and tribulation, and poverty (but you are rich)." The believers in Smyrna were not just enduring general hardship; they were facing intense persecution from the Roman Empire and hostile religious fractions. Their poverty was likely due to economic oppression, where they were excluded from trade, employment, and society for refusing to worship the emperor or pagan gods. This mirrors what is foretold in Revelation 13, where those who refuse the mark of the beast will be unable to buy or sell. The suffering of Smyrna foreshadows the global persecution of faithful believers in the end times. Yet Jesus reminds them—and us—that true riches are found not in earthly wealth, but in Him (Matthew 6:20).

"And I know the blasphemy of them which say they are Jews, and are not, but are the assembly of Satan." Jesus exposes false religious leaders who claimed to be faithful Jews but were persecuting His followers. True Jewish identity is not merely about ethnicity or religious rituals, but about faith in God's promises (Romans 2:28–29). By opposing Christ's followers, these individuals had aligned themselves with Satan's agenda, making them a spiritual adversary to God's people.

The term "assembly of Satan" does not refer to all Jews but specifically to those who opposed the gospel and persecuted the Church. This mirrors, Jesus' confrontation with religious leaders in John 8:44, where He said, "You are of your father the devil"—because they rejected God's truth and sought to silence His messengers.

Despite their trials, Jesus gives no rebuke to the church in Smyrna—only encouragement. He sees their faithfulness and assures them that eternal victory is theirs.

OLD TESTAMENT FORESHADOWS REVELATION:

Hear the Word of the LORD, you that tremble at His Word. Your brethren that hated you, that cast you out for My name's sake, said, Let the LORD be glorified: but He shall appear to your joy, and they shall be ashamed. (Isaiah 66:5)

Just as Isaiah encouraged faithful believers to endure opposition from false brethren, Jesus encourages the persecuted Christians in Smyrna to remain steadfast, reminding them that true spiritual riches belong to them—not their persecutors.

THE REVELATION OF JESUS CHRIST REVEALS:

$2:10$ Fear none of those things which you shall suffer. Behold, the devil will cast some of you into prison, that you may be tried; and you shall have tribulation ten days: be you faithful to death, and I will give you a crown of life.

In Revelation 2:10, Jesus encourages the believers in Smyrna, a heavily persecuted church, not to fear the coming tribulation. He acknowledges their suffering, warns them of further trials, and calls them to remain faithful even unto death, promising them the crown of life as a reward for their endurance.

"Fear none of those things which you shall suffer." Jesus does not promise deliverance from persecution but instead prepares them to endure it. Throughout Scripture, believers are warned that suffering is part of the Christian walk (John 16:33; 2 Timothy 3:12). However, He reassures them not to fear—for though they may suffer in this world, their eternal reward is secure.

"The devil will cast some of you into prison, that you may be tried." Jesus directly attributes the persecution to Satan, revealing that the enemy is actively working against the Church. Satan's strategy is to use earthly authorities to imprison, oppress, and try believers, hoping to weaken their faith. Yet, as seen throughout history, persecution often strengthens the faith of believers, rather than destroying it (James 1:2–3).

"You shall have tribulation ten days." The "ten days" of tribulation is often interpreted as either:

- A literal ten-day period of intense suffering in Smyrna.
- A symbolic representation of a complete but limited time of persecution.
- A prophetic reference to the ten periods of persecution under Roman emperors, as later chronicled in *Fox's Book of Martyrs*. *Fox's Book of Martyrs* tells historically of ten great primitive persecutions of the people of God in the days of pagan Rome:

    1. Nero (AD 54–68)—Major persecution (Paul and Peter martyred).
    2. Domitian (AD 81–96)—John exiled to Patmos.
    3. Trajan (AD 98–117)—Ignatius of Antioch martyred.
    4. Marcus Aurelius (AD 161–180)—Justin Martyr executed.
    5. Severus (AD 193–211)—Persecution spreads to North Africa.
    6. Maximinus (AD 235–238)—Targeted Christian clergy.
    7. Decius (AD 249–251)—Forced sacrifices to Roman gods.
    8. Valerian (AD 253–260)—Executed church leaders.
    9. Aurelian (AD 270–275)—Brief but intense persecution.
    10. Domitian (AD 303–313)—The Great Persecution, the most severe.

"Be you faithful to death, and I will give you a crown of life." The crown of life is a victor's crown, promised to those who endure suffering and remain faithful to Christ (James 1:12). Many early Christians in Smyrna, including Polycarp, the city's bishop, were martyred but refused to renounce Christ. Jesus does not promise an earthly rescue but a heavenly reward that far outweighs any earthly suffering.

Unlike other churches, Jesus has no word of correction—only encouragement—for Smyrna. Their suffering purified their faith. They remained faithful under extreme persecution. Their endurance exemplified true discipleship.

OLD TESTAMENT FORESHADOWS REVELATION:

Fear you not; for I am with you: be not dismayed; for I am your God: I will strengthen you; yea, I will help you; yea, I will uphold you with the right hand of My righteousness. (Isaiah 41:10)

Just as Jesus urges the believers in Smyrna not to fear suffering (Revelation 2:10), Isaiah reminds God's people that He will uphold them through trials—reinforcing the themes of endurance, divine testing, and faithfulness through trials. The suffering of the church in Smyrna is not in vain—it refines them, strengthens their faith, and secures their eternal reward.

THE REVELATION OF JESUS CHRIST REVEALS:

^{2:11} He that has an ear, let him hear what the Spirit says unto the churches; He that overcomes will not be hurt of the second death.

This verse is both an exhortation and a promise.

1. **A Call to Listen and Understand**—Jesus begins with a familiar phrase used throughout His teachings: "He that has an ear, let him hear." This phrase is not just a literal call to listen, but an appeal for spiritual discernment. It urges believers to pay attention to what the Holy Spirit is revealing, not just to the church in Smyrna but to all who will heed His words.

2. **The Promise to Overcomers**

   - "He that overcomes" refers to those who remain faithful in the face of persecution and trials. Overcoming means enduring suffering, standing firm in faith, and remaining true to Christ even unto death.
   - "Will not be hurt of the second death"—This phrase points to the final judgment in Revelation 20:14–15, where the second death is described as the Lake of Fire, the eternal separation from God.
   - The persecuted church in Smyrna was facing physical death, but Jesus reassures them that their faithfulness secures eternal life. Though they may suffer and die for their faith, they will never face eternal death.

3. **The Second Death: What It Means**—The first death is physical, the natural end of earthly life. The second death is spiritual and eternal, reserved for those who reject Christ (Revelation 21:8). Jesus assures believers that, no matter what happens to their bodies, their souls are eternally secure in Him.

Revelation 2:11 is a word of encouragement, assurance, and eternal security for those who stand firm in Christ. The second death has no power over those who belong to Jesus. The overcomers will live forever in His presence, free from fear, pain, and judgment.

OLD TESTAMENT FORESHADOWS REVELATION:

And many of them that sleep in the dust of the earth shall awake, some to everlasting life, and some to shame and everlasting contempt. (Daniel 12:2)

Daniel 12:2 and Revelation 2:11 both warn of final judgment while offering hope and assurance to the faithful. Those who stand firm in God's truth will inherit eternal life, escaping the second death and dwelling in His presence forever.

CHRIST'S LETTER TO THE CHURCH OF PERGAMOS

The third letter in Revelation is addressed to Pergamos, representing the Political (Orthodox) Church era (AD 313–590)—a time when Christianity merged with state power, leading to compromise and corruption.

The name *Pergamos* carries a striking meaning: "elevated marriage" or "mixed marriage." This reflects the church's unholy union with political power, a turning point in history when Christianity, once persecuted, became entangled with imperial authority.

In AD 313, Roman Emperors Constantine I and Licinius issued the Edict of Milan, granting tolerance to Christianity. While Constantine did not declare it the empire's official religion, his third successor did—transforming the faith from a persecuted movement into a state-controlled institution.

By AD 366, Damasus I, bishop of Rome, adopted the Babylonian priestly title "Pontifex Maximus"—a title historically used for pagan high priests. This marked a shift where bishops, particularly in Rome, sought power and influence, elevating clergy over laity. Christianity, once a grassroots faith, now functioned as a political machine, trading spiritual authority for worldly prestige.

This era also saw pagan traditions woven into church practices, diluting the purity of the gospel. Instead of spreading Christ's message, church leaders built grand cathedrals—monuments of power that outlasted their faithfulness. Political dominance overshadowed spiritual vitality, leading to the Dark Ages, where truth was suppressed, and the Church drifted from its mission.

Christ's warning to Pergamos is clear: Stay faithful. Reject compromise. Repent. No matter how powerful the world's systems seem, only Christ, the risen King, has true authority. Through Him, we can overcome.

Leaning forward, intrigued. "Ann, so I get that the church of Pergamos represents the time when Christianity and politics merged, but what I don't get is—when did the Dark Ages actually start?"

I nodded. "That's a great question, Irene. The Dark Ages, or the early Middle Ages, generally began after the fall of the Western Roman Empire in AD 476. Rome had been the backbone of civilization, and when it collapsed, Europe plunged into centuries of instability—education, trade, and centralized government fell apart."

Raising an eyebrow. "So was it just chaos?"

"Pretty much. The roads fell into disrepair, cities shrank, and without a strong central government, feudalism became the dominant system—meaning power shifted to local lords instead of a strong empire. But here's the thing—the Church actually became the most powerful institution during this time."

Frowning. "Wait, I thought Christianity was persecuted. How did the Church go from being hunted to being in charge?"

Smiling knowingly. "That brings us to the Edict of Milan in AD 313. Constantine and Licinius issued this decree, which legalized Christianity and ended its persecution."

Raising a hand dramatically. "Oh wow, so Christianity went from being outlawed to . . . running the world?"

"In a way, yes. After the Edict of Milan, Christianity didn't just gain freedom—it gained political power. Over time, emperors aligned with the Church, and by AD 380, Emperor Theodosius I made Christianity the official state religion of the Roman Empire. This was huge because it meant Christianity was no longer a grassroots movement—it was institutionalized."

Nodding slowly. "So, at first, this sounds like a good thing—no more persecution, right?"

"Right, but there was a catch. The merging of Church and State led to a compromised faith. The Church became more focused on political influence than on biblical truth. Pagan practices mixed with Christianity, and eventually, doctrine was controlled by religious leaders instead of Scripture. That's how we ended up with the spiritual corruption that helped fuel the Dark Ages."

Sitting back, arms crossed. "So, the Edict of Milan gave Christianity power, but that power led to compromise . . . and then the Dark Ages came after Rome fell?"

"Exactly. The Papal system rose to fill the power vacuum left by Rome's collapse. By AD 590, Pope Gregory I centralized Church authority, and from there, tradition, rather than Scripture, dominated. Education declined, and the Church controlled access to the Bible."

Shaking her head. "Wow. It's crazy how something that seemed like a blessing—freedom from persecution—ended up bringing spiritual darkness."

Flipping a page in my Bible. "And that's why the letter to Pergamos is so important. Jesus warned them about compromise—and history shows exactly where that compromise led."

Smirking. "I knew you were going to tie it back to Revelation."

Laughing. "Of course! History and prophecy go hand in hand."

Sighing. "Alright, let's get into it. What did Jesus say to Pergamos?"

Grinning. "Let's find out."

———◆◆◆———

THE REVELATION OF JESUS CHRIST REVEALS:

²:¹² And to the angel of the church in Pergamos write these things says He which has the sharp sword with two edges.

Jesus begins His message to the church in Pergamos by identifying Himself as the One who holds "the sharp sword with two edges." This imagery is significant because the sword represents divine truth, judgment, and authority.

In the Roman world, the sword was a symbol of imperial power and military dominance—and Pergamos was a city deeply tied to Rome. It was home to a powerful government seat and a center for pagan worship, including emperor worship, where believers faced pressure to compromise their faith. However, Christ reminds the church that it is not Rome's sword that holds true power, but rather His Word, which cuts deeper than any earthly authority.

The two-edge sword is a recurring biblical symbol for God's Word (Hebrews 4:12), which pierces through deception, exposes sin, and separates truth from falsehood. Unlike human rulers who wield political power, Christ's sword represents ultimate, divine justice—one that will both defend the faithful and judge those who distort the truth.

By using this imagery, Jesus is preparing Pergamos for a strong warning. Though they have remained faithful in some ways, they are allowing compromise and corruption to creep into the church. His sword is both a weapon of correction and a call to repentance, urging them to stand firm in the unchanging truth of God's Word rather than succumbing to the pressures of the world.

Christ's authority is absolute, and His Word will ultimately judge all things. The church must stand on the foundation of truth, rejecting compromise and remaining faithful, for only His word has the power to separate righteousness from sin.

OLD TESTAMENT FORESHADOWS REVELATION:

And He has made my mouth like a sharp sword; in the shadow of His hand has He hid me, and made me a polished shaft; in His quiver has He hid me. (Isaiah 49:2)

Both passages emphasize the power of God's Word—it is not just a message of salvation but also a weapon of judgment and authority. Christ's warning to Pergamos echoes Isaiah's prophecy: those who remain faithful to God's truth will be protected, while those who distort or compromise it will face the sword of His judgment.

THE REVELATION OF JESUS CHRIST REVEALS:

²˙¹³ I know your works, and where you dwell, even where Satan's throne is: and you hold fast My name, and have not denied My faith, even in those days wherein Antipas was My faithful martyr, who was slain among you, where Satan dwells.

Jesus acknowledges the faithfulness of the church in Pergamos despite their difficult circumstances. This verse highlights four key themes.

1. **"Where Satan's throne is"**—the center of pagan worship. Pergamos was a hub of idol worship and imperial cult activity, earning its reputation as a city where Satan's influence was strong. It was home to the great altar of Zeus, one of the most significant pagan altars in the ancient world, often called "Satan's throne" due to its prominence in emperor worship. The city also had a massive temple dedicated to Asclepius, the serpent god of healing, whose symbol (a serpent entwined around a staff) is still associated with medicine today. This serpent imagery directly contrasts with the biblical portrayal of Satan as the serpent in Genesis 3. Christians were expected to swear allegiance to Rome and worship the emperor as a god. Failure to comply led to persecution, imprisonment, or execution.

2. **"You hold fast My name, and have not denied My faith"**—the Church's loyalty. Despite living in an atmosphere dominated by evil, the believers in Pergamos remained steadfast in their faith. They refused to renounce Christ, even under pressure. Their faithfulness mirrors the call of Matthew 10:32: "Whoever acknowledges Me before men, I will also acknowledge before My Father in heaven." In a culture that demanded compromise, Pergamos stood firm, testifying to Christ's power even in a hostile world.

3. **"Even in those days wherein Antipas was My faithful martyr, who was slain among you"**—the cost of faith. Antipas is the only named martyr in the letters to the seven churches. Early church tradition says he was burned alive in a bronze bull under Domitian's reign, making him one of the first victims of state persecution. The title "faithful martyr" aligns with how Jesus Himself is described in Revelation 1:5—showing that Antipas followed in Christ's footsteps, standing for truth even unto death.

4. **"Where Satan dwells"**—spiritual opposition. The phrase is repeated for emphasis—Pergamos was deeply entrenched in satanic influence. It was a city of compromise, where many blended paganism with Christianity.

Though some remained faithful, others struggled against the temptation to conform to the surrounding culture.

OLD TESTAMENT FORESHADOWS REVELATION:

And he said, I have been very jealous for the Lord GOD of hosts: for the children of Israel have forsaken your covenant, thrown down your altars, and slain your prophets with the sword; and I, even I only, am left; and they seek my life, to take it away. (1 Kings 19:10)

A strong Old Testament parallel to Revelation 2:13 is found in 1 Kings 19:10, where Elijah laments his isolation and persecution for standing against the false worship of Baal. Pergamos was a center of paganism, just as Israel had turned to Baal worship in Elijah's time. The believers in Pergamos remained loyal to Christ, just as Elijah stayed faithful despite widespread apostasy. Antipas was martyred in Pergamos, just as many prophets were killed during Elijah's time for opposing idolatry. Both passages highlight the spiritual battle between truth and deception and affirm that God sees and honors those who remain steadfast in their faith, even in the strongholds of darkness.

THE REVELATION OF JESUS CHRIST REVEALS:

2:14 But I have a few things against you, because you have there them that hold the doctrine of Balaam, who taught Balac to cast a stumbling block before the children of Israel, to eat things sacrificed to idols, and to commit fornication (immorality).

In Revelation 2:14, Jesus rebukes the church at Pergamos for tolerating the doctrine of Balaam, an Old Testament figure who led Israel into sin. Though the believers in Pergamos had remained faithful in some ways, they had allowed compromise to enter their midst.

Who was Balaam? Balaam was a prophet in Numbers 22–25, hired by Balak, the king of Moab, to curse Israel. However, since God would not allow him to curse His people, Balaam devised a different strategy—he counseled Balak to seduce Israel into sin. The Moabite women lured Israelite men into idolatry and sexual immorality, leading to divine judgment (Numbers 25:1–3). This act of spiritual and moral corruption became known as the doctrine of Balaam.

Just as Balaam led Israel into compromise with the world, the church in Pergamos allowed false teachings to take root. Some believers tolerated idolatry and immorality, justifying them under the guise of cultural adaptation. This reflects the dangers of blending Christianity with pagan practices, which intensified after the church gained state approval under Constantine.

Jesus' rebuke to Pergamos is a warning to the Church today. Compromise can lead to spiritual corruption. Just as Balaam tempted Israel into sin, modern believers face the temptation to blend worldly values with faith, tolerating sin rather than standing firm in righteousness.

Christ's call remains the same: reject false teachings; avoid moral and spiritual compromise; and stay faithful to God's Word, no matter the pressure to conform. In other words, Jesus calls His Church to purity and truth, warning that failure to repent will result in judgment. Therefore His message is clear: stand firm in faith, or risk falling into deception.

OLD TESTAMENT FORESHADOWS REVELATION:

> And Israel abode in Shittim, and the people began to commit whoredom with the daughters of Moab. And they called the people unto the sacrifices of their gods: and the people did eat, and bowed down to their gods. And Israel joined himself unto Baal-peor; and the anger of the LORD was kindled against Israel. (Numbers 25:1–3)

This passage details the stumbling block Balaam placed before Israel— enticing them to worship idols and engage in sexual immorality. This same pattern of spiritual compromise is what Jesus warns the church in Pergamos about in Revelation 2:14. Just as Israel fell into sin through seduction, Pergamos was tolerating false teachings that led believers away from pure devotion to Christ and into worldliness.

THE REVELATION OF JESUS CHRIST REVEALS:

> [2:15] So have you also them that hold the doctrine of the Nicolaitanes, which thing I hate.

In this verse, Jesus delivers a strong rebuke to the church in Pergamos as he did to the church of Ephesus (Revelation 2:6), condemning them for tolerating the doctrine of the Nicolaitans—a belief system that He explicitly says He hates.

Who Were the Nicolaitans? The name "Nicolaitans" comes from two Greek words: *nikos* meaning to conquer or dominate and *laos* meaning the people or laity. Together, "Nicolaitan" means "conquerors of the people." This suggests a system where a hierarchical religious class (clergy) dominated the common believers (laity). The Nicolaitans exalted religious leaders over the people, creating a division between the clergy and the congregation.

The early church was founded on spiritual equality—all believers had direct access to God through Christ (1 Peter 2:9). The Nicolaitan system, however, introduced religious hierarchy, priestly control, and a power structure that placed leaders above the congregation. This led to spiritual oppression and a system where church leaders wielded authority over people's faith and even their salvation.

- The priesthood replaced personal faith—people were required to go through priests rather than directly to God.
- The church controlled doctrine and access to Scripture, making the common believer dependent on religious leaders.
- Sacraments and rituals replace the simple gospel of salvation by grace through faith.

This doctrine eventually evolved into the hierarchical system of the Roman Catholic Church, where popes, bishops, and priests held absolute authority over salvation, confession, and access to God's Word.

Again, this period marked the marriage of church and state—a political-religious system where Christianity became intertwined with imperial power. The Edict of Milan (AD 313) legalized Christianity, but this led to compromise. Instead of remaining pure and separate, the Church absorbed pagan practices, hierarchy, and worldly influence.

Jesus' hatred of this doctrine shows that He desires a church free from human control, hierarchy, and manipulation. He calls believers to return to personal faith, spiritual purity, and direct communion with God. The warning to Pergamos serves as a reminder that any system that elevates religious leaders above Christ and controls believers' faith is a Nicolaitan system—and Jesus hates it.

OLD TESTAMENT FORESHADOWS REVELATION:

There are six things does the LORD hate: yes, seven are an abomination unto Him: A proud look, a lying tongue, and hands that shed innocent blood, a heart that devises wicked imaginations, feet that be swift in running to mischief, a false witness that speaks lies, and he that sows discord among brethren. (Proverbs 6:16–19)

The Nicolaitans sowed discord by corrupting the purity of the Church, much like those whom God hates in Proverbs. Their false teachings led believers away from truth, similar to a lying tongue and a false witness mentioned in this verse. Their hierarchical domination created prideful religious leaders who sought power rather than servanthood, mirroring, the "proud look" that God despises. By perverting grace into license for sin, they led believers into moral and spiritual compromise, much like "feet that run to mischief." Thus, Proverbs 6:16–19 aligns with Revelation 2:15, as both passages highlight God's hatred for deception, pride, and corruption within His people.

THE REVELATION OF JESUS CHRIST REVEALS:

2:16 Repent; or else I will come to you quickly and will fight against them with the sword of My mouth.

In Revelation 2:16, Jesus commands the church at Pergamos to repent—a clear and urgent call to turn away from the compromises they had made with false teachings, particularly the doctrines of Balaam and the Nicolaitans. These teachings led to idolatry, immorality, and spiritual corruption, blending pagan practices with Christian faith.

"Repent; or else I will come to you quickly." Jesus warns that if they do not repent, He will intervene personally and swiftly. The phrase "I will come to you quickly" does not refer to His Second Coming, but rather a direct act of judgment against those who refuse to turn back to Him. This echoes the many times in Scripture where God brings divine discipline upon His people when they stray from His ways.

"And will fight against them with the sword of My mouth." The sword of His mouth is a symbol of divine truth and judgment. This imagery is drawn from Hebrews 4:12, where the Word of God is described as sharper than any two-edged sword. The sword represents His authority to judge with absolute righteousness—not with human weapons, but with the power of His word.

Jesus is making it clear that compromise with false doctrine and moral corruption will not be tolerated. If they do not repent, they will face the disciplining power of Christ's Word, which exposes, convicts, and brings judgment. This is a serious warning to the Church—compromise with the world leads to spiritual ruin, but true repentance restores our relationship with Christ.

OLD TESTAMENT FORESHADOWS REVELATION:

But with righteousness shall He judge the poor, and reprove with equity for the meek of the earth: and He shall smite the earth with the rod of His mouth, and with the breath of His lips shall He slay the wicked. (Isaiah 11:4)

This verse aligns with Revelation 2:16 in the following ways: Both passages depict the power of God's Word as a weapon of judgment. The "rod of His mouth" in Revelation, signifying divine authority and judgment through His spoken Word. Jesus, as the righteous Judge, will confront and destroy wickedness, just as prophesied in Isaiah.

THE REVELATION OF JESUS CHRIST REVEALS:

2:17 He that has an ear, let him hear what the Spirit says to the churches; To him that overcomes will I give to eat of the hidden manna, and will give him a white stone, and in the stone a new name written, which no man knows except he that receives it.

"To him that overcomes will I give to eat of the hidden manna." Manna, the supernatural bread from heaven, sustained the Israelites in the wilderness (Exodus

16:4). Jesus later identified Himself as the true bread of life (John 6:31–35), emphasizing that spiritual sustenance comes from Him. The hidden manna represents the deep, divine provision and intimate fellowship with Christ, reserved for those who faithfully endure. Unlike the physical manna, which was temporary, this hidden manna is eternal, symbolizing the spiritual nourishment and eternal satisfaction found in Christ.

"And will give him a white stone." In ancient times, white stones were used in legal trials, voting, and awards:

1. **Acquittal**—Judges would cast a white stone for innocence and a black stone for guilt. The white stone signifies forgiveness and justification in Christ.

2. **Victors' Token**—Athletes and gladiators who won contests were given a white stone, granting them access to a great feast. This parallels the believer's invitation to the marriage supper of the Lamb (Revelation 19:9).

3. **Covenant Sign**—White stones were also used as tokens of friendship and special favor, symbolizing a personal and eternal relationship with Christ.

"And in the stone a new name written, which no man knows except he that receives it." A new name signifies transformation, identity, and divine calling. Throughout Scripture, God changed the names of His chosen servants to reflect their new destiny (Abram to Abraham, Jacob to Israel, Simon to Peter). The unknown nature of this name suggests an intimate, personal revelation between Christ and the believer. It is a name known only by its recipient, highlighting the unique relationship each believer has with Christ.

Revelation 2:17 reassures believers that overcoming faithfulness leads to spiritual sustenance, divine favor, and a new identity in Christ. These promises contrast the compromised faith of Pergamos, where worldly corruption infiltrated the Church. The hidden manna points to a deeper walk with Christ, the white stone signifies victory and belonging, and the new name affirms our personal transformation in Him.

OLD TESTAMENT FORESHADOWS REVELATION:

And the Gentiles (non-Jews) shall see your righteousness, and all kings your glory: and you shalt be called by a new name, which the mouth of the LORD shall name. (Isaiah 62:2)

A new name given by God—Just as Isaiah 62:2 prophesies that God will give His people a new name, Revelation 2:17 speaks of a new name written on a white stone, personally bestowed upon the overcomer by Christ. In Isaiah, the new name signifies a new identity and status before God, just as in Revelation, the overcomer receives a new identity that is known only between them and God. Isaiah's passage describes the coming glory and special recognition for God's people, just as Revelation 2:17 promises hidden manna (divine provision), a white stone (favor and victory), and a secret name (personal relationship with Christ).

CHRIST'S LETTER TO THE CHURCH OF THYATIRA

The fourth letter in Revelation is addressed to Thyatira, prophetically representing the Papal (Pagan) Church era (AD 590–Tribulation Age)—a period when false religion and corruption infiltrated the Church, leading to centuries of spiritual darkness.

The name *Thyatira* is significant. The city was once called Semiramis, linking it to Babylonian idolatry. In biblical history, Babylon represents both a political and a spiritual system of corruption. Nimrod, Babylon's first king, built political Babylon, but his wife, Semiramis, established spiritual Babylon, introducing the worship of the queen of heaven (Genesis 10:8–10). This false system of worship persisted for centuries and influenced the Roman Catholic Church's transformation into a powerful religious empire.

Thyatira was also the home of Lydia, the first European convert to Christianity (Acts 16:14). However, by the time of Revelation, the church in Thyatira had become deeply compromised, tolerating false teachings and immorality, much like the era it represents.

The Papal Church era began in AD 590 when Gregory I became the first official Pope of the Roman Catholic Church. While Gregory himself was a strong leader, later popes abused power, suppressed biblical truth, and persecuted true believers. From AD 858–1085, historians refer to this period as the midnight of the Dark Ages, marked by corruption, bribery, and the near-extinction of gospel preaching.

The most ruthless Pope, Innocent III (AD 1198–1216), waged wars of extermination against Bible-believing Christians in France and Italy, forbade the reading of Scripture in common languages, and instituted the Inquisition, where anyone caught reading the Bible faced torture and execution. Under his orders, entire Christian communities—such as the Albigensians—were slaughtered in one of history's most diabolical acts.

For over a thousand years, the Holy Roman Empire ruled Europe, using religion as the means of control. Eventually, in 1806, Napoleon Bonaparte dismantled it. However, the damage was done—Europe's deep resentment of the

Catholic Church's brutality led to widespread anti-Christian sentiment, which continues today.

Thyatira symbolizes a corrupt church—one that tolerated idolatry, false doctrine, and immorality. Babylonian mysticism, astrological divination, and pagan rituals replaced biblical truth. Yet, Jesus still called individuals within this era to remain faithful. Christ's message to Thyatira is clear: Hold fast to love, faith, and endurance. Do not tolerate false teachings. Repent. Through Christ, the risen King, we can overcome.

———◆◆◆———

"Ann, you mentioned something called the 'midnight of the Dark Ages' just now. What exactly does that mean?"

"It refers to the period between AD 858 and 1085—often called the darkest chapter of church history. Corruption, bribery, and bloodshed were rampant, and biblical truth was nearly extinguished. The Church became less about faith and more about power. Popes and bishops held political control, sold indulgences, and lived in luxury while ordinary people suffered under oppressive religious rule."

"That sounds terrifying. But wasn't the Church supposed to be leading people to Christ?"

"It should have been, but instead, it became an empire concerned with control. One of the most infamous acts of this era was the Inquisition, a system designed to root out 'heresy.' Anyone suspected of disagreeing with the Church's teachings could be arrested, tortured, and executed—often without even knowing their accuser."

"Wait—executed? For what? Just for reading the Bible?"

"Yes, Irene. Pope Innocent III, reigned from AD 1198 to 1216, was one of the worst persecutors. He forbade people from reading the Bible in their own language. If you were caught with a Bible, you were labeled a heretic. His orders led to the massacre of entire Christian communities, like the Albigensians in France. Families—men, women, and children—were slaughtered simply for following biblical teachings instead of Church traditions."

"That's horrifying. And people say the Church was doing this in the name of God?"

"That was their claim. But in reality, it was about maintaining power. The Church wanted absolute control over salvation—only priests could interpret Scripture, forgive sins, or grant absolution. The idea of personal faith and direct access to God was seen as a threat."

"So, the Inquisition was basically a system of religious oppression?"

"Exactly. It started in the 12th century and lasted for hundreds of years, spreading across Europe. The Spanish Inquisition was especially brutal, targeting Jews, Muslims, and anyone suspected of not being a 'true Christian'—which really just meant anyone who didn't conform to the Church's authority."

"That explains why so many people in Europe today are anti-Christian. They're not rejecting Jesus—they're rejecting the history of the institutional Church."

"Yes, and that's the tragic part. The corruption of the Thyatira church era still affects how people see Christianity today. But Jesus never called us to rituals, political power, or forced conversions. He called us to love, faith, and truth. That's why His message to Thyatira still matters—He calls His true followers to stand firm, reject false teaching, and remain faithful."

"Wow . . . I never knew how much history was tied to this. It makes me even more grateful for the freedom to read the Bible for myself today."

"And that's exactly why knowing this history is so important. We must learn from the past and make sure the Church today doesn't repeat the same mistakes."

———◆◆◆———

THE REVELATION OF JESUS CHRIST REVEALS:

2:18 And to the angel of the church in Thyatira write these things says the Son of God, who has His eyes like to a flame of fire, and His feet are like fine brass.

In Revelation 2:18, Jesus addresses the church in Thyatira, introducing Himself with striking imagery that emphasizes His divine authority and judgment.

"These things says the Son of God." This is the only place in Revelation where Jesus directly refers to Himself as the Son of God. This title asserts His deity and supreme authority, contrasting with the church's compromise with false teachings and worldly influences. It is also significant in Thyatira, a city known for its worship of Apollo, and so-called son of Zeus. Jesus makes it clear: He, and He alone, is the true Son of God.

"Who has His eyes like a flame of fire." This description conveys His omniscience, penetrating gaze, and righteous judgment. Fire in Scripture often represents purification and judgment (Malachi 3:2; Hebrews 12:29). Jesus sees beyond outward appearances—He discerns the hearts and intentions of His people, exposing sin and hypocrisy. No corruption, false teaching, or secret sin can escape His watchful eyes.

"And His feet are like fine brass." In biblical symbolism, brass represents strength, purity, and judgment through fire (Daniel 10:6). In the Old Testament, the brazen altar was used for sacrifices, signifying atonement for sin. Here,

Christ's brass-like feet symbolize His unwavering righteousness and power to tread down evil. His authority is firm, and His judgment is unshakable.

OLD TESTAMENT FORESHADOWS REVELATION:

But who may abide the day of His coming? And who shall stand when He appears? For He is like a refiner's fire and like fullers' soap: And He shall purify the sons of Levi, and purge them as gold and silver, that they may offer unto the LORD an offering in righteousness. (Malachi 3:2–3)

Malachi's prophecy describes the coming of the LORD as a refining fire, purging His people so that they may serve Him in righteousness. In Revelation 2:18, Jesus is presented as the Son of God with fiery eyes of judgment and feet like refined brass, showing His authority to purify and discipline the church in Thyatira, which had tolerated corruption and false teaching.

THE REVELATION OF JESUS CHRIST REVEALS:

2:19 I know your works, and charity, and service, and faith, and your patience, and your works; and the last to be more than the first.

Jesus begins His message to the church in Thyatira with commendation, acknowledging their works, love (charity), service, faith, and patience. Unlike the church of Ephesus, which had lost its first love (Revelation 2:4), Thyatira is praised for increasing in good works, as "the last to be more than the first" indicates their growth in spiritual efforts.

"I know your works." Jesus sees all that they do, both the good and the bad. The church was active in ministry and service to others.

"Charity (love)." Unlike some other churches, Thyatira exhibited love, the most important virtue (1 Corinthians 13:1–3).

"Service." Their love was expressed through acts of serving others. This was a caring, ministry-minded church.

"Faith." They remained faithful despite external pressures. Their trust in God led them to act on their faith.

"Patience." They endured hardships with perseverance, likely under persecution or societal opposition.

"And the last to be more than the first." Unlike some churches that stagnated or declined, Thyatira's good works increased over time, showing spiritual growth.

The church of Thyatira had much to commend—it was a growing, active, and loving church. However, as the next verses reveal, despite their outward good, they tolerated corruption within. This is a warning to believers today: spiritual growth in service must not come at the expense of doctrinal purity. Good works must be accompanied by truth and holiness to be fully pleasing to Christ.

OLD TESTAMENT FORESHADOWS REVELATION:

Trust in the LORD, and do good; so shalt you dwell in the land, and verily you shalt be fed. (Psalm 37:3)

This verse in Psalms reflects the righteous living, faith, and perseverance that Jesus commended in Thyatira, even though later verses reveal that their good deeds were undermined by their tolerance of false teachings.

THE REVELATION OF JESUS CHRIST REVEALS:

2:20 Notwithstanding I have a few things against you, because you suffered that woman Jezebel, which calls herself a prophetess, to teach and to seduce my servants to commit fornication, and to eat things sacrificed to idols.

In Revelation 2:20, Jesus rebukes the church in Thyatira for tolerating a false prophetess, symbolically referred to as Jezebel—a reference to the infamous queen of Israel who led the nation into idolatry and immorality (1 Kings 16:31; 2 Kings 9:22). Just as Jezebel corrupted Israel by promoting Baal worship, this "Jezebel" in Thyatira seduced the church into spiritual adultery through false teaching, idolatry, and moral corruption.

Jesus calls this a whore church, a harlot church, because it compromised with the world instead of remaining faithful to Christ. The Church, which was meant to be the pure Bride of Christ, was instead committing adultery with the nations of the earth—entangled in political power, wealth, and false religion.

This period of church history (the Papal Church era, AD 590–Tribulation Age) saw the rise of a religious system that merged with political kingdoms, exercising worldly influence and control. The golden chains, religious artifacts, rituals, and idols became symbols of this corruption, drawing people away from the true gospel.

Jezebel's spirt works not just through false doctrine, but through seduction and deception—drawing people into spiritual compromise. Nations aligned with her represent religious corruption replacing true faith.

Jesus' rebuke is a warning to all believers—to reject false teachings, spiritual compromise, and the blending of pagan practices with Christian worship. Those who allow themselves to be seduced by religious deception will face judgment. However, those who remain faithful to Christ and His Word will be counted as His true Church—the pure Bride of Christ, not the harlot who rides the beast (Revelation 17:3–5).

OLD TESTAMENT FORESHADOWS REVELATION:

And it came to pass, as if it had been a light thing for him to walk in the sins of Jeroboam the son of Nebat, that he took to wife Jezebel the daughter of Ethbaal king of the Zidonians, and went and served Baal, and worshiped him. And he reared up an altar for Baal in the house of Baal, which he had built in Samaria. And Ahab made a grove; and Ahab did more to provoke the Lord GOD of Israel to anger than all the kings of Israel that were before him. (1 Kings 16:31–33)

This passage reveals Jezebel's role in leading Israel into idolatry and spiritual adultery, just as Jesus condemns the Thyatira church for tolerating the spirit of Jezebel, which promotes compromise, false teaching, and immorality.

Irene, deep in thought, sets down her notes and looks up at me.

Curious. "Okay, I have to ask—wasn't this the time of the crusades? I mean, we're talking about the Church becoming corrupt, wielding power, and getting entangled with politics. Weren't the crusades a huge part of that?"

I nodded. "Absolutely, the crusades were a major symptom of the spiritual decay Jesus was warning about in Revelation 2:20. This was when the Church, instead of spreading the gospel, started using military force in the name of God. It all began in 1095 when Pope Urban II called for the First Crusade to reclaim the Holy Land from Muslim control."

Raising an eyebrow. "So, it wasn't really about faith—it was about power?"

"Exactly. The Church offered absolution of sins to anyone who joined the fight, which meant that criminals, mercenaries, and even ordinary peasants took up the sword, believing they were earning their way into heaven. What started as a so-called 'Holy war' quickly turned into something else—violence, greed, and conquest."

Shaking her head. "That's crazy. I always thought the crusades were about defending Christianity, but it sounds more like political maneuvering and a religious excuse."

"That's the heartbreak part. Some crusaders genuinely believed they were fighting for God, but others were simply after land and wealth. And the worst part? The violence wasn't just against Muslims and Jews. During the Fourth Crusade, they attacked Constantinople—a Christian city. Instead of liberating the Holy Land, they looted and destroyed one of Christianity's greatest centers."

Stunned. "Wait, they attacked their own people? That's the ultimate betrayal!"

"It was. And that's why Jesus had such strong words of Thyatira—because the church had lost its way. They weren't spreading Christ's love. They were wielding a sword in His name, but for all the wrong reasons."

Sighing. "So this was part of the same corruption—selling indulgences, persecuting believers, controlling people through fear—and now adding war to the mix?"

I nodded. "Exactly. The Church went from being persecuted in the early centuries to becoming persecutor. The same leaders who suppressed the Bible and burned so-called 'heretics' also led armies in battle. It was about controlling not just people's faith, but entire nations."

Thoughtful. "No wonder people today still hold so much skepticism toward Christianity. It's like the Church traded its mission for power."

Softly. "That's why this warning in Revelation is so important. Jesus wasn't just speaking to the church of Thyatira—He was speaking to every generation. When the Church aligns itself with worldly power instead of God's truth, it always leads to corruption."

Nodding. "And yet, Jesus still called them to repent. That means there's always a way back."

Smiling. "Exactly. No matter how far the Church strays, Christ still invites His people to return to Him."

———◆◆◆———

THE REVELATION OF JESUS CHRIST REVEALS:

2:21 And I gave her space to repent of her fornication; and she repented not.

This verse demonstrates both God's patience and His justice. Despite the corruption, immorality, and idolatry within the church at Thyatira, Jesus extends an opportunity for repentance. The phrase "I gave her space" reveals that God is merciful, allowing time for correction before judgment falls. However, Jezebel—symbolizing false religion, spiritual seduction, and idolatry—refuses to repent.

The refusal to turn from sin is a grave warning. When people continually reject God's call to repentance, their hearts become hardened, and judgment becomes inevitable. This mirrors Romans 2:4–5, where Paul warns that God's kindness is meant to lead us to repentance, but stubbornness stores up wrath.

This verse also echoes God's dealings with ancient Israel. The nation repeatedly turned to idols despite God sending prophets to call them back to Him. Eventually, divine judgment came upon them. Likewise, Thyatira's tolerance of false teaching—symbolized by Jezebel—would lead to severe consequences if they failed to repent.

The lesson is clear: God is patient, but His patience is not infinite. When we ignore His warnings, we risk facing His righteous judgment. This verse serves as a sobering reminder to respond to God's call while there is still time.

OLD TESTAMENT FORESHADOWS REVELATION:

Since the day that your fathers came forth out of the land of Egypt unto this day
I have even sent unto you all My servants the prophets, daily rising up early and

sending them: Yet they listened not unto Me, nor inclined their ear, but hardened their neck: they did worse than their fathers. (Jeremiah 7:25–26)

Just as God gave Israel time to repent by sending prophets to warn them, Jesus gave Jezebel (symbolizing false religion in Thyatira) space to repent. Despite repeated warnings, Israel refused to listen, just as Jezebel "repented not." Both passages emphasize God's patience and the consequences of ignoring His mercy. This parallel highlights the pattern of rebellion throughout history—when people continually reject God's call to repentance, judgment inevitably follows.

THE REVELATION OF JESUS CHRIST REVEALS:

2:22 Behold, I will cast her into a bed, and them that commit adultery with her into great tribulation, except they repent of their deeds.

In Revelation 2:22, Jesus issues a solemn warning to the church in Thyatira, which had embraced corruption, idolatry, and spiritual adultery through the influence of Jezebel, a false prophetess. He declares that judgment is imminent unless repentance occurs.

"Behold, I will cast her into a bed." The word "bed" is symbolic. While a bed can represent rest and intimacy, here it signifies judgment—likely a reference to suffering, affliction, or even death. Jezebel, and those who follow her ways, will be cast into a place of torment rather than comfort. This could be both a literal judgment in history and a prophetic foreshadowing of the Great Tribulation.

"And them that commit adultery with her into great tribulation." This phrase does not refer solely to physical immorality but also to spiritual adultery—a metaphor used throughout Scripture for idolatry and unfaithfulness to God (James 4:4; Hosea 4:12). Those who align with false religious systems and turn from true worship will face severe consequences.

"Except they repent of their deeds." Even in His righteous judgment, Jesus extends mercy. Repentance is still possible. This shows that God's desire is always for restoration rather than destruction (2 Peter 3:9). However, if they refuse to turn back to the truth, tribulation and judgment are inevitable.

OLD TESTAMENT FORESHADOWS REVELATION:

And they shall deal with you hatefully, and shall take away all your labor, and shall leave you naked and bare: and the nakedness of your whoredoms shall be discovered, both your lewdness and your whoredoms. I will do these things unto you, because you have gone a whoring after the Gentile nations, and because you are polluted with their idols. (Ezekiel 23:29–30)

Both passages speak of those who have betrayed God by engaging in spiritual fornication, meaning they have compromised with false religions and idolatry. Just as Revelation warns that Jezebel and her followers will be cast into great tribulation, Ezekiel speaks of how Israel was stripped and judged for following after false gods. In both cases, God gives time for repentance, but if they refuse, judgment follows. This parallel reinforces God's consistent warning throughout Scripture: spiritual compromise leads to divine discipline, and only repentance can bring restoration.

THE REVELATION OF JESUS CHRIST REVEALS:

2:23 And I will kill her children with death; and all the churches shall know that I am He which searches the minds and hearts: and I will give to every one of you according to your works.

This verse is a severe warning from Christ to those who follow the corrupt and idolatrous teachings of Jezebel—the false prophetess influencing the church in Thyatira. Here, "her children" refers to her followers, those who embrace her false doctrines and immoral practices.

"I will kill her children with death." The consequences of spiritual corruption. This is a divine judgment against those who refuse to repent. "Kill with death" is an emphatic phrase, meaning utter destruction—not just physical death but eternal separation from God. This echoes God's judgment on Ahab and Jezebel's literal children (2 Kings 9:22–37), where they were violently removed from power due to their idolatry and wickedness. The same principle applies to spiritual "children"—those who follow false teachers and rebel against God.

"All the churches shall know that I am He which searches the minds and hearts." Christ's divine authority. Jesus declares His omniscience—He sees beyond outward actions and looks deep into the thoughts, motives, and desires of every person. This phrase is a reference to Jeremiah 17:10. This reinforces that judgment is based on the true condition of the heart, not just outward religious acts.

"I will give to every one of you according to your works." Judgment based on deeds. This does not imply salvation by works, but rather that actions reveal the true state of a person's heart. Those who are faithful to Christ will be rewarded, while those who persist in rebellion will face judgment. This principle is consistent throughout Scripture, including Romans 2:6, which states, "Who (God) will render to every man according to his deeds."

This verse is a stark reminder that Jesus sees all, knows all, and will judge all. While He offers grace to those who repent, He will bring judgment upon those who persist in sin. The churches are warned: tolerating false teaching leads to devastating consequences—but those who remain faithful will receive their due reward.

OLD TESTAMENT FORESHADOWS REVELATION:

I the LORD search the heart, I try the reins, even to give every man according to his ways, and according to the fruit of his doings. (Jeremiah 17:10)

Revelation 2:23 and Jeremiah 17:10 both highlight God's righteous judgment, His omniscience, and His call to accountability. Christ, as the divine Judge, sees all and will render to each according to their works.

THE REVELATION OF JESUS CHRIST REVEALS:

2:24 But to you I say, and to the rest in Thyatira, as many as have not this doctrine, and which have not known the depths of Satan, as they speak; I will put upon you none other burden.

In this verse, Jesus addresses the faithful remnant in Thyatira—those who have not embraced the corrupt teachings and practices of Jezebel. Unlike those who have been deceived by false doctrine and immoral practices, these believers have not delved into the so-called "deep things of Satan," and reference to the hidden, esoteric, or occult knowledge that false teachers claimed to possess.

Jesus reassures them that He will not impose any further burden on them beyond what they are already enduring. This statement echoes Acts 15:28, where the apostles determined not to lay unnecessary burdens on Gentile believers but to encourage them to remain faithful. In contrast to those who face severe judgment for their rebellion, the faithful are called to persevere and continue working in truth.

This verse is a reminder that even in times of widespread corruption and apostasy, God preserves a faithful remnant. For them, the call is to stand firm in their devotion to Christ, rejecting false teachings, and remaining steadfast in His truth.

OLD TESTAMENT FORESHADOWS REVELATION:

Therefore thus says the Lord GOD, Behold, I lay in Zion for a foundation a stone, a tried stone, a precious corner stone, a sure foundation: he that believes shall not make haste. (Isaiah 28:16)

Just as Revelation 2:24 highlights a faithful remnant in Thyatira who resist false doctrine and the "depths of Satan," Isaiah 28:16 speaks of Zion as the anchor point of true faith. Zion is a place, a people, and a promise—representing Jerusalem, the presence of God, and the eternal home of the redeemed. Christ is the cornerstone laid in Zion, and those who believe in Him and stand firm will not be shaken. In both passages, God assures the faithful that they will be upheld and will not face the same judgment as those who have embraced deception. The faithful in Thyatira are like those in Isaiah who trust in God's foundation rather than being caught up in falsehood.

THE REVELATION OF JESUS CHRIST REVEALS:

2:25 But that which you have already hold fast till I come.

In this verse, Jesus exhorts the faithful remnant in Thyatira to remain steadfast in their faith and commitment to Him. Despite the corruption and false teachings that have infiltrated the church, there are still believers who have not succumbed to the deception of Jezebel and the so-called "deep things of Satan" (Revelation 2:24). To these faithful ones, Christ gives a simple yet profound command: "Hold fast."

OLD TESTAMENT FORESHADOWS REVELATION:

Take fast hold of instruction; let her not go: keep her; for she is your life. (Proverbs 4:13)

Both verses emphasize endurance, faithfulness, and the importance of holding onto what God has given until the fulfillment of His promises.

THE REVELATION OF JESUS CHRIST REVEALS:

2:26 And he that overcomes, and keeps My works to the end, to him will I give power over the nations.

Jesus promises authority over the nations to those who remain faithful to Him until the end. This verse highlights perseverance, obedience, and reward for believers who do not compromise with false teachings or worldly influences.

"He that overcomes." Throughout Revelation, overcoming refers to remaining faithful in the face of persecution, temptation, and false doctrine (Revelation 12:11). True believers persevere in their devotion to Christ.

"Keeps My works to the end." This emphasizes active obedience to Christ's commands. It's not just about belief, but about continually living out one's faith until the very end (Matthew 24:13).

"To him will I give power over the nations." This refers to the future millennial reign of Christ (Revelation 20:4–6), where believers will rule with Christ as co-heirs (Romans 8:17). This is a fulfillment of Psalm 2:8–9, where the Messiah is given dominion over the nations.

OLD TESTAMENT FORESHADOWS REVELATION:

Ask of Me, and I shall give You the nations for Your inheritance, and the uttermost parts of the earth for Your possession. You shalt break them with a rod of iron; You shalt dash them in pieces like a potter's vessel. (Psalm 2:8–9)

Psalm 2 is a Messianic prophecy where God grants dominion to the Son (Jesus Christ) over the nations. Revelation 2:6 extends this promise to believers who overcome and remain faithful to Christ. Just as Christ will rule with divine authority, His faithful followers will co-reign with Him in the Millennial Kingdom (Revelation 20:4–6). This verse affirms God's sovereign plan to establish Christ's Kingdom, where righteousness will prevail and His faithful will share in His rule.

THE REVELATION OF JESUS CHRIST REVEALS:

$^{2:27}$ And He will rule them with a rod of iron; as the vessels of a potter will they be broken to shivers: even as I received of My Father.

This verse is a direct reference to Psalm 2:8–9, where God grants the Messianic King authority over the nations. Jesus, having received dominion from the Father, extends this promise to those who overcome—believers who remain faithful to Him until the end.

The phrase "rule them with a rod of iron" signifies absolute authority and righteous judgment over the nations. Christ's rule will be firm, unyielding, and just—ensuring that sin and rebellion are no longer tolerated. The Greek word for "rule" *poimanei* actually means "to shepherd." This implies that Christ's authority, while firm, is also meant to guide and care for His people.

The imagery of pottery being shattered speaks to the complete destruction of opposition. Just as fragile clay cannot resist a blow, the rebellious nations will not stand against Christ's reign when He establishes His Kingdom. This breaking symbolizes judgment on the ungodly and the removal of corruption before the righteous rule of Christ begins.

Christ received this authority from the Father (Matthew 28:18), and He grants it to His faithful followers who endure until the end. This points to the Millennial Kingdom (Revelation 20:4–6), where believers will co-reign with Christ and participate in His righteous governance of the earth.

OLD TESTAMENT FORESHADOWS REVELATION:

And He shall break it as the breaking of the potters' vessel that is broken in pieces; He shall not spare: so that there shall not be found in the bursting of it a shred to take fire from the hearth, or to take water withal out of the pit. (Isaiah 30:14)

Both passages describe complete destruction using the imagery of shattered pottery. Isaiah speaks of judgment against those who rebel against God, just as Jesus promises to break the rebellious nations with a rod of iron. The breaking of the potter's vessel in Isaiah illustrates God's decisive judgment, leaving nothing useful behind—mirroring the divine authority Christ wields in Revelation. Just as nations that reject God's rule will be shattered, those who remain faithful will share in Christ's dominion over them. This verse reinforces the theme of Christ's absolute authority and justice in establishing His Kingdom.

THE REVELATION OF JESUS CHRIST REVEALS:

$^{2:28}$ And I will give him the morning star.

Jesus concludes His promise to the overcomer in Thyatira with a profound reward—the morning star. This imagery holds deep biblical and prophetic significance.

In Revelation 22:16, Jesus declares, "I am the Root and the Offspring of David, and the bright and morning star." This confirms that the morning star is Christ Himself. To the one who overcomes, Jesus is offering the ultimate gift— Himself, His presence, and intimate fellowship with Him in eternity.

The morning star appears just before dawn, signaling the coming of a new day. Spiritually, "the morning star" represents hope, victory, and the promise of Christ's return. In 2 Peter 1:19, the apostle writes, "We have also a more sure word of prophecy; whereunto you do well that you take heed, as unto a light that shines in a dark place, until the day dawns, and the morning star arises in your hearts."—linking it to the fullness of revelation and the coming of Christ's Kingdom.

Jesus' promise in the preceding verse (Revelation 2:27) speaks of ruling with a rod of iron. The morning star complements this promise—it is a symbol of the believer's future reign with Christ. Just as Christ will rule in the Millennial Kingdom, those who remain faithful will share in His authority and glory (2 Timothy 2:12).

Thyatira had been infiltrated by false teachings, particularly the corrupt influence of "Jezebel." In contrast to spiritual darkness, Jesus offers Himself as the morning star, the light that dispels darkness. Overcomers will receive the fullness of His light, truth, and righteousness in the age to come.

OLD TESTAMENT FORESHADOWS REVELATION:

I shall see Him, but not now: I shall behold Him, but not near: there shall come a Star out of Jacob, and a Scepter shall rise out of Israel, and shall smite the corners of Moab, and destroy all the children of Sheth. (Numbers 24:17)

This verse, spoken by the prophet Balaam, foretells the coming of the Messiah as a "Star" from Jacob, pointing directly to Jesus Christ. Jesus later identifies Himself as "the bright and morning star" (Revelation 22:16), fulfilling this prophecy. The mention of the "scepter" in Numbers 24:17 aligns with Revelation 2:27, where Christ promises the overcomers authority over the nations, reinforcing the reward of reigning with Him. Thus, Numbers 24:17 serves as a prophetic foundation for Revelation 2:28, foretelling Christ's coming reign and His promise to give Himself (the morning star) to those who overcome.

THE REVELATION OF JESUS CHRIST REVEALS:

[2:29] He that has an ear, let him hear what the Spirit says to the churches.

This verse concludes Christ's message to the church of Thyatira and follows a pattern seen in all seven letters. It is both an invitation and a command. The phrase "He that has an ear" emphasizes that not everyone will truly listen—understanding requires spiritual discernment.

Jesus calls for attentive hearing, not just with physical ears but with a receptive heart. The Spirit is speaking, revealing divine truth, correction, and promise. Each church, though addressed specifically, carries lessons for all believers throughout history.

This verse reminds us that God's Word is living and active, meant for those willing to receive it. The question is not whether God is speaking—but whether we are listening.

OLD TESTAMENT FORESHADOWS REVELATION:

Incline your ear, and come unto Me: hear, and your soul shall live; and I will make an everlasting covenant with you, even the sure mercies of David. (Isaiah 55:3)

Just as Jesus calls the churches to *hear* what the Spirit is saying in Revelation; Isaiah urges people to "incline their ear" and listen to God's voice. Both verses emphasize that true life—spiritual renewal and covenant blessings—comes through attentively hearing and responding to God's Word.

CHRIST'S LETTER TO THE CHURCH OF SARDIS

The fifth letter in Revelation is addressed to Sardis, prophetically representing the Protestant Church era (AD 1517–Tribulation Age). This was the period of Reformation, when believers began breaking away from the Roman Catholic Church, seeking a return to biblical truth. However, while the Protestant movement started strong, over time, much of it became spiritually stagnant—a church that appeared alive but was hollow within.

The name *Sardis* means "remnant" or "escaping ones," reflecting those who broke free from the corruption of the medieval (papal) church. The Reformation was ignited by Martin Luther (1483–1546), who in 1517 nailed his Ninety-five Theses to the church door in Wittenberg, Germany, protesting the sale of indulgences and the false belief that salvation could be purchased. His revelation came from Romans 1:17: "For therein is the righteousness of God revealed from faith to faith: as it is written, The just shall live by faith."

Luther, like many in his time, had wrestled with guilt, believing he had to earn salvation through fasting, penance, and confession. Yet, through Scripture, he discovered that justification comes by faith alone—not by works, sacraments, or church decrees. This led to a massive shift in Christianity, challenging centuries of tradition and control.

The Reformation brought many positive changes:

- The Bible was translated into common languages.
- The doctrine of salvation by faith alone was restored.
- Believers were taught to pray directly to God instead of relying on priests.

However, over time, many Protestant churches fell into the same trap of spiritual complacency that they had once protested against. Rituals replaced genuine faith, denominations divided over doctrine, and many churches became spiritually dead—Christian in name, but lacking power and true devotion to Christ.

Christ's message to Sardis is clear: Wake up! Strengthen what remains. Do not settle for an appearance of life—seek true revival. Through Christ, the risen King, we can overcome.

"So, Ann, I get why the Reformation was necessary. The Catholic church had basically become a religious empire, selling indulgences like some kind of spiritual marketplace. But was Martin Luther really expecting to start a revolution?"

"Not at all. Luther wasn't trying to break away from the Church—at least, not at first. He was a Catholic monk, deeply devoted, but he couldn't ignore what he saw in Scripture. When he read Romans 1:17, it shook him.

> For therein is the righteousness of God revealed from faith to faith: as it is written, The just shall live by faith. (Romans 1:17)

He realized that salvation wasn't something the Church could sell—it was a free gift from God."

"And that's when he nailed his Ninety-five Theses to the church door?"

"Exactly—October 31, 1517. Luther meant to spark discussion, not rebellion. But with the new printing press, his message spread fast. Suddenly, people who had never questioned Church doctrine were reading the Bible for themselves."

"And the Church wasn't happy about that."

"Not at all. The Pope demanded that Luther recant, but he refused. In 1521, he stood before the Diet of Worms—a formal imperial council, not just a church trial—and was ordered to take back his writings. His response? 'Here I stand, I can do no other. God help me. Amen.'"

Irene amazed. "That took guts! But even though the Reformation was about faith, it still ended up dividing the Church."

"That's the irony. The movement started with a return to biblical truth, but over time, Protestantism fractured into hundreds of denominations. The Reformation freed people from religious oppression, but in some ways, it also led to spiritual complacency. Some churches fell into the same lifeless traditions they once protested against."

"So that's why the church of Sardis is a warning? A church that looks alive but is spiritually dead?"

"Exactly. Christ's message is clear—wake up! Strengthen what remains. It's not enough to have the name of being alive. True faith is more than tradition; it's a daily walk with Christ."

"And that's what we're about to read, right?"

"That's right. Let's get into it."

THE REVELATION OF JESUS CHRIST REVEALS:

^{3:1} And to the angel of the church in Sardis write these things says He that has the seven Spirits of God, and the seven stars; I know your works, that you have a name that you live, and are dead.

This letter is directed to the church in Sardis, a congregation that represents the Protestant Church era (AD 1517–Tribulation Age). While Sardis had a reputation for being a thriving church, Jesus reveals the harsh reality—they were spiritually dead.

"These things says He that has the seven Spirits of God, and the seven stars." Christ introduces Himself as the One who holds the seven Spirits of God (a reference to the fullness of the Holy Spirit, as seen in Isaiah 11:2) and the seven stars (the leaders of the churches, as explained in Revelation 1:20). This imagery emphasizes His complete authority over the Church, both in spiritual power and leadership. Sardis, despite its external religious reputation, lacked the Holy Spirit's power.

"I know your works, that you have a name that you live, and are dead." This is a sobering rebuke. Sardis had the appearance of life—perhaps large gatherings, respected traditions, and a well-known name. However, Christ saw the truth: they were spiritually lifeless. This is a warning to all churches that rely on reputation, tradition, or religious activity without true spiritual vitality.

Sardis reflects the Protestant movement, which started as a powerful return to biblical truth but, over time, became fragmented and, in many cases, spiritually stagnant. Many churches bore the name of Christ but lost their fire, replacing true faith with formality.

OLD TESTAMENT FORESHADOWS REVELATION:

Wherefore the LORD said, Forasmuch as this people draw near Me with their mouth, and with their lips do honor Me, but have removed their heart far from Me, and their fear toward Me is taught by the precept of men. (Isaiah 29:13)

Both passages rebuke spiritual hypocrisy—appearing righteous outwardly while being spiritually dead inside. Sardis had a name that they lived but were dead, just as Israel honored God with their lips but had hearts far from Him. Isaiah 29:13 condemns empty religious rituals and traditions taught by men, much like Sardis, which had the form of godliness but lacked true spiritual life.

This parallel highlights God's desire for authentic faith over outward religiosity. Sardis, like ancient Israel, needed to wake up and return to true devotion before it was too late.

THE REVELATION OF JESUS CHRIST REVEALS:

[3:2] Be watchful, and strengthen the things which remain, that are ready to die: for I have not found your works perfect before God.

Jesus issues a wake-up call to the church in Sardis, urging them to recognize their spiritual condition. While they have a reputation for being alive, they are actually near spiritual death. Yet, all hope is not lost—there are still remnants of faith and obedience that can be revived.

"Be watchful." The church is called to wake up and remain vigilant. Sardis was historically known for its complacency, having been conquered twice because its watchmen failed to stay alert. Spiritually, they had become just as careless, allowing their faith to grow lifeless. Jesus frequently warned about the need for spiritual watchfulness (Matthew 24:42).

"And strengthen the things which remain, that are ready to die." While much of their faith is lifeless, there are still some embers of spiritual life that can be reignited. This is a call to revival, urging them to nurture what is left before it perishes completely.

"For I have not found your works perfect before God." Their deeds were incomplete—perhaps outwardly good but lacking true devotion, faith, and spiritual fruit. This reflects a superficial faith—religion without true relationship, duty without passion.

OLD TESTAMENT FORESHADOWS REVELATION:

> Now therefore thus says the LORD of hosts; Consider your ways. You have sown much, and bring in little; you eat, but you have not enough; you drink, but you are not filled with drink; you clothe you, but there is none warm; and he that earns wages earns wages to put it into a bag with holes. Thus says the LORD of hosts; Consider your ways. (Haggai 1:5–7)

Just as Jesus tells Sardis to wake up and examine their spiritual condition, Haggai calls the people of Israel to consider their ways—to reflect on their actions and return to God's purpose. Haggai rebukes Israel for focusing on their own pursuits while neglecting the unfinished work of rebuilding God's Temple. Similarly, Jesus urges Sardis to revive what little remains of their faith before it completely fades. The people in Haggai's time had labored without true spiritual devotion, just as the church in Sardis had works that were incomplete and imperfect before God. Both passages emphasize self-examination, repentance, and the urgency of returning to God before it is too late. They remind us that outward religious activity is not enough—God desires true devotion, spiritual renewal, and a commitment to His will.

THE REVELATION OF JESUS CHRIST REVEALS:

> 3:3 Remember therefore how you have received and heard, and hold fast, and repent. If therefore you will not watch, I will come on you as a thief, and you will not know what hour I will come upon you.

"Remember therefore how you have received and heard, and hold fast, and repent." Jesus calls the church of Sardis to remember the truth they had once received. This suggests that Sardis had been given the gospel, sound teaching, and spiritual riches, yet they had neglected them. They are commanded to hold fast—to cling to the truth they once embraced—and to repent, meaning they must turn away from their spiritual deadness and return to the life-giving power of the Spirit.

"If therefore you will not watch, I will come on you as a thief, and you will not know what hour I will come upon you." This warning reflects the suddenness of Christ's judgment upon those who are spiritually complacent. The imagery of a thief in the night is often used in Scripture to describe the unexpected arrival of divine judgment (Matthew 24:42–44; 1 Thessalonians 5:2). Sardis, known for its overconfidence and history of sudden military defeats due to a lack of watchfulness, would have understood this warning well. The church had fallen into spiritual complacency, much like the city had fallen due to its own carelessness.

OLD TESTAMENT FORESHADOWS REVELATION:

But if the watchman sees the sword come, and blow not the trumpet, and the people be not warned; if the sword come, and take any person from among them, he is taken away in his iniquity; but his blood will I require at the watchman's hand. (Ezekiel 33:6)

In both passages, there is a warning to remain vigilant. In Ezekiel, the watchman is responsible for alerting the people to impending danger, just as Christ commands the church in Sardis to stay spiritually awake. If the church of Sardis does not remain watchful, Christ will come upon them like a thief, suddenly and without warning. Similarly, in Ezekiel, if the watchman fails to sound the alarm, destruction will come unexpectedly. Just as the watchman is held responsible for failing to warn the people, the church in Sardis will face consequences if they do not heed Christ's command to repent and remain alert.

This parallel emphasizes the urgent need for spiritual vigilance, warning that neglecting God's call can lead to sudden and unforeseen judgment.

Irene paused, adjusting her glasses before looking up.

"You know, Ann, Revelation 3:3 says they 'received and heard' the gospel. But for centuries, the common people didn't even have access to the Bible. It was locked away—literally."

I nodded. "Exactly. The church of Thyatira kept the Scriptures in Latin, which most people couldn't read. Only the clergy had access, and they controlled how it was interpreted."

Irene sighed. "And that's why the invention of the Gutenberg press was so revolutionary. When Johannes Gutenberg developed movable type around 1440, it changed everything. Before that, books were copied by hand, making them rare and expensive. But the printing press allowed for mass production. By 1455, Gutenberg had printed the first Bible—the Latin Vulgate."

I leaned forward. "But even then, the problem remained—the Bible was still in Latin. The people still couldn't read it for themselves. That's where the Reformation changed everything."

Irene smiled. "Right. In 1517, Martin Luther nailed his Ninety-five Theses to the church door in Wittenberg. His message spread like wildfire, thanks to the printing press. It gave people direct access to his writings, and soon, there was a demand for the Bible in common languages."

"Luther himself translated the Bible into German in 1522. But in England, the battle was even tougher. The Catholic church fought hard to keep the Bible in Latin. Translating it into English was illegal—it was considered heresy."

Irene nodded. "Which brings us to William Tyndale. He was determined to give the English people a Bible they could read. In 1526, he printed the first English New Testament. But because it was illegal, the copies had to be smuggled into England."

I sighed. "And he paid the ultimate price. In 1536, he was arrested, strangled, and burned at the stake. But his work wasn't in vain. His translation became the foundation for future English Bibles."

Irene paused, flipping through her notes.

"So, we know that William Tyndale printed the first English New Testament in 1526, but that was only half the battle. What about the Old Testament?"

I nodded. "Exactly, Tyndale wanted to translate the whole Bible, but he was constantly hunted by the authorities. He managed to translate the first five books of the Old Testament—Genesis through Deuteronomy—by 1530. He kept working, but before he could finish the entire Old Testament, he was arrested in 1535 and executed in 1536."

Irene sighed. "Such a tragedy. But his work wasn't in vain. I remember reading that before Tyndale died, he cried out, 'Lord, open the King of England's eyes!'"

I smiled. "And that's exactly what happened. Just a year later, in 1537, King Henry VIII approved the first officially recognized English Bible—the Matthew Bible—which was actually based on Tyndale's work!"

Irene raised an eyebrow. "Wait, the 'Matthew Bible?' Who was Matthew?"

I laughed. "It was a pseudonym. The translator was actually John Rogers, a close friend of Tyndale. Since Tyndale's name was still dangerous, Rogers published it under the name 'Thomas Matthew.' This Bible contained Tyndale's New Testament and his Old Testament up to 2 Chronicles. The rest of the Old Testament was finished using another translation."

Irene leaned forward. "So now, for the first time, England had an official English Bible. But it wasn't the final version, was it?"

I shook my head. "No, not at all. In 1539, King Henry authorized the Great Bible, which was an improved version of the Matthew Bible. It was called the 'Great Bible' because of its large size, meant to be read in churches. But it was still based largely on Tyndale's work."

Irene tapped her pen. "So that was under King Henry. But what happened after him?"

I sighed. "Well, after Henry died, things got complicated. England went back and forth between Protestant and Catholic rule. Queen Mary, a staunch Catholic, banned the English Bible entirely and burned Protestants at the stake—including

John Rogers, the man behind the Matthew Bible. But when Elizabeth I became queen, she restored the English Bible."

Irene nodded. "That must have set the stage for the King James Bible."

I smiled. "Exactly! By 1560, English Protestant scholars in exile in Geneva produced the Geneva Bible. It was the first English Bible to include numbered verses and study notes. The Puritans loved it because it was very readable, but Queen Elizabeth's bishops weren't happy with the notes, so they created the Bishops' Bible in 1568."

Irene laughed. "So now there were multiple English Bibles floating around?"

I chuckled. "Pretty much! By the time King James I came to the throne in 1603, he saw the division caused by different Bible versions. So, in 1604, he commissioned a new translation that would unite the church. Over 50 scholars worked on it for seven years, using the best available manuscripts. And in 1611, the King James Bible was finally completed."

Irene exhaled. "So it wasn't just one moment in history—it was a whole process! Tyndale's work laid the foundation, then came the Matthew Bible, the Great Bible, the Geneva Bible, the Bishops' Bible, and finally, the King James Version."

I nodded. "Exactly. And through it all, the key was accessibility. The printing press, the Reformation, and the work of these translators meant that for the first time in centuries, people could read the Bible for themselves—not just rely on the Church's interpretation."

Irene smiled. "Which ties right back to Revelation 3:3. Jesus told the church of Sardis to 'remember what they had received and heard.' After centuries of being kept in darkness, they finally had the Word of God in their own hands."

I leaned back. "But having the Bible wasn't enough. The danger for Sardis was complacency—having the truth but not living by it. Just like today."

Irene nodded. "A powerful warning. Just because we have access to the Bible doesn't mean we're spiritually alive. That's what Jesus was telling Sardis. They needed to wake up."

———◆◆◆———

THE REVELATION OF JESUS CHRIST REVEALS:

3:4 You have a few names even in Sardis which have not defiled their garments; and they will walk with Me in white: for they are worthy.

In this verse, Jesus acknowledges that even within a spiritually lifeless church, there remain a faithful remnant—those who have not defiled their garments (righteousness) with sin, compromise, or worldliness. This speaks to the biblical principle that God always preserves a remnant of true believers, no matter how corrupt or dead a church or society may become.

Despite Sardis being described as a church that has "a name that it lives, but is dead" (Revelation 3:1), Jesus recognizes that there are still a few who remain true to Him. This is a reminder that even in times of widespread apostasy or lukewarm faith, there will always be those who stand firm in righteousness.

Garments in Scripture often symbolize righteousness and purity (Isaiah 61:10; Zechariah 3:3–5). To have defiled garments means to be stained with sin, corruption, or compromise with the world. Conversely, walking in white represents holiness, victory, and eternal life in Christ. This imagery is later reinforced in Revelation 7:14, where the saints have "washed their robes and made them white in the blood of the Lamb."

The phrase "they will walk with Me" signifies intimacy, fellowship, and eternal life in the presence of Christ. It echoes the promise of being with Him in His Kingdom, much like how Enoch "walked with God" and was taken up (Genesis 5:24).

The worthiness mentioned here is not about human merit but about faithfulness and perseverance in Christ. The ones who remain untainted by spiritual complacency will be honored and rewarded by the Lord.

OLD TESTAMENT FORESHADOWS REVELATION:

Let your garments be always white; and let your head lack no ointment. (Ecclesiastes 9:8)

In Revelation 3:4, the faithful in Sardis are described as those who have not defiled their garments—a metaphor for maintaining spiritual purity and righteousness. Ecclesiastes 9:8 similarly instructs believers to always keep their garments white, symbolizing holiness, wisdom, and walking rightly before God. The white garments in both verses indicate those who are set apart for God, living in a way that pleases Him. Those in Sardis who remain faithful will "walk with Christ in white," much like how white garments in the Old Testament were associated with divine favor and righteousness.

Ecclesiastes 9:8 also mentions that one's head should not lack oil, which often represents the anointing of the Holy Spirit. Similarly, in Revelation 3:4, those who remain faithful are not spiritually empty but are prepared to walk in Christ's presence.

Both Revelation 3:4 and Ecclesiastes 9:8 emphasize living a pure and consecrated life, clothed in righteousness, and remaining prepared for God's presence. The message is clear—those who stay undefiled will walk in the light of God's holiness.

THE REVELATION OF JESUS CHRIST REVEALS:

[3:5] He that overcomes, the same will be clothed in white raiment; and I will not blot out his name out of the Book of Life, but I will confess his name before My Father, and before His angels.

This verse contains a powerful promise to the faithful believers in Sardis—those who remain steadfast and overcome spiritual complacency will be eternally secure in Christ.

"He that overcomes." Throughout the letters to the churches in Revelation, Jesus calls believers to overcome—to remain faithful, resist spiritual apathy, and stand firm in the truth. Overcoming here specifically refers to remaining spiritually awake in a church that had the reputation of being alive but was spiritually dead (Revelation 3:1).

"The same will be clothed in white raiment." White garments symbolize righteousness, purity, and victory in Christ (Revelation 7:9, 13–14). In Sardis, a city known for its luxury and fine garments, Christ contrasts worldly riches with the true garments of righteousness that only He can provide. Those who overcome will be dressed in holiness of Christ and welcomed into His eternal presence.

"And I will not blot out his name out of the Book of Life." The Book of Life is a record of those who belong to God and will inherit eternal life (Exodus 32:32–33; Daniel 12:1; Revelation 20:12, 15). This phrase suggests a warning as well as a promise—those who remain faithful will have their names permanently secured in the Book of Life, while those who turn away risk being blotted out. This does not imply that salvation is easily lost but rather emphasizes the importance of remaining in Christ. True believers demonstrate their faith by persevering to the end (John 10:27–29).

"But I will confess his name before My Father, and before His angels." This echoes Matthew 10:32: "Whoever confesses Me before men, him I will also confess before My Father who is in heaven." Jesus stands as our mediator and advocate (1 John 2:1), publicly acknowledging the faithful before God's throne. Just as earthly rulers would honor their loyal subjects, Christ will declare the names of those who have overcome, recognizing them as His own in the presence of the Father and the angels.

Revelation 3:5 is both a promise and a challenge. Those who remain faithful, overcoming spiritual complacency and clinging to Christ, will receive eternal righteousness, security in the Book of Life, and public recognition in heaven. It is a call to stay spiritually vigilant, to walk in holiness, and to look forward to the day when Christ Himself will declare our names before the Father.

OLD TESTAMENT FORESHADOWS REVELATION:

Yet now, if You will forgive their sin—; and if not, blot me, I pray You, out of
Your book which You have written. And the LORD said unto Moses, Whosoever
has sinned against Me, him will I blot out of My book. (Exodus 32:32–33)

In both passages, there is a reference to a divine book that records the names
of those who belong to God. Moses pleads with God to either forgive Israel or
remove his name from "the book," signifying a record of those in covenant with
God. Revelation 3:5 affirms that the names of the faithful will not be blotted out
but will be confessed before the Father.

Exodus 32:33 teaches that those who sin against God will be removed from
His book. Revelation 3:5 provides the contrast—those who overcome will remain
in the Book of Life, clothed in white raiment. Both verses highlight that God alone
determines who is recorded in His book. This book is associated with salvation
and eternal life (Psalm 69:28; Daniel 12:1).

This parallel emphasizes God's faithfulness to the righteous and the
seriousness of remaining steadfast in Him.

THE REVELATION OF JESUS CHRIST REVEALS:

3:6 He that has an ear, let him hear what the Spirit says to the churches.

This verse, repeated throughout the messages to the seven churches,
serves as a universal call to spiritual discernment. It emphasizes the need for
believers to listen attentively to the Holy Spirit's guidance and apply Christ's
warnings, corrections, and promises to their lives.

OLD TESTAMENT FORESHADOWS REVELATION:

Yet the LORD has not given you a heart to perceive, and eyes to see, and ears to
hear, unto this day. (Deuteronomy 29:4)

Deuteronomy 29:4 highlights the spiritual blindness and deafness of Israel
despite witnessing God's miracles. Revelation 3:6 urges the churches to listen and
respond to what the Spirit is saying. In Deuteronomy, Israel saw God's wonders
but failed to grasp their true significance. In Revelation, Christ warns the churches
that hearing without obedience leads to judgment. Both verses stress that spiritual
perception is a gift from God—but it requires a willing heart to receive it.

Jesus' warning to the churches echoes Moses' warning to Israel: Do not
harden your hearts. Hear, understand, and obey—before it is too late.

CHRIST'S LETTER TO CHURCH OF PHILADELPHIA

The sixth letter in Revelation is addressed to Philadelphia, prophetically representing the Missionary Church era (AD 1730–Rapture). The name *Philadelphia* means "brotherly love," reflecting the spirit of revival, evangelism, and global missions that defined this church age.

Beginning with the Great Awakenings in Europe and America, this era saw unprecedented spiritual renewal, as passionate believers took the gospel to the ends of the earth. From the rise of modern missionary movements to the explosion of evangelism and Bible translations, countless men and women walked through the "open door" set before them.

Unlike the previous churches that faced rebuke, Philadelphia receives only commendation. They kept His Word, remained faithful to His name, and are promised deliverance from the hour of trial—a reference to the coming Tribulation. Christ's message to Philadelphia is clear: Hold fast! You have been faithful—keep going. Through Christ, you will overcome.

Irene pauses for a moment, thoughtfully flipping through the pages of my manuscript before looking up.

"So, we're in the Philadelphia church era now, the age of missions and revival. You mentioned the Great Awakenings in Europe and America—when exactly did they begin? I always thought it was just an American movement."

"It actually started in Europe before making its way to America. The first Great Awakening began in the early 1700s, around 1730. The spark? A spiritual dryness had settled over the Protestant churches—Christianity had become routine, more about formality than transformation. People attended church, but their hearts weren't truly engaged. Then, something changed."

"What happened?"

"Enter men like Count Nikolas Zinzendorf and the Moravians in Germany. They were small in number, but their prayers ignited a missionary movement that influenced the world. At the same time, in England, John Wesley and George Whitefield were preaching salvation and grace through faith, calling people to a personal relationship with Christ rather than just church attendance."

"Wesley—he's the founder of Methodism, right?"

"Exactly. He and Whitefield took preaching beyond the pulpit. Instead of waiting for people to come to church, they went to the fields, the marketplaces, wherever the people were. Crowds in the thousands would gather to hear them preach. It was radical—unheard of at the time."

"And then America?"

"Yes. Whitefield made multiple trips across the Atlantic and brought the revival to the American colonies. This is when you see Jonathan Edwards rise up. His sermon, 'Sinners in the Hands of an Angry God,' became one of the most famous messages of the movement. But it wasn't just fiery preaching—it was an outpouring of the Holy Spirit. People were weeping, repenting, and turning their lives to Christ in ways that hadn't been seen in generations."

"It must have changed society."

"It absolutely did. The Great Awakening didn't just renew personal faith—it reshaped the colonies. It broke down denominational barriers, emphasizing unity in Christ rather than religious hierarchy. It laid the foundation for religious freedom and, ultimately, influenced the American Revolution."

Curious. "American Revolution?"

"Yes, the American Revolution took place from 1775 to 1783. It began with the battles of Lexington and Concord on April 19, 1775, and officially ended with the Treaty of Paris on September 3, 1783, when Britain recognized the independence of the United States."

"So the revival wasn't just spiritual—it had political consequences too?"

"It did. The idea that people didn't need a State Church to connect with God gave them the confidence to challenge the idea that they needed a king to rule over them. Many of the founding fathers were influenced by this awakening. It was the birth of both a renewed Church and a new nation."

"That's powerful. And this continued with the Second Great Awakening?"

"Yes, about fifty years later. While the first Great Awakening shook colonial America, the second Great Awakening in the early 1800s spread even further—sparking revival across the frontier. It was during this time that camp meetings became popular, where thousands would gather for days at a time to experience revival. It led to a rise in missionary work, social reforms, and the expansion of the Church across America."

"So Philadelphia—the missionary church—is marked by this explosion of evangelism and revival. No rebuke, just encouragement."

"Exactly. Unlike the other churches, Philadelphia is commended for keeping His Word and not denying His name. It was a church walking in obedience, and because of that, Jesus set before them an 'open door'—opportunities to spread the gospel across the world."

"And that *open door* is still open, right?"

"Yes, and that's the challenge. The Philadelphia era is still unfolding—we are part of this mission, part of the calling to keep His Word, to reach the lost, and to hold fast to the faith. Until the door closes, the work continues."

"That's both inspiring and convicting. We have a responsibility to carry on what they started."

"Absolutely. And that's what makes this church so unique. It's a call to keep moving forward—to remain faithful, knowing that through Christ, we will overcome."

———◆◆◆———

THE REVELATION OF JESUS CHRIST REVEALS:

3:7 And to the angel of the church in Philadelphia write these things says He that is holy, He that is true, He that has the key of David, He that opens, and no man shuts; and shuts, and no man opens.

In Revelation 3:7, Jesus addresses the church in Philadelphia, describing Himself with distinct and powerful attributes:

"He that is holy, He that is true." Jesus decares His divine nature. Holiness is an essential attribute of God (Isaiah 6:3), and truth is His very essence (John 14:6). Unlike earthly rulers, He is flawless in character and completely trustworthy.

"He that has the key of David." This phrase connects to Isaiah 22:22, where Eliakim is given authority over the house of David. In this context, Christ is the ultimate fulfillment of this prophecy, holding sovereign authority over God's Kingdom—the power to grant or deny access to eternal life.

"He that opens, and no man shuts; and shuts, and no man opens." Jesus alone has the power to open doors of opportunity, salvation, and service that no one else can close. Likewise, He can shut doors—denying access to those who reject Him. This signifies His complete authority over entrance into the Kingdom of God.

OLD TESTAMENT FORESHADOWS REVELATION:

And the key of the house of David will I lay upon his shoulder; so he shall open, and none shall shut; and he shall shut, and none shall open. (Isaiah 22:22)

In Isaiah 22:22, God gives Eliakim, the steward of King Hezekiah's household, the key of the house of David, symbolizing authority, access, and governance. Jesus, in Revelation 3:7, declares that He possesses the ultimate fulfillment of this key—not just over an earthly kingdom, but over God's eternal Kingdom. The phrase "opens, and no man shuts; and shuts, and no man opens" emphasizes Christ's absolute power over salvation, opportunity, and divine authority. This verse in Isaiah foreshadows Christ as the true Messianic King, the one who alone controls entrance into God's Kingdom.

THE REVELATION OF JESUS CHRIST REVEALS:

³·⁸ I know your works: behold, I have set before you an open door, and no man can shut it: for you have a little strength, and have kept My Word, and have not denied My name.

The church of Philadelphia, known as the "faithful church," represents an era of revival, missions, and evangelism that began in the 18th century and continues until the present. This church did not receive rebuke, only commendation, because it remained faithful to God's Word and His name.

The phrase "I have set before you an open door" signifies a divine opportunity—a gateway to spread the gospel to the nations. This reflects the rise of global evangelism, the explosion of missionary work, and the spiritual awakenings that characterized this period. The church of Philadelphia embraced this calling, leading to the Great Awakenings, Azusa Street Revival, and global healing movements.

This open door was:

- A door of evangelism—The gospel spread worldwide, reaching the people who had never heard it before.
- A door of spiritual power—The church moved in the power of the Holy Spirit, leading to revivals and awakenings.
- A door of perseverance—Though the church had "a little strength," it endured through opposition and hardship.

Philadelphia remained true to Scripture, unlike the churches before it that had drifted into corruption and compromise. The Protestant Reformation had restored the authority of God's Word, and now, the *faithful church* was putting it into action by taking the message of salvation to the nations.

Jesus assures this church that no one can shut the door He has opened. The opposition of governments, religious institutions, or even persecution could not stop the gospel from advancing. Once God opens a door, no human force can close it.

Philadelphia is a model of faithfulness, perseverance, and mission-minded Christianity. As believers, we are called to walk through the open doors God provides, spreading His truth, standing firm in His Word, and never denying His name.

What open doors has God placed before you? How can you remain faithful, even in times of weakness? Are you actively sharing the gospel in your sphere of influence? Jesus calls His church to boldly step through the open doors of opportunity, knowing that His power sustains and His truth endures.

OLD TESTAMENT FORESHADOWS REVELATION:

Thus says the LORD to His anointed, to Cyrus, whose right hand I have held, to subdue nations before him; and I will loose the armor of kings, to open before him the two leaved gates; and the gates shall not be shut. (Isaiah 45:1)

In Isaiah 45:1, God declares that He will open doors before Cyrus, allowing him to conquer kingdoms and fulfill His divine plan. This symbolizes divine authority, access, and God-ordained opportunities. Similarly, in Revelation 3:8, Jesus tells the church of Philadelphia that He has set before them an open door that no man can shut. This represents divine favor, opportunity, and the unstoppable spread of the gospel.

Both passages emphasize that when God opens a door—whether for a king like Cyrus or for His faithful church—no earthly power can close it. Just as Cyrus was used as an instrument to fulfill God's purposes, the church of Philadelphia is given an open door to advance the Kingdom of God.

Irene leaned forward, intrigued.

"Ann, I've been hearing about the Azusa Street Revival, but I don't really understand what made it so significant. Was it just another Church movement, or was there something more?"

I smiled, knowing this was a pivotal moment in church history.

"Oh, Irene, the Azusa Street Revival was a movement like no other. It started in Los Angeles in 1906, led by a humble African American preacher named William J. Seymour. What happened there wasn't just a church gathering—it was an outpouring of the Holy Spirit; unlike anything people had seen in centuries."

Irene furrowed her brow. "So, what exactly happened?"

My eyes lit up. "It was revival in its purest form—a return to the power of Pentecost. People came from all over the world to a small, run-down mission on Azusa Street, and the Holy Spirit moved mightily. There were reports of miracles, healings, people speaking in tongues, and an overwhelming presence of God that transformed lives. It was the birth of the modern Pentecostal movement."

Irene leaned back, processing. "Wait . . . speaking in tongues? Like the Book of Acts?"

"Exactly!" I nodded. "Just like on the Day of Pentecost in Acts 2. People experienced the baptism of the Holy Spirit with signs and wonders, and it sparked a global missionary movement. Before Azusa, the power of the Holy Spirit had largely been neglected in mainstream Christianity. But after Azusa, it spread like wildfire. Today, most Pentecostal and Charismatic churches can trace their roots back to that revival."

Irene folded her arms. "So, this wasn't just some small event—it reshaped Christianity?"

"Completely," I affirmed. "It crossed racial, denominational, and social barriers. Men, women, black, white, rich, poor—everyone worshiped together, something unheard of in that time. It was a fulfillment of Joel 2:28:"

> And it shall come to pass afterward, that I will pour out My Spirit upon all flesh; and your sons and your daughters shall prophesy, your old men shall dream dreams, your young men shall see visions. (Joel 2:28)

"And just like the Philadelphian church in Revelation," I continued. "It was a season of open doors—missions exploded, churches multiplied, and believers were empowered like never before."

Irene was quiet for a moment, then nodded. "That explains why the Pentecostal movement is so strong today. The open door Jesus gave Philadelphia—it wasn't just for that time. It's still open."

"Exactly. And the question remains—are we ready to walk through it?"

THE REVELATION OF JESUS CHRIST REVEALS:

^{3:9} Behold, I will make them of the assembly of Satan, which say they are Jews, and are not, but do lie; behold, I will make them to come and worship before your feet, and to know that I have loved you.

In this verse, Jesus addresses the faithful church of Philadelphia, assuring them that their enemies—those who falsely claim to be Jews but are instead of the assembly of Satan—will one day recognize the truth.

Who are those who "say they are Jews, and are not?" These individuals are not true spiritual Jews (Romans 2:28–29), meaning they do not follow God in faith or obedience. While they may claim a Jewish identity or religious superiority, their actions align with Satan's deception rather than God's truth. This group is also mentioned in Revelation 2:9, where Jesus rebukes those who falsely claim to represent God but oppose His people.

What does it mean that they will worship at their feet? This does not mean that they will worship believers, but that they will acknowledge that God's favor rests upon His faithful followers. This is a fulfillment of Old Testament prophecies like Isaiah 60:14, where the enemies of God's people recognize their divine calling. It signifies the vindication of the faithful—those who have suffered persecution will one day be honored by those who opposed them.

The assurance of Christ's love. The most powerful promise in this verse is that Jesus Himself will ensure that the faithful are recognized as His beloved. Despite opposition, deception, and persecution, those who remain steadfast in Christ will receive ultimate validation—not from man, but from God Himself.

In other words, false religious claims do not go unnoticed by God; He exposes hypocrisy and deception. True believers will one day be vindicated and acknowledged by their persecutors. Jesus assures the faithful that they are deeply loved by Him, and that love will be evident to all.

OLD TESTAMENT FORESHADOWS REVELATION:

The sons also of them that afflicted you shall come bending unto you; and all they that despised you shall bow themselves down at the soles of your feet; and they shall call you, The City of the LORD, the Zion of the Holy One of Israel. (Isaiah 60:14)

In Isaiah 60:14, those who once persecuted God's people will come in humility, acknowledging God's favor upon them. Similarly, in Revelation 3:9, Jesus declares that those who falsely claim to be His chosen will one day recognize the truth and acknowledge the faithfulness of Christ's followers.

Both verses depict a future moment when the persecutors of God's people will be humbled. Just as in Isaiah's prophecy, where oppressors bow before God's chosen, Revelation 3:9 speaks of a future vindication where Christ's faithful ones will be recognized as His beloved.

Isaiah also describes Jerusalem as "The City of the LORD," highlighting God's special relationship with His people. In Revelation, Jesus assures the church of Philadelphia that even their enemies will come to recognize that they are deeply loved by God. This parallel reinforces the biblical theme that God will ultimately exalt His faithful ones and bring justice against those who oppose His truth.

Irene leans forward, a thoughtful look on her face.

"Ann, I keep hearing the term 'Zion' in the Bible, and I've also heard people talk about 'Zionists.' Are they related? What exactly does Zion mean?"

I nodded; smiling as I prepared to explain.

"That's a great question, Irene. 'Zion' appears throughout the Bible, and its meaning has evolved over time. Originally, it referred to a specific place—the stronghold of Jerusalem that King David conquered from the Jebusites. After David made it his capital, the name Zion became synonymous with Jerusalem as a whole."

"So, it started as a physical location?"

"Yes. But it didn't stay just that. Over time, Zion came to represent more than just a city—it symbolized the presence of God, His Kingdom, and His chosen people. In the prophets, Zion is used to describe the future restoration of Israel and even the heavenly Jerusalem."

"Wait, so when the Bible talks about Zion, sometimes it's talking about Jerusalem, and sometimes it's something bigger?"

"Exactly! Take Isaiah 60:14, for example—it says that those who once despised Zion will one day recognize it as 'the City of the LORD.' That's the prophetic view of Zion as the center of God's rule and blessing. In the New Testament, Zion is often tied to the heavenly Jerusalem, the ultimate dwelling place of God's people."

"Okay, that makes sense. But what about 'Zionists'? That term seems more political than spiritual."

"Good observation. Zionism is a modern political movement that began in the late 19th century, advocating for the Jewish people to return to their ancestral homeland—what we now call Israel. It was largely in response to persecution, especially in Europe. The movement gained momentum after the Holocaust, leading to the establishment of the modern State of Israel in 1948."

"So Zionism is about the physical return to the land of Israel, while Zion in the Bible is about both the land and something much greater?"

"Exactly. For many Jews, Zionism is about reclaiming their homeland, but for believers in Christ, Zion holds an even deeper meaning. It represents God's eternal Kingdom, the fulfillment of His promises, and ultimately, the New Jerusalem."

"That's fascinating! So when Jesus tells the church in Philadelphia that their enemies will acknowledge God's love for them, does that connect to Zion's future role?"

"Absolutely! Revelation 3:9 echoes Isaiah 60:14—both passages describe a time when those who oppose God's people will recognize His favor upon them. Zion represents God's faithfulness, both to Israel and to those who are grafted into His promises through Christ."

"Wow, Zion is so much more than I thought. It's not just a place—it's a promise."

"Exactly, Irene. And that promise isn't just about history—it's about the future of all who belong to God."

Irene sat back, taking it all in. "Well, that certainly gives me a new perspective. Zion isn't just ancient history—it's destiny."

"Amen!"

————◆◆◆————

THE REVELATION OF JESUS CHRIST REVEALS:

3:10 Because you have kept the word of My patience, I also will keep you from the hour of temptation, which shall come upon all the world, to try them that dwell upon the earth.

This verse contains one of the most significant promises in Scripture concerning divine protection in the end times. Christ is addressing the faithful church of Philadelphia, commending them for their endurance and steadfastness in keeping His Word despite opposition. In return, He offers a profound assurance—they will be kept from the "hour of temptation" that will come upon the whole world.

"Because you have kept the word of My patience." The believers in Philadelphia demonstrated endurance and faithfulness to Christ's teachings. The phrase "word of My patience" suggests they remained steadfast despite trials, refusing to compromise their faith. This reflects a key biblical principle: those who endure in faith will receive divine protection and reward.

"I also will keep you from the hour of temptation." The phrase "keep you from" (Greek: *tereo ek*) can mean to preserve, protect, or remove from a situation. Many scholars interpret this as an indication that the faithful believers will be spared from the Tribulation—supporting the belief in a pre-Tribulation Rapture. The "hour of temptation" refers to a future period of intense trial and testing that will affect the entire world. This aligns with biblical prophecies about the Tribulation Age (Matthew 24:21; Daniel 12:1).

"Which shall come upon all the world, to try them that dwell upon the earth." The scope of this trial is global—it is not a localized persecution but a worldwide event. The phrase "them that dwell upon the earth" is often used in Revelation to describe unbelievers (Revelation 6:10, 13:8, 17:8), implying that this testing is primarily aimed at those who reject God.

Ultimately, this verse offers great encouragement: those who remain steadfast in their faith will not be abandoned in the coming trials. Instead, they will be shielded by the One who holds all power over time, history, and eternity.

OLD TESTAMENT FORESHADOWS REVELATION:

Come, My people, enter into your chambers, and shut your doors about you: hide yourself as it were for a little moment, until the indignation be over past. (Isaiah 26:20)

In Revelation 3:10, Jesus promises to keep the faithful from the hour of trial that will come upon the whole world. This suggests divine protection for believers during a time of great tribulation. In Isaiah 26:20, God calls His people to hide themselves until the time of indignation (judgment) passes, showing His provision and shelter during a period of wrath. Both verses emphasize God's protection over His faithful ones—whether it be from judgment, tribulation, or divine wrath. Isaiah's prophecy foreshadows the promise in Revelation, indicating that God has always set apart and preserved His faithful remnant in times of great trial.

THE REVELATION OF JESUS CHRIST REVEALS:

3:11 Behold, I come quickly: hold that fast which you have, that no man takes your crown.

This verse is a call to perseverance and readiness. Jesus reminds the church in Philadelphia, and all believers, that His return is imminent. Though "quickly" in biblical terms does not always mean immediate, it does emphasize the sudden and unexpected nature of His coming. This echoes His words in Matthew 24:44:

Therefore be you also ready: for in such an hour as you think not the Son of Man comes. (Matthew 24:44)

The phrase "hold that fast which you have" is an exhortation to remain steadfast in faith, obedience, and devotion. The believers in Philadelphia had already demonstrated faithfulness, keeping His Word and not denying His name (Revelation 3:8). Now, they are urged to hold tightly to what they have—to their faith, their testimony, and their endurance—lest anyone take their crown.

The *crown* here symbolizes victory, reward, and eternal life. It is not referring to salvation itself, but to the rewards given to the faithful at Christ's return:

Henceforth there is laid up for me a crown of righteousness, which the Lord, the righteous Judge, shall give me at that day: and not to me only, but unto all them also that love His appearing. (2 Timothy 4:8)

The warning suggests that while a believer's salvation is secure in Christ, their heavenly reward can be diminished or lost through complacency, compromise, or falling away.

This verse serves as both encouragement and warning—an encouragement to those who remain faithful and a warning against letting go of spiritual diligence. The message is clear: Jesus is coming soon, and believers must stay faithful to their calling, not allowing trials, temptations, or deception to rob them of their reward.

OLD TESTAMENT FORESHADOWS REVELATION:

You shalt also be a crown of glory in the hand of the LORD, and a royal diadem in the hand of your God. (Isaiah 62:3)

In Isaiah 62:3, God speaks of His people as a *crown of glory* and a *royal diadem*, signifying their honored status before Him. This imagery represents reward, righteousness, and divine recognition. Revelation 3:11 continues this theme, urging believers to *hold fast* to what they have so that no one may take their crown. This emphasizes perseverance in faith to retain the honor and reward that God has promised. Both passages reflect God's desire to bestow His people with eternal honor, but they also highlight the need for faithfulness. The crown is not merely a status but a symbol of divine reward that must be guarded against spiritual complacency.

Just as Israel was called to remain faithful to receive God's promises, believers in Philadelphia (and today) are called to endure in faith so they do not lose their heavenly reward.

THE REVELATION OF JESUS CHRIST REVEALS:

3:12 Him that overcomes will I make a pillar in the temple of My God, and he will go no more out: and I will write upon him the name of My God, and the name of the city of My God, which is New Jerusalem, which comes down out of heaven from My God: and I will write upon him My new name.

In Revelation 3:12, Jesus makes profound promises to those who overcome— believers who remain steadfast in faith. This verse carries deep symbolism, reflecting eternal security, divine identity, and heavenly citizenship.

"Him that overcomes will I make a pillar in the temple of My God, and he will go no more out." A *pillar* is a symbol of strength, permanence, and stability. Unlike earthly structures that decay, those who overcome will be firmly established in God's presence forever. This imagery would have been significant to the Philadelphian believers, as their city was prone to earthquakes, forcing people to flee their homes. Jesus assures them that in His Kingdom, they will never be displaced or shaken. It also echoes the imagery of Solomon's Temple, where two pillars, *Jachin* ("He shall establish") and *Boaz* ("In Him is Strength"), stood at the entrance (1 Kings 7:21).

"And I will write upon him the name of My God." Receiving God's name signifies ownership, belonging, and divine protection. In ancient times, a master's name was often inscribed on servants or soldiers as a mark of loyalty. This reflects God's covenant promise to His people:

And they shall be Mine, says the LORD of hosts, in that day when I make up My jewels; and I will spare them, as a man spares his own son that serves him. (Malachi 3:17)

"And the name of the city of My God, which is New Jerusalem, which comes down out of heaven from My God." New Jerusalem represents the eternal dwelling place of God's people (Revelation 21:2). This promise assures believers of their heavenly citizenship—they are not of this world but are destined for the eternal city of God. This contrasts with the instability of earthly cities. Unlike Philadelphia, which had been rebuilt multiple times after earthquakes, the New Jerusalem is an everlasting city.

"And I will write upon him My new name." A *new name* signifies transformation and deeper revelation of Christ's nature. Just as Abram became Abraham and Jacob became Israel, the overcomers will receive a new identity reflecting their eternal relationship with Christ. This is a personal and intimate promise—believers will share in Christ's victory and divine inheritance.

This verse is a powerful encouragement for believers to hold fast in faith, knowing that their eternal reward is secure in Christ.

OLD TESTAMENT FORESHADOWS REVELATION:

Even unto them will I give in My house and within My walls a place and a name better than that of sons and of daughters: I will give them an everlasting name, that shall not be cut off. (Isaiah 56:5)

"I will make a pillar in the temple of My God" (Revelation 3:12). "I will give in My house and within My walls a place" (Isaiah 56:5). In Isaiah, God promises a permanent place in His house to those who are faithful, just as Jesus promises to make the overcomers pillars in His eternal temple. Both passages highlight spiritual stability, permanence, and inclusion in God's Kingdom.

"I will write upon him the name of My God" (Revelation 3:12). "I will give them an everlasting name" (Isaiah 56:5). In Isaiah, God grants an everlasting name, while in Revelation, Christ writes God's name on the faithful, marking them as His own. This signifies divine ownership, identity, and covenant blessing.

"And the name of the city of My God, which is New Jerusalem" (Revelation 3:12). The promise of being included "within My walls" (Isaiah 56:5). Isaiah's prophecy speaks of a secure place in God's house, while Revelation reveals New Jerusalem, the eternal dwelling place of God's people. Both verses emphasize belonging to the Heavenly Kingdom.

"I will write upon him My new name" (Revelation 3:12). "A name that shall not be cut off" (Isaiah 56:5). The promise of a new name in Revelation reflects transformation and a deeper relationship with God, just as Isaiah's promise of an eternal name signifies unchanging favor. Both passages reinforce the promise that faithful believers will be eternally established in God's Kingdom, bearing His name and dwelling securely in His presence. Isaiah's prophecy foreshadows Christ's promise to the overcomers in Philadelphia—a permanent place in the New Jerusalem, a new identity in Christ, and eternal security in God's presence.

THE REVELATION OF JESUS CHRIST REVEALS:

³:¹³ He that has an ear, let him hear what the Spirit says to the churches.

This verse is a repeated exhortation in Christ's messages to the seven churches, emphasizing the universal call to spiritual discernment.

Key themes and meaning:

1. **A Call to Spiritual Awareness**—The phrase "He that has an ear" is not referring to physical hearing but to spiritual receptivity. Many hear words, but few truly listen with understanding and obedience. Jesus calls for those who have spiritual sensitivity to pay attention to what the Holy Spirit is saying.

2. **A Message for All Churches**—Though this letter is addressed to the church in Philadelphia, the command is for all believers. The seven letters in Revelation are prophetic, historical, and personal, making them applicable to individuals, churches, and the entire body of Christ.

3. **The Role of the Holy Spirit**—"What the Spirit says to the churches" underscores that Christ speaks through the Holy Spirit. The Spirit convicts, guides, warns, and instructs, but it is up to believers to listen and respond.

4. **Hearing versus Obeying**—Many people hear God's Word but do not act on it. Jesus' words echo James 1:22, which reminds us to be doers of the Word, not just hearers.

5. **Warning and An Invitation**—This phrase is both a warning and an invitation. A warning to those who ignore God's voice. An invitation to those willing to listen and respond.

Revelation 3:13 is a timeless command. God is speaking—are we listening? The Spirit's voice is still calling the Church today to be faithful, discerning, and obedient. Let us open our hearts, hear His voice, and respond in faith.

OLD TESTAMENT FORESHADOWS REVELATION:

Incline your ear, and come unto Me: hear, and your soul shall live; and I will make an everlasting covenant with you, even the sure mercies of David. (Isaiah 55:3)

Isaiah 55:3, like Revelation 3:13, urges people to incline their ear—not just physically hear but actively listen and respond to God's voice. Both passages emphasize that spiritual life and blessing come through hearing and obeying God. In Isaiah, the promise is that those who listen will live. In Revelation, the message to the churches is a call to awaken spiritually, to receive correction and reward by responding to Christ's words. Isaiah speaks of an everlasting covenant—God's promise of mercy to those who turn to Him. Revelation calls the churches to hear the Spirit's message, leading to victory and eternal reward.

Just as Isaiah 55:3 calls God's people to hear, respond, and receive life, Revelation 3:13 urges the Church to listen to the Spirit and walk in obedience. Both verses highlight the critical importance of spiritual discernment and responsiveness to God's voice.

CHRIST'S LETTER TO THE CHURCH OF LAODICEA

The seventh and final letter in Revelation is addressed to Laodicea, prophetically representing the Apostate Church era (AD 1900–Tribulation Age). The name *Laodicea* means "rule of the people," reflecting a self-governed, self-sufficient church—one that prioritizes human opinion over God's authority. This is the final church era before Christ's return, marked by spiritual lukewarmness, pride, and complacency.

Unlike the previous churches, Jesus has no praise for Laodicea. While they believe themselves to be rich and in need of nothing, Jesus exposes their true condition—wretched, miserable, poor, blind, and naked (Revelation 3:17). Their wealth and success have blinded them to their spiritual poverty.

Historically, Laodicea was a thriving financial and medical hub in southwest Turkey. It was famous for its banking industry, its luxurious black wool, and its medicinal eye salve—all symbols Jesus later uses to reveal their deeper spiritual needs. Even after a devastating earthquake in AD 61, Laodicea refused imperial aid from Rome, choosing to rebuild itself without assistance—a fitting picture of its self-reliant attitude.

Paul hinted at their spiritual decline in Colossians 2:1–2, warning that wealth and knowledge do not equate to true spiritual depth. They had a form of godliness, yet their hearts were far from God. This mirrors today's modern church, which often prioritizes social acceptance, material success, and cultural relevance over genuine faith, repentance, and dependence on Christ.

Jesus' call to Laodicea is urgent: Repent. Return to true faith. Be zealous. Open the door to Him before it's too late. This is the last warning before judgment.

Christ's message to Laodicea is clear: the lukewarm church—neither hot nor cold—must wake up, be diligent, and repent. In Christ, there is still hope to overcome.

THE REVELATION OF JESUS CHRIST REVEALS:

^{3:14} And to the angel of the church of the Laodiceans write; These things says the Amen, the Faithful and True Witness, the Beginning of the creation of God.

Jesus introduces Himself to the church of Laodicea with a powerful declaration of His authority, truth, and divine nature. His titles in this verse carry significant meaning, particularly for a church that had lost its spiritual fervor and become self-reliant.

"These things says the Amen." The word *Amen* means "so be it" or "truth." In Isaiah 65:16, God is called the "God of truth" (literally, "the God of Amen"). Jesus identifies Himself as the Amen, signifying that He is the fulfillment of God's promises, the embodiment of truth, and the final authority over all things (2 Corinthians 1:20). This is particularly relevant for Laodicea, a church that was deceived into believing it was spiritually rich while, in reality, it was blind and destitute.

"The Faithful and the True Witness." Jesus is not only the *Amen* but also the Faithful and True Witness. This title emphasizes His absolute reliability and truthfulness. In contrast, Laodicea had become spiritually compromised, believing in its own strength and sufficiency rather than the truth of Christ. Jesus, as the true witness, exposes their deception and calls them back to genuine faith. This echoes John 14:6, where Jesus declares:

Jesus says unto him, I am the way, the truth, and the life: no man comes unto the Father, but by Me. (John 14:6)

"The Beginning of the creation of God." This phrase does not mean that Jesus was created, as some heretical teachings claim. The Greek word *arche* (translated as "beginning") means the source, origin, or ruler. Jesus is the *originator* of creation—the One through whom all things were made (John 1:3; Colossians 1:15–17). This was especially relevant to Laodicea, a church that had become so focused on its material wealth and self-sufficiency that it had forgotten its dependence on Christ, the true Creator and Sustainer of all things.

Jesus addresses Laodicea with firm authority, reminding them of who He is: the final Word (Amen), the true standard (Faithful and True Witness), and the sovereign Creator (the Beginning of God's creation). His introduction alone is a wake-up call to a church that had become complacent, worldly, and spiritually blind.

This message extends to today's modern church, which often mirrors Laodicea—comfortable, wealthy, yet spiritually lukewarm. Christ is calling His people to recognize their desperate need for Him, to reject self-sufficiency, and to return to faithfulness before it is too late.

OLD TESTAMENT FORESHADOWS REVELATION:

That he who blesses himself in the earth shall bless himself in the God of truth; and he that swears in the earth shall swear by the God of truth; because the former troubles are forgotten, and because they are hid from My eyes. (Isaiah 65:16)

In Isaiah 65:16, God is called the God of truth (literally, the God of *Amen* in Hebrew). In Revelation 3:14, Jesus identifies Himself as the Amen, signifying that He is the final confirmation of all God's promises (2 Corinthians 1:20). Both verses emphasize God's unchangeable truth and faithfulness.

Isaiah 65:16 speaks of God as the one in whom people will find their blessing and assurance. In Revelation 3:14, Jesus is described as the Faithful and True Witness, highlighting His perfect reliability in declaring God's truth.

Isaiah's prophecy anticipates a time when God will bring about renewal and a new creation. Jesus, as the Beginning of the creation of God, is the source and ruler over all creation (John 1:3; Colossians 1:15–17), reaffirming His divine authority.

Isaiah 65:16 and Revelation 3:14 both highlight God's unshakable truth, faithfulness, and power over creation. Jesus, as the Amen, the Faithful and True Witness, and the source of creation, fulfills the Old Testament revelation of God's eternal authority, making His call to the Laodicean church one of both warning and divine assurance.

THE REVELATION OF JESUS CHRIST REVEALS:

3:15 I know your works, that you are neither cold nor hot: I wish you were cold or hot.

Jesus, addressing the church of Laodicea, rebukes their spiritual condition. Unlike the churches of Philadelphia and Smyrna, which received praise, Laodicea receives a sharp warning.

Laodicea is described as neither cold nor hot—a metaphor drawn from their own city's water supply. Nearby Hierapolis had hot springs, valued for their healing properties. Colossae, another neighboring city, had cold, refreshing water, useful for drinking. Laodicea's water, however, was lukewarm, carried by aqueducts from hot springs miles away. By the time it arrived, it was tepid, unpalatable, and often filled with minerals that made it undrinkable. Just as their water was undesirable, their faith was neither fervent nor refreshing—it was stagnant, compromised, and useless.

Laodicea represents a self-sufficient but spiritually bankrupt church. Their wealth and comfort had blinded them to their true condition. They were Christian in name, but without passion, conviction, or deep commitment.

- Cold—This could represent those completely distant from faith, who at least recognize their need for salvation.
- Hot—This represents a burning zeal for God, a life transformed by faith.
- Lukewarm—This is the most dangerous state—a person who believes they are fine, but is actually in spiritual decay.

Jesus would rather they be *cold* or *hot*—either fully rejecting the truth and realizing their lost state, or fully embracing the gospel and living in its power. But the *lukewarm* deceive themselves into thinking they are safe, while in reality, they are in grave danger.

This verse is one of the most striking indictments against nominal Christianity—faith that is shallow, compromised, and driven more by culture than by Christ. Many churches today, like Laodicea, are wealthy and influential but have lost their spiritual power. Many focus on social acceptance rather than biblical truth. They compromise on doctrine to avoid conflict. They lack true passion for Christ, content with a comfortable, lukewarm faith.

Jesus' words to Laodicea serve as a wake-up call: faith without zeal is useless. True Christianity is not about comfort—it requires commitment, transformation, and devotion. Therefore this verse sets the stage for the following warning, where Jesus threatens to spit out the lukewarm—showing just how serious spiritual apathy is in His eyes.

OLD TESTAMENT FORESHADOWS REVELATION:

And Elijah came unto all the people, and said, How long will you be between two opinions? If the LORD be God, follow Him: but if Baal, then follow him. And the people answered him not a word. (1 Kings 18:21)

In 1 Kings 18:21, the prophet Elijah rebukes Israel for wavering between two choices—God or Baal. They refused to fully commit, remaining in spiritual indecision. Similarly, in Revelation 3:15, Jesus rebukes Laodicea for being neither hot nor cold—a picture of half-hearted, compromised faith. Both verses call for a decisive commitment. Just as Elijah challenged Israel to choose whom they would serve, Jesus challenges the Laodicean church to fully commit to Him rather than remaining spiritually lukewarm.

This parallel emphasizes the danger of spiritual complacency, where people acknowledge God but refuse to fully follow Him. Jesus, like Elijah, calls for a choice—to be either zealous and on fire for Him or to fully recognize their lost state and repent.

THE REVELATION OF JESUS CHRIST REVEALS:

[3:16] So then because you are lukewarm, and neither cold nor hot, I will vomit you out of My mouth.

Laodicea's spiritual condition mirrors its geographical reality. The city was known for its lukewarm water supply—unlike the cold, refreshing springs of Colossae or the hot, healing waters of Hierapolis, Laodicea's water was tepid and unpalatable. Similarly, their faith was neither refreshing (cold) nor zealous (hot), but indifferent and complacent.

- Jesus expresses disgust at their spiritual condition, using the imagery of vomiting—a strong word symbolizing rejection and divine judgment.
- Lukewarm faith is self-sufficient and apathetic, lacking true passion for God.
- Jesus would rather they be hot (on fire for Him) or even cold (fully aware of their lost state), rather than being spiritually indifferent.

This warning applies to modern Christianity, where comfort, compromise, and worldly success often take precedence over true devotion to Christ. Many churches have lost their fervor, becoming more focused on cultural acceptance than on biblical truth. Jesus calls believers to wholehearted commitment, warning that lukewarmness leads to separation from Him. The only cure for spiritual complacency is repentance and renewed zeal for God.

OLD TESTAMENT FORESHADOWS REVELATION:

That the land spue not you out also, when you defile it, as it spued out the nations that were before you. (Leviticus 18:28)

In Leviticus 18:28, God warns Israel that if they follow the abominable practices of the pagan nations, the land itself will vomit them out, signifying divine rejection and judgment. Similarly, in Revelation 3:16, Jesus warns the lukewarm church in Laodicea that their spiritual compromise makes them unfit for His Kingdom, leading to Him vomiting them out—a direct parallel to the judgment upon unfaithful nations in the Old Testament. Both passages highlight God's intolerance for complacency, impurity, and half-hearted devotion—whether in Israel's conduct or in the spiritual condition of the Laodicean church.

This parallel underscores that God's standard has not changed—He demands wholehearted commitment, and those who remain spiritually lukewarm will face His rejection just as the disobedient nations before them.

THE REVELATION OF JESUS CHRIST REVEALS:

^{3:17} Because you say, I am rich, and increased with goods, and have need of nothing; and knows not that you are wretched, and miserable, and poor, and blind, and naked.

The church of Laodicea is the only church in Revelation that receives no commendation from Christ—only rebuke. Their greatest spiritual deception is their self-sufficiency—they believe they are wealthy, successful, and in need of nothing, yet Christ exposes their true condition: they are wretched, miserable, poor, blind, and naked.

The Laodicean church is a picture of spiritual pride and blindness. Their material wealth has deceived them into thinking that they are spiritually rich, but in reality, they are spiritually bankrupt. Their prosperity has given them a false sense of security, making them unaware of their desperate need for Christ.

- They say, "I am rich," yet Jesus says they are poor—meaning they lack true spiritual riches (faith, wisdom, and holiness).
- They believe they "have need of nothing," yet Jesus says they are miserable—because without Him, they are spiritually destitute.
- They live in a city known for its famous medical eye salve, yet Jesus says they are blind—unable to see their own sin and their need for repentance.
- They are famous for their luxurious black wool, yet Jesus says they are naked—lacking the righteous garments only He can provide.

The Laodicean church represents the final stage of church history, a time of lukewarm faith, spiritual decline, and apostasy before the return of Christ. This church reflects many aspects of the modern church, where material success, social acceptance, and self-reliance often take precedence over true faith, repentance, and dependence on Christ.

Jesus' words serve as a final warning to the Laodicean church—and to all believers in the last days: material prosperity is no substitute for spiritual vitality. A church that values comfort over conviction, success over sanctification, and self-sufficiency over surrender is on the brink of being rejected by Christ.

This verse calls every believer to examine their heart—are we truly rich in Christ, or are we deceived by worldly wealth?

OLD TESTAMENT FORESHADOWS REVELATION:

And Ephraim said, Yet I am become rich, I have found me out substance: in all my labors they shall find none iniquity in me that were sin. (Hosea 12:8)

In Hosea 12:8, Ephraim (a reference to Israel) boasts in its wealth and prosperity, believing that its material riches prove its righteousness. Similarly, the

Laodicean church claims to be rich and self-sufficient, blind to its spiritual poverty. Both Ephraim and Laodicea fail to recognize their true condition before God. Ephraim assumes no iniquity can be found in them, just as Laodicea believes it "has need of nothing," yet Christ calls them wretched, miserable, poor, blind, and naked. Both passages warn against self-reliance and the illusion that wealth equals God's favor. In reality, riches can blind people to their need for repentance, leading to spiritual complacency and eventual judgment.

Hosea 12:8 and Revelation 3:17 reveal a timeless warning: material success does not equal spiritual health. A false sense of self-sufficiency can lead to spiritual blindness, causing people to reject their need for God. Jesus calls the Laodicean church (and all believers) to recognize their true condition, repent, and seek true spiritual riches in Him.

THE REVELATION OF JESUS CHRIST REVEALS:

3:18 I counsel you to buy gold from Me tried in the fire, that you may be rich; also buy white raiment, that you may be clothed, and that the shame of your nakedness does not appear; and anoint your eyes with eye-sap, that you may see.

In Revelation 3:18, Jesus, in His mercy, offers the Laodicean church the solution to their spiritual blindness, poverty, and nakedness. Despite their self-sufficiency and material wealth, He exposes their true condition—they are spiritually bankrupt. Christ counsels them to "buy" three essential things from Him:

1. **Gold Tried in the Fire**—True spiritual riches, refined and purified through trials, unlike the fleeting wealth of the world. This represents genuine faith, tested and proven (1 Peter 1:7).

2. **White Raiment**—Symbolizing righteousness, which comes not from self-effort but through Christ alone (Isaiah 61:10). The Laodiceans prided themselves on their fine black wool garments, yet Christ reveals their true state—naked before God. Only His righteousness can cover their shame.

3. **Eye Salve**—The city of Laodicea was famous for its medical eye ointment, yet its people were spiritually blind. Jesus urges them to receive true spiritual sight, enabling them to discern truth and see things from God's perspective.

This verse is a loving rebuke and an invitation to true spiritual restoration. Christ warns that worldly wealth and self-sufficiency are empty without Him. Only through refined faith, His righteousness, and divine wisdom can they overcome their lukewarm, deceived state.

This message is just as relevant today. Many churches and believers rely on prosperity, comfort, and self-reliance, thinking they need nothing. Yet, Christ calls us to recognize our need for His refining fire, His righteousness, and His spiritual insight. Only by coming to Him can we be truly rich, clothed, and able to see.

OLD TESTAMENT FORESHADOWS REVELATION:

Ho, every one that thirsts, come you to the waters, and he that has no money; come you, buy, and eat; yea, come, buy wine and milk without money and without price. (Isaiah 55:1)

In both passages, God calls His people to "buy" what is spiritually valuable, yet this purchase is not made with earthly wealth. Instead, it requires humility, repentance, and faith. Jesus offers the Laodiceans gold refined in fire (true faith), white garments (righteousness), and eye salve (spiritual sight).

Isaiah 55:1 calls people to seek the eternal rather than temporary earthly satisfaction, just as Jesus warns the Laodicean church that material wealth does not equal spiritual riches. They must see God's provision, not their own self-sufficiency.

The call in Isaiah is for the thirsty to come to the waters, symbolizing spiritual refreshment and cleansing. Likewise, Jesus offers Laodicea true riches, righteousness, and clarity of vision—all of which can only come through Him.

Both passages emphasize that spiritual riches, righteousness, and wisdom cannot be obtained through material means but must be received through faith and surrender to God. Christ's counsel to Laodicea mirrors Isaiah's prophetic call: Come, seek, and receive what only God can provide.

THE REVELATION OF JESUS CHRIST REVEALS:

3:19 As many as I love, I rebuke and chasten; be zealous therefore, and repent.

In this verse, Jesus reassures the Laodicean church that His harsh rebuke is not out of anger but out of love. Divine correction is an act of grace, not rejection (Hebrews 12:6). Though they are lukewarm, self-reliant, and spiritually blind, He still cares for them deeply. His call to repentance is not one of condemnation but an invitation to renewal and restoration.

This verse reminds us that God's discipline is always rooted in love. He does not expose sin to destroy but to restore. If we find ourselves spiritually dull or complacent, we must embrace His correction, rekindle our zeal, and return to Him with sincere repentance. His love is relentless, and He calls us to a faith that is alive, passionate, and ever-growing.

OLD TESTAMENT FORESHADOWS REVELATION:

My son, despise not the chastening of the LORD; neither be wary of His correction: For whom the LORD loves He corrects; even as a father the son in whom he delights. (Proverbs 3:11–12)

In both passages, God's correction is an expression of His love for His people. Just as a father disciplines a child for their good, so God rebukes and chastens those He loves. The Lord's discipline is not to punish, but to restore and strengthen His people. It is a call to growth, refinement, and deeper fellowship with God.

Proverbs urges believers not to despise God's correction, while Revelation calls the Laodiceans to be zealous and repent. Both passages emphasize the need for a heart willing to change, recognizing that discipline leads to spiritual renewal.

God's discipline is proof of His love. He corrects not to destroy but to refine, awaken, and restore. Those who respond with repentance and renewed passion will experience spiritual revival and deeper fellowship with Him.

THE REVELATION OF JESUS CHRIST REVEALS:

3:20 Behold, I stand at the door, and knock: if any man hears My voice, and opens the door, I will come into him, and will sup with him, and he with Me.

This verse is one of the most personal and intimate invitations from Jesus in the Bible. It is a direct appeal to individuals, not just the church as a whole.

Jesus stands at the door and knocks. Jesus is outside, standing at the door waiting to be invited in. The imagery reflects a patient and persistent Savior, longing for fellowship with His people. It also highlights the Laodicean church's self-sufficiency—they had shut Him out with their complacency and spiritual blindness.

"If any man hears My voice." This reveals the personal nature of salvation. It is not about a group or institution, but an individual response to Christ. It requires spiritual sensitivity—hearing His voice means recognizing the conviction of the Holy Spirit and responding in faith.

"And opens the door." Jesus does not force Himself in—He waits for the door to be opened. The responsibility lies on the individual to respond to His call. Opening the door symbolizes repentance, faith, and surrender.

"I will come into him, and will sup with him." The act of sharing a meal in biblical times was a sign of deep fellowship and intimacy. Jesus is offering more than just entry—He is offering a relationship, communion, and transformation.

This verse summarizes the entire message of salvation—the heart of the gospel—Jesus calls, we respond, and He enters into intimate fellowship with us. It also serves as a warning to those who have pushed Christ out of their lives, urging them to return and restore their relationship with Him.

Revelation 3:20 is both an invitation and a warning. It calls for personal repentance, faith, and restoration of a relationship with Christ. The Laodicean church had shut Jesus out, but He was still lovingly calling to them to return. This verse remains a timeless reminder that Jesus stands ready to enter any heart that welcomes Him.

OLD TESTAMENT FORESHADOWS REVELATION:

I sleep, but my heart wakes: it is the voice of my beloved that knocks, saying, Open to me, my sister, my love, my dove, my undefiled: for my head is filled with dew, and my locks with the drops of the night. (Song of Solomon 5:2)

In Song of Solomon, the bridegroom (a picture of Christ) calls to his bride, longing for fellowship with her. In Revelation 3:20, Jesus stands at the door of the believer's heart, calling them into deeper communion. In Song of Solomon 5:2, the bride hesitates, and by the time she responds, her beloved has departed. This is a warning not to delay responding to Christ. In Revelation 3:20, Jesus patiently knocks, waiting for the one who will hear and respond.

Both passages emphasize the intimacy of relationship between Christ and His people. In Revelation, Jesus promises to "sup" (share a meal) with the one who opens the door, signifying deep personal fellowship. In Song of Solomon, the bridegroom's words reflect the tenderness and love of Christ for His people.

Song of Solomon 5:2 foreshadows the invitation of Christ in Revelation 3:20—a call to personal intimacy and communion. Both verses highlight the urgency of responding to God's call without delay. Just as the bride delayed and found her beloved gone, those who ignore Christ's knock risk missing out on the depth of fellowship He desires to share.

THE REVELATION OF JESUS CHRIST REVEALS:

3:21 To him that overcomes will I grant to sit with Me in My throne, even as I also overcame, and am set down with My Father in His throne.

In this final promise to the overcomer, Jesus offers the greatest reward yet—co-reigning with Him on His throne. This verse not only speaks of victory but of ultimate exaltation and authority for those who remain faithful to Christ.

The overcomer refers to the one who remains faithful in Christ, resisting sin, spiritual complacency, and false doctrine. Just as Christ overcame sin, the world, and death, believers are called to persevere in faith, endure trials, and walk in victory.

Jesus invites believers to sit with Him on His throne, meaning they will share in His authority and rule in His coming Kingdom (Revelation 20:6). This parallels Jesus' own victory, as He overcame and is now seated at the right hand of the

Father (Psalm 110:1; Hebrews 1:3). Believers are called not only to be servants of Christ but co-heirs and rulers alongside Him in the millennial reign and beyond (Romans 8:17; 2 Timothy 2:12).

Jesus sets Himself as the model for overcoming. His path of obedience, suffering, death, and resurrection is the blueprint for all who would reign with Him. This verse highlights that glory follows suffering, as seen in Philippians:

> And being found in fashion as a man, He humbled Himself, and became obedient unto death, even the death of the Cross. Wherefore God also has highly exalted Him, and given Him a name which is above every name. (Philippians 2:8–9)

The Laodiceans had become spiritually passive and self-sufficient, but Christ calls them to true victory—not material wealth but eternal reign with Him. He offers them not a seat of comfort in their own luxury, but a seat in His throne—a place of divine authority, given to those who remain faithful.

This verse serves as a final encouragement and challenge to believers. Christ does not merely call us to avoid spiritual complacency but to rise above it, pursue holiness, and live with the expectation of reigning with Him. The promise of co-reigning with Christ should drive us to faithfulness, endurance, and unwavering devotion.

Jesus, the King of kings, offers the highest honor to those who overcome: to rule and reign with Him. This verse is a reminder that our present struggles are temporary, but our reward in Christ is eternal. Are we living as overcomers, or are we settling into spiritual complacency? The invitation is before us—the choice is ours.

OLD TESTAMENT FORESHADOWS REVELATION:

> The LORD said unto my LORD, Sit you at My right hand, until I make Your enemies Your footstool. (Psalm 110:1)

In Psalm 110:1, God the Father invites the Messiah (Jesus) to sit at His right hand, signifying supreme authority, victory, and rulership. In Revelation 3:21, Jesus extends a similar invitation to believers—to sit with Him on His throne, sharing in His rule and reign. Psalm 110:1 prophesies the Messianic rule of Christ after His victory over sin and death. Revelation 3:21 parallels this by promising those who overcome a seat alongside Christ, just as He overcame and was exalted.

In both passages, the key to exaltation is victory and obedience. Psalm 110:1 shows Christ's reward for fulfilling God's plan. Revelation 3:21 reveals that believers who overcome through faith will also share in Christ's reward.

Psalm 110:1 is one of the most quoted messianic prophecies in the New Testament, emphasizing Jesus' enthronement at God's right hand (Matthew

22:44; Hebrews 1:3). Revelation 3:21 extends this enthronement promise to believers, linking their destiny to Christ's.

Psalm 110:1 establishes Christ's divine authority and reign, while Revelation 3:21 extends this privilege to those who remain faithful. Just as Christ overcame and was seated in victory, we too are called to overcome, persevere, and reign with Him.

THE REVELATION OF JESUS CHRIST REVEALS:

[3:22] He that has an ear, let him hear what the Spirit says to the churches.

This verse is a recurring phrase throughout the letters to the seven churches in Revelation, serving as a final call to *attention* and *obedience*. It emphasizes the universal relevance of Christ's message—not just to one church, but to all believers throughout history.

Revelation 3:22 is a final plea for every believer to be attentive, discerning, and obedient to Christ's words. It is a reminder that spiritual deafness leads to complacency, but those who listen and respond will walk in truth and victory.

OLD TESTAMENT FORESHADOWS REVELATION:

Give ear, O you heavens, and I will speak; and hear, O earth, the words of my mouth. (Deuteronomy 32:1)

Both verses command an audience to listen attentively to God's message. In Deuteronomy, Moses calls upon the heavens and the earth as witnesses to God's declaration. In Revelation, Jesus calls the churches to hear what the Spirit is saying, emphasizing that the message is not optional but urgent and binding.

In Deuteronomy, the message is directed at all creation, symbolizing the unchanging and eternal nature of God's Word. In Revelation, the Spirit speaks to all churches, representing the universal Church throughout all ages.

In both passages, hearing requires action. Israel was expected to obey God's commands and remain faithful. The churches in Revelation are warned to heed the Spirit's message, repent, and remain faithful until Christ's return.

Deuteronomy 32:1 and Revelation 3:22 both emphasize that God's voice demands a response. Whether addressing ancient Israel or the end-time Church, His words are life-giving, urgent, and transformative—but only for those who truly have ears to hear.

———◆◆◆———

Irene leaned back, shaking her head. "I can't believe how much history is packed into just two chapters of Revelation. Through the seven churches, Jesus didn't just speak to the past—He laid out a prophetic timeline of the entire 2,000-year Church Age. It's like a divine puzzle unfolding right before our eyes."

"Exactly. If you don't study history, you won't understand the future."

She nodded. "I always thought prophecy was just about what's coming, but it's also about what's already happened."

"Yes! God declares the end from the beginning. Take Daniel 2, for example—Nebuchadnezzar's dream wasn't just a warning; it mapped out 2,500 years of history in advance. It revealed five key kingdoms: Babylon, Medo-Persia (Medes and Persians), Greece, Rome, and—prophetically—America. When you include Egypt and Assyria, which came before Babylon, you get a complete prophetic timeline of seven world empires—from Genesis to Revelation—leading up to Christ's return."

"So history is God's pattern for how He works in the world?"

"Exactly. That's why we can trust Him. He's the same God who parted the Red Sea, spoke to Daniel, and fulfilled every prophecy about Christ. He's still in control."

"That's comforting, especially with everything happening in the world."

"Nothing catches Him off guard. If we focus only on what we see, we'll lose sight of His greater plan."

Softly, she said, "That's where faith comes in."

"Yes. The world sees chaos, but believers see God's hand. The question isn't whether prophecy will be fulfilled—it's where we'll stand when it happens."

With conviction, she answered, "Then I choose Him."

Smiling, I picked up my Bible. "That's the only choice that matters. Now . . . let's step into Revelation 4:1."

SUMMARY OF REVELATION 2–3

Revelation chapters 2 and 3 contain Christ's letters to the seven churches, representing the spiritual conditions of churches throughout history and offering prophetic insight into the Church Age. Each letter includes commendations, rebukes, warnings, and promises, revealing Christ's deep concern for His Church and His call to faithfulness.

Jesus addresses:

1. **Ephesus**—The apostolic church that had forsaken its first love, despite its works and perseverance (Revelation 2:1–7).

2. **Smyrna**—The persecuted church, encouraged to remain faithful even unto the death (Revelation 2:8–11).

3. **Pergamos**—The compromising church, rebuked for tolerating false teachings (Revelation 2:12–17).

4. **Thyatira**—The corrupt church, condemned for allowing immorality and idolatry (Revelation 2:18–29).

5. **Sardis**—The dead church, warned to wake up and strengthen what remains (Revelation 3:1–6).

6. **Philadelphia**—The faithful church, commended for keeping God's Word and promised deliverance from the coming Tribulation (Revelation 3:7–13).

7. **Laodicea**—The lukewarm church, neither hot nor cold, warned to repent before being rejected (Revelation 3:14–22).

Each church is called to *overcome*—to remain steadfast in faith, rejecting compromise and spiritual complacency. The rewards promised to the overcomers reflect the restoration of what was lost in Eden, culminating in eternal life, authority, and fellowship with Christ.

KEY TAKEAWAYS

- Jesus sees and knows the spiritual condition of His Church—nothing is hidden from His eyes.
- Each church represents different challenges believers face—persecution, compromise, corruption, deadness, faithfulness, and lukewarmness.
- Christ calls for repentance and perseverance—warning against spiritual decline and promising eternal rewards.
- The Church Age is a time of testing and refinement—but it will come to an end.

As Revelation chapter 3 concludes, the Church's time on earth is nearly finished. With the opening of Revelation 4:1, the Church disappears from the earth and enters heaven, signaling the transition into God's prophetic plan for the end times.

Chapter 4

Revelation 4:1:
The Rapture of the Church

THE MOMENT THAT CHANGES EVERYTHING—The next major event on God's prophetic calendar is the Rapture of the Church. Unlike other prophetic events that require specific signs, the Rapture is imminent—it could occur at any moment. As Jesus warned:

> Therefore be you also ready: for in such an hour as you think not the Son of Man comes. (Matthew 24:44)

No further prophecy must be fulfilled before this glorious event occurs.

With Revelation 4:1, we reach a pivotal turning point in biblical prophecy—a shift from the Church Age to God's final dealings with a rebellious world. Until this moment, Revelation has centered on Christ and His messages to the seven churches, which represent distinct eras in Church history. But now, the focus moves to "the things which shall be hereafter" (Revelation 1:19).

What happens here?

Many scholars believe that John's sudden calling up to heaven in Revelation 4:1 is a symbolic foreshadowing of the Rapture. This doesn't mean the Rapture itself happens in this verse, but that John's experience serves as a prophetic picture of what the Church will soon experience—being called up to meet Christ before judgment begins.

Come up here, and I will show you things which must be hereafter. (Revelation 4:1)

This heavenly summons closely parallels Paul's description in 1 Thessalonians 4:16–18, where the Lord descends *for* His Church with a shout, the voice of the archangel, and the trumpet of God—and the Church is caught up to meet Him in the air:

> For the Lord Himself shall descend from heaven with a shout, with the voice of the archangel, and with the trump of God: and the dead in Christ shall rise first. Then we which are alive and remain shall be caught up together with them in the clouds, to meet the Lord in the air: and so shall we ever be with the Lord. Wherefore comfort one another with these words. (1 Thessalonians 4:16–18)

For nearly 2,000 years—since the outpouring of the Holy Spirit at Pentecost (Acts 2, around AD 30)—the Church has been central to God's redemptive work on earth, faithfully carrying out the Great Commission. In Revelation 2–3, Christ addresses the Church directly—encouraging faithfulness, warning against compromise, and offering promises to those who overcome.

But now, something changes.

Revelation 4:1 marks the close of the Church Age. From this point forward, the Church is no longer seen on earth until Revelation 19, when she returns *with* Christ at His Second Coming. This dramatic absence strongly implies that the Church has been taken to heaven—rescued before the Tribulation Age begins.

> For God has not appointed us to wrath, but to obtain salvation by our Lord Jesus Christ. (1 Thessalonians 5:9)

> Much more then, being now justified by His blood, we shall be saved from wrath through Him. (Romans 5:9)

> And to wait for His Son from heaven, whom He raised from the dead, even Jesus, which delivered us from the wrath to come. (1 Thessalonians 1:10)

What follows is a sobering revelation of life on earth without the Church: the opening of the seven seals, the sounding of the seven trumpets, the pouring out of the seven bowls of wrath, and the rise of global rebellion. Meanwhile, the Bride of Christ is safely with the Lord in heaven, awaiting her return in glory.

THE REVELATION OF JESUS CHRIST REVEALS:

> 4:1 After this I looked, and, behold, a door was opened in heaven: and the first voice which I heard was as it were of a trumpet talking with me; which said, Come up here, and I will show you things which must be hereafter.

Revelation 4:1 marks a dramatic transition in the Book of Revelation, shifting from the messages to the seven churches (chapters 2–3) to the unfolding prophetic events of the future. This verse is one of the strongest biblical indicators of the Rapture of the Church—the moment when believers are taken up to be with Christ before the judgments of the Tribulation.

"After this I looked, and, behold, a door was opened in heaven." The phrase "after this" (Greek: *meta tauta*) signals a new section in John's vision. It follows Jesus' messages to the churches and transitions into "the things which shall be hereafter" (Revelation 1:19). This phrase suggests that the Church Age has concluded, and the events that follow take place after the Church is removed from the earth.

John then sees a door opened in heaven, a clear indication of divine invitation and access. Throughout Scripture, an open door symbolizes an opportunity or transition (Isaiah 26:2; John 10:9). In this case, it represents the entrance of the Church into heaven, paralleling Christ's promise to His followers:

> I am the door: by Me if any man enter in, he shall be saved, and shall go in and out, and find pasture. (John 10:9)

This open door suggests that a major dispensational shift has occurred—from the Church Age to the events that lead to the Second Coming of Christ.

"And the first voice which I heard was as it were of a trumpet talking with me." John hears a voice like a trumpet. This imagery is significant because trumpets are often associated with divine announcements, war, or a call to gather God's people (Numbers 10:1–3; 1 Corinthians 15:51–52; 1 Thessalonians 4:16–18). The trumpet-like voice immediately brings to mind Paul's description of the Rapture:

> Behold, I show you a mystery; We shall not all sleep, but we shall all be changed. In a moment, in the twinkling of an eye, at the last trump: for the trumpet shall sound, and the dead shall be raised incorruptible, and we shall be changed. (1 Corinthians 15:51–52)

The voice, resembling a trumpet, calling John up to heaven, serves as a symbolic foreshadowing of the Rapture of the Church. Just as John is taken up to heaven to witness the future events, so too will the Church be removed from the earth before the Tribulation begins.

"Which said, Come up here, and I will show you things which must be hereafter." The command "Come up here" mirrors the promise of Christ that His people will one day be caught up to be with Him (John 14:2–3). John's ascent symbolizes the transition from the Church Age to the Tribulation, foreshadowing the Church's removal before God's judgment is poured out on the earth.

The phrase "I will show you things which must be hereafter" reinforces the dispensational shift. John is now witnessing the prophetic timeline of the end times, beginning with the heavenly scene in chapters 4 and 5, followed by the Tribulation judgments in chapters 6–19.

From this point forward, the Church is no longer mentioned on earth throughout the Tribulation (Revelation 6–19). The focus shifts to Israel, the nations, and God's judgment and plan for restoration on the earth. This absence supports the pre-Tribulation Rapture view—that believers are removed before God's wrath is poured out.

OLD TESTAMENT FORESHADOWS REVELATION:

Though He had commanded the clouds from above, and opened the doors of heaven, And had rained down manna for them to eat, and had given them of the bread of heaven. (Psalm 78:23–24)

1. **An Opened Door in Heaven**—In both passages, heaven's doors are opened. In Revelation 4:1, John sees a door opened in heaven, symbolizing divine access, revelation, and transition from earth to the heavenly realm. In Psalm 78:23, God opens the doors of heaven to pour out divine provision, demonstrating His supernatural intervention.

2. **A Call from Above**—In Revelation 4:1, John hears a voice from heaven, calling him to "Come up here." Similarly, in Psalm 78:24, God's provision comes down from above—both signify divine communication and intervention.

3. **Heaven's Provision and Revelation**—The manna from heaven in Psalm 78:24 represents God's supernatural sustenance, just as John is invited into heaven to receive divine revelation. Both depict heaven as the source of life-giving truth—manna for physical sustenance and prophecy for spiritual guidance.

4. **A Transition to Something Greater**—Psalm 78 recalls the wilderness journey of Israel, where they were sustained by heavenly bread, but Revelation 4:1 marks a transition from the Church Age to the heavenly realm, where the faithful will experience the fulfillment of God's promises.

Psalm 78:23–24 parallels Revelation 4:1 in that both describe heaven opening to reveal God's purposes. In the Old Testament, God opened heaven to sustain Israel with manna. In Revelation, God opens heaven to call John (and symbolically, the Church) into His presence before the coming judgments. This emphasizes the heavenly invitation extended to the faithful—first in the form of provision, and ultimately, in the form of eternal communion with God.

Irene leaned forward, a curious look in her eyes. "Ann, I've got a question that's been bugging me. I heard someone say that the 'last trump' in 1 Corinthians 15 might refer to Donald Trump's final term as president. Is that even possible? Could that be what Paul was talking about?"

I smiled gently, my Bible already open. "I know that theory has made the rounds, especially during election seasons. But no, Irene—that's not what Paul meant. The 'last trump' in 1 Corinthians 15:52 isn't political at all. It's a divine trumpet—a signal from heaven that marks the moment of the Rapture, when the dead in Christ are raised and we who are alive are changed in the twinkling of an eye."

Irene nodded slowly. "So it has nothing to do with Trump . . . the man?"

I shook my head. "No connection whatsoever. It's a homonym—'trump' is simply short for 'trumpet.' In the context of Paul's letters, especially 1 Thessalonians 4:16, it's clear he's talking about the 'trump of God.' It's a supernatural call, not a political metaphor."

Irene chuckled softly. "I guess that makes sense. Sometimes we want prophecy to fit our headlines instead of the other way around."

I leaned in. "Exactly. We have to let Scripture interpret Scripture. The trumpet in Paul's writing is always tied to God gathering His people—not human elections or presidents. If we're not careful, we can start bending prophecy to suit our preferences instead of preparing our hearts for His return."

Irene sighed. "That's a good word. It's easy to get distracted."

Smiling. "That's why we watch, stay sober, and rightly divide the Word. He's coming—but not on Air Force One."

"Ann, what about the different views on the Rapture—pre-Tribulation, mid-Tribulation, post-Tribulation? It's so confusing! Why are there so many interpretations? Shouldn't it be obvious from Scripture?"

"You'd think so, but Bible prophecy is one of the most debated topics in theology. It's been that way for centuries. People argue over the timing of the Rapture because they have different interpretations of Scripture. But the key thing to remember is this: all Rapture views fall under pre-Millennialism—which means everyone who believes in the Rapture agrees that it happens before the Millennium. The debate is just about when it happens in relation to the Tribulation."

"Okay, so at least they agree that the Rapture happens before the 1,000-year reign of Christ on earth. But why do some people believe the Church will have to go through part or all of the Tribulation?"

"Well, let's break it down. The pre-Tribulation Rapture view teaches that the Church will be taken to heaven before the Tribulation begins. This is the belief that Christ comes *for* His Church before the world experiences seven years of divine judgment. This was the uncontested view of the early church for 354 years before any other theory emerged."

"Really? The early church believed in a pre-Tribulation Rapture?"

"Yes! The apostle Paul and the early church fathers held to this view. It's grounded in passages like 1 Thessalonians 4:16–17, which says:"

For the Lord Himself shall descend from heaven with a shout, with the voice of the archangel, and with the trump of God: the dead in Christ shall rise first: Then we which are alive and remain shall be caught up together with them in the clouds, to meet the Lord in the air: and so shall we ever be with the Lord. (1 Thessalonians 4:16–17)

"That does sound like a pre-Tribulation Rapture! But what about the mid-Trib and post-Trib views?"

"The mid-Tribulation Rapture view teaches that the Church will go through the first three and a half years of the Tribulation before being raptured at the halfway point. They believe that the Church will suffer some of the judgments but will be taken before the worst of God's wrath begins."

"So, they think the Church will experience some of the Tribulation but not all of it?"

"Exactly. And then there's the post-Tribulation Rapture view, which teaches that the Church will endure all seven years of the Tribulation and be raptured right before Christ's Second Coming."

"That doesn't make sense. If the Church is raptured right before Jesus returns, when do believers go through the Judgment Seat of Christ and the marriage supper of the Lamb?"

"One of the key challenges with the post-Tribulation view is that it leaves no time for important events Scripture places in heaven. After the Rapture, believers will stand before Christ at the Bema Seat Judgment to receive rewards for their faithful service (2 Corinthians 5:10). Then, just before returning with Christ at His Second Coming, the Church—the Bride—will be united with the Bridegroom in a wedding ceremony, followed by the marriage supper of the Lamb, where Old Testament and Tribulation saints—the redeemed from other ages—are invited as honored guests (Revelation 19:9). This sequence affirms that these heavenly events require a span of time—time not afforded in a post-Tribulation scenario."

"I see what you mean! And what about those newer views, like the Partial Rapture or Pre-Wrath views?"

"The Partial Rapture theory says that only the *spiritually mature* believers will be raptured, while the others will have to go through the Tribulation to 'prove' themselves."

I continued. "The Pre-Wrath Rapture theory teaches that the Church will be raptured during the last half of the Tribulation—after the Antichrist declares himself to be God, but before God's final wrath is poured out. However, this view is not supported by Scripture, because Jesus promised to keep us from the hour of trial that is coming upon the whole world (Revelation 3:10)."

"Wow, so many interpretations! But from everything you're saying, the pre-Tribulation Rapture makes the most sense. It fits with Scripture, allows time for the rewards and wedding ceremony in heaven, and seems to reflect what the early church believed."

"Exactly! Jesus promised to take His Bride before God's wrath is poured out on the earth. The Church is not appointed to wrath, but to receive salvation through Him (1 Thessalonians 5:9). When the Tribulation begins, the Church will already be in heaven—safe with Christ—awaiting His return at the Second Coming."

"That's such a comforting thought! No wonder Paul said, 'Comfort one another with these words.'"

HOW DID THE CHURCH GET UP INTO HEAVEN?

Revelation 4:1 marks a pivotal moment in biblical prophecy—the transition from the Church Age to the events that follow. But the question arises: How did the Church get into heaven?

John, in this passage, is a symbol of the Church being caught up. The phrase "after this" signifies the conclusion of the Church Age. The door to heaven opens, and John is called up—a prophetic picture of the Rapture. While we do not see a mass gathering of the Church explicitly in this passage, John serves as a representative, showing us what will happen when Christ calls His Church home.

The Mystery Revealed

The Rapture has been widely debated, misunderstood, and even mocked—but it remains a profound biblical truth. The apostle Paul, writing under divine revelation, referred to it as a "mystery" (*mysterion* in Greek)—a truth once hidden but now revealed by God.

Paul unveils this mystery in 1 Corinthians 15:51–57:

Behold, I show you a mystery; We shall not all sleep, but we shall all be changed. In a moment, in the twinkling of an eye, at the last trump: for the trumpet shall sound, and the dead shall be raised incorruptible, and we shall be changed. For this corruptible must put on incorruption, and this mortal must put on immortality. So when this corruptible shall have put on incorruption, and this mortal shall have put on immortality, then shall be brought to pass the saying that is written, Death is swallowed up in victory. O death, where is your sting? O grave, where is your victory? The sting of death is sin; and the strength of sin is the law. But thanks be to God, which gives us the victory through our Lord Jesus Christ. (1 Corinthians 15:51–57)

This truth was hidden from the Old Testament saints. The prophets wrote about the Messiah, His coming Kingdom, and the end of the age, but the Rapture of the Church was never disclosed—until Paul. He received this revelation directly from the Lord, and it changed everything.

What Happens at the Rapture?

Paul describes seven key aspects of this mystery:

1. Not all believers will die—some will be taken alive.
2. The dead in Christ will be resurrected—New Testament saints who believed in God's promises.
3. Living believers will be transformed instantly—translated like Enoch:

And Enoch walked with God: and he was not; for God took him. (Genesis 5:24).

4. We will become immortal—receiving incorruptible bodies.
5. We will be glorified—given bodies like Christ's resurrected body.
6. We will be changed at the sound of the trumpet—the signal of our gathering to Christ.
7. It will be instantaneous—happening in the "twinkling of an eye."

The Trumpet Call of God

The term "rapture" does not appear explicitly in the Bible; however, the concept is deeply rooted in Scripture. The phrase "caught up" in 1 Thessalonians 4:17 comes from the Greek word *harpazo*, which means to seize by force, snatch away suddenly, or transport from one place to another.

Our English word *rapture* comes from the Latin translation of the Bible, where "harpazo" was rendered as *rapiemur*—meaning to be caught up, taken swiftly, or snatched away. This translation shaped our modern understanding of the Rapture as the moment when believers—both those who have died in Christ and those still living—are supernaturally gathered to meet the Lord in the air.

Many critics argue that because the word *rapture* is not found in the Bible, the event itself is unbiblical. However, the same could be said of other commonly accepted theological terms. For example:

- The word "Bible" is not found in the Bible.
- The word "Trinity" does not appear in Scripture, yet we believe in God the Father, God the Son, and God the Holy Spirit.

Likewise, though the word *rapture* is not directly written in Scripture, the event itself is clearly described. The Bible repeatedly speaks of a sudden gathering, a forceful taking away, and a divine transformation of believers at Christ's return.

The *harpazo* of the Church means that:

- All believers who have died in Christ will be resurrected.
- All living believers will be instantly transformed.
- Together, they will be caught up to meet Christ in the air.

This is the blessed hope of the Church—the promise that Jesus will return *for* His Bride, delivering us from the coming Tribulation. The Rapture is not just an idea—it is a divine appointment, a moment in history yet to be fulfilled, when Christ will gather His people to Himself in an instant, just as He promised.

What About Those Who Have Died?

Many ask, "What happens to those who have been cremated, lost at sea, or whose bodies have completely decayed?" The answer is simple: God is not limited by earthly constraints. The same God who formed man from the dust (Genesis 2:7) can reassemble every molecule of those who have died. Whether buried, burned, or lost, nothing is beyond His power. The dead in Christ will rise—their bodies will be glorified, just as Christ's was.

A Hidden Truth Now Revealed

The Rapture was not revealed in the Old Testament because it was a divine mystery, hidden from the foundation of the world. But in due time, God revealed it through Paul, giving the Church a hope beyond death—a promise that Christ will return for His Bride before the Tribulation.

This truth is not just theological—it is personal. The promise of the Rapture is a call to be ready, be watchful, and be faithful. The trumpet could sound at any moment. Are you ready?

———◆◆◆———

Irene sat back, flipping through her Bible with a bewildered look. She tapped a pen against the pages, sighed, and shook her head. I, sipping my tea, watched with a knowing smile.

Rubbing her temples. "Ann, I'm trying to make sense of this, but my brain feels like it's short-circuiting. If the dead in Christ rise at the Rapture, and that includes all believers, then . . . how do the Old Testament saints fit in? Weren't they already taken to heaven when Jesus died? Or are they waiting for something else? My head hurts."

Chuckling, I set my tea down. "I get it, Irene. It's a lot. But let's break it down. You're right—when Jesus died, He descended to Sheol, the Hebrew term often translated as Hades in Greek and loosely as 'hell' in English. But He didn't go there to suffer. He went to the side known as Abraham's Bosom—or paradise—where the righteous souls who had died before Him were waiting."

Irene's eyes widening. "So they weren't in heaven?"

"No, not yet. Before Jesus paid for sin, heaven wasn't open to them. They were saved by faith in the coming Messiah, but their sins weren't yet atoned for. The Day of Atonement sacrifice was only for the *covering* of sins—a foreshadowing of Jesus' Second Coming. They had to wait. But then Jesus comes, proclaims victory, and leads them out when He rises. That's what Ephesians 4:8 means when it says, 'Wherefore He says, When He ascended up on high, He led captivity captive, and gave gifts unto men,' meaning He liberated the souls of the righteous Old Testament saints and relocated paradise to heaven."

Slowly nodding. "Okay . . . so their souls went to heaven with Him. But what about their bodies? Are they part of the Rapture?"

"Nope. The 'dead in Christ' at the Rapture are only New Testament believers. The Old Testament saints' bodies are still in the grave and won't be resurrected until Christ's Second Coming at the end of the Tribulation."

Throwing her hands up. "Wait—what? Why? Why wouldn't they be included?"

Grinning. "Because the Church and Israel have different roles in God's prophetic plan. The Old Testament saints are part of Israel, not the Church."

Grabbing her tea for comfort. "I need a flow chart."

I laughed. "Fair enough. Let's lay it out."

There are two major resurrections:

1. **The First Resurrection**—for the righteous. This happens in stages:

   - Jesus was the 'firstfruits' when He rose (1 Corinthians 15:20).

- The Church is resurrected at the Rapture (1 Thessalonians 4:16–17).
- The Tribulation martyrs and Old Testament saints are resurrected at Christ's Second Coming (Daniel 12:1–2; Isaiah 26:19; Revelation 20:4–6).

2. **The Second Resurrection**—for the unrighteous. This happens at the Great White Throne Judgment (Revelation 20:11–15), when the unbelievers are resurrected for judgment.

Staring blankly. "So the Old Testament saints . . . aren't part of the Rapture because the Rapture is just for the Church?"

"Bingo. The Rapture is the removal of the Church Age believers before the Tribulation. The Old Testament saints were saved before the Church Age, so their resurrection is at the Second Coming after the Tribulation, right before the Millennial Kingdom starts."

Tapping her fingers. "So, they're already in heaven in spirit, but their bodies are still waiting?"

"Exactly! The same way we go to heaven if we die now, but our bodies remain in the grave until the Rapture. The Old Testament saints are waiting for their resurrection bodies too, but theirs come later."

Letting out a long breath. "Whew . . . that makes sense. Complicated, but it makes sense."

Smiling. "You're not alone. This was a mystery—Paul literally calls it a *mysterion* in 1 Corinthians 15:51. It wasn't revealed in the Old Testament, which is why it's so debated."

She pointed at me. "So you're telling me that whether it's the Old Testament or the New Testament, everyone will see Jesus at some point—either at the Rapture, the Second Coming, or the Great White Throne Judgment?"

"Absolutely. Church Age believers will see Him in the air at the Rapture and stand before Him at the Bema Seat. At the Second Coming, surviving nations will face the Sheep and Goat Judgment. Then, after the Millennial Kingdom, all unbelievers will stand before Him at the Great White Throne Judgment. In the end, no one will escape standing before Christ."

Leaning back. "Wow. That puts everything into perspective."

Nodding. "It does. And it also reminds us that God's plan is precise. Nothing is random. Every resurrection is exactly where it should be."

Smirking. "Alright, Ann . . . I think my brain needs a break. Let's talk about something easy now. Like, oh I don't know . . . the Trinity?"

Laughing. "Oh, Irene, you don't know what you're asking!"

———◆◆◆———

OLD TESTAMENT MYSTERY? OR HIDING IN PLAIN SIGHT?

The tale of the two kings—King Solomon and Christ, the King of kings—reveals one of the most profound and often overlooked mysteries in the Old Testament: the foreshadowing of the Rapture. The Song of Songs, written by King Solomon and often misunderstood as merely a poetic romance, is in fact a prophetic narrative about the maturing of the Bride—those called to be with the Messiah. It is a story of longing, delay, preparation, and, ultimately, transformation.

Solomon, as a type of the anti-Messiah, represents the earthly rule Israel chose over God at Sinai. In contrast, the Shepherd—the true Beloved—calls to His Bride throughout the Song, drawing her away from attachment to an earthly king and back to Himself. The Bride's internal struggle mirrors that of both Israel and the Church: longing for the Shepherd, yet entangled in the comforts and distractions of the world.

In Song of Songs 2:10–13, the Shepherd calls the Bride to "rise up and come away." The winter is past; the rain is over and gone—spring has arrived. This imagery closely parallels the language of the Rapture in 1 Thessalonians 4:16–17, where the Bridegroom calls His beloved to meet Him in the air. Yet, like many today, the Bride hesitates. She delights in the warmth of the Shepherd's love but is reluctant to leave the comfort of the familiar behind.

The pattern continues as she repeatedly falls asleep at crucial moments. In Song of Songs 5:2–6, her Beloved knocks, but she delays in responding. By the time she opens the door, He is gone. This mirrors the warning of the parable of the ten virgins in Matthew 25—some will be ready when the Bridegroom comes, and some will miss the moment. When she finally seeks Him, she is met with rebuke and stripped of her veil—a sign of unfaithfulness. Like many in the Church today, she professes love for Him but is unwilling to leave the comfort of the world to labor in the harvest beside Him.

But the story does not end in failure. The Song of Songs is a journey of transformation. By Song of Songs 6:3, the Bride has matured: "I am my Beloved's, and my Beloved is mine." No longer does she see Him as belonging to her first—she understands that true love begins with surrender. By Song of Songs 7:10–12, she has fully yielded, declaring, "I am my Beloved's, and His desire is toward me." She is eager, rising early, calling Him to move forward— ready to labor at His side. This is the Bride made ready.

Finally, in Song of Songs 8:5, she is seen coming up out of the wilderness, leaning on her Beloved. No longer asleep, no longer delaying, no longer clinging to her own way—she is now fully dependent on Him. This is the image of those who will be caught up in the first resurrection—those who are watching, waiting, and ready.

The Song of Songs reveals the spiritual condition of the Bride—her immaturity, her delays, her awakenings, and ultimately, her readiness for the Shepherd's call. It is both a warning and an invitation. Will we be found prepared at His first call, or, like the Bride in her early state, will we awaken too late?

The mystery of the Rapture was hidden in the Old Testament, but for those with eyes to see, it was always there. The Bridegroom is calling. The question remains: Will we rise and come away with Him?

THE RAPTURE: TWO DISTINCT FUTURE COMINGS OF CHRIST

The Bible speaks of two distinct future comings of Christ: one secret and one visible to all. Understanding this distinction is essential in grasping the full scope of biblical prophecy.

First Coming: The Rapture—Jesus Comes as a Thief in the Night

The Rapture is an event where Christ comes secretly to take His Church out of the world before the coming Tribulation. This event is described as happening suddenly and without warning, like a thief in the night.

Jesus Himself warned of this sudden event:

> Remember therefore, how you have received and heard, and hold fast, and repent. If therefore you shalt not watch, I will come on you as a thief, and you shalt not know what hour I will come upon you. (Revelation 3:3)

> Watch therefore: for you know not what hour your Lord does come. (Matthew 24:42)

> For yourselves know perfectly that the Day of the Lord so comes as a thief in the night. (1 Thessalonians 5:1–2)

> But the Day of the Lord will come as a thief in the night. (2 Peter 3:10)

When a thief comes, he comes quietly, unseen, and takes what is most valuable. In the same way, Jesus will come unannounced to gather His jewels—the Church, His Bride—removing all those in Christ from the earth.

At this moment, the graves of all Church Age believers—those who died in Christ—will burst open as they are resurrected. The living believers will be instantly transformed and caught up together with them in the clouds to meet the Lord in the air (1 Thessalonians 4:16–17).

This event will be invisible to the world. Only those taken will witness Christ in the air. The rest of the world will be left behind, confused and unaware of what has just taken place.

While the earth endures the darkest time in human history—the Tribulation—Church Age saints will be in heaven, standing before the Judgment Seat of Christ to receive their rewards for faithfulness, and participating in the marriage ceremony of the Lamb.

Second Coming: The Visible Return of Christ

Seven years after the Rapture, Christ will return—this time openly, for all to see. This is the event described in Revelation when Jesus descends from heaven with His saints and His holy angels, riding on white horses in great power and glory (Matthew 25:31; Jude 1:14; Revelation 19:11–16). At this moment, every person on earth—believers and unbelievers alike—will see Him coming in the clouds. No one will be able to deny it.

Key differences between the Rapture and the Second Coming:

- Rapture—Jesus comes as a thief in the night, secretly *for* His Church.
- Second Coming—Jesus comes openly *with* His saints and angels, in power and glory, visible to all.

The first event is private, seen only by those taken to heaven. The second event is global, seen by every nation, tribe, and person on earth.

The Church—The Called-Out Ones

The word "Church" comes from the Greek word "*Ecclesia,*" meaning "called-out assembly." It refers to those who have been called out of darkness and into the light—redeemed from sin and gathered unto Christ. This term was not exclusive to the New Testament. In Acts 7:38, *ecclesia* is used to describe the assembly of Israel in the wilderness during Moses' time, and could just as accurately be translated "assembly" rather than "church" in that context.

Interestingly, the Greek word for "synagogue" is *sunagoge*, which also means "assembly." Both *ecclesia* and *sunagoge* refer to gatherings of people—but *ecclesia* in the New Testament context specifically designates the Body of Christ, a distinct spiritual community.

Just as we have been called out of sin into salvation, we will also be called out of this world before God's wrath is poured out. This is the blessed hope of the Rapture—a divine rescue mission. It is not just an escape, but an act of love and mercy, removing those in Christ before the judgment begins on the earth.

The Final Act: Jesus as King Over All

The Book of Revelation culminates in Christ's triumphant return as King of kings and Lord of lords. He will restore the earth, establish His Kingdom, and reign forever. From the garden of Eden to this very hour, the drama of redemption has been unfolding—and now we stand on the edge of the final chapter. Soon, the

Lord will return in two phases: first, to secretly gather His Bride in the Rapture; then, to openly return in power and glory to judge the world, restore creation, and establish His eternal reign. The question remains: will you be ready?

Sitting in our favorite spot, Bibles open, coffee cups in hand. Irene looks deep in thought, flipping through pages, and finally sighs, exasperated.

"Okay, Ann, I've got to ask you something. I believe in the pre-Tribulation Rapture—I really do. But I keep seeing all these verses about believers being left behind. And I thought all Christians get raptured? Like, the pure and holy ones, as well as those who, you know . . . the ones who live however they want all week, then show up at church on Sunday like nothing's wrong."

"Ahh, now you're getting into the purpose of the Rapture. Not all believers will be taken at the Rapture—only the ones who are truly ready."

"Wait. So you're telling me not all Christians get raptured?"

"Exactly. Look at Jesus' parable of the ten virgins in Matthew 25. All ten were waiting for the Bridegroom, which means they were all expecting Him—likely representing believers. But only five were ready and went in to the wedding ceremony, while the other five were left behind when the door was shut."

"So that means some Christians won't be taken in the Rapture?"

"Yes. Jesus talks about different levels of readiness—some producing thirtyfold, sixtyfold, and hundredfold returns (Mark 4:8, 20). The hundredfold believers—the ones truly watching, waiting, and walking in obedience—are the Bride. The lukewarm believers? They'll have to endure part—or even all—of the seven-year Tribulation before they wake up and get serious about their faith."

"Hold on, hold on. Are you saying there are Christians who won't be at the wedding at all?"

"That's right. Some will be at the wedding ceremony, some will only attend the wedding supper, and some won't make it at all."

"What? Where in the Bible does it say that?"

"Okay, look at Matthew 22:2–14—the parable of the wedding feast. Some guests were invited but refused to come. Others showed up without the proper garments—without righteousness—and were cast out. It's not just about being invited; it's about being ready."

"So, let me get this straight . . . the Bride—the hundredfold believers—are taken in the Rapture. The foolish virgins—the lukewarm believers—are left behind. And then there are others who don't even make it to the marriage supper?"

"Exactly. And guess what? There are two marriage suppers."

"Two?"

"Yep. Revelation 19:9 talks about the marriage supper of the Lamb—that's for the Bride and the wedding guests, including the Old Testament saints and Tribulation martyrs, often referred to as 'guests' or 'friends of the Bridegroom' (John 3:29; Matthew 22:1–14; Revelation 19:9). But Revelation 19:17–18 describes a very different supper—the supper of the great God—where the birds feast on the flesh of those who rejected Christ."

"Wait . . . So you're telling me that everyone will be at a supper . . . but some will be eating and others will be eaten?"

"Exactly. Everyone will be somewhere—either celebrating with Jesus or facing judgment."

"Okay, this is blowing my mind. So what happens to the Christians who are left behind?"

"They will have to go through the Tribulation to be refined. Remember what Jesus told the Laodicean church in Revelation 3:18? He told them to buy gold refined in the fire. That fire is the Tribulation."

"So basically, they weren't fully committed to Christ before the Rapture, so they have to go through the fire to be purified?"

"Yes! Look at Zephaniah 1:7–8—it says some guests have to change their garments (from unrighteous to righteous) before they can attend the marriage supper. That means their righteousness wasn't complete."

"So let's say someone is a lukewarm Christian. They go to church, they believe in Jesus, but they're still living for the world. What happens to them?"

"If they truly belong to Christ, they won't lose their salvation, but they'll miss the Rapture. They'll have to prove their faith during the Tribulation—some by martyrdom (Revelation 6:9–11)."

"But won't that be terrible? The Tribulation is going to be awful!"

"Yes! That's why Jesus said to 'watch and pray that you may be counted worthy to escape' (Luke 21:36)."

"So how do we make sure we're ready?"

I pulled out my notes:

1. Watch and Pray (Luke 21:36)—Stay alert and don't get distracted by the world.
2. Keep Your Lamp Full (Matthew 24:4)—Be filled with the Holy Spirit.
3. Love His Appearing (2 Timothy 4:8)—Long for His return, and He will reward you.

"Wow. I feel like I need to step it up spiritually."

"We all do. The question isn't *if* Jesus is coming—it's who will be ready when He does?"

"And who will be at the right supper!"

"Exactly! Now, let's make sure we have our wedding garments on and our lamps full. We want to be part of the Bride—not just guests."

THE CHURCH IS NOT APPOINTED TO WRATH

From the beginning of time, God has never poured out His wrath on the righteous along with the wicked. This has been His pattern of divine protection, and it is no different when it comes to the Tribulation.

What is unleashed in the Tribulation period is not merely persecution—it is about Israel and a rebellious world. This is Daniel's 70th Week, the final seven years decreed for Israel (Daniel 9:24–27). The Church is not in focus—she has been raptured, delivered from the wrath to come.

God's Pattern of Protection Before Judgment

This pattern is clear throughout Scripture:

- Enoch was raptured before the flood (Genesis 5:24).
- Noah and his family were kept safe while God's wrath fell on the earth (Genesis 7).
- Lot and his family were removed before Sodom and Gomorrah were destroyed (Genesis 19).
- The Israelites were protected from the plagues in Egypt (Exodus 12:23).

God rescues the righteous before judgment falls. He does not pour His wrath on those He has redeemed.

Revelation 4:1—A Watershed Moment

Revelation 4:1 marks the dividing line—the moment when the Church disappears from the earth and is not mentioned again until Revelation 19, when she returns *with* Christ at His Second Coming. The phrase "Come up here" is a powerful echo of what Paul describes in 1 Thessalonians 4:16–18—the Rapture of the Church. It is both a comfort to those who are ready and a warning to those who are not.

Are You Ready?

This chapter closes with a pressing question: Are you ready for His return? Jesus warned, "Watch therefore, for you know not what hour your Lord does come" (Matthew 24:42).

The Rapture is imminent—it could happen at any moment. There is no prophecy left to be fulfilled before it occurs. The only uncertainty is whether you will be found ready. Will you be part of the Bride, caught up in the Rapture? Or will you be left behind to face the wrath of God?

This is not a question to answer someday. This is a question that must be answered today. "Choose this day whom you will serve" (Joshua 24:15). The final events of history are about to unfolded. Where will you stand?

———◆◆◆———

Irene and I retreat to my study, surrounded by open Bibles, commentaries, and scattered notes. She leans forward, eyes wide, clearly wrestling with the implications of what I've just explained.

"Okay, Ann. I get it. The Church is the Restrainer—the one thing holding back the full force of the Tribulation. But when the Rapture happens . . . what then? What happens when the Church is suddenly gone?"

"Chaos, Irene. Utter chaos. Imagine—millions, maybe even billions of people worldwide, just vanishing in an instant. Every believer, every true follower of Christ, gone in the blink of an eye."

"But . . . what happens to America? We've got millions of Christians. Wouldn't that cripple the country?"

"Absolutely. Think about it—pilots, drivers, doctors, law enforcement, military leaders, teachers, government officials—all gone. Planes will fall from the sky. Cars will crash. Hospitals will be overwhelmed. The stock market? Instant freefall. The economy? Collapse."

"But wouldn't governments step in? Wouldn't world leaders try to stabilize things?"

"They'll try—but remember, a lot of them will be gone too. The Rapture won't just wipe out church congregations; it'll strip away the moral backbone of society. Without the Church, there's no restraint on evil. Crime will explode. Governments will panic. Nations will turn against each other overnight."

"And America . . . ?"

"America as we know it? Gone. Our foundation was built on biblical principles, but with the Church removed, we'll spiral into moral, political, and economic ruin. What's left of the government will scramble to reorganize, probably under global leadership. And don't forget—the Rapture isn't just an American event. Every nation will be affected."

"So, it's not just America falling apart . . . it's global."

"Yes. The world will be in shock. Imagine the headlines."

MILLIONS MYSTERIOUSLY DISAPPEAR—MASS PANIC ENSUES

PLANES CRASH, CITIES BURN, GOVERNMENTS COLLAPSE

WORLD LEADERS CALL FOR GLOBAL UNITY AMID CRISIS

"The world will be desperate for answers. And that's when someone steps up—the Antichrist."

"Wait. You're telling me this is how he rises to power?"

"Exactly. The world will be so broken, so desperate for stability, that they'll accept any leader who promises peace. He'll look like a savior—someone who has all the answers, who can unite the nations. But it's a deception."

"And people will believe him?"

"Most will. He'll be charismatic, powerful, and 'miraculously' able to restore order. He'll offer a new system, a new economy, a new world order. And with the Restrainer gone—no Church, no Holy Spirit restraining evil—there's nothing stopping him."

"But there will still be people left—people who knew the truth but weren't truly walking with Christ before the Rapture. What happens to them?"

"Some will wake up and realize what happened. The Bible calls them Tribulation saints—those who come to Christ *after* the Rapture. But it won't be easy. They'll be persecuted, hunted, forced to choose between loyalty to Christ or the Antichrist."

"So, no more middle ground. No more 'I'll decide later.'"

"Nope. It's either take the mark of the beast or die for your faith."

Shaking her head. "This is terrifying. And people just . . . ignore it? They mock it?"

"That's exactly what Jesus warned about—people will be eating, drinking, going about life, thinking none of this will ever happen . . . until it does. Just like in the days of Noah."

Exhaling slowly. "So, if America collapses, if the world descends into darkness, if the Antichrist rises, then what's left for those who missed the Rapture?"

"Only two choices: stand for Christ and face persecution or bow to the Antichrist and be eternally lost."

Whispering. "Ann, people need to know this. They need to be ready."

Nodding. "Exactly. That's why we warn, we preach, and we pray. Because once the Rapture happens, there's no second chance to be part of it. You're either taken . . . or left behind."

A heavy silence fills the room. Irene stares at her Bible, her mind racing. At last, she looks up, eyes filled with urgency.

"Ann, we need to tell as many people as possible."
"Yes. Before it's too late."

SUMMARY OF REVELATION 4:1

Revelation 4:1 marks a pivotal shift in biblical prophecy—the transition from the Church Age to the unfolding of end-time events. Up until this moment, the focus has been on Christ and His message to the seven churches, representing different stages of church history. But now, the scene shifts.

John hears a voice like a trumpet, saying, "Come up here, and I will show you things which must be hereafter" (Revelation 4:1). This divine call mirrors the promise of the Rapture (1 Thessalonians 4:16–17), when Christ will remove His Church before the coming Tribulation. From this point forward, the Church is absent from the earth and does not reappear until Revelation 19—returning *with* Christ at His Second Coming.

With the Church now in heaven, God's prophetic timeline moves forward. The Tribulation period begins, bringing God's wrath upon the world. The righteous are safely in His presence, receiving their rewards and partaking in the wedding, while the earth faces judgment.

KEY TAKEAWAYS

- The end of the Church Age—The Church is removed from the earth, signaling the end of the dispensation of grace.
- The Rapture—John's calling up to heaven symbolizes the catching away of the Church before the Tribulation.
- God's wrath begins—The Tribulation is not for the Church but for a world that has rejected Christ.
- Christ's return—The next time the Church appears in Revelation is in glory, returning *with* Christ to establish His Kingdom.

Revelation 4:1 is a defining moment—a call to be ready. The time of the Church on earth is coming to a close. The question is:

Are you ready for His return?

Chapter 5

Revelation 4:
The Church in Heaven

THE CHURCH'S HEAVENLY HOME—The Book of Revelation is a divine unveiling—a grand, prophetic panorama of the future orchestrated by God Himself. It is a book of hope and assurance, illuminating the certainty of God's plan amidst a chaotic world. Within its pages, the apostle John is transported beyond time and space, witnessing the majesty of heaven and the unfolding events of the last days. Now, as we enter Revelation chapter 4, we shift from the Church's earthly presence to its glorious position in heaven. The transition is dramatic, as the scene moves from the Rapture of the Church on earth to the breathtaking vision of God's throne.

At this pivotal moment, John is caught up "in the Spirit" and ushered into the very throne room of heaven. His words vividly describe an awe-inspiring reality—one that no human eye has fully seen and no mind can completely comprehend. It is here, in Revelation 4:2–11, that we are given an unparalleled glimpse into the throne of God, the worship of celestial beings, and the triumphant presence of the redeemed.

This passage confirms a crucial biblical truth: the Church is in heaven before the Tribulation unfolds on earth. The absence of any mention of the Church in the subsequent chapters dealing with God's judgment affirms the promise that believers are not appointed to wrath (1 Thessalonians 5:9). The events described in Revelation chapters 4 and 5 set the stage for the judgments to come, but they do so from a heavenly perspective, revealing the Church's secured position in the presence of God.

In this chapter, we will explore the vision of heaven that John beheld—the indescribable glory of God's throne, the radiant splendor surrounding it, and the unceasing worship of the heavenly hosts. We will uncover the significance of the twenty-four elders, the four living creatures, and the anthems of praise that echo throughout the heavens. This scene is a powerful reminder that heaven is not merely a distant hope; it is a present reality, where Christ reigns and His Church will one day dwell in eternal worship.

The vision given to John serves to strengthen the faith of every believer. As we delve into the details of this extraordinary revelation, we will see that heaven is not only a place of unimaginable beauty but also the seat of divine authority, where God's sovereign plan unfolds in perfect harmony. Let us open our hearts and minds to the wonders of this heavenly vision, for in doing so, we embrace the blessed hope that awaits all who belong to Christ.

———◆◆◆———

"Ann, I've been studying Revelation, and I keep seeing people use the phrases 'last days' and 'end times' like they're the same thing. Are they?"

"That's a great question, Irene! A lot of people confuse the two, but they actually refer to different periods. *Last days* specifically relates to the end of the Church Age—the time we are in right now, before the Rapture happens. It began at Pentecost when the Holy Spirit was given to the Church, and it will continue until the Rapture of those in Christ."

"So when Peter said in Acts 2:17, 'In the last days, God says, I will pour out My Spirit on all people,' he was talking about the Church Age?"

"Exactly! The last days started when Jesus ascended into heaven, and they continue as the gospel is preached to all nations. But then, once the Church is removed from the earth at the Rapture, we enter a new phase called the *end times*—which includes the Tribulation, the Second Coming of Christ, and the Millennial Kingdom."

"So, the *end times* don't start until after the Rapture?"

"Correct! The Tribulation is the beginning of the end times. It's a seven-year period of judgment, as outlined in Daniel's prophecy and described in Revelation. The final portion of the end times includes Christ's return to establish His thousand-year reign, known as the Millennial Kingdom (Revelation 20:1–6)."

"That makes sense! The last days are about the Church on earth, and the end times are about what happens after the Church is taken to heaven."

"You got it! That's why understanding the timeline is so important. Right now, we are still in the *last days*, but soon, the Church will be called up, and the world will enter the prophetic events of the *end times*."

THE REVELATION OF JESUS CHRIST REVEALS:

4:2 And immediately I was in the Spirit: and, behold, a throne was set in heaven, and One sat on the throne.

This verse marks a pivotal moment in the Book of Revelation, as John experiences an instantaneous transformation, shifting from the earthly realm into the spiritual dimension. The phrase "immediately I was in the Spirit" underscores the suddenness and supernatural nature of John's experience. It is a divine summons, one that transcends human capability, as John is lifted beyond time and space to witness the heavenly realm.

The central focus of this verse is the throne in heaven, a symbol of divine sovereignty, ultimate authority, and unshakable power. The throne represents God's absolute rule over creation, demonstrating that history unfolds under His command. John does not immediately describe the details of heaven but first directs our attention to the foundational truth—God is seated on His throne. This imagery echoes similar visions found in Isaiah 6:1, Ezekiel 1:26–28, and Daniel 7:9, all of which emphasize the grandeur and majesty of God's throne.

The phrase "One sat on the throne" is a deliberate declaration of divine kingship. Unlike earthly rulers, who rise and fall, God's reign is eternal and unchallenged. This passage reminds us that, despite the turmoil of the world, heaven remains unshaken, and God remains sovereign.

For the Church, this vision brings immense comfort. It affirms that believers are not abandoned amid earthly trials but are part of a divine plan that culminates in heavenly glory. Before the judgments of the Tribulation begin, John first sees the certainty of God's rule, reinforcing the hope and security found in Christ. This verse serves as a reminder that all things—past, present, and future—are under God's control, and His purposes will be fulfilled in their appointed time.

OLD TESTAMENT FORESHADOWS REVELATION:

And above the firmament that was over their heads was the likeness of a throne, as the appearance of a sapphire stone: and upon the likeness of the throne was the likeness as the appearance of a man above upon it. And I saw as the color of amber, as the appearance of fire round about within it, from the appearance of His waist even upward, and from the appearance of His waist even downward, I saw as it were the appearance of fire, and it had brightness round about. As the appearance of the bow that is in the cloud in the day of rain, so was the appearance of the brightness round about. This was the appearance of the likeness of the glory of the LORD. And when I saw it, I fell upon my face, and I heard a voice of One that spoke. (Ezekiel 1:26–28)

Ezekiel describes a breathtaking heavenly vision with the throne of God at its center—much like John in Revelation. Both prophets are "in the Spirit" and receive a divine revelation that begins with the glory and majesty of God seated on His throne, emphasizing God's sovereign rule.

THE REVELATION OF JESUS CHRIST REVEALS:

4:3 And He that sat was to look upon like a jasper and a sardine stone: and there was a rainbow round about the throne, in sight like to an emerald.

John describes the One seated on the throne as having an appearance like jasper and sardine stone (sardius), surrounded by a rainbow like an emerald. These elements carry significant biblical and symbolic meanings.

- Jasper—This stone, often associated with clarity and radiance, is symbolic of God's purity and perfection. In Revelation 21:11, the New Jerusalem is described as having a brilliance like jasper, further reinforcing the connection between God's holiness and His eternal Kingdom.
- Sardine (Sardis) Stone—This deep red stone is linked to judgment, sacrifice, and redemption. It may represent both God's wrath against sin and the redemptive blood of Christ. The high priest's breastplate contained both jasper and sardius stones, signifying that these colors are tied to divine authority and the atonement of God's people.
- Emerald Rainbow—Unlike the multicolored rainbow given to Noah as a sign of God's covenant, this emerald rainbow suggests a dominant shade of green, which is often associated with mercy, new life, and renewal. It encircles the throne, indicating that even amidst judgment, God's mercy remains ever-present.

Together, these descriptions reinforce that God's throne is not only a seat of absolute power and judgment but also of covenant faithfulness and mercy. The imagery builds on Old Testament descriptions of God's throne while emphasizing the impending fulfillment of His divine plan.

OLD TESTAMENT FORESHADOWS REVELATION:

And you shalt set in it settings of stones, even four rows of stones: the first row shall be a sardius, a topaz, and a carbuncle: this shall be the first row. And the second row shall be an emerald, a sapphire, and a diamond. And the third row a ligure, an agate, and an amethyst. And the fourth row a beryl, and an onyx, and a jasper: they shall be set in gold in their enclosings. And the stones shall be with the names of the children of Israel, twelve, according to their names, like the engravings of a signet (signature ring); every one with his name shall they be according to the twelve tribes. (Exodus 28:17–21)

This passage describes the breastplate of judgment worn by the high priest, which was adorned with twelve precious stones, including jasper and sardius (sardine). These stones represent the tribes of Israel and are symbolic of God's covenant with His people—possibly suggesting that the appearance of God in Revelation 4:3 evokes His faithfulness and covenantal glory.

"Ann, this verse in Exodus refers to the twelve tribes in the Old Testament, and now John describes the One on the throne as having the appearance of jasper and sardius. Is there a connection?"

"Absolutely, Irene! When John sees the One seated on the throne and describes Him as looking like jasper and sardius, he's making a profound connection to the twelve tribes of Israel. These stones were part of the high priest's breastplate, which represented the twelve tribes."

"The high priest's breastplate? That sounds significant."

"It is! In Exodus 28:15–21, God commanded Moses to have the high priest wear a breastplate with twelve stones, each engraved with the name of a tribe of Israel. The sardius stone represented Reuben, the firstborn son of Jacob, and the jasper stone represented Benjamin, the youngest. These two stones were the first and the last on the breastplate, essentially encompassing all the tribes in between."

"So when John describes God's throne using these two stones, he's pointing to Israel?"

"Exactly! It's as if John is saying that the One seated on the throne carries Israel upon His heart, just as the high priest did when he ministered before the LORD in the Old Testament. The high priest would bear the names of the twelve tribes over his heart as a sign that he was interceding for them. When John gets to heaven and sees this imagery, he realizes that Israel is still central to God's plan."

"That's incredible! So this confirms that the Church Age is over at this point in Revelation, and now God is dealing with Israel?"

"Yes, that's precisely what's happening. At this moment in the vision, the Church has already been raptured, and God's attention is turning back to Israel. The Tribulation is also called 'the time of Jacob's trouble' (Jeremiah 30:7), which means that it's focused on Israel. The presence of these stones in the vision is a reminder that God has not forgotten His covenant with Israel."

"And what about the rainbow that John sees around the throne? What does that represent?"

"That's another powerful image! The rainbow is a reference to God's covenant with Noah in Genesis 9:12–16. After the Flood, God placed a rainbow in the sky as a sign that he would never again destroy the earth with water. But here, John sees a rainbow like an emerald, meaning it's a dominant shade of green, which symbolizes life, mercy, and renewal."

"Where does it say that in the Bible?"

"Green in Scripture often symbolizes life and vitality—'I am like a green olive tree . . .' (Psalm 52:8); fruitfulness—Psalm 1:3 and Jeremiah 17:8; and renewal and hope—Isaiah 55:12–13, where life returns to a barren land. Emerald is also one of the twelve stones on the high priest's breastplate (Exodus 28:17–20) and one of the foundation stones of the New Jerusalem (Revelation 21:19), further reinforcing its heavenly association."

"So is the rainbow a sign of God's mercy in the midst of judgment?"

"That's exactly right! Even as the judgments of Revelation are about to unfold, the rainbow is a reminder that God is a covenant-keeping God. He is faithful to His promises, not only to the Church but also to Israel. The storm may be coming, but the rainbow reminds us that God's mercy is still present."

"That makes so much sense. It's like John is witnessing a shift—God turning His attention back to Israel while still upholding His promises."

"Yes! And this is why understanding the symbolism of the high priest's breastplate is so crucial. In the Old Testament, the high priest interceded for Israel. In the New Testament, Jesus is our High Priest (Hebrews 4:14–16), interceding for both Israel and the Church. His role as High Priest never ends."

"That's an amazing picture! So when we get to heaven, will we see the rainbow like John did?"

"Yes, I believe so! The rainbow around the throne signifies that for the Church, the storm is over. Just like after a storm on earth, we see a rainbow as a sign that the trial has passed, John sees the rainbow in heaven, signaling that the Church's trials are over, and a new day is dawning."

"That's such a powerful image—both a reminder of God's promises and a declaration that His plan is unfolding exactly as He said it would."

"Yes! And this is why prophecy is so important. It reassures us that God's Word is true and that He is in control of history. When John sees the jasper and sardius, the rainbow, and the throne, he is witnessing the faithfulness of God in full display—His promise to Israel, mercy, and sovereignty over all things."

———◆◆◆———

THE REVELATION OF JESUS CHRIST REVEALS:

^{4:4} And round about the throne were four and twenty seats: and upon the seats I saw four and twenty elders sitting, clothed in white raiment; and they had on their heads crowns of gold.

John's vision now expands to include twenty-four elders, seated on twenty-four thrones around the throne of God. These elders are clothed in white raiment and wear golden crowns upon their heads. Their presence in heaven is significant, offering insight into God's redemptive plan and the rewards of the faithful.

The twenty-four elders represent both Old and New Testament saints, forming a complete picture of God's redeemed people. The number twenty-four is symbolic—likely comprising the twelve tribes of Israel, representing the faithful of the Old Testament, and the twelve apostles, representing Church Age believers. This connection is confirmed in Revelation 21:12–14, where the New Jerusalem is described as having twelve gates inscribed with the names of the twelve tribes of Israel and twelve foundations bearing the names of the twelve apostles of the Lamb.

The presence of the twenty-four elders in heaven at this moment reinforces the pre-Tribulation Rapture of the Church, as they are already seated and rewarded before God's judgment begins on the earth. Clothed in white raiment—a symbol of purity, righteousness, and victory—the elders reflect imagery consistently used throughout Scripture to describe the redeemed. These garments signify that the elders have been justified by faith and clothed in the righteousness of Christ, confirming their status as those who have already been redeemed.

The golden crowns on their heads symbolize victory and reward. Throughout the New Testament, believers are promised crowns as rewards for faithfulness and perseverance. The crowns mentioned in Scripture include:

- The Crown of Life—For those who endure trials (James 1:12).
- The Incorruptible Crown—For those who exercise self-discipline in their faith (1 Corinthians 9:25).
- The Crown of Righteousness—For those who eagerly await Christ's return (2 Timothy 4:8).
- The Crown of Glory—For faithful shepherds (1 Peter 5:4).
- The Crown of Rejoicing—For those who lead others to Christ (1 Thessalonians 2:19).

These golden crowns signify that the saints have received their heavenly rewards at the Judgment Seat of Christ (2 Corinthians 5:10). However, their crowns are distinct from those of Christ Himself. In Revelation 19:12, Jesus is described as wearing many crowns (diadems), which signify His supreme authority over all creation.

It is important to note that these twenty-four elders are not angels. Angels do not sit on thrones, receive crowns, or wear white garments as a sign of redemption. The elders are distinct from the angelic beings and later appear in John's vision (Revelation 5:11). Their position around the throne and their rewards indicate that they are redeemed human beings, representing both Israel and the Church.

The elders are seated on thrones, which suggests a role of co-rulership with Christ. In Revelation 3:21, Jesus promises that those who overcome will sit with Him on His throne. This promise is fulfilled in these elders, who now have a position of authority and honor in God's Kingdom.

Their presence around the throne highlights the fulfillment of God's covenant with both Old Testament saints and New Testament believers. It is a picture of completion—the redeemed have been gathered, rewarded, and given their rightful place in the presence of God before the Tribulation begins.

The vision of the twenty-four elders in Revelation 4:4 reveals the completeness of God's redemptive work. These elders symbolize the faithful of all ages, clothed in righteousness, rewarded for their faithfulness, and seated in positions of honor before God's throne. Their presence confirms that the Church is in heaven before the Tribulation, and their crowns remind us that faithfulness to Christ will be rewarded in eternity.

This passage is a powerful affirmation of God's promises to His people. It reminds believers that their trials and struggles on earth are not in vain—those who endure will receive a place in His Kingdom, a crown of gold, and the joy of eternal fellowship with Christ.

OLD TESTAMENT FORESHADOWS REVELATION:

Then the moon shall be confounded, and the sun ashamed, when the LORD of hosts shall reign in Mount Zion, and in Jerusalem, and before His ancients gloriously. (Isaiah 24:23)

In Isaiah 24:23, the "ancients" (elders) are seen in the presence of God's glory as He reigns, just as the twenty-four elders surround the throne in Revelation 4:4. Both passages emphasize the heavenly reign of God and the presence of honored representatives who witness His majesty. Isaiah's vision foreshadows the heavenly court in Revelation, where God's reign is fully realized with elders seated around His throne, reflecting divine governance and worship.

This Old Testament verse reinforces the continuity between the prophetic visions of Isaiah and John, linking the idea of God's rule, divine council, and honored elders surrounding Him in both the Old and New Testaments.

◆ ◆ ◆

The scent of old books lingered in the air as sunlight streamed through the tall windows of my study, casting golden rays over the wooden desk cluttered with open Bibles, notebooks, and a steaming cup of tea. Irene sat across from me, flipping through the pages of her Bible, brow furrowed in deep concentration. The subject we had been discussing—judgment and rewards in heaven—had left her with more questions than answers.

"I don't understand," Irene sighed, looking up from the pages of Revelation. "The Bible talks about the Bema Seat of Christ and the Judgment Seat of Christ—are they the same thing? And if we're saved, why do we even have to be judged at all?"

I smiled gently, recognizing the familiar confusion. "That's a great question, Irene. A lot of people struggle with this. The Bema Seat of Christ and the Judgment Seat of Christ are actually the same thing—just different ways of describing it. The word *bema* comes from the Greek term for a raised platform where rewards were given to victorious athletes in the ancient Olympic games. It's not a place of condemnation, but a place of reward."

Irene's eyes widened. "So it's not like the Great White Throne Judgment?"

"Not at all," I confirmed, leaning forward. "The Great White Throne Judgment in Revelation 20 is for unbelievers—those who rejected Christ. They will stand before God to be judged for their sins and ultimately face eternal separation from Him. But believers—those who accepted Christ—won't be at that judgment. Instead, we'll stand before the Bema Seat of Christ, which is the place of reward, not punishment."

Irene exhaled in relief, but then her brow creased again. "Okay, but what exactly are we being judged for? If Jesus already forgave our sins, what's left to judge?"

I picked up my Bible and turned to 2 Corinthians 5:10.

"Paul explains it perfectly:"

> For we must all appear before the Judgment Seat of Christ; that every one may receive the things done in his body, according to that he has done, whether it be good or bad. (2 Corinthians 5:10)

"This judgment isn't about salvation—it's about what we did with our lives after we were saved."

"So . . . kind of like a rewards ceremony?" Irene asked hesitantly.

"Exactly!" I nodded. "Think of it like the Olympics. When a race is over, the athletes don't get punished for how they ran—they get rewarded for how well they competed. Some receive gold medals, some silver, some bronze, and some may leave empty-handed. But they're all still Olympians. At the Bema Seat, Jesus will reward us for our faithfulness, obedience, and how we used our lives to serve Him."

Irene slowly nodded, the concept beginning to take shape. "So, does that mean some people will get more rewards than others?"

"Yes, but not in a way that will make anyone jealous or ashamed," I reassured her. "Remember, heaven is a place of joy. Jesus Himself spoke of rewards in Luke 19:15–19, where He describes servants being given different levels of authority based on their faithfulness. Some will rule over ten cities, some over five. Our rewards are based on how well we lived out our faith."

Irene leaned back in her chair, deep in thought. "So, what kinds of things will Jesus reward us for?"

I smiled and started listing them. "The Bible mentions several things—how we treated others (Matthew 10:41–42), how we used our resources (Matthew 6:1–4), how we endured suffering and persecution (Matthew 5:11–12), and even how much we longed for His return (2 Timothy 4:8). Everything we do for Christ, no matter how small, matters. Even giving someone a cup of water in His name is recorded in heaven."

Irene's eyes misted. "That's . . . beautiful. I guess I never realized how much God sees. Every little thing."

I reached across the table and squeezed her hand. "He sees it all, and He treasures it. That's why the Bema Seat is not something to fear—it's something to look forward to. Imagine standing before Jesus and hearing Him say, 'Well done, good and faithful servant.' That moment alone will be worth everything."

Irene let out a deep breath, her heart lighter than before. "I want to live my life with that moment in mind."

I nodded; my smile warm. "That's exactly why He tells us about it. To give us hope and purpose. And one day, when we stand before Him, every sacrifice, every act of love, every unseen moment of faithfulness will be worth it."

————◆◆◆————

THE REVELATION OF JESUS CHRIST REVEALS:

4:5 And out of the throne proceeded lightnings and thunderings and voices: and there were seven lamps of fire burning before the throne, which are the seven Spirits of God.

John's vision of the throne of God is one of awe-inspiring majesty and power. The lightnings and thunderings that proceed from the throne signify divine authority, judgment, and the overwhelming presence of God. This imagery recalls the scene at Mount Sinai, where God's presence was revealed amid thunder, lightning, and a thick cloud (Exodus 19:16). Just as these signs at Sinai demonstrated the holiness and power of God, their presence in John's vision underscores His sovereignty over all creation.

The voices proceeding from the throne likely represent the divine decrees and proclamations of God's will. Throughout Scripture, God's voice is described as powerful and commanding, shaking the heavens and the earth (Psalm 29:3–9). The voices in this vision remind us that all things in heaven and earth are subject to His word.

The seven lamps of fire burning before the throne symbolize the seven Spirits of God—a representation of the fullness and perfection of the Holy Spirit (Revelation 1:4, 3:1). This imagery is connected to Isaiah 11:2, where the Spirit of the Lord is described in sevenfold attributes: the Spirit of wisdom, understanding, counsel, might, knowledge, fear of the Lord, and divine presence. The lamps serve as a reminder that the Holy Spirit is ever-present before God's throne, illuminating His will and empowering His people.

Together, these elements present a picture of God's throne as a place of absolute power, perfect justice, and divine revelation. They remind us that while God is merciful, He is also a righteous judge. This vision prepares us for the unfolding of events in Revelation, where His authority and holiness will be revealed in their fullness.

OLD TESTAMENT FORESHADOWS REVELATION:

And it came to pass on the third day in the morning, that there were thunders and lightnings, and a thick cloud upon the mountain, and the voice of the trumpet exceedingly loud; so that all the people that were in the camp trembled. And Moses brought forth the people out of the camp to meet with God; and they stood at the foot of the mountain. And Mount Sinai was completely in smoke, because the LORD descended upon it in fire: and the smoke thereof ascended as the smoke of a furnace, and the whole mountain quaked greatly. (Exodus 19:16–18)

This scene parallels the lightnings, thunderings, and fire proceeding from God's throne in Revelation. Both passages portray God's awesome, fearsome presence—one on earth (Mount Sinai), the other in heaven (the throne).

THE REVELATION OF JESUS CHRIST REVEALS:

4:6 And before the throne there was a sea of glass like unto crystal: and in the midst of the throne, and round about the throne, were four beasts full of eyes before and behind.

John's description of the sea of glass before the throne presents an image of unparalleled clarity and calmness. The sea, often representing chaos and turmoil in Scripture, now appears perfectly still and crystalline, symbolizing God's unshakable peace, purity, and divine order. This imagery reflects Exodus 24:10, where Moses and the elders of Israel saw under God's feet a pavement like sapphire stone, as clear as the heavens. It is also reminiscent of Ezekiel 1:22, where the prophet describes a firmament like an awe-inspiring crystal stretched over the heads of the cherubim. The sea of glass, then, serves as a visual metaphor for the transcendent holiness of God's throne room, a place untouched by the corruption of the fallen world.

The four living creatures, or "beasts," surrounding the throne are angelic beings of immense power and significance. Their description—full of eyes before and behind—symbolizes divine omniscience and vigilance. These creatures resemble the cherubim of Ezekiel 1:5–14 and the seraphim of Isaiah 6:1–3, beings that continually minister in God's presence and declare His holiness. Their many eyes indicate an all-seeing awareness, a readiness to execute God's will, and an unwavering focus on His glory.

These creatures play a vital role in heavenly worship, crying out day and night in reverence to God. Their presence highlights the ceaseless adoration of God in heaven, reinforcing the reality that all creation exists to glorify Him. They also remind us that in the throne room of God, there is no ignorance or blindness—everything is seen, known, and governed by divine wisdom.

The sea of glass and the four living creatures together create a striking contrast: the former represents perfect peace, while the latter embody divine energy and purpose. This passage gives believers a glimpse into the majesty of heaven, where God reigns supreme, unshaken and exalted above all things.

OLD TESTAMENT FORESHADOWS REVELATION:

And the likeness of the firmament upon the heads of the living creatures was as the color of the awesome crystal, stretched forth over their heads above. (Ezekiel 1:22)

This corresponds to the "sea of glass like unto crystal"—a clear, awe-inspiring expanse before God's throne, reflecting His purity, majesty, and separation from creation.

THE REVELATION OF JESUS CHRIST REVEALS:

4:7 And the first beast was like a lion, and the second beast like a calf, and third beast had a face as a man, and the fourth beast was like a flying eagle.

These four living creatures symbolize different aspects of God's divine nature and Christ's ministry. They parallel the four faces of the cherubim in Ezekiel 1:10 and reflect the fourfold depiction of Christ in the gospels.

The gospels present a fourfold portrait of Christ, each revealing a unique aspect of His identity and mission:

- King—The lion represents Christ as King (Matthew), emphasizing His majesty and rule.
- Suffering Servant—The calf (ox) symbolizes Christ as the Suffering Servant (Mark), highlighting His sacrifice and service.
- Son of Man—The man points to Christ's humanity (Luke), showcasing His connection to mankind.
- Son of God—The eagle signifies Christ's divine nature (John), soaring above all in power and eternity.

These creatures not only worship before the throne but also represent the fullness of Christ's role as King, Servant, Man, and God. Their presence emphasizes the completeness of God's plan for redemption and His sovereignty over all creation.

OLD TESTAMENT FORESHADOWS REVELATION:

As for the likeness of their faces, they four had the face of a man, and the face of a lion, on the right side: and they four had the face of an ox on the left side; they four also had the face of an eagle. (Ezekiel 1:10)

This passage describes the four-faced cherubim in Ezekiel's vision, which closely aligns with the four living creatures John sees in Revelation. Both visions emphasize God's majesty, divine authority, and the completeness of His rule—represented through these symbolic creatures. The lion represents power and kingship, the ox signifies service and sacrifice, the man reflects wisdom and relationship, and the eagle symbolizes swiftness and divinity. These images reveal the omnipotence and multifaceted nature of God's presence.

THE REVELATION OF JESUS CHRIST REVEALS:

[4:8] And the four beasts had each of them six wings about him; and they were full of eyes within: and they rest not day and night, saying, Holy, holy, holy, LORD God Almighty, which was, and is, and is to come!

This verse presents an awe-inspiring image of unceasing heavenly worship and the divine attributes of God. The four living creatures—already described as having distinct forms resembling a lion, an ox, a man, and an eagle—are now depicted with six wings, mirroring the seraphim in Isaiah 6:2–3, who also proclaim God's holiness. The six wings symbolize divine speed and readiness to act upon God's will, while their many eyes reflect God's omniscience, seeing all things past, present, and future.

Their unceasing proclamation—"Holy, holy, holy, LORD God Almighty"—is a direct parallel to Isaiah's vision of God's throne, where the seraphim cry out the same words (Isaiah 6:3). The threefold declaration of holiness signifies the absolute purity, perfect, and separateness of God. It also alludes to the Triune nature of God—Father, Son, and Holy Spirit. This repetition emphasizes His unchanging nature and eternal authority over creation.

The title "LORD God Almighty" exalts God's omnipotence, affirming His sovereign control over all things. The phrase "which was, and is, and is to come" reinforces His eternal existence, echoing Revelation 1:8, where Christ is declared the Alpha and Omega. This emphasizes that God is beyond time, reigning from eternity past to eternity future.

The ceaseless worship of the four living creatures underscores the constant adoration and reverence that God receives in heaven. Unlike earthly worship, which is limited by time and human weakness, heavenly worship is eternal, unhindered, and fully devoted. Their presence around the throne reminds us that God is the center of all existence, and everything in creation exists to glorify Him.

This vision calls believers to recognize the holiness and sovereignty of God, urging us to live in reverence and awe. It also reminds us that true worship is not just an action but a state of being, where our hearts, like these heavenly creatures, are continually focused on God's majesty and glory.

OLD TESTAMENT FORESHADOWS REVELATION:

Above it stood the seraphims: each one had six wings; with two he covered his face, and with two he covered his feet, and with two he did fly. And one cried unto another, and said, Holy, holy, holy, is the LORD of hosts: the whole earth is full of His glory. (Isaiah 6:2–3)

Both passages describe heavenly beings with six wings, continually declaring the holiness of God. The threefold repetition of "holy, holy, holy" in both verses emphasizes God's absolute purity, transcendence, and divine perfection. Additionally, both accounts place these angelic beings in direct proximity to God's throne, reinforcing the continuity of worship between the Old and New Testament revelations.

THE REVELATION OF JESUS CHRIST REVEALS:

[4:9] And when those beasts give glory and honor and thanks to Him that sat on the throne, who lives forever and ever.

The four living creatures, continuously praising God, lead the heavenly host in worship. Their expressions of glory, honor, and thanks reflect their complete awareness of God's infinite majesty and eternal nature. Their worship is an acknowledgment of God's supreme authority, a declaration that He alone is worthy of all adoration.

The phrase "who lives forever and ever" affirms God's eternal existence, a truth emphasized throughout Scripture (Psalm 90:2; Daniel 7:9). Unlike created beings, whose existence is bound by time, God is unchanging, beyond time, and everlasting. The worship of these creatures reveals a profound truth—true adoration springs from recognizing God's sovereignty and eternity.

This moment of worship sets the stage for the twenty-four elders' response in the next verses, where they cast their crowns before the throne. The unceasing worship in heaven serves as a model for believers, reminding us that our lives, too, should be a continual offering of praise to the One who reigns forever.

OLD TESTAMENT FORESHADOWS REVELATION:

And at the end of the days I Nebuchadnezzar lifted up my eyes unto heaven, and my understanding returned unto me, and I blessed the Most High, and I praised and honored Him that lives forever, whose dominion is an everlasting dominion, and His Kingdom is from generation to generation. (Daniel 4:34)

This verse echoes the eternal reign of God, acknowledging His sovereignty, just as the four living creatures in Revelation give glory, honor, and thanks to the One who lives forever and ever. Both passages emphasize that worship is directed toward the eternal and unchanging nature of God, who rules over all creation.

THE REVELATION OF JESUS CHRIST REVEALS:

[4:10] The four and twenty elders fall down before Him that sat on the throne, and worship Him that lives forever and ever, and cast their crowns before the throne, saying.

This verse presents a profound act of heavenly worship—the twenty-four elders, representing the redeemed from both the Old and New Covenants, falling before God and casting their crowns at His feet. Their response signifies humility, reverence, and acknowledgment that all glory belongs to God alone.

The crowns they cast are victor's crowns (stephanos), rewards given for faithful service (2 Timothy 4:8; James 1:12). However, rather than holding onto them as symbols of personal achievement, the elders surrender them to the One truly worthy of all honor. This act symbolizes:

- God as the true source of all victories—No reward is obtained apart from His grace and power.
- Selfless worship—In heaven, there is no comparison or pride, only complete devotion to God.

- A declaration of divine sovereignty—All authority and dominion belong to Him alone.

Their prostration before the throne mirrors the posture of deep submission and awe, seen throughout Scripture (Psalm 95:6; Philippians 2:10). The emphasis on God's eternal nature ("who lives forever and ever") reinforces His unmatched supremacy—He alone is the Alpha and Omega, the Beginning and the End.

This verse paints a stunning image of heaven's worship, reminding believers that all we accomplish is by God's grace. Our ultimate response should be to lay everything at His feet, offering Him our lives in gratitude and devotion.

OLD TESTAMENT FORESHADOWS REVELATION:

Yours, O LORD, is the greatness, and the power, and the victory, and the majesty: for all that is in the heaven and in the earth is Yours; Yours is the Kingdom, O LORD, and You are exalted as head above all. (1 Chronicles 29:11)

This verse aligns with the elders' act of casting their crowns, showing that all honor and authority ultimately belong to God alone. The twenty-four elders, representing the redeemed, acknowledge this truth by surrendering their crowns before the throne in total humility and worship.

THE REVELATION OF JESUS CHRIST REVEALS:

4:11 You are worthy, O Lord, to receive glory and honor and power: for You have created all things, and for Your pleasure they are and were created.

This verse is the grand conclusion of the celestial worship scene, where the twenty-four elders—representing the redeemed—fall before God's throne and cast their crowns in surrender and adoration. Their proclamation affirms that God alone is worthy to receive all glory, honor, and power because He is the Creator of all things.

The word "worthy" (Greek: *axios*) denotes absolute worthiness and authority. The elders recognize that no one else—not angels, not mankind, not any other being—deserves worship like the One who created all things. This echoes Psalm 96:4–5:

For the LORD is great and greatly to be praised: He is to be feared above all gods. For all the gods of the nations are idols: but the LORD made the heavens. (Psalm 96:4–5)

Unlike the false gods of the world, the God of Revelation is the true Creator. His creation alone testifies to His divine sovereignty.

The phrase "for Your pleasure they are and were created" reveals a foundational truth: everything in existence was made for God's will and delight.

Creation was not an accident but an act of divine purpose and intentionality. This aligns with Colossians 1:16, where Paul writes:

> For by Him were all things created, that are in heaven, and that are in earth, visible and invisible, whether they be thrones, or dominions, or principalities, or powers: all things were created by Him, for Him. (Colossians 1:16)

Every aspect of existence—from the smallest atom to the vast galaxies—was made for God's glory. The elders casting their crowns signify a willing surrender to God's purpose, acknowledging that all achievements, authority, and rewards belong to Him.

This verse serves as a model of worship for believers. Just as the elders in heaven surrender their crowns, we too are called to surrender our lives in reverence to our Creator. Every breath, every act of obedience, and every moment of praise is an offering to the One who made us for His purpose.

Thus, Revelation 4:11 is a powerful reminder that God alone is the center of existence, and our highest calling is to glorify Him forever.

OLD TESTAMENT FORESHADOWS REVELATION:

> Let them praise the name of the LORD: for He commanded, and they were created. He has also established them forever and ever; He has made a decree which shall not pass. (Psalm 148:5–6)

> Let them praise the name of the LORD: for He commanded, and they were created. He has also established them forever and ever; He has made a decree which shall not pass. (Isaiah 43:7)

This passage aligns closely with Revelation 4:11 in several ways: It acknowledges God as the Creator of all things. It affirms that creation exists by His command. It highlights God's eternal authority and sovereignty, just as Revelation 4:11 declares that all things were created for His pleasure. Additionally, Isaiah 43:7 echoes this theme. Isaiah reinforces that creation exists for God's glory and pleasure, which is the central message of Revelation 4:11.

SUMMARY OF REVELATION 4:2–11

Revelation chapter 4 marks a pivotal moment in John's vision, shifting the focus from the Church on earth to the throne room in heaven. The Church Age has ended, and John is transported "in the Spirit" to witness the heavenly realm where God reigns in glory. This transition represents the prophetic fulfillment of the Rapture, placing the redeemed in God's presence before the Tribulation unfolds on earth (Revelation 4:1).

John sees God's throne, surrounded by lightnings, thunderings, and voices, demonstrating His power and impending judgment. Before the throne, a sea of glass reflects divine peace (Revelation 4:2–5), while the four living creatures continuously worship, declaring His holiness (Revelation 4:6–8). Around them, the twenty-four elders, symbolizing the redeemed, fall in worship and cast their crowns before God, acknowledging that all glory belongs to Him alone (Revelation 4:4, 9–11).

This scene confirms that the Church is in heaven during the seven-year Tribulation, witnessing the unfolding of God's wrath upon a rebellious world. But our time in heaven is not the end of the story. After seven years, we return *with* Christ to the earth at His Second Coming (Revelation 19), where He establishes His Millennial Kingdom—a reign that lasts one-thousand years. Only after this Kingdom Age will eternity begin in the new heaven and new earth.

KEY TAKEAWAYS

- The Church in heaven—The Rapture removes believers before the Tribulation, placing them in God's presence.
- The throne of God—A display of divine sovereignty, judgment, and unshakable authority.
- The four living creatures—Angelic beings declare God's holiness, representing His watchful governance over creation.
- The twenty-four elders casting crowns—Worship is central in heaven, as all rewards and victories belong to God.
- Christ's worthiness—Revelation 4 concludes with an exaltation of God as the Creator and the rightful ruler of all things.

This chapter presents a glimpse of heaven's glory and the destiny of the redeemed, not as a final resting place, but as a prelude to Christ's return and reign on earth. Our future is not only in heaven but also on the earth restored under Christ's rule, fulfilling God's ultimate plan for His Creation.

Chapter 6

Revelation 5:
The Seven-Sealed Book

THE SEALED SCROLL AND THE FATE OF CREATION—
Revelation chapter 5 stands as one of the most powerful chapters in the entire
Book of Revelation, unveiling a profound moment in God's redemptive plan. This
chapter presents a scene of divine majesty, as John witnesses the continuation of
his vision from Revelation chapter 4. Having described the glory of God's throne
and the worship surrounding His throne, John now turns his attention to a
mysterious scroll—sealed with seven seals—held in the right hand of the One
seated upon the throne.

This chapter introduces a search for someone worthy to open the book—a
task no one in heaven, on earth, or under the earth could fulfill—until the Lion of
the tribe of Judah, the Root of David, is revealed. This moment marks the
beginning of God's final judgments, the restoration of all things, and the unfolding
of redemption for creation. It sets the stage for the rest of Revelation's prophecies.

John's vision in this chapter is deeply rooted in Old Testament imagery,
particularly that of the kinsman-redeemer in Jewish law. Just as Boaz redeemed
Ruth and her inheritance (Ruth 4:1–10), Christ, as our Kinsman-Redeemer, has
the right to reclaim what was lost—the earth itself, which fell under the curse of
sin. The sealed scroll represents the title deed to Creation, and only Christ, through
His sacrifice, is worthy to open it.

As we delve into this chapter, we gain a greater understanding of Christ's supreme authority, the significance of His redemptive work, and the destiny of the world as God's plan unfolds.

KINSMAN REDEEMERS

Before diving into the specific verses of Revelation 5, we must first understand the biblical concept of a kinsman-redeemer, a role that directly parallels Christ's work of redemption.

Levitical Law and Redemption

In the Levitical law given to Moses, God made provisions for redeeming individuals, property, and inheritance when a person had fallen into debt. This law covered three key areas:

1. **A Slave**—If someone became a slave to pay off debt, a kinsman-redeemer had the right to purchase their freedom (Leviticus 25:47–49).

2. **A Widow and Her Land**—If a husband died, his closest male relative (a kinsman) could redeem the widow and restore her inheritance (Deuteronomy 25:5–10).

3. **Land**—If a family's land was lost due to debt, a kinsman-redeemer could purchase it back (Leviticus 25:25).

For one to be a kinsman-redeemer, they had to meet three qualifications:

1. **Be related**—Only a family member had the right to redeem.
2. **Be willing**—Redemption was a choice, not an obligation.
3. **Be able**—The redeemer had to have the resources to pay the price.

These laws were not just practical but prophetic, pointing to Christ, who would redeem humanity and Creation itself.

Jeremiah's Redemption of Land

Jeremiah 32 provides a real-life example of kinsman redemption. As Jerusalem was about to fall to the Babylonians, God instructed Jeremiah to purchase land from his cousin, Hanameel, despite its impending occupation.

> So Hanameel my uncle's son came to me in the court of the prison according to the word of the LORD, and said unto me, 'Buy my field, I pray you, that is in Anathoth, which is in the country of Benjamin: for the right of inheritance is yours, and the redemption is yours; buy it for yourself.' Then I knew that this was the word of the LORD. (Jeremiah 32:8)

Jeremiah, being related, willing, and able, paid the redemption price of seventeen shekels of silver, fulfilling the role of a kinsman-redeemer.

Boaz: A Picture of Christ

Another well-known kinsman-redeemer was Boaz, who redeemed Ruth and secured Naomi's inheritance.

> And the kinsman said, 'I cannot redeem it for myself, lest I mar my own inheritance: Redeem you my right to yourself; for I cannot redeem it.' (Ruth 4:6)

Boaz then legally redeemed the land and took Ruth as his wife, securing her future and continuing the lineage that would lead to Christ. Boaz met all three requirements: He was related, willing, and able. His actions foreshadow Jesus, who would redeem not just one family, but all of creation.

The scent of parchment and candle wax filled the library as Irene turned the pages of her study notes. I, scribbling furiously in my leather journal, glanced up and saw her eyes alight with curiosity.

"Ann, I know the basics of Ruth's story, but refresh my memory—how does it tie into redemption?"

"Oh, it's one of the most beautiful redemption stories in Scripture. Naomi's husband dies, leaving her and her two sons in Moab. The sons marry Moabite women, Ruth and Orpah, but then they die too, leaving all three widows."

"Right. And Naomi decides to return to Bethlehem?"

"Exactly. She tells Ruth and Orpah to go back to their families. Orpah does, but Ruth clings to Naomi, saying, 'Your people shall be my people, and your God my God.'"

"And that's how Ruth ends up meeting Boaz?"

"Yes. Boaz is a relative of Naomi's late husband, and as a kinsman-redeemer, he has the right to redeem her land and marry Ruth to preserve the family line."

"That's incredible. So the whole book is really a picture of Christ and His Bride."

"Exactly! Just as Boaz was related, willing, and able to redeem Ruth, Jesus is our ultimate Kinsman-Redeemer, redeeming us from sin."

Irene leaned back, contemplating the significance. "That makes this whole concept of the sealed book in Revelation 5 even more profound."

I nodded. "It does. And I'm hoping this manuscript captures that depth. I want it to be not only something that educates but also moves people."

Irene smiled. "You're onto something, Ann. Just make sure to keep it accessible. Revelation is heavy, but if people can see the love story of redemption in it, they'll be drawn in."

I tapped my pen against the journal. "Then that's what I'll do."

ADAM'S FALL AND THE UNFOLDING OF REDEMPTION

God originally gave Adam authority over the earth—a divine lease, if you will, for 6,000 years. However, through deception in the garden of Eden (Genesis 3), Adam effectively transferred his authority to Satan, plunging Creation under the curse of sin and death. From that moment, Satan became the "prince of this world" (John 12:31), holding claim over the kingdoms of the earth.

Jesus's temptation in the wilderness further reveals this reality:

> Then the devil, taking Him up on a high mountain, showed Him all the kingdoms of the world in a moment of time. And the devil said to Him, 'All this authority I will give You, and their glory; for this has been delivered to me, and I give it to whomever I wish.' (Luke 4:5–6)

Satan, a deceiver and usurper, claims dominion over what was originally entrusted to humanity. Yet Scripture affirms that the earth still belongs to God:

> The earth is the LORD's and the fullness thereof; the world, and they that dwell therein. (Psalm 24:1)

Satan's authority is temporary. He is an interloper—one who encroaches on another's rights. He is also a squatter, unlawfully occupying what is not his. But he refuses to acknowledge the true Owner: God.

Now, in Revelation 5, we see a pivotal moment—God holds a sealed scroll, a document of redemption. Before anything can move forward in God's divine plan, someone must be found worthy to break the seals and reclaim the earth.

Just as Boaz redeemed Ruth, and Jeremiah redeemed his cousin's land, someone must step forward to legally redeem the earth and overthrow Satan's rule. That someone is Jesus Christ—the only One who is related to us (through the Incarnation—born of Mary by the power of the Holy Spirit), willing to redeem us (through His sacrifice), and able to do so (through His divine authority).

Revelation 5 presents the moment where the search for a worthy redeemer reaches its climax. Heaven holds its breath as John weeps—until the Lion of Judah, the Lamb who was slain, steps forward.

The battle for dominion over the earth is not over. But the rightful King is about to reclaim what is His.

———◆◆◆———

The library was quieter than usual, the late afternoon sun casting long streaks of gold across the wooden floor. I flipped through my notes and adjusted my glasses, while Irene sat back, her expression thoughtful.

"Ann, I need you to clarify something for me. You've mentioned this 6,000-year lease before—but has it really been 6,000 years since Adam? How do we calculate that?"

Nodding. "Great question. The first 4,000 years of human history are covered in the Old Testament—from Adam to Christ. Then Jesus arrives and literally splits time into two eras: BC and AD. That adds another 2,000 years from His time until now."

"Right, but how can we be sure that Jesus lived exactly 2,000 years ago?"

"Some historians and scholars have proposed that Jesus was born on September 11, 3 BC, aligning with the Jewish Feast of Trumpets (Yom Teruah). According to Jewish custom, a man began his public ministry at 30 years old, and it is widely held that Jesus was crucified at approximately 33½ years old, placing His death around 30 AD. If this timeline is correct, we are nearing the 2,000-year mark since He completed His redemptive work on the Cross."

Irene, referencing Hosea 6:2. "So if a day is like a thousand years to the LORD, and we're now at the end of the second 'day,' wouldn't that mean the third day—'the millennial reign'—is right around the corner?"

"Exactly! Hosea 6:2 prophesies that after two days—or 2,000 years—the LORD will revive Israel and restore all things. We are right on schedule for that prophecy to unfold."

"And if we add 2,000 years to 30 AD, we land at 2030." Irene paused, her eyes widening. "That's only a few years away!"

"Yes. No one knows the day or hour, but we do know that God works in patterns. The 6,000-year lease is nearly up, which means Satan's rule on earth is coming to an end. The next prophetic event is Christ's return *for* His Church at the Rapture—before He later returns to establish His Kingdom."

"That would also explain why everything in the world is accelerating—wars, deception, immorality. It's all leading to something."

"Exactly. The devil knows his time is almost up, and he's desperate. But here's the good news—just like God had a plan in the days of Noah, just like He had a plan to send Jesus at the perfect time, He has a plan to defeat Satan and redeem the earth. That's what we're about to see unfold in Revelation 5."

Irene exhaled slowly, gripping her Bible. "This just got a lot more real. If we're truly approaching the end of the 6,000 years, then everything happening in the world right now suddenly makes perfect sense."

Irene continued. "But if we really want to understand where we are on God's prophetic calendar, how do we even begin? It all feels so complicated."

"That's actually why I wrote *The Vanishing: The Day Will Be Like Any Other—Until the Rapture Silences the World*. It picks up where *The Trumpet* leaves off—moving from America's prophetic destiny into the divine timeline of the Rapture."

"So you're saying there's a pattern? A timeline we can actually follow?"

"Yes. In the book, I explore how God's calendar—through the feasts, the Shemitah cycles, and prophetic signs—has laid out patterns and harbingers that have played out all throughout history. Each one points more urgently to Christ's return *for* His Church."

"Do you really think we're that close?"

"I believe we are. I ask the hard questions: Are we living in the final moments before the Rapture? Could 2028/2029 fulfill some of the Bible's most urgent prophecies?"

"But Jesus said we wouldn't know the day or the hour . . ."

"He did—but He also said we should watch, discern, and recognize the season. What if God has already given us all the clues—through His feasts, His calendar, and the rhythm of the Shemitah—to know when His return is near?"

Irene leaning in. "That sounds fascinating. So you're saying that God's calendar—not just world events—actually gives us a framework for when things will unfold?"

"Yes. The Bible is full of patterns, and God's appointed times are more precise than most people realize. The book explores how the Shemitah years align with past biblical events and major world shifts, pointing toward a major prophetic fulfillment in the coming years. It's not about setting dates—it's about recognizing that God's timeline is unfolding right in front of us."

Nodding. "Well, count me in. I want to know exactly where we are in God's timeline."

—————◆◆◆—————

THE LAW OF REDEMPTION AND THE COMING JUDGMENT

From the beginning, God established a divine judicial system governing the land, inheritance, and redemption. When the Israelites entered the Promised Land, God set laws in place and ensured land ownership would always revert to its original family. This system, dictated by God's judicial mind, was a foreshadowing of a much greater redemption—the reclaiming of the earth itself.

The Law of the Jubilee

Under Jewish law, as given to Moses, the land could never be sold permanently because it belonged to God (Leviticus 25:23). The Year of Jubilee occurred every 50 years, serving as a divine reset—ensuring that land, property, and inheritance were returned to their rightful owners. It marked both the completion of a 49-year cycle (seven sets of seven years) and a year of rest and restoration before the next cycle began, emphasizing God's provision and sovereignty over the land.

> The land shall not be sold permanently, for the land is Mine; for you are strangers and sojourners with Me. (Leviticus 25:23)

This legal principle made it clear: God owns everything, including the land and its people. Israel was simply entrusted as stewards of His creation. But when sin entered the world, that stewardship was compromised. Adam relinquished his authority, and Satan took over as an illegal ruler—a squatter refusing to acknowledge the true Owner.

What happened during the Jubilee Year?

1. **Land Restoration**—On the first day of the 50th year, all land that had been sold reverted back to its original owners or their families (Leviticus 25:10).

2. **Debt Cancellation and Freedom for Slaves**—Those who had become indentured servants due to debt were released, and financial burdens were lifted, restoring people to their rightful place in society (Leviticus 25:39–41).

3. **A Year of Rest for the Land**—Like the Sabbatical Year (which occurred every seven years), the Jubilee was a year of no sowing, reaping, or harvesting. The people relied on stored provisions and naturally growing produce for food (Leviticus 25:11–12, 21–22).

4. **A Proclamation of Liberty**—On the Day of Atonement (the 10th day of the 50th year), a trumpet sounded throughout the land to announce the start of the Jubilee, signifying complete freedom and restoration (Leviticus 25:9–10).

The Day of Atonement (Yom Kippur) was an annual observance—not every seven years. It was held once a year, on the 10th day of the seventh month, Tishri 10 (Leviticus 16:29–30, 23:26–32). However, in the Jubilee Year—every 50th year—the trumpet was blown specifically on the Day of Atonement to proclaim liberty throughout the land. That particular Day of Atonement was especially significant, as it marked the beginning of the Jubilee restoration: debts were canceled, slaves were freed, and land was returned to its original owners. The Jubilee Year was more than an economic reset—it was a powerful spiritual reminder that the land, the people, and all creation ultimately belong to God. It declared His sovereignty, justice, and faithfulness in providing for His people, ensuring that no family or tribe would be left destitute forever.

Why the Earth Must Be Redeemed

Satan has held dominion over the earth since Adam's fall. He refuses to release his grip, and as a result, the entire world remains under a curse. Not just humanity, but even nature itself suffers under this curse (Romans 8:22). Before Jesus can establish His millennial reign, the earth must first be redeemed. This is the purpose of Revelation 5—the legal reclaiming of the earth by its rightful Owner. Jesus Christ is the only one qualified to take back what Adam lost.

The Coming Tribulation Judgments

Because Satan refuses to relinquish his hold over creation, Jesus must remove him by force. This is why the judgments of Revelation are necessary. God will unleash twenty-one judgments over seven years:

- Seven Seal Judgments
- Seven Trumpet Judgments
- Seven Bowl (Vial) Judgments

Each judgment is part of God's divine process to reclaim what is rightfully His. The ultimate goal is to break Satan's hold over the earth, fulfill God's promise of justice, and usher in the Kingdom of Christ on earth.

The Earth's Future: Christ's Reign and Our Role

Once the final judgment is complete, Satan will be bound in the bottomless pit, and Christ will return with His saints to rule the earth for 1,000 years.

Jesus not only redeemed us from hell, but He also redeemed us to reign with Him on earth. This is the ultimate fulfillment of God's plan—restoring the earth, removing sin, and re-establishing His Kingdom.

With this foundation, we now turn to Revelation 5:1, where John sees the sealed book—the legal document that holds the conditions for the redemption of the world. The question remains: Who is worthy to open it?

THE REVELATION OF JESUS CHRIST REVEALS:

5:1 And I saw in the right hand of Him that sat on the throne a book written within and on the backside, sealed with seven seals.

As the scene in heaven continues from Revelation 4, John now beholds a striking image—God seated on the throne, holding a book (or scroll) in His right hand. This moment introduces the most pivotal element in the unfolding of the end times: the seven-sealed book (scroll), which represents the divine title deed and legal document of redemption and judgment.

The fact that the scroll is in God's right hand is significant. In Scripture, the right hand symbolizes power, authority, and dominion (Psalm 110:1; Isaiah 41:10). The placement of the scroll in God's hand indicates that He alone holds the authority over history, judgment, and the fate of creation. It is a divine decree that no one can alter apart from the One who is worthy.

"A book written within and on the backside." The Greek word *biblion* (translated as "book") more accurately describes a scroll, a common format for important legal documents in biblical times. The scroll is written on both sides, which was unusual, as most scrolls contained writing only on one side. This detail conveys a few key meanings:

1. **The Fullness of God's Plan**—The fact that it is completely written on both sides suggests that nothing can be added to it or taken away. God's sovereign plan is complete.

2. **A Legal Contract or Title Deed**—In the ancient world, legal contracts, such as land deeds or wills, were sometimes written on the inside with a summary on the outside. This imagery aligns with Jeremiah 32:6–15, where a sealed deed is used in a land redemption transaction. Similarly, this scroll represents the title deed to the earth—which was lost when Adam forfeited dominion (Genesis 3) and which only Christ can reclaim.

3. **The Decrees of Judgment**—The contents of the scroll likely contain the decrees of God's final judgment on the world, as the opening of each seal in Revelation 6 triggers catastrophic events. The scroll contains the destiny of the world, the unfolding of history, and the ultimate fulfillment of God's purposes.

"Sealed with seven seals." The scroll is sealed with seven seals, emphasizing divine completeness and perfection—seven being the number of completion in biblical numerology. Seals in ancient times were used to:

-   Secure the contents—No one could break the seals except an authorized person.
-   Authenticate a legal document—Only the rightful owner or a legally designated redeemer could open a sealed contract.

- Prevent tampering—The fact that the scroll is completely sealed implies that its judgments and decrees cannot be altered by man.

These seven seals will be broken one by one in Revelation 6, unleashing the events of the Tribulation—God's judgments upon the earth.

- The Significance of This Scroll—This is no ordinary book. It is the divine title deed to the world, the document outlining both God's final judgment on evil and His plan for the restoration of all things through Christ. No one in heaven or earth is worthy to open it—except for the Lamb of God (Revelation 5:5–7).
- The Prophetic Connection—This scroll ties into Daniel 12:4, 9, where the prophet Daniel was told to seal up the vision until the end of time. Now, in Revelation, that sealed vision is about to be revealed. What was hidden in Daniel is now being disclosed in Revelation.

This verse sets the stage for one of the most powerful moments in Scripture: the search for the only One who is worthy to open the book—the Lion of Judah, the Lamb who was slain (Revelation 5:5–6).

OLD TESTAMENT FORESHADOWS REVELATION:

And when I looked, behold, a hand was sent unto me; and, lo, a scroll of a book was therein; And He spread it before me; and it was written within and without: and there was written therein lamentations, and mourning, and woe. (Ezekiel 2:9–10)

Both Ezekiel and John see a scroll (or book) that is written on both sides—a rare detail emphasizing its completeness and divine significance. In Ezekiel, the scroll contains lamentations, mourning, and woe, signifying judgment—just as the breaking of the seals in Revelation unleashes God's judgments upon the earth. Like in Revelation, Ezekiel's scroll represents God's decrees that are not yet fully revealed, emphasizing that God's plan is sealed until the appointed time.

This Old Testament passage confirms that the scroll in Revelation 5:1 is both a record of judgment and the divine plan for redemption, sealed until the appointed time when Christ alone is worthy to open it.

THE REVELATION OF JESUS CHRIST REVEALS:

5:2 And I saw a strong angel proclaiming with a loud voice, Who is worthy to open the book, and to loose the seals thereof?

In Revelation 5:2, John sees a strong angel making a proclamation with a loud voice—a divine call echoing across the heavens, the earth, and even the realm of the dead. The question he asks is of utmost significance: "Who is worthy to open the book, and to loose the seals thereof?"

This verse marks a crucial moment in the unfolding of God's redemptive plan. The scroll in the right hand of God represents the title deed to the earth and the divine plan for judgment and restoration. However, before the plan can be executed, a kinsman-redeemer must be found—one who meets the divine qualifications to legally reclaim what was lost.

This diligent and desperate search mirrors two key Old Testament precedents, both involving the redemption of land and inheritance: (1) Jeremiah and the sealed scroll (Jeremiah 32:6–15). Just as Jeremiah was the rightful redeemer for his family's land, a redeemer must be found to reclaim the earth in Revelation 5. (2) Boaz, Ruth, and the kinsman-redeemer (Ruth 4:1–10). Boaz serves as a foreshadowing of Christ—who alone can redeem the earth and its inhabitants.

The angel's proclamation is not just a call for someone to act—it is a challenge. It underscores the incomparable worthiness required to take the scroll and execute God's divine justice.

- This is not merely about opening a book.
- It is about reclaiming the earth from the power of sin and Satan.
- It is about restoring creation to its rightful Owner—God.

At this moment, all of creation awaits an answer: Is there anyone worthy?

The coming verses will reveal that only One can answer this call—Jesus Christ, the Lion of Judah and the Lamb who was slain.

OLD TESTAMENT FORESHADOWS REVELATION:

And the vision of all is become unto you as the words of a book that is sealed, which men deliver to one that is learned, saying, Read this, I pray you: and he says, I cannot; for it is sealed. And the book is delivered to him that is not learned, saying, Read this, I pray you: and he says, I am not learned. (Isaiah 29:11–12)

In both passages there is a sealed book. The question is who is worthy or able to open or read it. The Isaiah passage emphasizes inaccessibility of divine knowledge without revelation, while Revelation highlights that only Christ is worthy to break the seals and reveal God's final plan.

THE REVELATION OF JESUS CHRIST REVEALS:

5:3 And no man in heaven, nor in earth, neither under the earth, was able to open the book, neither to look thereon.

This verse underscores the absolute inability of any created being—whether in heaven, on earth, or under the earth—to open the sealed book in God's hand.

The weight of this moment is profound, as the book represents the title deed to creation and the unfolding of God's redemptive and judicial plan for the world.

A comprehensive search is conducted throughout the created order:

- In Heaven—No angel, saint, or heavenly being is found worthy. Not even the most righteous figures of biblical history—Abraham, Moses, Elijah, or even John himself—can open it.
- On Earth—No living human has the qualifications. No king, prophet, or priest possess the authority.
- Under the Earth—Even in the realm of the dead, no one is found capable. This excludes all human souls who have passed on, as well as fallen angels and demons.

Despite the greatness of angelic beings and the faithfulness of the saints, not a single created being is worthy to take the book or even look inside it—emphasizing the immense holiness and divine authority required.

Why is no one worthy? The reason no one can open the book is that this is a matter of redemption, not mere power. The scroll represents the legal right to reclaim creation. Since Adam forfeited dominion to Satan (Gensis 3), only a kinsman-redeemer—one who is both fully human and divinely worthy—can reclaim it. Sin has disqualified all of creation. Humanity, angels, and all living things are under the curse of sin. No one can stand before God and claim the authority to redeem the world.

This verse builds tension—creation is trapped in the curse, and no one can break its chains. Without someone worthy to open the book, there is no hope for redemption, no restoration, and no future beyond sin's dominion.

Revelation 5:3 sets the stage for one of the most triumphant moments in Scripture—the revelation of the Lamb of God, the only One worthy to redeem the earth and fulfill God's plan.

OLD TESTAMENT FORESHADOWS REVELATION:

And I sought for a man among them, that should make up the hedge, and stand in the gap before Me for the land, that I should not destroy it: but I found none. (Ezekiel 22:30)

In Revelation 5:3, no one is found worthy to open the scroll. In Ezekiel 22:30, God searches for someone to intercede for Israel but finds none. Both passages emphasize the inability of man to meet divine requirements. In both cases, the absence of a worthy individual creates a crisis—in Ezekiel, it results in judgment; in Revelation, it leaves the earth seemingly without hope of redemption. Though Ezekiel finds no man, the ultimate answer comes through Jesus Christ, who in

Revelation 5:5 is revealed as the One worthy to open the scroll—just as He is the ultimate intercessor who stands in the gap for humanity.

Thus, Ezekiel 22:30 serves as a foreshadowing of Revelation 5:3, both emphasizing the failure of humanity and the necessity of divine intervention.

THE REVELATION OF JESUS CHRIST REVEALS:

5:4 And I wept much, because no man was found worthy to open and to read the book, neither to look thereon.

John's reaction to the unworthiness of all created beings to open the sealed book is one of deep sorrow. His weeping reflects the gravity of the moment—if no one is found worthy, the redemption of creation cannot proceed. The sealed book represents the title deed to the earth, which was forfeited through sin. If no redeemer steps forward, God's plan of restoration remains unfulfilled, and judgment and renewal cannot take place.

John's distress underscores the desperate need for a kinsman-redeemer, one who is worthy to break the seals and reclaim what was lost. His weeping is not merely an emotional reaction but a realization of the cosmic implications— without a redeemer, the promises of God remain unfulfilled, and creation remains in bondage to sin and corruption.

But John's weeping does not last. This moment of despair is necessary to emphasize the magnitude of the One who will step forward. Just as in biblical history, where redemption seemed impossible until God provided a way— whether through Boaz redeeming Ruth, Jeremiah purchasing land in Israel, or Christ's atoning sacrifice—so too will a worthy Redeemer emerge in Revelation 5. The stage is set for the triumphant unveiling of the Lamb who was slain, the only One worthy to open the book and reclaim what rightfully belongs to God.

OLD TESTAMENT FORESHADOWS REVELATION:

Oh that my head were waters, and my eyes a fountain of tears, that I might weep day and night for the slain of the daughter of my people! (Jeremiah 9:1)

A strong Old Testament parallel for Revelation 5:4 can be found in Jeremiah 9:1, where the prophet Jeremiah, often called the "weeping prophet," mourns over the fate of his people because of their sin and impending judgment.

Just as John weeps in Revelation 5:4 because no one is found worthy to open the sealed book, Jeremiah weeps over the spiritual condition and coming judgment upon Israel. Both men experience deep sorrow at the seeming hopelessness of the situation—John because redemption seems out of reach without a worthy Redeemer, and Jeremiah because of the people's rejection of God. Yet, in both cases, God's plan does not end in despair. In Revelation, the

Lamb is revealed as worthy to open the book, just as Jeremiah later sees God's promise of restoration beyond judgment (Jeremiah 31:31–34).

THE REVELATION OF JESUS CHRIST REVEALS:

5:5 And one of the elders says to me, Weep not: behold, the Lion of the tribe of Judah, the Root of David, has prevailed to open the book, and to loose the seven seals thereof.

In Revelation 5:5, John's sorrow is interrupted by one of the elders, who proclaims the glorious truth: One has been found worthy—the Lion of the tribe of Judah, the Root of David—who has prevailed to open the book and break its seven seals.

This moment marks a turning point. John, overwhelmed with despair over the seeming impossibility of redemption, is now directed to look upon the One who has conquered—Jesus Christ. The elder's words reveal two significant Messianic titles that affirm Christ's identity and His authority to reclaim the earth:

1. **The Lion of the Tribe of Judah**—This title finds its origin in Genesis 49:9–10, where Jacob prophesies over his son Judah, likening him to a lion and declaring that "the scepter shall not depart from Judah." Jesus, as a descendant of Judah, is the fulfillment of this prophecy—the ultimate ruler and King who will reign in power and justice.

2. **The Root of David**—This title is drawn from Isaiah 11:1, 10, signifying that Christ is both the offspring and the source of David's lineage. As the Root of David, He holds the divine right to rule, fulfilling God's covenant with David that his throne would be established forever (2 Samuel 7:12–16).

Throughout history, Christ has been known as the Lamb of God, meek and humble, the sacrificial atonement for the sins of the world (John 1:29). But now, in this moment of divine justice, He takes on the role of the Lion, the mighty warrior-King who comes to reclaim what is rightfully His.

Unlike before, when He stood silently before Pilate, now He roars in power. The time of mercy is giving way to righteous judgment. He is coming not as a Suffering Servant but as a conquering King, bringing vengeance upon those who rejected Him, opposed His Father, and defied His rule (2 Thessalonians 1:7–9).

The word "prevailed" (Greek: *nikao*) means "to overcome, to conquer, to be victorious." Christ defeated sin, death, and Satan through His sacrificial death and resurrection (Colossians 2:15; Hebrews 2:14–15). Because of this victory, He alone is worthy to open the scroll, reclaiming the dominion Adam forfeited and executing God's final plan for redemption and judgment.

This moment signals that the Lion is ready to act. The breaking of the seals will initiate the Tribulation judgments that will culminate in Christ's return to defeat His enemies and establish His Kingdom (Revelation 19:11–16). The days of grace are coming to an end—Jesus is no longer offering salvation but preparing to pour out His wrath upon the earth.

John's weeping is turned to hope and triumph—for the rightful King is about to take back what belongs to Him.

OLD TESTAMENT FORESHADOWS REVELATION:

Judah is a lion's whelp: from the prey, my son, you are gone up: he stooped down, he couched as a lion, and as an old lion; who shall rouse him up? The scepter shall not depart from Judah, nor a lawgiver from between his feet, until Shiloh (messianic title referring to Jesus Christ) comes; and unto Him shall the gathering of the people be. (Genesis 49:9–10)

And there shall come forth a Rod out of the stem of Jesse, and a Branch shall grow out of his roots. And in that day there shall be a Root of Jesse, which shall stand as a banner to the people; to it shall the Gentiles seek: and His rest shall be glorious. (Isaiah 11:1, 10)

Revelation 5:5 draws on Genesis 49 and Isaiah 11, linking Jesus directly to Judah (kingly authority) and David (messianic lineage)—establishing His divine right to open the scroll and unleash God's final plan.

Irene furrowed her brow as she stirred her coffee. "Okay, Ann, I understand Jesus' birth, ministry, death, burial, and resurrection. But one thing I've always wondered about—He didn't ascend to heaven right away, right? How long was He on earth after His resurrection?"

I set down my pen and nodded. "That's a great question. Jesus remained on earth for forty days after His resurrection before ascending to heaven."

Irene's eyes widened. "Forty days? That's significant, isn't it? I mean, Moses spent forty days on Mount Sinai, the Israelites wandered for forty years, and Jesus fasted in the wilderness for forty days."

I smiled. "Exactly. The number forty often represents a period of testing, preparation, or transition in Scripture. After His resurrection, Jesus didn't just vanish—He intentionally appeared to His followers, proving that He was alive and preparing them for what was to come."

Irene leaned in. "So, who actually saw Him during those forty days?"

I picked up my binder and flipped through the pages. "The New Testament records multiple appearances of the risen Christ, leaving no doubt that He truly rose from the dead."

I began listing them out:

- In or around Jerusalem:
  o To Mary Magdalene in the garden (Mark 16:9; John 20:11–18).
  o To other women who came to the tomb (Matthew 28:8–10).
  o To Peter (Luke 24:34).
  o To ten disciples in the Upper Room (Luke 24:36–43; John 20:19–25).
  o To the eleven apostles, including Thomas, a week later (Mark 16:14; John 20:26–29).
  o At the ascension, when He gave His final instructions (Mark 16:19–20; Luke 24:50–53; Acts 1:4–12).
  o To the disciples on the road to Emmaus (Mark 16:12–13; Luke 24:13–35).
- In Galilee:
  o To the disciples at the Sea of Galilee (John 21:1–24).
  o To Cephas, then by the twelve (1 Corinthians 15:5).
  o To over five hundred people at once (1 Corinthians 15:6).
  o To James, then by all the apostles (1 Corinthians 15:7).
- After His ascension:
  o To Paul on the road to Damascus (Acts 9:1–6, 22:1–10, 26:12–18; 1 Corinthians 15:8).

Irene sat back in her chair, shaking her head in amazement. "That's a lot of appearances! And to over five hundred people at once? How do people still doubt the resurrection with all this evidence?"

I nodded. "It's one of the most well-documented events in history. And notice, Jesus didn't just appear to His followers—He ate with them, let them touch Him, and even cooked breakfast for them by the sea. He wanted to make it abundantly clear that He had truly risen, body and all."

Irene tapped her fingers on the table, deep in thought. "So after forty days of proving He was alive, He ascended to heaven. And that's when the disciples were told to wait for the Holy Spirit at Pentecost, right?"

I grinned. "Exactly. Ten days later, on the Feast of Pentecost, the Holy Spirit came, just as Jesus promised. That's when the Church was born."

Irene exhaled. "Wow. It's incredible how everything connects. So much meaning packed into those forty days."

I nodded. "And it all points to one truth—Jesus lives. And because He lives, everything changes."

THE REVELATION OF JESUS CHRIST REVEALS:

5:6 And I beheld, and, lo, in the midst of the throne and of the four beasts, and in the midst of the elders, stood a Lamb as it had been slain, having seven horns and seven eyes, which are the seven Spirits of God sent forth into all the earth.

In this pivotal verse, John shifts his gaze from his weeping to behold a stunning and paradoxical sight—the Lamb as it had been slain standing in the center of the throne, among the four living creatures and the elders. This moment marks the dramatic revelation of who is worthy to open the sealed scroll.

The image of the Lamb is one of the most profound symbols in all of Scripture. Jesus Christ, the Lion of Judah from the previous verse, now appears as a Lamb, emphasizing His sacrificial role in redemption. The phrase "as it had been slain" highlights that although He bears the marks of sacrifice, He is standing, alive and victorious. This is a direct reference to His atoning death and resurrection.

John's vision places the Lamb in the midst of the throne, which is highly significant. The throne belongs to God, yet the Lamb stands at its center, revealing His divine authority and oneness with God. Jesus is not a distant or secondary figure; He shares the throne of God.

The Lamb is described as having seven horns and seven eyes, which represent His perfect attributes:

- Seven Horns—In biblical imagery, horns symbolize power and authority (Psalm 89:17; Daniel 7:24). The number seven represents completeness and perfection. Thus, the seven horns of the Lamb indicate complete, omnipotent power—Jesus possesses all authority in heaven and on earth (Matthew 28:18).
- Seven Eyes—Eyes symbolize wisdom, insight, and omniscience. The seven eyes reflect perfect knowledge and understanding, meaning that Christ sees all things and knows all things.

The seven Spirits of God are a reference to the fullness of the Holy Spirit, as seen in Isaiah 11:2, where the Spirit of the Lord is described with seven attributes—wisdom, understanding, counsel, might, knowledge, fear of the Lord, and the Spirit of the Lord itself. The Spirit is not confined to heaven but is sent forth into all the earth, demonstrating God's presence and active work throughout the world.

What makes this revelation so remarkable is the contrast between the Lion (Revelation 5:5) and the Lamb (Revelation 5:6). The world expects a conquering king, but instead, victory comes through the suffering and sacrifice of the Lamb. Jesus prevails not through brute force but through self-giving love, through the Cross.

This imagery is deeply rooted in the Old Testament:

- The Passover Lamb—Jesus is the ultimate Passover Lamb (Exodus 12:5–13; 1 Corinthians 5:7), whose blood brings deliverance.
- Isaiah 53:7—"He was led as a lamb to the slaughter." This prophecy of the Suffering Servant finds its fulfillment in Christ.
- Zechariah 4:10—A reference to the seven eyes of the LORD, which scan the earth.

Revelation 5:6 is one of the most profound Christological revelations in Scripture. It confirms the deity, authority, and sacrificial victory of Christ. He is the slain Lamb, but He is also the sovereign King. His sacrifice purchased the right to redeem the earth, and His resurrection establishes His eternal reign.

The Lion has conquered by becoming the Lamb—and through Him, redemption is assured.

OLD TESTAMENT FORESHADOWS REVELATION:

He was oppressed, and He was afflicted, yet He opened not His mouth: He is brought as a lamb to the slaughter, and as a sheep before her shearers is silent, so He opens not His mouth. (Isaiah 53:7)

For who has despised the day of small things? For they shall rejoice, and shall see the plummet in the hand of Zerubbabel with those seven; they are the eyes of the LORD, which run to and fro through the whole earth. (Zechariah 4:10)

Revelation 5:6 draws deeply from Isaiah 53:7 and Zechariah 4:10. Together, these passages present Jesus as the Lamb, slain yet triumphant, filled with perfect wisdom (seven eyes) and power (seven horns), and empowered by the fullness of the Spirit of God—sent out into all the earth.

THE REVELATION OF JESUS CHRIST REVEALS:

5:7 And He came and took the book out of the right hand of Him that sat upon the throne.

This verse marks a turning point in the heavenly vision, where Jesus Christ, the Redeemer, steps forward to take the scroll from the right hand of God. This scroll, sealed with seven seals, represents the title deed to the earth—the legal document containing the full plan of redemption and judgment. Jesus alone is worthy to take the scroll, signifying His authority to execute God's final plan for the restoration of creation.

For Jesus to be the Redeemer, He had to fulfill the qualifications of a kinsman redeemer, as outlined in the Old Testament (Leviticus 25:25; Ruth 4:4–10). Three qualifications were necessary:

1. **He Had to Be Related**—Jesus became human, taking on flesh and becoming one of us. Hebrews 2:16–17 affirms this, stating that He was made like His brethren so He could intercede on our behalf. As both the Root and Offspring of David (Revelation 22:16), He fulfills the prophecy of a Messiah who would come from Judah's lineage (Genesis 49:10).

2. **He Had to Be Willing**—The work of redemption was not forced upon Christ; He chose it willingly. In Luke 22:42, He prayed, "Father, if it is Your will, take this cup away from Me; nevertheless, not My will, but Yours, be done." This demonstrates His complete submission to the Father's will, willingly accepting the suffering of the Cross to redeem mankind.

3. **He Had to Be Able**—Not only did Jesus have the willingness, but He was also the only one qualified to redeem us. He was sinless (2 Corinthians 5:21), the perfect Passover Lamb (1 Peter 1:18–19), whose precious blood was the only acceptable price for sin. Unlike earthly transactions, this redemption was not paid with corruptible things like silver or gold, but with the spotless sacrifice of Christ.

When Jesus takes the scroll, it signifies several crucial events:

*   The Final Phase of Redemption Begins—While Jesus has already redeemed His people spiritually, the physical redemption of creation is yet to take place. The earth, still under the curse of sin, awaits full restoration (Romans 8:19–22). The breaking of the seals will initiate God's final judgments, paving the way for Christ's reign.
*   The Overthrow of Satan's Dominion—The world, given over to Satan's rule through Adam's fall (Luke 4:5–6), will now be reclaimed. Jesus, the rightful heir, asserts His authority over all creation.
*   Christ's Role as the Supreme Judge and King—By taking the scroll, Christ is assuming His role as the executor of divine judgment and the fulfillment of all prophecy regarding His Second Coming (Psalm 2:8–9).

Jesus did not take the scroll presumptuously—He was given the authority by God. This act reflects Daniel 7:13–14, where the Son of Man approaches the

Ancient of Days (God the Father) and receives an everlasting Kingdom. His authority is absolute, and no one can challenge His right to rule.

Revelation 5:7 is a moment of triumph. Jesus Christ, the Lamb who was slain, now steps forward as the Lion of Judah, ready to reclaim what was lost. Through His life, death, and resurrection, He has proven Himself worthy, willing, and able to open the scroll and complete the work of redemption. The stage is now set for the unfolding of God's final plan—the redemption of the earth, the judgment of the wicked, and the establishment of Christ's Kingdom.

OLD TESTAMENT FORESHADOWS REVELATION:

The LORD said unto My LORD, Sit you at My right hand, until I make Your enemies Your footstool. The LORD shall send the rod of Your strength out of Zion: rule in the midst of Your enemies. (Psalm 110:1–2)

This passage parallels Revelation 5:7, where Jesus approaches the throne of God and takes the book from His right hand, symbolizing the transfer of divine authority to execute God's final judgment and redemption plan. Just as Psalm 110:1–2 speaks of the Messiah ruling from Zion and subduing His enemies, Revelation 5 depicts Jesus taking His rightful place as the Lamb who is worthy to open the sealed book, setting in motion the events of the end times. Both passages highlight Christ's exaltation, kingship, and dominion over all things.

THE REVELATION OF JESUS CHRIST REVEALS:

5:8 And when He had taken the book, the four beasts and four and twenty elders fell down before the Lamb, having every one of them harps, and golden vials full of odors, which are the prayers of saints.

This moment marks the culmination of worship, prophecy, and answered prayer as the heavenly elders fall before the Lamb. The significance of the harps and golden vials reveals two major themes:

1. **The Golden Vials—The Prayers of the Saints**. The golden vials filled with incense symbolize the accumulated prayers of God's people throughout the ages. These prayers, described as "odors" or fragrant incense, are offered in the presence of the Lamb.

    These are not just any prayers but the prayers for God's Kingdom to come, for justice, redemption, and the fulfillment of His promise. This echoes the Lord's Prayer: "Thy Kingdom come. Thy will be done in earth, as it is in heaven." (Matthew 6:10)

Every cry for justice, every plea for deliverance, every intercession for God's reign on earth is now answered. The long-awaited fulfillment of the prayers of saints throughout history is at hand.

2. **The Harps—Prophetic Worship and Fulfilled Prophecy.** The harps symbolize the power of prophetic worship and proclamation. Throughout the Old Testament, harps were associated with prophecy:

- 1 Samuel 10:5—The prophets would prophesy while playing harps.
- 2 Kings 3:15—Elisha received prophetic revelation while music was played.
- 1 Chronicles 25:1—David appointed musicians who prophesied through their instruments.

In Revelation 5:8, the harps represent the prophetic words spoken through the ages regarding the coming Kingdom. Every prophecy declaring that Christ would rule and reign is about to be fulfilled. The elders holding the harps symbolize the prophets and the faithful who declared God's Word, pointing to this moment in time.

The combination of prayers and harps signals the ultimate fulfillment of God's plan: The prayers of the saints have reached their fulfillment. The prophecies spoken throughout history are about to be realized. The Lamb has taken the scroll, signaling the redemption of creation. This scene represents the greatest moment in history—the beginning of Christ's reign. Every prophecy about His Kingdom, every prayer for redemption, every cry for justice is now being answered.

This verse is a powerful reminder that God hears every prayer and fulfills every promise. The prayers of the saints are not forgotten—they are collected, treasured, and will be answered in His perfect time. Likewise, every prophetic word given by God's faithful servants will come to pass.

The harps and vials together declare that the long-awaited moment has come—Christ is taking back the earth, and the Kingdom of God is at hand!

OLD TESTAMENT FORESHADOWS REVELATION:

Let my prayer be set forth before You as incense; and the lifting up of my hands as the evening sacrifice. (Psalm 141:2)

Revelation 5:8 reflects the priestly rituals of incense as does the psalmist's symbolic prayer in Psalm 141:2. The golden vials of incense in Revelation 5:8 represent the prayers of the saints—showing us that our prayers ascend before the throne of God like sacred offerings, treasured and powerful in heaven's courtroom.

Irene set her coffee down and leaned forward, an inquisitive expression on her face. "Ann, I was reading about the Lord's Prayer, and I noticed something—there are actually two versions of it. One in Matthew 6 and another in Luke 11. Are they the same prayer, or are they different?"

I nodded, flipping open my Bible. "Good observation. Both passages record Jesus teaching His disciples how to pray, but they were given in two different contexts. The one in Matthew 6:9–13 is part of the Sermon on the Mount, where Jesus is teaching a large crowd. The one in Luke 11:2–4 happens later when one of His disciples asks Him specifically, 'Lord, teach us to pray.'"

Irene furrowed her brow. "So, was Jesus just repeating the same lesson?"

"Yes and no. The content is similar, but the wording in Luke is slightly shorter. This shows that Jesus wasn't giving a rigid prayer to be recited verbatim, but rather offering a model for how to pray. That's why He says, 'After this manner, therefore, pray' in Matthew. He wasn't saying, 'Recite these exact words every time,' but teaching a pattern for prayer."

Irene nodded, intrigued. "A pattern? So each part of the prayer teaches us something?"

"Exactly! Let's break it down." I pointed to Matthew 6:9–13 in my Bible:

1. Our Father which art in heaven, Hallowed be Thy name.

"Begin with worship and acknowledging who God is. Prayer starts by focusing on Him, not us."

2. Thy Kingdom come. Thy will be done in earth, as it is in heaven.

"We align ourselves with God's will, surrendering our plans and desires to Him."

3. Give us this day our daily bread.

"Then, we present our needs, asking God for provision—not just physically, but spiritually."

4. And forgive us our debts, as we forgive our debtors.

"Confession and forgiveness. We seek God's mercy and commit to forgiving others."

5. And lead us not into temptation, but deliver us from evil.

"We ask for spiritual protection and strength against the enemy."

6.   For Yours is the Kingdom, and the power, and the glory, forever. Amen.

"We end in praise, reaffirming God's authority and sovereignty over all things."

Irene's eyes widened. "So the Lord's Prayer isn't just something we recite—it's a template for how to pray?"

"Exactly," I affirmed. "It's a guide that shows us the right order—worship, submission, provision, forgiveness, protection, and praise."

Irene hesitated for a moment. "But that brings me to another question. If this prayer is a model, is it enough to just recite it, like some churches do?"

I shook my head. "Reciting the words isn't wrong, but it's not meant to be a ritual. Jesus warned against 'vain repetitions' (Matthew 6:7). If we pray the Lord's Prayer without meaning, just as an obligation, then we miss the whole point. The prayers of the saints in Revelation 5:8 aren't just repeated phrases—they are heartfelt intercessions lifted up before God. What matters isn't just saying the words, but praying with understanding, sincerity, and faith."

Irene sat back in thought. "So prayer isn't about just going through the motions—it's about connecting with God."

I smiled. "Exactly. The Lord's Prayer is a starting point, but our conversations with God should be personal and genuine. It's not about reciting words; it's about relationship."

Irene exhaled deeply. "That makes so much sense. I think I've been saying prayers instead of praying prayers."

I chuckled. "We've all been there. But now that you see the pattern, you can pray the way Jesus taught—not just with words, but with your heart."

Irene nodded with determination. "No more empty recitations. From now on, I'm going to pray like Jesus meant it."

———◆◆◆———

THE REVELATION OF JESUS CHRIST REVEALS:

5:9 And they sung a new song, saying, You are worthy to take the book, and to open the seals thereof: for You were slain, and have redeemed us to God by Your blood out of every kindred, and tongue, and people, and nation.

In Revelation 5:9, the twenty-four elders and the four living creatures burst forth in a new song—a song of redemption, declaring Christ's worthiness to take the scroll and open its seals. This song encapsulates the entirety of God's redemptive plan, emphasizing Christ's atoning sacrifice and the universality of salvation.

The phrase "They sang a new song" is significant. In Scripture, a new song often accompanies a major act of divine deliverance (Psalm 33:3, 40:3, 144:9). Here, the "new song" marks the final act of redemption, as Christ prepares to reclaim the earth from sin and judgment. Unlike the old songs of Israel, which celebrated past deliverances (such as the Exodus), this new song celebrates the consummation of redemption—not just for Israel, but for every nation, tribe, and tongue.

"You are worthy to take the book, and to open the seals thereof." The worthiness of Christ is the central theme of this passage. No one else in heaven, on earth, or under the earth was found worthy (Revelation 5:3–4). Only Christ—the slain Lamb—has the authority to take the scroll because He alone paid the redemption price. His worthiness is rooted in His sacrifice, not just His divine nature.

"For You were slain, and have redeemed us to God by Your blood." This statement explicitly links redemption to the sacrificial death of Christ. The Greek word for "redeemed" (*exegorasas*) means to purchase or ransom—a direct reference to the price Christ paid for humanity's salvation. This language echoes Old Testament redemption laws, particularly the kinsman-redeemer (Leviticus 25:25; Ruth 4:1–10). Just as Boaz redeemed Ruth and her inheritance, Christ redeemed humanity by paying the price with His own blood (1 Peter 1:18–19).

"Out of every kindred, and tongue, and people, and nation." This passage affirms that salvation is not limited to Israel but extends to all nations, ethnicities, and languages. The four descriptors—kindred, tongue, people, and nation—represent the complete inclusivity of the gospel. This fulfills God's covenant with Abraham that through his seed "all the nations of the earth shall be blessed" (Genesis 22:18). It also aligns with Jesus' Great Commission to make disciples of all nations (Matthew 28:19).

Past, Present, and Future in the Song:

- Past—"You have redeemed us"—Christ's work on the Cross is already accomplished.
- Present—"You are worthy"—Christ is currently reigning in heaven, ready to take the scroll.
- Future—"We shall reign on the earth" (Revelation 5:10)—The final fulfillment comes when believers rule with Christ in the Millennial Kingdom (Revelation 20:4).

Revelation 5:9 bridges the past and future of God's redemptive plan. Christ's sacrifice at Calvary sealed the victory, but the final restoration of creation is yet to come.

This verse affirm that:

- Jesus is the Redeemer (Isaiah 53:5; Ephesians 1:7).
- Salvation is available to all people (Romans 10:12–13).
- Believers are made kings and priests, with a future reign (1 Peter 2:9; Revelation 20:6).

The new song in Revelation 5:9–10 is a hymn of victory, gratitude, and anticipation. It proclaims that the Lamb has already redeemed His people, and because of this, He alone is worthy to open the scroll and bring about the final fulfillment of God's Kingdom. This verse is both a celebration and a declaration—a reminder that Christ's work is complete, but the fullness of His reign is still to come.

OLD TESTAMENT FORESHADOWS REVELATION:

O sing unto the LORD a new song: sing unto the LORD, all the earth. Sing unto the LORD, bless His name; show forth His salvation from day to day. Declare His glory among the nations, His wonders among all people. (Psalm 96:1–3)

Psalm 96:1 calls for a "new song" to be sung to the LORD, just as Revelation 5:9 describes a new song being sung in heaven. Psalm 96:2 speaks of declaring God's salvation, which aligns with Revelation 5:9, where Christ is praised for redeeming people by His blood. Psalm 96:3 emphasizes declaring God's glory "among the nations" and "all people," mirroring the Revelation passage, which states that Christ redeemed people from every kindred, tongue, people, and nation.

This passage in Psalms anticipates the universal reign of God and the praise of the Redeemer by all nations, ultimately fulfilled in Revelation 5:9 when Christ is glorified as the Lamb who redeemed the world.

THE REVELATION OF JESUS CHRIST REVEALS:

5:10 And has made us to our God kings and priests: and we will reign on the earth.

Revelation 5:10 continues the triumphant declaration of the redeemed, emphasizing their new identity and destiny in Christ. This verse highlights three key aspects of the believer's role in God's Kingdom:

1. **Kings and Priests—A Royal Priesthood**. This passage fulfills the promise made in Exodus 19:6, where God tells Israel, "And you shall be to Me a kingdom of priests and a holy nation." The redeemed—both Jews and Gentiles—are now part of this royal priesthood through Christ.

   - As kings, believers are given authority in Christ's Kingdom, ruling with Him in righteousness. This authority is not for personal gain but to administer God's justice and truth.

- As priests, believers serve as intercessors, worshipers, and ministers before God, bridging the gap between Him and the world, much like the Levitical priests of the Old Testament.

2. **A Future Reign on Earth**—This verse affirms the coming millennial reign of Christ, where the redeemed will rule with Him on earth for 1,000 years (Revelation 20:6). The idea of reigning with Christ is also echoed in 2 Timothy 2:12, "If we suffer, we shall also reign with Him: if we deny him, he also will deny us."

   The reign of believers is not abstract—it is literal. This counters the belief that the Kingdom of God is only spiritual. While Christ reigns spiritually in our hearts today, His physical reign over the earth will be fulfilled in the Millennial Kingdom.

3. **A Promise Already Given, Yet to Be Fully Realized**—The wording "has made us" indicates a completed work—through Christ's death and resurrection, we are already kings and priests in position. However, "we will reign on the earth" is future, pointing to the coming fulfillment of this promise in the Messianic Kingdom.

   This dual reality—already redeemed but awaiting our full inheritance—is a common theme in Scripture. 1 Peter 2:9 confirms this identity, calling believers "a chosen generation, a royal priesthood, a holy nation."

Revelation 5:10 is a powerful declaration of the redeemed's purpose and destiny. Through Christ, we are both kings and priests, called to reign and serve. Our ultimate reign will be realized when Christ returns, establishing His Kingdom on earth. Until then, we walk in this calling spiritually—interceding, worshiping, and exercising kingdom authority through faith and obedience.

This verse is a reminder that salvation is not just about personal redemption; it's about being restored to a divine role in God's eternal Kingdom.

OLD TESTAMENT FORESHADOWS REVELATION:

And you shall be unto Me a kingdom of priests, and a holy nation. These are the words which you shalt speak unto the children of Israel. (Exodus 19:6)

Exodus 19:6 foreshadows God's plan for His redeemed people. Just as Israel was called to be a kingdom of priests under the Old Covenant, believers in Christ—both Jew and Gentile—are made kings and priests in His eternal Kingdom, reigning with Him on the earth. It reveals that believers are restored to their original calling: to rule and serve with Christ in His coming Kingdom on earth.

—◆ ◆ ◆—

Irene swirled her coffee, deep in thought.

"Ann, I was reading about the millennial reign of Christ, and something's been bothering me. Revelation 5:10 says that we—all the redeemed—will be made kings and priests and will reign on the earth. But here's what I'm struggling with: does that include women? Because in the New Testament, Paul says women should be silent in the church. And when he talks about the fivefold ministries, most preachers say those roles are only for men."

I set down my Bible and leaned in. "I can see why that's confusing. But let's start with the bigger picture—God's original plan for both men and women. In Genesis 1:27–28, we see that God created man and woman in His image and gave them both dominion over the earth. That tells us His intention wasn't for one gender to rule over the other, but for both to walk in their God-given authority."

Irene nodded. "Okay, so if men and women were created equal in God's image, then why does Paul say women should be silent in church? And why do so many preachers say women can't be in ministry?"

I sighed. "Paul's words in 1 Corinthians 14:34–35—where he says women should be silent—are often misunderstood. In the early church, women typically sat separately from men, and because they were less formally educated at the time, they would occasionally call out during the teaching, disrupting the service. Paul wasn't saying women should never speak; he was addressing a specific cultural issue. In fact, in 1 Corinthians 11:5, he acknowledges that women were prophesying in the church—so clearly, he didn't mean they had to be completely silent."

Irene raised an eyebrow. "That makes sense. But what about the fivefold ministry? I've always heard it was only for men."

I smiled. "The fivefold ministry—apostles, prophets, evangelists, pastors, and teachers—is outlined in Ephesians 4:11–12. And nowhere in that passage does it say these roles are limited to men. In fact, Scripture gives us examples of women serving in these very capacities."

Irene leaned in. "Really? Like who?"

I counted on my fingers. "Let's start with apostles—Paul mentions Junia in Romans 16:7, calling her 'outstanding among the apostles.' Then there are prophets: the Bible specifically names Deborah in Judges 4:4 and Anna in Luke 2:36. What about evangelists? The Samaritan woman at the well became one of the first, bringing her entire town to Jesus in John 4. As for pastors and teachers, Priscilla—alongside her husband Aquila—taught Apollos the way of God more accurately in Acts 18:26."

Irene's eyes widened. "So women were leaders in the early church?"

I nodded. "Absolutely. And let's not forget Galatians 3:28: 'There is neither Jew nor Greek, slave nor free, male nor female, for you are all one in Christ Jesus.' God's call isn't based on gender—He calls both men and women to serve His Kingdom."

Irene exhaled. "Wow. That changes everything. So during the millennial reign, women will reign as kings and priests alongside men?"

I smiled. "Yes. When Revelation 5:10 says we will reign with Christ, it includes all the redeemed. Our authority in the Kingdom isn't based on being male or female—it's based on being in Christ. Women won't be 'queens and priestesses'; they will be kings and priests, reigning with the same authority as men."

Irene sat back, shaking her head. "So all this time, people have been limiting what God never limited?"

I grinned. "Exactly. The real question isn't whether women can serve—it's whether they'll answer the call."

Irene picked up her Bible, a fire in her eyes. "Then I'm ready to answer it."

———◆◆◆———

THE REVELATION OF JESUS CHRIST REVEALS:

5:11 And I beheld, and I heard the voice of many angels round about the throne and the beasts and the elders: and the number of them was ten thousand times ten thousand, and thousands of thousands.

John's vision in Revelation 5:11 shifts to a magnificent heavenly scene, where he witnesses an overwhelming number of angels, elders, and living creatures gathered around the throne of God. The sheer vastness of this assembly emphasizes the importance and magnitude of the moment—the unveiling of the scroll, which signifies the final redemption of the earth.

In this verse John describes the number of angels as "ten thousand times ten thousand, and thousands of thousands." This phrase symbolizes an innumerable host, signifying an incalculable number beyond human comprehension. In biblical times, *ten thousand* was often used to represent the largest conceivable number (Daniel 7:10). This implies that the angelic host surrounding God's throne is beyond counting, reinforcing the vast heavenly authority and power present in this moment.

Here, the angels are positioned around the throne, as well as around the four living creatures (cherubim) and the twenty-four elders (who likely represent the redeemed saints). This setup suggests a divine hierarchy in worship—angels encircling the redeemed and the throne, acknowledging the worthiness of the

Lamb. The positioning also signifies that while angels play a significant role in God's plan, their role is distinct from that of the redeemed—they are not the ones who needed redemption, but they celebrate and witness it.

Hebrews 1:14 describes angels as *ministering spirits* sent to serve those who will inherit salvation. For thousands of years, they have protected, guided, and fought on behalf of God's people. Now, in this moment, their mission shifts— they are not carrying out tasks but rather observing and rejoicing as the final stages of God's redemption plan unfold. The angels have witnessed the fall of man, the redemptive work of Christ, and now they see the culmination of God's plan. The celebration in heaven is a response to this divine moment.

Revelation 5:11 paints a breathtaking vision of heaven's response to Christ's authority. The sheer vastness of the angelic host reflects the cosmic significance of this moment. The ministry of angels, which has spanned thousands of years, now takes a backseat as Christ, the Lamb of God, steps forward to reclaim creation.

OLD TESTAMENT FORESHADOWS REVELATION:

A fiery stream issued and came forth from before Him: thousand thousands ministered unto Him, and ten thousand times ten thousand stood before Him: the judgment was set, and the books were opened. (Daniel 7:10)

Revelation 5:11 draws directly from Daniel 7:10, reinforcing the continuity of prophetic visions from Old to New Testament. Both describe countless angelic beings surrounding the throne of God, worshiping and serving in anticipation of divine judgment and the unfolding of redemptive history.

THE REVELATION OF JESUS CHRIST REVEALS:

5:12 Saying with a loud voice, Worthy is the Lamb that was slain to receive power, and riches, and wisdom, and strength, and honor, and glory, and blessing.

In this verse, the angels, elders, and living creatures in heaven erupt in a resounding declaration of worship, proclaiming that the Lamb—Jesus Christ— is worthy of all honor and divine attributes. This marks a pivotal moment in the heavenly scene, emphasizing that the Lamb, who was slain, alone is worthy to open the sealed book and bring redemption to completion.

The phrase "saying with a loud voice" signifies the majesty, urgency, and total unity of the worship in heaven. There is no hesitation, no division—every being in the heavenly realm is proclaiming the worthiness of the Lamb in unison. This loud, thundering praise reflects the overwhelming joy and victory of Christ's finished work.

"Worthy is the Lamb that was slain." The worthiness of Christ is directly tied to His sacrifice. He is not just worthy because He is the Son of God but because He chose to be slain, to suffer, and to die for the redemption of humanity. The phrase "was slain" underscores His sacrificial death, fulfilling Isaiah 53:7: "He was oppressed, and He was afflicted, yet He opened not His mouth: He is brought as a lamb to the slaughter, and as a sheep before her shearers is silent, so He opens not His mouth." His worthiness to open the seals is not by force or status, but by His obedient sacrifice and atonement for sin.

Heaven's worshipers declare that Jesus is worthy to receive seven attributes, symbolizing completeness and divine perfection.

1. **Power**—Christ possesses supreme authority over all creation (Matthew 28:18).
2. **Riches**—He is the possessor of all spiritual and material wealth (Philippians 4:19).
3. **Wisdom**—Christ embodies perfect wisdom, guiding His people (Colossians 2:3).
4. **Strength**—His might and ability to accomplish redemption and rule as King (Isaiah 40:29).
5. **Honor**—The highest respect and reverence due to Him alone (Philippians 2:9–11).
6. **Glory**—The radiance and divine majesty of Christ (John 17:5).
7. **Blessing**—Every word of praise, adoration, and worship belongs to Him (Ephesians 1:3).

This proclamation fulfills Philippians 2:9–11, where every knee shall bow, and every tongue confess that Jesus Christ is Lord. It also mirrors the Messianic prophecy in Daniel 7:13–14, where the Son of Man is given dominion, glory, and an everlasting Kingdom. This moment is not just about heavenly beings; it represents the ultimate recognition of Christ's supremacy over all creation.

Revelation 5:12 reveals the heart of worship in heaven—a worship that is entirely centered on the Lamb who was slain. This worship acknowledges Christ's divine attributes, His sacrifice, and his ultimate rule over all things. It reminds believers that true worship is about exalting Jesus, recognizing His work, and surrendering all honor, glory, and praise to Him alone.

OLD TESTAMENT FORESHADOWS REVELATION:

All Your works shall praise You, O LORD; and Your saints shall bless You. They shall speak of the glory of Your Kingdom, and talk of Your power; To make known to the sons of men His mighty acts, and the glorious majesty of His

Kingdom. Your Kingdom is an everlasting Kingdom, and Your dominion endures throughout all generations. (Psalm 145:10–13)

Psalm 145:10–13 beautifully parallels Revelation 5:12, showing a continuity of divine praise, kingdom language, and heavenly worship that stretches from the Old Testament to the ultimate unveiling in the New Testament. It emphasizes that the Lamb (Jesus) is rightly worshiped with the same honor as Yahweh (God the Father), for He is the fulfillment of God's eternal redemptive plan.

THE REVELATION OF JESUS CHRIST REVEALS:

5:13 And every creature which is in heaven, and on the earth, and under the earth, and such as are in the sea, and all that are in them, heard I saying, Blessing, and honor, and glory, and power, be to Him that sits on the throne, and to the Lamb forever and ever.

In Revelation 5:13, we witness one of the most awe-inspiring moments in all of Scripture—a moment when every creature in the entire universe acknowledges the supremacy of Christ. At this moment, all of creation—angels, saints, earthly beings, and even those under the earth—cry out in unified praise. The entire cosmos pauses in reverence. This passage reveals the totality of Christ's dominion, affirming that He is not just the Redeemer of humanity but the Redeemer of all creation.

The universal chorus echoes the groaning of creation described in Romans 8:19–22, where Paul speaks of creation longing for the day of redemption. Since the fall of man, the natural world has been under the curse of sin (Genesis 3:17–18). Death, decay, and suffering entered into creation because of humanity's rebellion; but now, through Christ, all things will be restored. This passage confirms that the redemption of the world is not just for people but for everything God has made—the earth, the animals, the environment, and even the heavens.

The Lamb who was slain now takes His rightful place, receiving blessing, honor, glory, and power. This shows that Jesus Christ, though He came as a Suffering Servant, now reigns in absolute authority. His sacrifice was not just for personal salvation but for the restoration of all things.

The worship is not limited to believers or angels—it extends to every creature. This is a fulfillment of Philippians 2:10–11, which declares that one day:

That at the name of Jesus every knee should bow, of things in heaven, and things in earth, and things under the earth. And that every tongue should confess that Jesus Christ is Lord, to the glory of God the Father. (Philippians 2:10–11)

Even the rebellious will acknowledge Christ's supremacy. Those in hell, demons, and even Satan himself will have no choice but to recognize the authority of Jesus. However, their worship will be in forced submission, unlike the willing adoration of the saints and angels.

The curse that was placed upon creation will finally be lifted. The redeemed will reign with Christ on a renewed earth (Revelation 21:1–5). Just as the garden of Eden was a paradise before sin, the world will once again be restored to a state of peace and glory.

Revelation 5:13 is a triumphant declaration of Christ's victory over sin, death, and the curse. All of creation joins in the great celebration of His rule, declaring Him worthy of blessing, honor, glory, and power. This moment signals the beginning of the complete restoration of God's Kingdom, where Jesus Christ reigns supreme forever and ever.

OLD TESTAMENT FORESHADOWS REVELATION:

Let the heavens rejoice, and let the earth be glad; let the sea roar, and the fulness thereof. Let the field be joyful, and all that is therein: then shall all the trees of the wood rejoice before the LORD: For He comes, for He comes to judge the earth: He shall judge the world with righteousness, and the people with His truth. (Psalm 96:11–13)

Both passages depict all creation—heaven, earth, sea, and everything within them—praising God. Revelation 5:13 shows universal worship of Christ as Redeemer, while Psalm 96:11–13 anticipates joyful praise as God comes to judge and establish righteousness. This aligns with the fulfillment in Revelation, where every creature acknowledges Christ's eternal rule.

THE REVELATION OF JESUS CHRIST REVEALS:

5:14 And the four beasts said, Amen. And the four and twenty elders fell down and worshiped Him that lives forever and ever.

As the grand scene of heavenly worship reaches its climax, we see the four living creatures (beasts) confirming all that has been proclaimed about the Lamb with a resounding "Amen." The word *Amen* is a declaration of truth, certainty, and agreement, signifying that all creation acknowledges Christ's worthiness to redeem the earth and rule forever.

Following the affirmation of the four living creatures, the twenty-four elders—representing the redeemed of both the Old and New Testaments—fall prostrate before the throne in complete surrender and adoration. Their act of falling down symbolizes absolute submission, reverence, and recognition of God's eternal authority.

"Him that lives forever and ever." This phrase highlights the eternal nature of God and Christ. He is the Alpha and Omega, the one who was, who is, and who is to come (Revelation 1:8). Unlike earthly rulers who rise and fall, Christ reigns eternally, securing not only our redemption but the restoration of all things.

This final verse in Revelation 5 serves as the concluding act of worship in response to the Lamb taking the sealed scroll. Heaven and earth have now declared His supremacy, worthiness, and eternal dominion. The elders' worship affirms that Christ alone holds the authority to fulfill God's redemptive plan.

OLD TESTAMENT FORESHADOWS REVELATION:

You, even You, are LORD alone; You have made heaven, the heaven of heavens, with all their host, the earth, and all things that are therein, the seas, and all that is therein, and You preserve them all; and the host of heaven worships You. (Nehemiah 9:6)

In both passages, all of creation—heaven, earth, and the sea—recognizes God's sovereignty and worships Him. Nehemiah highlights God as the one who made and preserves all things, while Revelation 5:14 shows creation bowing before "Him that lives forever and ever." Nehemiah mentions "the host of heaven" worshiping God, which parallels the four living creatures and the twenty-four elders bowing in worship in Revelation 5:14.

Nehemiah 9:6 affirms the eternal dominion of God, much like Revelation 5:14, where all creation acknowledges His rule and falls down in worship before Him.

SUMMARY OF REVELATION 5

Revelation 5 is a pivotal chapter that shifts the focus from God's throne (Revelation 4) to the unfolding of His divine plan through the Lamb of God, Jesus Christ. The chapter opens with John seeing a scroll in the right hand of God, sealed with seven seals—representing God's decreed judgment and redemption of the world. A strong angel proclaims a challenge: "Who is worthy to open the book, and to loose the seals thereof?" (Revelation 5:2). A deep sense of despair fills John as no one in heaven, on earth, or under the earth is found worthy to open the scroll (Revelation 5:3–4).

Then, one of the twenty-four elders comforts John, revealing that the Lion of the tribe of Judah, the Root of David, has prevailed (Revelation 5:5). But instead of a lion, John sees a Lamb as though it had been slain—a striking image of Christ's sacrifice and victory (Revelation 5:6). Jesus takes the scroll from the Father's hand (Revelation 5:7), affirming His authority to execute God's final plan of judgment and restoration. This moment ignites worship in heaven, as the four living creatures and the twenty-four elders fall before the Lamb, singing a new song of redemption (Revelation 5:8–9). They declare that Jesus, through His blood, has redeemed people from every nation and made them kings and priests to reign on earth (Revelation 5:10).

A breathtaking scene unfolds as millions of angels join in, declaring the Lamb's worthiness to receive power, riches, wisdom, strength, honor, glory, and blessing (Revelation 5:11–12). Then, every creature in heaven, on earth, under the earth, and in the sea unites in worship, giving blessing, honor, and glory to God and the Lamb forever (Revelation 5:13). The chapter concludes with the four living creatures affirming with "Amen" and the twenty-four elders falling down in worship before the eternal King (Revelation 5:14).

KEY TAKEAWAYS

- The scroll and seven seals—Represents God's divine plan for judgment and redemption.
- The worthiness of the Lamb—Jesus alone is worthy because of His sacrificial death and victory.
- Heavenly worship—The chapter emphasizes universal adoration of Christ by all creation.
- The role of the redeemed—Believers are called kings and priests to reign with Christ.
- God's sovereign plan unfolding—The events of Revelation hinge on Christ opening the scroll, leading to the coming judgments and ultimate redemption.

Revelation 5 reveals that redemption and judgment are in the hands of Christ. The chapter offers comfort to believers, affirming that Jesus has already won the victory and will bring all things to completion. This chapter is a call to worship, trust, and anticipate the fulfillment of God's Kingdom on earth. The Lamb who was slain is also the Lion who will reign.

Chapter 7

Revelation 6:
The Seal Judgments
The Tribulation Age—
Daniel's 70th Week: First 3½ Years

UNLEASHING THE APOCALYPSE—Revelation 6 marks a dramatic shift in the narrative. Up until now, John's vision has been centered in heaven—witnessing the glorified Christ, the worship of the heavenly host, the raptured saints, and the throne of God. The focus has been on the majesty and sovereignty of God, the Lamb's worthiness, and the preparation for the events that will unfold. But now, the scene shifts to earth, and with the breaking of the first seal, the Tribulation Age officially begins—called Daniel's 70th Week.

The scroll, held by the Ancient of Days (God the Father), represents the title deed to the earth—sealed with seven seals, waiting to be opened by the only One worthy: Jesus Christ, our Kinsman-Redeemer. The act of breaking these seals is not just the unveiling of future events but the very process of reclaiming creation from the usurper, Satan. This is the moment when Christ begins to execute judgment, setting in motion the final countdown to His return and the establishment of His Kingdom on earth.

However, what unfolds is not immediate restoration but a series of catastrophic events—war, famine, death, and divine wrath. Many today focus solely on Jesus as a Savior, full of mercy and love, but Revelation 6 reveals another undeniable truth: Jesus is also the righteous Judge. The same Jesus who came as the Lamb of God will now act as the Lion of Judah, bringing judgment upon a world that has rejected Him. Just as God once judged the world in the days of Noah, leaving only a remnant to survive, so too will He bring judgment upon the earth again in the final days.

Each seal that is opened unleashes an act of divine justice, intensifying the chaos on earth. This is not random destruction; it is the sovereign plan of God unfolding, bringing history to its destined climax. What follows in the seal judgments is not merely an account of the Tribulation but a call to wake up—a warning that the world is on a collision course with judgment, and only those who belong to Christ will escape His wrath.

As John watches these events unfold, we are reminded that prophecy is not just a warning—it is a call to decision. The world will face the full measure of God's justice, but for those who are in Christ, there is the promise of deliverance. This chapter marks the transition from the glory of heaven to the devastation on earth—a sobering yet necessary reality in God's redemptive plan.

THE 70 WEEKS OF DANIEL

In Daniel 9:24–27, the angel Gabriel tells the prophet Daniel:

> Seventy weeks are determined upon your people and upon your Holy City, to finish the transgression, and to make an end of sins, and to make reconciliation for iniquity, and to bring in everlasting righteousness, and to seal up the vision and prophecy, and to anoint the Most Holy. (Daniel 9:24)

Daniel 9:24 describes the purpose of the 70 weeks, introducing the full 70 weeks (490 years) and outlines six key purposes for Israel and Jerusalem, including the end of sin and the arrival of everlasting righteousness.

In Hebrew, the term "weeks" refers to units of seven, and in this context it clearly means weeks of years (seven years per "week"). So:

- 1 week = 7 years.
- 70 weeks x 7 years = 490 years total

Therefore this remarkable prophecy outlines 490 prophetic years in God's plan for Israel and Jerusalem—not the Church or the Gentile world. It serves as a divine timeline for major redemptive events, including the coming of the Messiah and the final seven-year period to come, the Tribulation Age.

Daniel's 69 Weeks (483 Years)

> Know therefore and understand, that from the going forth of the commandment to restore and to build Jerusalem unto the Messiah the Prince shall be seven weeks, and threescore and two weeks: the streets shall be built again, and the wall, even in troublous times. (Daniel 9:25)

Daniel 9:25 outlines the beginning and length of the first 69 weeks of the prophecy. It speaks of "seven weeks and threescore and two weeks"—with "threescore" meaning 60. This totals 7 + 60 + 2 = 69 weeks. Since each "week" represents a period of seven years, 69 x 7 equals 483 years. Using the biblical prophetic calendar, where a year is 360 days, this amounts to 173,880 days. This remarkable time span begins with the decree to rebuild Jerusalem and ends with the arrival of the Messian, Jesus Christ.

In Bible prophecy—particularly in books like Daniel and Revelation—a year is often measured as 360 days rather than the 365.25 days of the solar calendar or the fluctuating months of the Jewish lunisolar calendar. This is known as the "prophetic year," and it is supported by passages such as Genesis 7:11 and 8:3–4, where the Flood is described as lasting 150 days over a five-month span—indicating 30-day months. Additionally, Revelation 11:2–3 and 12:6, 14 equate 42 months with 1,260 days, reinforcing the 360-day prophetic year model.

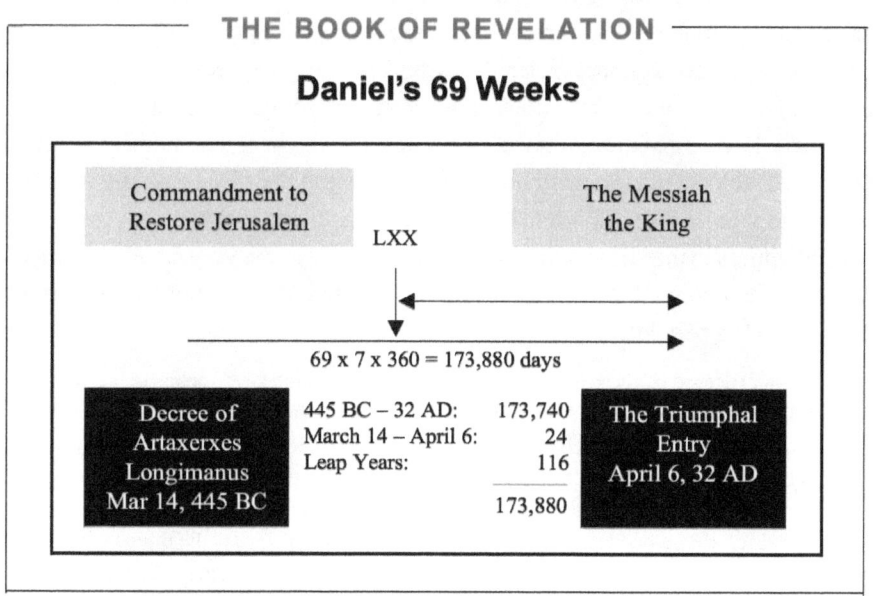

- Start Date: March 14, 445 BC—The decree of Artaxerxes Longimanus to restore and rebuild Jerusalem (Nehemiah 2).
- End Date: April 6, 32 AD—Often interpreted as the Triumphal Entry of Jesus into Jerusalem (Palm Sunday).

- Calculations:
  - 69 weeks x 7 years = 483 years.
  - 483 years x 360-day prophetic years = 173,880 days.
  - Days spanning the years from 445 BC to 32 AD = 173,740.
  - Days between March 14 and April 6 = 24.
  - Leap year days = 116.

When combined, these components result in a total of 173,880 days, perfectly aligning with the 69 prophetic weeks (483 years x 360 days) in Daniel's prophecy.

From March 14, 445 BC (decree) to April 6, 32 AD (triumphal entry), this period fits precisely—ending on the very day Jesus rode into Jerusalem on a donkey, fulfilling Zechariah 9:9:

> Rejoice greatly, O daughter of Zion; shout, O daughter of Jerusalem: behold, your King comes unto you: He is just, and having salvation; lowly, and riding upon an ass, and upon a colt the foal of an ass. (Zechariah 9:9)

This was no ordinary day—it was the prophesied First Coming of Jesus Christ as King. Zechariah 9:9 had foretold that the Messiah would come humbly, riding on a donkey. Now, centuries later, Jesus fulfilled this prophecy to the very letter as He entered Jerusalem to the cries of the people shouting, "Blessed be the King!"

Luke 19 captures the emotional and prophetic weight of that moment. Though the crowd welcomed Him, many in Israel—including their leaders—did not truly recognize who He was or what day it was. Jesus wept over the city, mourning their blindness to the "time of their visitation." This was the very day that Daniel's 69 weeks had pointed to—the day the long-awaited Messiah publicly presented Himself to His people.

> Saying, Blessed be the King that comes in the name of the Lord: peace in heaven, and glory in the highest. And some of the Pharisees from among the multitude said unto Him, Master, rebuke Your disciples. And He answered and said unto them, 'I tell you that, if these should hold their peace, the stones would immediately cry out.' And when He drew near, He beheld the city, and wept over it, saying, 'If you had known, even you, at least in *this your day*, the things which belong unto your peace! But now they are hidden from your eyes. For the days shall come upon you, that your enemies shall cast a trench about you, and surround you, and close you in on every side, And shall lay you even with the ground, and your children within you; and they shall not leave in you one stone upon another; because you knew not the time of your visitation.' (Luke 19:38–44)

Jesus held the Jews accountable for recognizing "this your day" (Luke 19:42). Because they did not, He pronounced judgment upon them (Luke 19:43–44).

The Gap After the 69th Week

> And after threescore and two weeks shall Messiah be cut off, but not for Himself: and the people of the prince that shall come shall destroy the city and the sanctuary; and the end thereof shall be with a flood, and unto the end of the war desolations are determined. (Daniel 9:26)

Daniel 9:26 foretells two key events after the 69th week: the crucifixion of the Messiah—"cut off, but not for Himself"—and the destruction of Jerusalem and the temple by the people of a coming prince. Both were fulfilled: Christ was crucified for the sins of the world, and in AD 70, the Romans destroyed the city and temple.

This verse also points to a prophetic gap between the 69th and 70th weeks—representing the Church Age, a mystery later revealed in the New Testament (Ephesians 3:3–9). During this time, God's focus is on building the Church, until "the fullness of the Gentiles comes in" (Romans 11:25), after which He will turn again to Israel in the final 70th week.

Daniel's 70th Week: The Tribulation Age (7 Years)

> And he (the Antichrist) shall confirm the covenant with many for one week: and in the midst of the week he shall cause the sacrifice and the oblation to cease, and for the overspreading of abominations he shall make it desolate, even until the consummation, and that determined shall be poured upon the desolate. (Daniel 9:27)

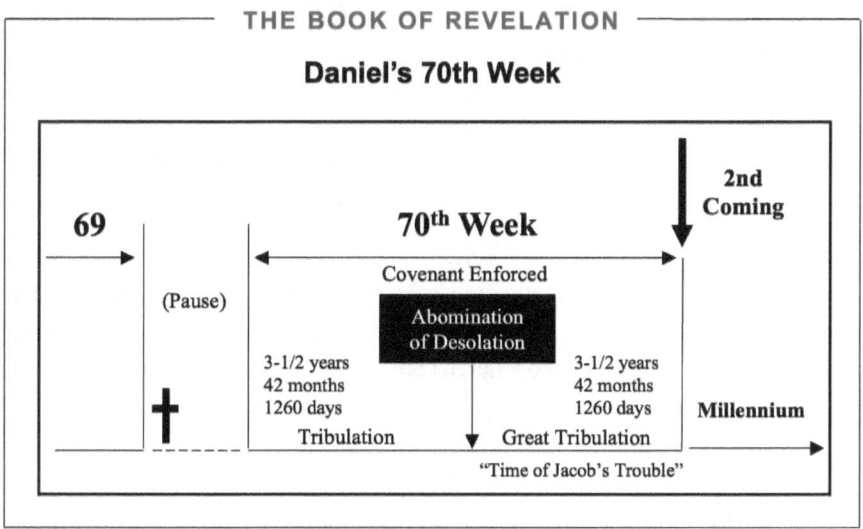

Daniel 9:27 describes the final 70th week—a seven-year period that is still future and commonly referred to as the Tribulation period. During this time, a powerful world leader—understood by many as the Antichrist—will confirm or enforce a covenant with many, likely involving Israel. However, at the midpoint of the seven years—after 3½ years—he will break this agreement and commit what Jesus called the "abomination of desolation" (Matthew 24:15), an act later echoed in Revelation 13:5. This event marks the beginning of the Great Tribulation—a time of unprecedented judgment and turmoil on earth. The 70th week will culminate in the return of Jesus Christ, who will bring an end to the rebellion and establish His righteous Kingdom.

This final seven-year period described in Daniel's prophecy corresponds precisely with other prophetic timelines in Scripture:

- 42 months / 1,260 days (Revelation 11–13).
- Time, times, and half a time (Daniel 7:25, 12:7).

This period is known as the Tribulation Age, also referred to as "the time of Jacob's trouble" (Jeremiah 30:7). It is a time of intense judgment and global upheaval, distinct from the present Church Age, and it culminates in the Second Coming of Jesus Christ.

Theological Implications: Israel and the Church Are Distinct

A proper understanding of biblical prophecy requires us to distinguish between Israel and the Church—two separate entities in God's redemptive plan.

- The Seventy Weeks were determined for Israel and Jerusalem (Daniel 9:24), not the Church.
- The Church was a "mystery" in the Old Testament, later revealed through the apostles (Ephesians 3:1–9).
- Paul affirms a threefold division of humanity in 1 Corinthians 10:32: Jews, Gentiles (nations), and the Church of God.

To fully grasp God's prophetic timeline, we must recover a robust Israelology—a biblical understanding of Israel's unique and ongoing role in redemptive history. This is not just a branch of eschatology (end times doctrine) or ecclesiology (doctrine of the Church) but a distinct and necessary study in its own right.

THE REVELATION OF JESUS CHRIST REVEALS:

[6:1] And I saw when the Lamb opened one of the seals, and I heard, as it were the noise of thunder, one of the four beasts saying, Come and see.

Revelation 6:1 marks a dramatic shift in the Book of Revelation, transitioning from the glorious worship scenes in heaven to the unleashing of divine judgment upon the earth. John, positioned as a witness to these unfolding events, describes how the Lamb—Jesus Christ—opens the first of the seven seals.

The significance of the Lamb opening the seals cannot be overstated. In Revelation 5, John wept when no one was found worthy to take the scroll, but then the Lamb—Jesus—stepped forward as the only one who could. This moment signifies His absolute authority over history and judgment. The opening of the seals initiates the events of the Tribulation, bringing about divine retribution and the final fulfillment of God's plan for humanity.

John describes hearing a noise like thunder. Thunder in Scripture often signals divine power, judgment, and impending action (Psalm 29:3–4; Job 37:2–5). The ominous sound foreshadows the catastrophic events that will follow, emphasizing the severity of what is about to be unleashed. It is not a gentle revelation but an overwhelming force that will shake the earth.

John then hears one of the four living creatures say, "Come and see." These four creatures were introduced in Revelation 4:6–8, described as being around the throne of God, full of eyes and having different appearances resembling a lion, an ox, a man, and an eagle. They represent God's creation and His supreme authority over all living things.

Their command to "Come and see" is both an invitation and an announcement—John is being called to bear witness to the unfolding judgments. Some translations simply say "Come," which could indicate a summoning of the rider that follows in the next verse.

With the breaking of the first seal, the stage is set for the beginning of the Tribulation. This moment marks the transition from the age of grace to the age of wrath, as Christ begins to reclaim the earth from the dominion of sin and evil. What follows in the next verses is the arrival of the four horsemen of the apocalypse, each representing different aspects of destruction that will be unleashed upon the world.

This verse is the calm before the storm, a powerful moment in which heaven moves to initiate judgment. The world has long rejected the Lamb as Savior; now, they will see Him as Judge. The thunder rolls, the seals are broken, and the time of reckoning begins.

OLD TESTAMENT FORESHADOWS REVELATION:

And when they went, I heard the noise of their wings, like the noise of great waters, as the voice of the Almighty, the voice of speech, as the noise of a host: when they stood, they let down their wings. (Ezekiel 1:24)

And the sound of the cherubims' wings was heard even to the outer court, as the voice of the Almighty God when He speaks. (Ezekiel 10:5)

Both Revelation 6:1 and Ezekiel's prophetic visions highlight the powerful sound that marks divine action. In Ezekiel 1:24 and Ezekiel 10:5, the sound of the cherubim's wings is compared to the voice of the Almighty—loud, commanding, and unmistakable. Likewise, in Revelation 6:1, a thunderous voice accompanies the opening of the first seal. This sound signals the start of God's judgment and matches the divine authority seen in Ezekiel. The cherubim in Ezekiel and the four living creatures in Revelation both serve at God's throne. They announce His will and act as messengers of His power.

Together, these passages show a strong connection between Old Testament prophecy and New Testament fulfillment. God's voice, whether in thunder or wings, always carries authority, purpose, and power.

THE REVELATION OF JESUS CHRIST REVEALS:

6:2 And I saw, and behold a white horse: and he that sat on him had a bow; and a crown was given unto him: and he went forth conquering, and to conquer.

The First Seal Judgment—White Horse and False Christ. The opening of the first seal reveals a rider on a white horse, symbolizing a powerful global figure who emerges on the world stage. This is the Antichrist, a counterfeit Christ, who appears as a savior but ultimately brings deception and destruction.

At first glance, the rider may resemble Christ, who also appears on a white horse in Revelation 19:11–16. However, there are key differences:

- The Rider in Revelation 6:2 has a bow but no arrows. This suggests he conquers through diplomacy, deception, and political maneuvering rather than outright war.
- The Rider in Revelation 6:2 wears a "stephanos" (a victor's crown), while Christ in Revelation 19:12 wears "diadems" (royal crowns). The Antichrist's authority is given to him temporarily, while Christ's rule is eternal.
- The Rider in Revelation 6:2 is followed by war, famine, and death. This aligns with the Antichrist's deceptive peace, which quickly dissolves into chaos. Jesus, however, brings true peace and justice.
- Christ's weapon is a sword (Revelation 19:15), not a bow. The Antichrist's bow without arrows signifies a political conquest rather than military force at first.

The Antichrist rises to power after the Rapture of the Church, filling the vacuum left by the sudden disappearance of millions of believers. With the world in turmoil—economies collapsing, governments in chaos, and mass confusion—he presents himself as a man of peace and unity. He may initially broker a false peace treaty, particularly with Israel, fulfilling Daniel 9:27, where a seven-year covenant is made but later broken.

The Tribulation Age—Daniel's 70th Week begins. For the first three and a half years, the Antichrist appears as a benevolent leader, bringing a temporary calm to a shattered world. However, this peace is short-lived, as the following three seals introduce war, famine, and death.

The bow without arrows suggests that the Antichrist's early conquests are achieved without force—through diplomacy, deception, and strategic alliances rather than open warfare. He is likely a charismatic leader who unites the nations under a new world order:

- An intellectual genius—Daniel 7:20, 8:23; Ezekiel 38:3.
- A persuasive orator—Daniel 7:20; Revelation 13:2.
- A shrewd politician—Daniel 11:21, 8:25.
- A financial genius—Revelation 13:17; Ezekiel 28:4–5; Psalm 52:7; Daniel 11:38, 43.
- A forceful military leader—Daniel 8:24; Revelation 6:2, 13:4; Isaiah 4:16.
- A powerful organizer—Revelation 13:1–2, 17:17.
- A unifying religious guru—2 Thessalonians 2:4; Revelation 13:3, 14–15.

However, this false peace is a deceptive trap leading to greater destruction.

Let no man deceive you by any means: for that Day shall not come, except there comes a falling away first, and that man of sin be revealed, the son of predition (the Antichrist); who opposes and exalts himself above all that is called God, or that is worshiped; so that he as God sits in the temple of God, showing himself that he is God. (2 Thessalonians 2:3–4)

The crown ("stephanos") is given to him, indicating that his power is not self-made but granted by the world and ultimately permitted by God for a time.

The four horsemen of the apocalypse (Revelation 6:1–8) represent sequential judgments upon the earth.

1. **The White Horse**—Deception and False Peace (the Antichrist).
2. **The Red Horse**—War and Bloodshed.
3. **The Black Horse**—Famine and Economic Collapse.
4. **The Pale Green Horse**—Death and Pestilence.

The fact that war, famine, and death follow this rider confirms that his conquest is not of righteousness but of destruction. The Antichrist may begin as a man of peace, but his rule will spiral into tyranny, suffering, and global devastation.

The breaking of the first seal marks the beginning of the seven-year Tribulation (Daniel's 70th Week). The world has rejected Christ, and now it receives a counterfeit messiah who ushers in a temporary peace but ultimately leads to global catastrophe.

- This rider represents deception. The world will believe it has found a savior, but he is a false Christ (Matthew 24:5).
- His rise is the first act in God's final judgment. The Tribulation is now officially underway, and the judgments will escalate.
- The Church is absent. This aligns with the pre-Tribulation Rapture view, as believers are not appointed to wrath (1 Thessalonians 5:9).

The world longed for peace without God, and now they have it—a counterfeit peace under the rule of the Antichrist. But his reign will soon give way to chaos, proving that only Christ can bring true and lasting peace.

OLD TESTAMENT FORESHADOWS REVELATION:

I saw by night, and behold a man riding upon a red horse, and he stood among the myrtle trees that were in the bottom; and behind him were there red horses, speckled, and white. (Zechariah 1:8)

These horses in Zechariah, like those in Revelation 6, represent divine judgments and movements upon the earth. While Revelation 6:2's rider on the white horse is often interpreted as a counterfeit Christ or the Antichrist—going out to conquer with deceptive peace—Zechariah's horses also depict agents of God going out into the world to execute His will. The symbolism of colored horses, riders, and their global activity ties these prophetic passages together.

Irene sat across from me, her brow furrowed. "Ann, something about all this unsettles me. If the Rapture is a global event—people vanishing everywhere in an instant—then why is the Antichrist's first major move a peace treaty with Israel? Wouldn't the whole world be in chaos? Wouldn't everyone be desperate for peace?"

"That's a good question, Irene. Yes, it will be global chaos—planes falling from the sky, cars crashing, markets collapsing. Every nation will feel it. But here's the key: God's prophetic clock has always revolved around Israel. Not America. Not Europe. Israel."

"Right, I get that—Israel is the centerpiece of Bible prophecy. But why only Israel? Why not a global treaty?"

"Actually, the treaty has global implications, but it's confirmed—or finalized—with Israel. That's the key word in Daniel 9:27: the Antichrist 'confirms' a covenant with many, but the focus is on Israel. Think of it like this—Israel is the epicenter of the earthquake, but the shockwaves are felt around the world."

"So, you're saying this treaty is already on the table before the Rapture?"

"Possibly. Some scholars believe the treaty may already be in development—perhaps disguised as peace talks or buried within international diplomacy. But the Antichrist will rise after the Rapture as a charismatic global leader. The world will be desperate for answers—and for peace. Confirming a treaty with Israel, the most contested land in human history, will be his crowning achievement. He'll look like a genius."

"But if it's specific to Israel, how does it affect everyone else?"

"Because peace in the Middle East—especially in Jerusalem—isn't just a regional issue; it's a global one. The world's three major religions all have deep-rooted ties to the land. (Christianity: 2.4 billion; Islam: 1.9 billion; and Hinduism: 1.2 billion.) So, stabilizing Israel would impact energy markets, military alliances, and global political stability. Nearly every nation has a vested interest in what happens in that small but explosive piece of land."

"And that's when the Tribulation officially begins?"

"Yes. Not at the Rapture—the Rapture ends the Church Age. The Tribulation countdown begins with the signing—or confirming—of that seven-year treaty. That's when Daniel's 70th Week officially begins."

"So the Antichrist will look like a peacemaker?"

"Exactly. He'll appear to be the answer to all the world's problems. But halfway through that seven-year period, he'll break the treaty, desecrate the rebuilt temple, and demand to be worshiped. That's when all hell breaks loose—the Great Tribulation."

"So while the Church is gone, Israel becomes the center stage again?"

"Right. The focus shifts back to Israel. The Tribulation is designed to bring her to the point of surrender—so she'll recognize Jesus as the true Messiah. That's why it's called 'the time of Jacob's trouble.' It's not about punishing the Church—that part is finished. It's about God completing His plan for Israel."

"And what about the rest of the world during all this?"

"The rest of the world will suffer under God's judgment, yes. But Israel is where the spiritual battle reaches its peak. Jerusalem becomes ground zero for the final conflict between good and evil. That's why Satan wants it. That's why the Antichrist signs the treaty. And that's why Jesus returns—to reclaim it."

Irene sighed. "Ann . . . I have to admit, it's a lot. I always knew Israel was important in Bible prophecy, but this . . . this goes deeper than I imagined. A rebuilt temple? A peace treaty that triggers the Tribulation? And now—looking at your notes—you're saying there's a red heifer that plays a role?"

"Yes—and believe me, I felt just as overwhelmed when I first started studying all of this. But the more I learned, the clearer it became: nothing God does is random. The temple is key. And the red heifer? It's one of the final puzzle pieces before it can be rebuilt."

"Okay, walk me through this slowly. Why does the temple need to be rebuilt? And what's so special about the red heifer?"

"Let's start with the temple. Right now, there's no Jewish temple in Jerusalem. The first one—Solomon's Temple—was destroyed in 586 BC. The second—Herod's Temple, the one Jesus visited—was destroyed in AD 70, just as He said it would be. But according to Bible prophecy, a Third Temple will be rebuilt."

"During the Tribulation?"

"That's right. Scripture doesn't say exactly when—before or after the Rapture—but the temple must be standing by the midpoint of the Tribulation. That's when the Antichrist enters it, sets up what's called the 'abomination of desolation,' and demands to be worshiped as God. Jesus mentioned that in Matthew 24:15."

"And the red heifer—what does that have to do with rebuilding the temple?"

"According to Numbers 19, the ashes of a red heifer are required to purify both the Temple Mount and the priesthood. It's a ritual of purification. And Irene—this is where it gets wild—there hadn't been a certified red heifer in over 1600 years. But today, Israel has identified one. Pure. Without blemish. Not a single white hair. And it's being closely monitored by the Temple Institute."

"So you're saying they already have everything they need?"

"Almost everything. The temple is already prepared—in pieces—ready to be assembled. The priestly garments are made. Over 500 Levitical priests have been trained in ritual law. The temple vessels—menorahs, altars, utensils, shofars—they're all ready. The only thing holding them back is the site itself—and the international tension surrounding the Temple Mount."

"And you really think this red heifer could be the one?"

"I do. And the Jewish people do too. In their tradition, the red heifer appears just before the Messiah comes. For them, it signals His First Coming. But we know it will actually mark His second."

"It's just so surreal. I mean, how can one little cow . . . end up affecting the whole world?"

"Because it represents something bigger. It's not really about the cow—it's about the countdown. Every detail is falling into place, just as the Bible said it would. And the fact that it's happening in our lifetime? That should make us sit up straight. Jesus is coming soon, Irene."

"So . . . the Rapture could really happen any day?"

"Any moment. There's nothing in Bible prophecy that needs to be fulfilled before it happens. The Rapture ends the Church Age. Then the Antichrist rises. The treaty is signed. The Third Temple is rebuilt. The judgments begin. But we won't be here for that."

"Unless someone's not ready . . ."

"Exactly. And that's why I'm so passionate about sharing this—not to scare people, but to wake them up. This isn't some ancient myth. It's real. Prophecy isn't just history told in advance—it's God's love letter: warning us, inviting us to be ready. Just like Noah and the ark . . . once the door is shut, it's shut."

I sighed. "Irene, I'll never forget the moment I realized we were living in the final generation. I grew up hearing about prophecy—my godmother used to talk about the end times, the Rapture, the Antichrist—but it always felt far off, like a mystery only pastors and theologians could understand."

I continued. "But then one day, I started seeing the pieces fall into place. It was May 14, 2018—exactly 70 years after Israel became a nation. I remember reading the headlines: THE UNITED STATES RECOGNIZES JERUSALEM AS ISRAEL'S CAPITAL. It was all over the news. Some people cheered. Others rioted. But most had no idea they were witnessing Bible prophecy being fulfilled."

"And that's when it hit me. Jesus said in Matthew 24:32–34:"

Now learn a parable of the fig tree; When his branch is yet tender, and puts forth leaves, you know that summer is near. So likewise you, when you shall see all these things, know that it is near, even at the doors. Verily I say unto you, This generation shall not pass, till all these things be fulfilled. (Matthew 24:32–34)

"Israel is the fig tree. It was reborn May 14, 1948. And Jesus said the generation that sees this happen will not pass away until all is fulfilled."

"And I thought, Lord . . . how long is a generation?"

"Psalm 90:10 says:"

The days of our years are threescore years and ten (70 years); and if by reason of strength they be fourscore years (80 years), yet is their strength labor and sorrow; for it is soon cut off, and we fly away. (Psalm 90:10)

"Seventy to eighty years."

I did the math.

1948 + 70 = 2018

1948 + 80 = 2028

I felt a chill run down my spine.

"If Israel is the prophetic time clock . . . and a biblical generation is seventy to eighty years . . . and the Rapture happens before the Tribulation . . ."

"Irene, I dropped to my knees.

I started praying like never before.

Because that meant we were standing on the absolute edge of time. The Church Age is about to close. We are living in the final seconds before midnight.

Then, in 2019, something else happened.

I saw an article that made my heart stop: the Jewish population in Israel had officially surpassed the number of Jews living outside it.

For the first time since AD 135, the majority of Jews had returned to their homeland. Ezekiel 36 and 37—the dry bones coming to life—were being fulfilled right before my eyes.

And then came 2020.

The world shut down.

The economy collapsed.

Nations were on edge.

And suddenly, everything in Revelation 13—the push for global government, digital currencies, tracking systems, control over buying and selling—it wasn't some distant prophecy anymore. It was being implemented.

That's when I knew: there was no turning back.

Jesus is coming soon.

That's why I don't stay silent. I can't. I tell people—wake up! Open your eyes! We are the final generation.

If Israel is God's prophetic time clock . . . if the fig tree generation is nearing its end . . . if the red heifer has appeared . . . if the Third Temple is ready to rise—

Then tell me, Irene . . . what's left?"

Whispers. "Nothing."

"Nothing."

Tears in her eyes. "Ann, what if people don't listen? What if they don't believe?"

I said softly, "Then they'll be left behind.

And I don't want that for anyone.

Because the second that trumpet sounds, it's over. The Church is gone. And the world will have no idea what just happened."

I met Irene's eyes. "That's why I'm telling you now—why I tell everyone: Don't wait. Don't risk it. If we really are the final generation . . . then the Rapture could happen at any moment.

And when it does?

The Antichrist rises.

The peace treaty is signed.

And the clock on the Tribulation begins."

Irene leaned in, eyes wide. "So if the Rapture triggers the Tribulation . . . what happens next? I mean, after the peace treaty?"

I nodded and turned the page of my manuscript. "Then the Lamb opens the second seal."

Irene blinked. "That's Revelation 6, right?"

"Yes," I said quietly. "Revelation 6:3. The red horse appears. War breaks out. Peace vanishes from the earth. People turn on each other. It's the end of false security . . . and the beginning of global chaos."

THE REVELATION OF JESUS CHRIST REVEALS:

6:3 And when He had opened the second seal, I heard the second beast say, Come and see.

"And when He had opened the second seal." This continues the divine unveiling of end-time events. Jesus Christ, the Lamb who is worthy (Revelation 5:9), is the only one able to open the seals of the scroll handed to Him by God the Father. Each seal represents a stage of judgment or unfolding prophecy, and now we move to the second in this sequence.

"I heard the second beast say." The second living creature, or "beast," is one of the four living beings around the throne described in Revelation 4:6–8. These creatures are likely angelic or cherubic beings, symbolic of the authority and presence of God. Each beast calls forth a new rider with each seal, acting as heavenly announcers.

"Come and see." This phrase, repeated with the opening of the first four seals, is both an invitation and a declaration. John is being called to witness a new phase in the prophetic timeline. The phrase also carries urgency—these events are not hypothetical but are divinely appointed realities that must come to pass.

This verse is a transition; it prepares us for the second horseman of the apocalypse, who is revealed in the next verse (Revelation 6:4). While Revelation 6:3 by itself is brief, it is the key that opens the door to one of the most devastating global judgments: widespread war and bloodshed.

The second seal reminds us that human history is under divine orchestration. As chaotic as war and conflict appear on earth, God is not surprised or caught off guard. Each seal is part of God's sovereign plan, not random disaster. It also shows us that Christ is not only Savior but Judge. His authority includes the unfolding of justice on a global scale.

OLD TESTAMENT FORESHADOWS REVELATION:

And I turned, and lifted up my eyes, and looked, and, behold, there came four chariots out from between two mountains; and the mountains were mountains of brass. In the first chariot were red horses; and in the second chariot black horses, and in the third chariot white horses; and the fourth chariot grisled and bay horses. (Zechariah 6:1–3)

Just as in Revelation 6, Zechariah sees a prophetic vision of colored horses coming out at God's command. These horses in Zechariah represent spirits or angelic agents that go out to patrol and carry out God's will across the earth. The red horse in Zechariah, like the one in Revelation, is associated with war and bloodshed. In both books, God is revealing His sovereign control over future events through symbolic imagery. The visions are not just descriptive—they are predictive and declarative of divine judgment.

THE REVELATION OF JESUS CHRIST REVEALS:

6:4 And there went out another horse that was red: and power was given to him that sat thereon to take peace from the earth, and that they should kill one another: and there was given unto him a great sword.

The Second Seal Judgment—Red Horse of War. When the Lamb (Jesus Christ) opens the second seal, John hears the second living creature—one of the four surrounding the throne—say, "Come and see." What follows is a vision of a red horse, a fiery emblem of war, violence, and bloodshed.

The color red in Scripture is frequently associated with blood, violence, and judgment: Isaiah 63:2–3 describes the LORD coming with garments stained red from treading the winepress of His wrath. Nahum 2:3: "The shield of His mighty men is made red; the valiant men are in scarlet." This horse is no longer white and deceptive like the first (the Antichrist's illusion of peace); instead, it reveals the true face of human rebellion and divine judgment—war unleashed.

"And power was given to him that sat thereon to take peace from the earth." Note the language: "power was given." This rider operates only by permission of the Sovereign God. Just as Jesus allows the first rider to go forth in deceptive peace, He now allows this second rider to follow. The phrase emphasizes divine control—God is orchestrating judgment as He pulls back restraint.

This peace is not a localized ceasefire. It is worldwide. The Antichrist's supposed global peace, promised in the first seal, quickly crumbles. The second seal exposes that false peace never lasts—especially when it is rooted in deception.

"And that they should kill one another." What follows is widespread bloodshed. This points not only to international warfare, but also civil wars, racial conflicts, tribal violence, and personal hatred unleashed on a massive scale. Society begins to collapse from within. People turn on one another. Nations turn on nations. Trust is shattered.

This echoes Jesus' own prophecy:

> And you shall hear of wars and rumors of wars: see that you be not troubled: for all things must come to pass, but the end is not yet. For nation shall rise against nation, and kingdom against kingdom: and there shall be famines, and pestilences, and earthquakes, in diverse places. (Matthew 24:6–7)

Also echoed in:

> And because iniquity shall abound, the love of many shall wax cold. (Matthew 24:12)

This is a violent unraveling of human civilization—a preview of what happens when God removes His hand of restraint.

"And there was given unto him a great sword." The great sword represents unprecedented warfare. The Greek word for sword here is "*machaira*," often referring to a short sword or dagger used in close combat—symbolizing personal, hand-to-hand violence. Yet the fact that it is a "great" sword suggests this violence is not only personal—it is also widespread, devastating, and global.

This could encompass:

- Civil unrest and riots.
- Ethnic cleansing and genocide.
- Global warfare and mass destruction.
- Terrorism and lawlessness.

What began as a promise of unity under the Antichrist quickly turns to chaos and conflict, proving once again that peace apart from Christ is unsustainable.

This verse reminds us that true peace comes only from Jesus Christ, the Prince of Peace (Isaiah 9:6). Any peace that the world offers—especially from deceptive figures like the Antichrist—is fleeting and false. This red horseman is a solemn warning: without Christ, man always returns to conflict, and without the restraining hand of God, evil escalates uncontrollably.

OLD TESTAMENT FORESHADOWS REVELATION:

And I will call for a sword against him throughout all My mountains, says the Lord GOD: every man's sword shall be against his brother. (Ezekiel 38:21)

This verse echoes the same imagery found in Revelation 6:4: "Take peace from the earth . . . that they should kill one another." In Ezekiel 38:21: "Call for a sword . . . every man's sword against his brother." God's judgment involves turning people against each other—civil war, betrayal, and chaos—just as we see with the red horse of war in Revelation.

THE REVELATION OF JESUS CHRIST REVEALS:

6:5 And when He had opened the third seal, I heard the third beast say, Come and see. And I beheld, and lo a black horse; and he that sat on him had a pair of balances in his hand.

The Third Seal Judgment—Black Horse of Famine. Just as with the first two seals, it is Jesus Christ—the Lamb—who opens the third seal. The scroll He holds in Revelation 5 contains the judgments of God, and with each broken seal, another layer of end-time judgment unfolds on the earth. This is not chaos unfolding randomly—this is divine, ordered justice.

John again hears a voice—this time, the third of the four living creatures around God's throne (Revelation 4:6–8). With the same invitation—"Come and see"—John is drawn into yet another vivid and terrifying vision.

The rider appears on a black horse, the color of famine, despair, and economic collapse. Just as red symbolized bloodshed and war in the second seal, black represents the consequences of that war—famine (Matthew 24:7). In Lamentations 5:10, blackness is a poetic image of hunger:

Our skin was black like an oven because of the terrible famine. (Lamentations 5:10)

The rider holds a pair of balances (scales) in his hand—used for measuring food. This tells us two things:

1. **Scarcity**—Food is no longer sold in abundance but is measured precisely, even rationed.

2. **Economic Control**—The balances also symbolize a controlled economy, possibly manipulated under the direction of the coming world ruler—the Antichrist.

This imagery suggests a global economic crisis marked by hyperinflation, rationing, and extreme poverty. It paints a world where even basic sustenance becomes a luxury.

War doesn't just bring bloodshed—it disrupts agriculture, destroys supply chains, and cripples economies. Famine always follows war. That is what we are seeing in this judgment: a world in collapse, one seal at a time. Each judgment escalates in intensity, setting the stage for the Great Tribulation and the unveiling of the Antichrist's full authority.

OLD TESTAMENT FORESHADOWS REVELATION:

Moreover He said unto me, Son of man, behold, I will cut off the supply of bread in Jerusalem: and they shall eat bread by weight, and with care; and they shall drink water by measure, and with astonishment: That they may want bread and water, and be dismayed one with another, and waste away for their iniquity. (Ezekiel 4:16–17)

Just like the black horse's rider holds scales or balances, this passage from Ezekiel describes rationing food and water in Jerusalem as a sign of famine and judgment. It's a prophetic image of scarcity measured out—echoing the precise "measure of wheat for a penny" language in Revelation 6:6.

THE REVELATION OF JESUS CHRIST REVEALS:

6:6 And I heard a voice in the midst of the four beasts say, A measure of wheat for a penny, and three measures of barley for a penny; and see you hurt not the oil and the wine.

The black horse appears as the third seal is opened by the Lamb (Jesus Christ). The rider carries a pair of balances, signifying weighing and measuring—economic control and scarcity. This is a time of severe famine and inflation during the first half of the Tribulation.

"A measure of wheat for a penny, and three measures of barley for a penny." "Measure" (Greek: *choinix*) was about one quart—just enough for one person's daily food. "Penny" (Greek: *denarius*) was a full day's wage in New Testament times (Matthew 20:2). This means a full day's labor will earn just enough food for one person—no surplus, no provision for family. The alternative? Three measures of barley—cheaper but lower in nutrition. The poor will resort to this just to stay alive.

What would normally buy a family's groceries will only buy a single portion. Money loses its value. Food becomes a luxury. This signals a global famine, worsening the aftermath of the wars brought by the red horse (Revelation 6:4). This will be a prime opportunity for the Antichrist to rise and offer "solutions," seizing greater global control as people cry out for relief.

"And see you hurt not the oil and the wine." This mysterious phrase has prompted much study. Here's what it likely means:

1. **Preserved Luxuries**—Oil and wine were considered luxury items. This suggests the famine hits the poor hardest, while the wealthy continue to access finer things. A symbol of economic disparity: In a world collapsing, the elite are protected—highlighting the growing divide.

2. **Limited Destruction**—God places limits on judgment. Even in wrath, God controls the extent of famine. The oil and wine are spared, showing restraint in judgment—for now.

3. **Spiritual Symbolism**—Oil is often symbolic of the Holy Spirit. Wine is symbolic of joy, covenant, or even the blood of Christ.

Some scholars suggest this may hint at God's continued provision for His faithful—even during the Tribulation—but that interpretation would apply more directly to a remnant than the general population.

Though this is a future prophecy, it gives believers a sober reminder: God is in control of history. These seals are not random—they are opened by Christ Himself. The Church is called to watch and be ready, proclaiming the gospel while it is still the day of salvation.

> Behold, now is the accepted time; behold, now is the day of salvation. (2 Corinthians 6:2)

Revelation 6:6 is a sobering reminder that the Tribulation will be marked not only by war and chaos but also by deep economic distress. The black horse represents famine, inflation, and the collapse of stability—where even basic necessities become unaffordable, and daily survival becomes a burden.

This verse paints a world of growing inequality: many suffer, while a privileged few remain untouched. Yet even in this judgment, God shows restraint—setting limits so that His mercy tempers the unfolding justice.

OLD TESTAMENT FORESHADOWS REVELATION:

> And there was a great famine in Samaria: and, behold, they besieged it, until a donkey's head was sold for fourscore (eighty) pieces of silver, and the fourth part of a cab of dove's dung for five pieces of silver. (2 Kings 6:25)

This passage shows hyperinflation and desperation in a famine. People pay exorbitant prices for things that are normally worthless—mirroring the economic collapse seen in Revelation 6:6.

THE REVELATION OF JESUS CHRIST REVEALS:

^{6:7} And when He had opened the fourth seal, I heard the voice of the fourth beast say, Come and see.

This verse continues the dramatic unveiling of God's end-time judgments. With the opening of the fourth seal, another phase of divine wrath is released upon the earth.

"And when He had opened the fourth seal." Here, "He" refers to Jesus Christ, the only One found worthy to open the scroll and break its seals (Revelation 5:5–9). Each seal represents a prophetic event unleashed during the Tribulation period—a time of escalating judgment upon a rebellious and unrepentant world. The fourth seal marks a new level of severity, building upon the deception (white horse), war (red horse), and famine (black horse) that came before it. These judgments are cumulative and sequential, each one intensifying the devastation.

"I heard the voice of the fourth beast say, Come and see." The fourth living creature, one of the four cherubim surrounding God's throne (Revelation 4:6–8), calls John once again to observe the vision. The phrase "Come and see" invites John—and us—to behold what is not just a vision of judgment, but a warning, a revelation, and a call to repentance.

Each of the four living creatures is uniquely involved in unveiling the first four seals—signifying their heavenly authority and role in administering divine justice. Their voices thunder like a heavenly decree, granting permission for these end-time events to unfold.

This seal introduces the pale horse and its rider, death, with hell following (explored in Revelation 6:8). But verse 6:7 stands alone as the prelude, drawing our attention to the seriousness and sovereignty of this moment. Nothing is random—each seal is divinely timed and executed by Christ Himself.

God is not reacting; He is ruling.

This verse reminds us that Jesus remains in full control—every seal and rider acts under His authority. For believers, this brings comfort and urgency: comfort because our Savior reigns, and urgency because the world must be warned.

OLD TESTAMENT FORESHADOWS REVELATION:

For thus says the Lord GOD; How much more when I send My four severe judgments upon Jerusalem, the sword, and the famine, and the wild beast, and the pestilence, to cut off from it man and beast? (Ezekiel 14:21)

Ezekiel 14:21 is echoed directly in Revelation 6:7–8, where the fourth seal introduces Death riding a pale horse, with Hell following, and power is given over a fourth of the earth to kill "with sword, and with hunger, and with death, and with the beasts of the earth." These four judgments in Revelation reflect the same "four sore judgments" from Ezekiel:

1. Sword (war)
2. Famine (hunger)
3. Pestilence (death)
4. Beasts of the earth

Revelation 6:7–8 draws heavily from Ezekiel 14:21, showing that the judgments of the Tribulation are not new but consistent with God's historical dealings with unrepentant nations. The New Testament reveals the ultimate fulfillment of what was foreshadowed in the Old Testament.

THE REVELATION OF JESUS CHRIST REVEALS:

6:8 And I looked, and behold a pale horse: and his name that sat on him was Death, and Hell followed with him. And power was given to them over the fourth part of the earth, to kill with sword, and with hunger, and with death, and with the beasts of the earth.

The Fourth Seal Judgment—Pale Green Horse of Hell and Death. The Greek word for "pale" is *chloros*, denoting a greenish-sickly hue, the color of decay, disease, and decomposition. It's the color of death, reminiscent of a corpse. The rider atop this horse is not just symbolic—he is named: Death. And close behind him follows Hades (hell), the grave or the abode of the dead. This pair brings not only physical destruction but spiritual ruin, echoing Jesus' warning in Matthew 10:28:

Fear him which is able to destroy both soul and body in hell. (Matthew 10:28)

This is the only seal where the rider is named—"Death." But death doesn't ride alone. He is joined by Hades, personified as trailing behind him like a relentless undertaker, reaping souls that fall under his blade. Their mission is clear: mass destruction on a global scale.

A quarter of the earth's population will fall victim to this deadly judgment. Considering today's population, that would be nearly 1.5 billion people. This is not symbolic. The language in the text is *literal*, and it aligns with prophetic passages throughout Scripture warning of God's coming wrath.

This judgment arrives in four distinct waves, mirroring Ezekiel 14:21, which speaks of God's four severe judgments: ". . . the sword, and the famine, and the wild beast, and the pestilence." Revelation 6:8 names them specifically:

1. **The Sword**—Represents war, violence, and civil unrest.
2. **Hunger**—Following war, famine spreads, echoing the third seal.
3. **Death**—Possibly disease and pestilence—the natural result of war and starvation (Matthew 24:7).
4. **The Beasts of the Earth**—The Greek word *"therion"* suggests ferocious, untamed animals. Driven by desperation and hunger, animals will invade human spaces, attacking and killing. In a lawless, decaying world, nature itself turns hostile.

This passage evokes the image of the Grim Reaper—a chilling figure with a scythe who mows down humanity. But in Revelation, this is not folklore—it's a prophetic certainty. The fourth seal unleashes a supernatural and natural convergence of death, where human violence, natural disasters, spiritual judgment, and animal savagery work in harmony to execute divine wrath.

This is a wake-up call for the world. The pale horse signals that God's patience has run its course. The world's rejection of Christ results in judgment that comes swiftly, unmistakably, and severely. But even in this terrifying prophecy, there is a message: God is just, and He is faithful to His Word. The Book of Revelation doesn't just tell us what will happen—it urges us to repent and believe in the only One who can deliver us: Jesus Christ.

OLD TESTAMENT FORESHADOWS REVELATION:

And it shall come to pass, if they say unto you, Where shall we go forth? Then you shalt tell them, Thus says the LORD; Such as are for death, to death; and such as are for the sword, to the sword; and such as are for the famine, to the famine; and such as are for the captivity, to the captivity. And I will appoint over them four kinds, says the LORD: the sword to slay, the dogs to tear, the fowls of the heaven, and the beasts of the earth, to devour and destroy. (Jeremiah 15:2–3)

Revelation 6:8 aligns with Jeremiah 15:2–3. These warnings from God mirror the consequences of disobedience—again involving a strong fourfold judgment pattern—sword, famine, pestilence, and wild animals. This Old Testament verse forms the prophetic pattern of God's judgment—one that is intensified and expanded in the Tribulation narrative of Revelation.

Irene's eyes widened as she held her Bible open to Revelation 6. "Ann . . . have you ever noticed something strange about the four horsemen?"

I glanced up, intrigued. "What are you seeing?"

"Those colors—white, red, black, and green—they're the exact same ones you see in the flags of so many Middle Eastern nations. It's hard to ignore. I mean, seriously—it's like a divine fingerprint."

"You're absolutely right," I said, tilting my head thoughtfully. "Those colors—white, red, black, and green—are known as the Pan-Arab colors. They're deeply rooted in Arab history and Islamic tradition, and you'll find them in the flags of nations like Jordan, Kuwait, Palestine, Sudan, Syria, and the United Arab Emirates. They were chosen deliberately to represent Arab unity and Islamic identity."

I continued. "Interestingly, several non-Arab nations—like Iran, Afghanistan, Kenya, and South Africa—also include all four of these colors in their flags. Though not Pan-Arab in culture or ethnicity, the presence of these colors may still reflect powerful ideological or symbolic meaning."

"In total, there are at least thirteen national flags that feature all four of these colors," I clarified. "That's not just coincidence—it feels like prophetic design, aligning with biblical themes of regional alignment in the end times."

Irene nodded slowly. "And think about it . . . those colors aren't just there for dramatic effect. They represent conquest, war, famine, and death. And the nations that carry those colors? They're the very regions where turmoil, religious tension, and hostility toward Israel are most intense."

"Irene, that's no coincidence. It makes perfect sense when you trace the conflict all the way back to Abraham. Everything began with one pivotal decision—when Abraham and Sarah tried to fulfill God's promise in their own way by having a child through Hagar. That child was Ishmael."

"And God still blessed Ishmael—He promised that twelve princes would come from him. But the covenant—the everlasting covenant—that went to Isaac. That's the dividing line. Genesis 17:19–21 lays it out like a legal contract."

I nodded. "Exactly. Isaac was the son of promise. Through him came Jacob—and from Jacob, the twelve tribes of Israel. And through that line came the Messiah. Ishmael, on the other hand, became the father of many Arab nations. And ever since, the descendants of those two sons have been locked in a spiritual and geopolitical tug of war."

"You know what else blows my mind?" Irene continued. "God placed Israel right at the center of the world—strategically, geographically, spiritually. Ezekiel 5:5 says:"

> Thus says the LORD God; This is Jerusalem: I have set it in the midst of the nations and countries that are round about her. (Ezekiel 5:5)

"That's not a metaphor—it's a divine GPS marker from heaven."
I nodded, pulling out a map.

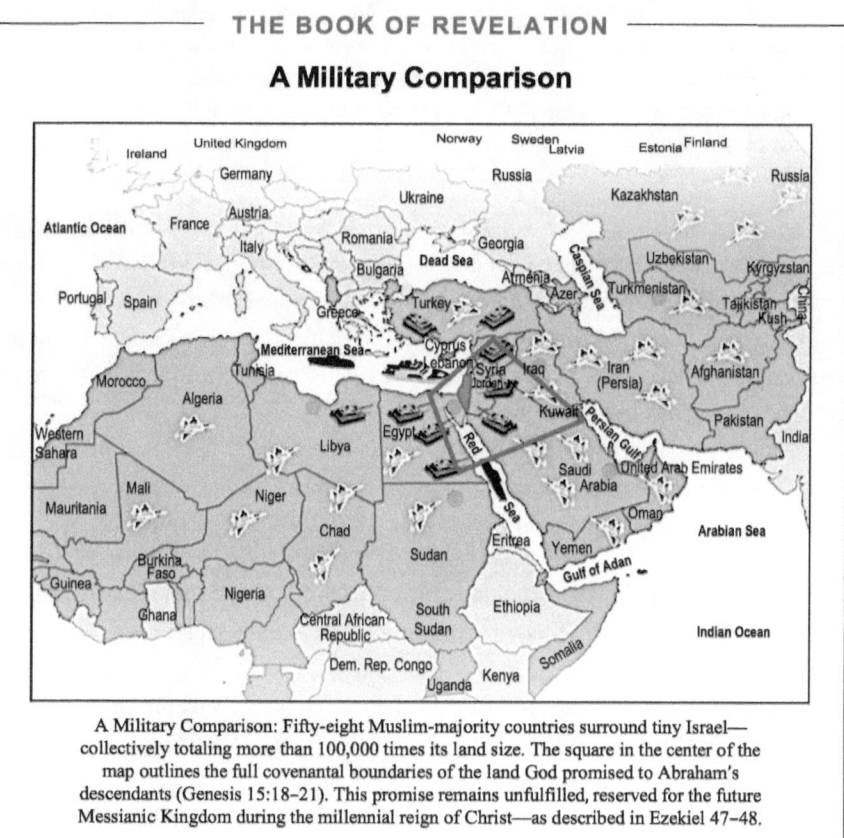

THE BOOK OF REVELATION

A Military Comparison

A Military Comparison: Fifty-eight Muslim-majority countries surround tiny Israel—collectively totaling more than 100,000 times its land size. The square in the center of the map outlines the full covenantal boundaries of the land God promised to Abraham's descendants (Genesis 15:18–21). This promise remains unfulfilled, reserved for the future Messianic Kingdom during the millennial reign of Christ—as described in Ezekiel 47–48.

"And even after all the persecution, exile, and attempted genocide—Israel is still here. Not just surviving, but thriving. May 14, 1948, marked the fulfillment of Amos 9:14–15. God brought them back, and He promised they would never again be uprooted."

> And I will bring again the captivity of My people of Israel, and they shall build the waste cities, and inhabit them; and they shall plant vineyards, and drink the wine thereof; they shall also make gardens, and eat the fruit of them. And I will plant them upon their land, and they shall no more be pulled up out of their land which I have given them, says the LORD your God. (Amos 9:14–15)

"That's what sets the Bible apart—its prophecies stand. They're not vague; they're detailed, time-stamped, and fulfilled in living color."

"And here's the kicker—God said He would bless those who bless Israel and curse those who curse her (Genesis 12:1–3). History proves it. Just look at the nations that turned against the Jews—Germany under Hitler is a prime example."

> Now the LORD had said unto Abram, Get you out of your country, and from your kindred, and from your father's house, unto a land that I will show you. And I will make of you a great nation, and I will bless you, and make your name great; and you shalt be a blessing. And I will bless them that bless you, and curse him that curses you: and in you shall all families of the earth be blessed. (Genesis 12:1–3)

Irene sighed. "And yet, even today, Israel is a global tech hub. Intel, Google, Apple—they're all there. The Iron Dome, Waze, voicemail, USB drives . . . all of it came out of that tiny strip of land—smaller than New Jersey."

I nodded. "And people still ask why the Bible focuses so much on Israel. Because God does. It's not about politics—it's about prophecy. Not about nationalism—it's about covenant."

"That's why I'm watching the Middle East so closely. The four horsemen's colors, the rebirth of Israel, the global shift toward digital currency—it's all converging. We're not just reading prophecy anymore. We're living it."

"Ann, I keep seeing the same theme come up in every article and video—this war in Ezekiel 38 and 39. Isn't that what they call the Gog and Magog war?"

"Yes, exactly. The war described in Ezekiel 38 and 39 is one of the most dramatic end times prophecies in the Bible. It speaks of a coalition of nations rising up against Israel in the last days—led by a figure called Gog from the land of Magog. That's why it's often called the Gog and Magog war."

"And that coalition of nations—doesn't it sound eerily like the very nations dominating today's headlines?"

"Absolutely, Irene. Magog is widely believed to be modern-day Russia. Persia? That's Iran. Then you have Cush—likely parts of modern-day Sudan; that was ancient Ethiopia—and Put, most often associated with Libya. Gomer and Beth Togarmah point to regions in Turkey and Central Asia. What's stunning is this: many of these nations were never close allies historically. And yet today, we're watching unprecedented alliances form—particularly between Russia, Iran, and Turkey. All of them openly hostile toward Israel."

"That's exactly what gave me chills! Ezekiel, Daniel, and John weren't writing fiction—they were recording divine previews of our day. These prophecies were written more than 2,500 years ago, yet it's like reading today's headlines. Every piece is falling into place."

"Yes, and what's even more remarkable is how the attack unfolds. Ezekiel tells us this invasion will come when Israel is living in perceived safety—likely after a temporary peace. But then, in a stunning display of divine power, God Himself steps in. He unleashes earthquakes, torrential hail, fire from heaven, and even causes the armies to turn on one another in confusion. It's not just military defeat—it's divine judgment."

Irene furrowed her brow. "So it's not Israel that saves herself?"

Shaking my head slowly. "No—Irene, God does. That's the point. It won't be military might or political strategy. It'll be unmistakably divine. So supernatural, the whole world will have no choice but to recognize it was the hand of the God of Israel. Like He says in Ezekiel 38:23:"

> Thus will I magnify Myself, and sanctify Myself; and I will be known in the eyes of many nations, and they shall know that I am the LORD. (Ezekiel 38:23)

"That reminds me of Psalm 83, too. Isn't that another war prophecy?"

I nodded. "Many scholars believe Psalm 83 could be either a distinct prophetic war or a prayer describing a confederation of enemies that have historically sought to wipe out Israel. The psalmist lists a coalition—Edom (southern Jordan), Moab (central Jordan), Ammon (northern Jordan), Amalek (southern Israel), Philistia (Gaza Strip), and others—all ancient enemies of Israel, which today correspond to modern Arab nations surrounding her."

"That really sounds like a prelude to Ezekiel's war."

"It could be. Some see Psalm 83 as a regional conflict involving Israel's immediate neighbors—possibly a setup for the larger coalition in Ezekiel 38–39. Psalm 83:4 says:"

> They have said, Come, and let us cut them off from being a nation; that the name of Israel may be no more in remembrance. (Psalm 83:4)

"That mindset is still very much alive today among many of Israel's enemies."

"It's sobering, Ann—and yet amazing—to see how God laid it all out in His Word."

"That's why watching Israel is so important prophetically. These aren't just isolated verses—they're threads in a vast, divine tapestry. And when you see all the threads coming together . . . you realize we truly are living in the final moments before Christ returns."

———◆◆◆———

THE REVELATION OF JESUS CHRIST REVEALS:

6:9 And when He had opened the fifth seal, I saw under the altar the souls of them that were slain for the Word of God, and for the testimony which they held.

The Fifth Seal Judgment—A Shift from Judgment to Witness. Unlike the first four seals, which unleash external judgments upon the earth—conquest, war, famine, and death—the fifth seal reveals something different: the heavenly scene of martyrs who have died for their faith. This is a pause in judgment and a glimpse behind the veil, showing the spiritual cost of faithfulness during the Tribulation.

"I saw under the altar the souls of them." The image of souls under the altar alludes to the Old Testament tabernacle and temple, where blood from sacrifices was poured out beneath the altar (Leviticus 4:7). These martyrs are not forgotten—they are honored as those whose lives were offerings for the cause of Christ. Their presence under the altar symbolizes that their death was a holy sacrifice.

"That were slain for the Word of God." This verse clearly states *why* they were killed: for holding onto God's Word and remaining faithful to the testimony of Jesus. During the Tribulation, access to Scripture and any proclamation of biblical truth will be met with violent opposition. These believers boldly refused to compromise, even under threat of death.

"And for the testimony which they held." They weren't martyred for vague spiritual ideals—they were slain because they clung to specific truths: that Jesus is Lord, that salvation is only through Him, and that the Antichrist system must be rejected, including the mark of the beast. These may include Tribulation saints who come to faith after the Rapture, often through the witness left behind by today's believers—such as Bibles, sermons, or warnings not to accept the mark.

This verse underscores a sobering reality: true faith will cost people their lives during the Tribulation. These individuals are not raptured saints, but those who believed during the Tribulation and stood against the Antichrist's system. Many may be former skeptics who find left behind Bibles, books, or videos and are convicted to stand for Christ even at the cost of death (Matthew 24:9–10).

The fifth seal reveals the souls of martyrs under the heavenly altar—those who gave their lives for the Word of God and the testimony of Jesus Christ. They represent the courageous believers of the Tribulation, who stood firm against the Antichrist and refused to deny Christ, even unto death. Their sacrifice is not forgotten. Instead, it's honored in heaven, and their blood cries out for justice, as we will see in the next verses.

OLD TESTAMENT FORESHADOWS REVELATION:

And the priest shall put some of the blood upon the horns of the altar of sweet incense before the LORD, which is in the tabernacle of the congregation; and shall pour all the blood of the bull at the bottom of the altar of the burnt offering, which is at the door of the tabernacle of the congregation. (Leviticus 4:7)

Just as blood was poured at the altar's base in the tabernacle, the souls under the altar in Revelation 6:9 symbolize lives offered in sacrifice—now they are remembered in the holy place of God's presence.

THE REVELATION OF JESUS CHRIST REVEALS:

6:10 And they cried with a loud voice, saying, How long, O Lord, holy and true, do You not judge and avenge our blood on them that dwell on the earth?

This powerful verse—the cry for justice from the martyrs—reveals the heartfelt plea of the souls under the altar; those who were slain for the Word of God and their unwavering testimony (Revelation 6:9). These are Tribulation martyrs, those who refused to bow to the Antichrist, take the mark of the beast, or deny the Lord—even at the cost of their lives.

They are not crying out for personal vengeance, but for divine justice—for God's holiness to be upheld and for the truth to be vindicated on the earth.

"How long, O Lord?" This question, "How long?" echoes the cries of the prophets and psalmists throughout the Old Testament:

- Psalm 94:3—"LORD, how long shall the wicked, how long shall the wicked triumph?"
- Habakkuk 1:2—"O LORD, how long shall I cry, and You will not hear!"

The longing for justice is not new—it's been on the hearts of the righteous throughout every age. But here, in Revelation 6:10, the cry is amplified, because these souls died in the most intense persecution the world has ever seen.

"Holy and true." They appeal to God's character, the two attributes of God most relevant in this moment:

- Holy—Set apart, righteous, unable to overlook evil.
- True—Faithful to His promise, especially His promise to judge the wicked and deliver the righteous.

Their question is a faith-filled plea, trusting that God will answer—but also recognizing the tension between His mercy and His justice. They are not accusing God, but waiting on His perfect timing.

"Do You not judge and avenge our blood." The martyrs are not seeking personal revenge. This is not bitterness; it is righteous indignation—a longing for

God to bring His justice against those who rebelled, persecuted, and killed His servants. Their blood, like Abel's, cries out for God to act (Genesis 4:10). In fact, in Romans 12:19, we are reminded:

> Dearly beloved, avenge not yourselves, but rather give place unto wrath: for it is written, Vengeance is Mine, I will repay, says the Lord. (Romans 12:19)

The time is coming when that repayment will begin—especially during the judgments of the trumpets and bowls to come in later chapters of Revelation.

"On them that dwell on the earth." This phrase is used repeatedly in Revelation to refer to the earth dwellers who are in rebellion against God, those who have rejected truth and embraced the Antichrist. These martyrs are no longer of the earth—their home is in heaven. They are calling on God to deal with those who continue to rebel, persecute, and destroy the people of God.

Though this verse speaks prophetically of a future group of martyrs, it reminds us that:

- God sees and hears the cries of the persecuted.
- Justice may be delayed, but it will not be denied.
- In the face of injustice, we must cling to the truth that God is holy, true, and just—and His judgment will be perfect.

OLD TESTAMENT FORESHADOWS REVELATION:

> O Lord GOD, to whom vengeance belongs—O God, to whom vengeance belongs, shine forth! Rise up, O Judge of the earth; render punishment to the proud. LORD, how long will the wicked, how long will the wicked triumph? (Psalm 94:1–3)

Just like the martyrs in Revelation, the psalmist calls out to the Judge of the earth, asking how long the wicked will be allowed to flourish.

THE REVELATION OF JESUS CHRIST REVEALS:

> [6:11] And white robes were given to every one of them; and it was said to them, that they should rest yet for a little season, until their fellow-servants also and their brethren, that should be killed as they were, should be fulfilled.

This verse offers a deeply moving glimpse into the divine response to the cry of the martyrs from the previous verse (Revelation 6:10). The souls of those who were slain for their unwavering testimony and for the Word of God are seen under the heavenly altar—a place symbolizing sacrifice and divine justice. God's answer to their cry is not immediate vengeance, but a robe, a promise, and a pause.

"And white robes were given to every one of them." The giving of white robes signifies vindication, purity, and heavenly reward. These martyrs, though killed by the world, are honored in heaven. The robe is not merely a garment but a declaration of their faithfulness and a sign that they belong to the Lamb (Revelation 7:14). It's a heavenly affirmation that their suffering was not in vain.

"And it was said to them, that they should rest yet for a little season." God tells them to rest, suggesting a period of peace and waiting. This echoes the divine pattern found throughout Scripture—God's judgment is certain, but often delayed to allow His purposes to unfold fully. In this case, the waiting points to the continuation of martyrdom during the Tribulation.

This delay does not mean God is inactive or indifferent. Rather, it reflects His mercy, allowing time for others to come to faith—even though it will cost them their lives. The phrase "a little season" reveals that God's timeline is purposeful and controlled. Justice will come. But for now, grace and prophecy must be fulfilled.

"Until their fellow-servants also and their brethren, that should be killed as they were, should be fulfilled." This sobering statement reveals a prophetic truth: the persecution is not yet over. Many more will come to faith in Christ during the Tribulation—and many of them will face martyrdom. This highlights both the severity of the Tribulation period and the cost of discipleship in a world ruled by the Antichrist and hostile to truth.

This portion of Scripture also dispels any false teaching that believers will be immune to suffering. Even after the Rapture, those who turn to Christ will pay dearly for their faith. Yet heaven honors them deeply.

Revelation 6:11 captures the mercy, justice, and divine patience of God. It reminds us that the road of faith may be costly, but God never forgets His own. The white robes represent eternal honor. The delay in judgment reveals a divine plan in motion. And the continuation of martyrdom points to the ongoing battle between light and darkness—a battle that will end in Christ's ultimate victory.

OLD TESTAMENT FORESHADOWS REVELATION:

I beheld, and the same horn made war with the saints, and prevailed against them; Until the Ancient of Days (God the Father) came, and judgment was given to the saints to the Most High; and the time came that the saints possessed the Kingdom. (Daniel 7:21–22)

Daniel 7:21–22 parallels Revelation 6:11 by depicting a time when the saints are persecuted—just as the martyrs under the altar are slain for their testimony. The phrase "judgment was given" mirrors their cry for justice in Revelation 6:10, and "until the time came" reflects the instruction to "rest yet for a little season." Both passages highlight persecution followed by God's promised vindication.

◆ ◆ ◆

Irene traced Revelation 6:9 with a furrowed brow. "Ann, it says the souls of the martyrs are under the altar. Aren't believers supposed to go straight to heaven when they die?"

I nodded. "They do—if they're in Christ. But these are Tribulation martyrs—those who came to faith after the Rapture and were killed. They're in heaven, but under the altar, symbolizing their sacrifice. In the Old Testament, blood was poured out at the base of the altar. These saints gave their lives for Christ—their souls cry out for justice."

Irene blinked. "So they can speak?"

"Yes. They're fully conscious—praying, crying out. And they're given white robes, which suggests they have some kind of intermediate body—not yet glorified, but visible and vocal. Like Moses and Elijah at the Transfiguration."

"She nodded. "So they're waiting for resurrection—just like the Old Testament saints?"

"Exactly. When Jesus rose, He moved *paradise* to heaven. Now, they're part of the great cloud of witnesses—watching, waiting, praying for justice and for the day their bodies are made new."

Irene whispered, "It's sobering."

I nodded. "And beautiful. The altar isn't just about sacrifice—it's about worship and victory."

THE REVELATION OF JESUS CHRIST REVEALS:

6:12 And I beheld when He had opened the sixth seal, and, lo, there was a great earthquake; and the sun became black as sackcloth of hair, and the moon became as blood.

The Sixth Seal Judgment—Cosmic and Earthly Upheaval. When the sixth seal is opened, we are no longer in the realm of symbolic horsemen—this seal unleashes literal, global cataclysms. The earth quakes violently, the sun turns black like sackcloth, and the moon becomes blood red. These signs are not mere natural disasters—they are divine disturbances. The imagery echoes Old Testament apocalyptic passages (Joel 2:31; Isaiah 13:10), where celestial changes announce God's direct intervention in human history.

This moment signals the beginning of the Day of the Lord—a time of judgment, cleansing, and preparation for Christ's return. The events described shake both the physical and spiritual order of creation. God is not just judging individuals—He is purging the earth and the heavens in preparation for His millennial reign. Those who have rejected Christ and ignored His gospel will be present on earth during the shaking. They will witness firsthand what it means to experience the wrath of the Lamb—not from the Antichrist, but from Christ Himself.

This passage is a stark reminder: the wrath of God is real, and it is coming. But for the Church, there is hope—we are not appointed unto wrath (1 Thessalonians 5:9). This is why the message must be preached. The time is short. The call is urgent.

OLD TESTAMENT FORESHADOWS REVELATION:

And I will show wonders in the heavens and in the earth, blood, and fire, and pillars of smoke. The sun shall be turned into darkness, and the moon into blood, before the great and terrible Day of the Lord come. (Joel 2:30–31)

Just like in Revelation 6:12, we see the sun darkened and the moon turning to blood—clear cosmic signs preceding God's final judgment.

THE REVELATION OF JESUS CHRIST REVEALS:

$^{6:13}$ And the stars of heaven fell unto the earth, even as a fig tree casts her untimely figs, when she is shaken of a mighty wind.

Revelation 6:13 continues the vivid, terrifying vision of the sixth seal being opened by the Lamb, Jesus Christ. This verse describes a cosmic upheaval that follows the great earthquake and the darkening of the sun and moon in the previous verse (Revelation 6:12). The imagery used here is both prophetic and poetic, illustrating judgment with unmistakable force.

"And the stars of heaven fell unto the earth." This phrase likely refers to a massive celestial disturbance. It may describe a meteor storm, an intense falling of heavenly bodies such as comets, meteors, or perhaps even something supernatural in origin. In prophetic language, "stars" often symbolize political or angelic powers (Isaiah 34:4; Revelation 12:4). Here, it may represent literal cosmic events or a symbolic collapse of earthly powers and rulers, all under divine judgment.

"Even as a fig tree casts her untimely figs." This simile highlights the sudden and violet nature of God's judgment. Just as unripe figs fall too soon in a storm, so the stars (or powers) fall before their time—symbolizing unpreparedness and loss.

"When she is shaken of a mighty wind." Wind, in prophetic literature, often signifies divine action (Jeremiah 4:11–13). Here, it represents the overwhelming power of God's judgment that shakes not only the earth but also the heavens.

Revelation 6:13 is a clear escalation of divine judgment. It reveals a world that is not only trembling beneath the feet of men but also above their heads. The heavens, once considered stable and eternal, are disturbed in a way that reflects the wrath of the Lamb. For those on earth, these signs will be terrifying evidence that the natural order is unraveling—and God is in control of it all.

OLD TESTAMENT FORESHADOWS REVELATION:

And all the host of heaven shall be dissolved, and the heavens shall be rolled together as a scroll: and all their host shall fall down, as the leaf falls off from the vine, and as a falling fig from the fig tree. (Isaiah 34:4)

This verse in Isaiah mirrors the same celestial chaos depicted in Revelation. Both passages describe the falling of heavenly bodies and use the fig tree as a symbol of sudden collapse. Isaiah is speaking of God's judgment against the nations, and Revelation expands that scope to a global, end times judgment initiated by the Lamb.

THE REVELATION OF JESUS CHRIST REVEALS:

6:14 And the heaven departed as a scroll when it is rolled together; and every mountain and island were moved out of their places.

This verse describes one of the most cataclysmic events in the entire Book of Revelation. As the sixth seal is opened, the world experiences a cosmic unraveling that goes beyond natural disaster—it is a supernatural disruption of creation itself.

When John writes that "the heaven departed as a scroll when it is rolled together," he's describing the violent upheaval of the sky—as if the very fabric of space is being peeled back. This could be interpreted literally or symbolically, but in either case, it reveals a divine unveiling—the barrier between heaven and earth is being removed, and the presence of God is drawing near. It's reminiscent of Isaiah 34:4, which uses almost identical language.

In fact, throughout the Old Testament, the Bible consistently speaks of God "stretching out the heavens." These aren't just poetic expressions—they may hint at profound truths about the fabric of the cosmos itself.

- "Who alone stretches out the heavens . . ."—Job 9:8.
- "Stretching out heaven like a tent curtain . . ."—Psalm 104:2.
- "Who stretches out the heavens like a curtain, and spreads them out like a tent to dwell in . . ."—Isaiah 40:22.
- "He has stretched out the heavens . . ."—Jeremiah 10:12.
- "The LORD who stretches out the heavens . . ."—Zechariah 12:1.

This repeated phrase appears not only in Isaiah, Jeremiah, and the Psalms, but also in books like Job, Zechariah, Ezekiel, and even 2 Samuel. The idea of the heavens being "stretched" is one of the most consistent cosmological descriptions in Scripture—and it aligns with modern concepts in astrophysics about the expansion of the universe.

But Scripture takes it further. The Bible describes space not as empty and void, but as something with physical properties.

- Torn—"Oh that you would rend the heavens . . ."—Isaiah 64:1.
- Worn out like a garment—Psalm 102:25–26.
- Shaken—Hebrews 12:26; Haggai 2:6; Isaiah 13:13.
- Burnt up—2 Peter 3:12.
- Split apart like a scroll—Revelation 6:14.
- Rolled up like a mantle or scroll—Hebrews 1:12; Isaiah 34:4.

These descriptions suggest that space is not merely an empty void, but a substance—something that can be stretched, shaken, worn out, or rolled up. If space can be torn or bent, then it implies that space exists within a larger framework—it has structure, tension, and perhaps even additional dimensions.

Modern physics now explores concepts like the curvature of space-time and higher dimensions—realities the Bible hinted at thousands of years ago. For example, Isaiah 40:22 refers to "the circle of the earth," and Paul speaks of a third heaven in 2 Corinthians 12:2—both suggesting truths beyond ancient understanding.

So, when Scripture describes God "stretching the heavens," it might not just be metaphorical language. It could be divine insight into a reality that modern science is only beginning to grasp.

The second part of the verse, "every mountain and island were moved out of their places," signals massive geological and planetary upheaval. It is not a localize event—it affects every continent and oceanic body. The imagery here conveys a shaking so profound that the entire structure of the earth is destabilized. This is not merely a natural earthquake but a divine act of judgment.

This verse also echoes Haggai 2:6:

> Yet once more, in a little while, I will shake the heavens and the earth and the sea and the dry land. (Haggai 2:6)

Together, these prophetic images show that the world as we know it will not just end gradually or politically—it will end dramatically and divinely, with creation itself reacting to the presence and power of the Lamb. The sixth seal is a terrifying preview of the Day of the Lord, when all earthly and heavenly security is stripped away, and no place remains to hide (Matthew 24:7, 29).

OLD TESTAMENT FORESHADOWS REVELATION:

The mountains quake at Him, and the hills melt, and the earth is burned at His presence, yea, the world, and all that dwell therein. (Nahum 1:5)

This emphasizes the global impact of God's presence—just as in Revelation, where the earth itself responds to divine wrath.

———◆◆◆———

"Ann, what you just said struck me. If the Tribulation isn't just about judgment—but also restoration—then could the sixth seal be more than wrath? Could it be the start of God's physical restoration of creation itself?"

THE BOOK OF REVELATION

Supercontinent—Pangaea

Supercontinent—Pangaea, the landmass that existed when all continents were joined as one.

My eyes lit up. "Exactly. Revelation 6:12–14 isn't just chaos—it reads like a reordering. A cosmic reset. The beginning of creation's restoration."

"Right! What if this isn't just judgment—but preparation? God resetting the earth for the Millennial Kingdom, for Christ's thousand-year reign."

I nodded. "Think about it—Genesis 1:9 says:"

And God said, Let the waters under the heaven be gathered together unto one place, and let the dry land appear: and it was so. (Genesis 1:9)

"That means the earth started with one landmass. Scientists call it Pangaea, but Scripture said it first—long before geology caught up."

"And then later in Genesis 10:25, it says:"

And unto Eber were born two sons: the name of one was Peleg; for in his days was the earth divided; and his brother's name was Joktan. (Genesis 10:25)

"That suggests the single landmass was broken apart during his lifetime— most likely after the Flood, through massive tectonic shifts."

THE BOOK OF REVELATION

The Seven Continents and the Oceans of the World

Supercontinent divides into seven continents in the days of Peleg (Genesis 10:25)—occurring around 100 years after Noah's Flood (2348 BC). This timeline places Peleg's life at a key point in early post-Flood history, when God was reshaping the world and dispersing the nations.

"So what if the massive earthquake in the sixth seal is the reversal of that?" I continued. "What if God is pulling the land back together—restoring creation to how it was in Eden? One land. One people. One King."

"And that ties in with the idea that the heavens are being purged too. Revelation says the sky recedes like a scroll. That's not just earthly—it's cosmic. It echoes Isaiah 34:4:"

> And all the host of heaven shall be dissolved, and the heavens shall be rolled together as a scroll: and all their host shall fall down, as the leaf falls off from the vine, and as a falling fig from the fig tree. (Isaiah 34:4)

"A powerful link between Old and New Testament prophecy."

"Yes, Irene! That line in Revelation 6:13—'the stars of heaven fell to the earth'—has often been seen as meteor showers or judgment. But what if it also points to atmospheric collapse or cosmic upheaval? Zechariah 14:6–7 talks about unpredictable changes in light. Think about it—if massive earthquakes trigger volcanic eruptions, ash could darken the sun and make the moon appear blood-red."

"So when it says the sun turns black and the moon like blood, that could literally be volcanic ash darkening the skies. It's not just poetic—it's a physical sign of global upheaval."

"Yes, Irene! The Lord isn't just purging sin—He's restoring creation. These judgments are part of His plan to prepare the earth for His Kingdom. That's what makes it so powerful—they're redemptive."

"It's like going from Eden . . . back to Eden. Full circle. The fall is being reversed, piece by piece, during the Tribulation. It's not just the wrath of the Lamb—it's His love, restoring what was lost."

"Exactly. And when judgment begins, people won't just fear destruction—they'll try to hide. Revelation 6:15–16 says they'll cry out for the rocks to fall on them, to shield them from the face of Him who sits on the throne. But what they're witnessing isn't just wrath—it's the unveiling of divine glory, authority, and the coming reign of Christ."

"Isn't it fitting? God always restores before He fills. In Genesis 1, He formed the earth before filling it. In salvation, He cleanses us before filling us with the Holy Spirit. And in Revelation, He's doing it again—restoring creation before establishing His Kingdom."

"I love that, Irene. Restoration always precedes glory—it's God's pattern. From Eden to Eden, from division to unity. The earth, once fractured by sin, will be made whole again under the reign of our King."

"It's so beautiful. Revelation isn't just about what we escape—it's about what He's preparing. That gives us so much more hope."

Smiling, I whispered, "Amen. Maranatha. Come, Lord Jesus—restore it all."

Irene, thoughtfully: "Can you imagine it? One land. No borders. No more war. Christ reigning from Jerusalem in justice and peace."

"And the nations will come to Him, just like Isaiah said. They'll beat their swords into plowshares—and learn war no more."

"A world finally at rest—not because of human effort, but because the Creator Himself stepped in and set all things right."

"It truly is the restoration of all things. From Genesis to Revelation—He is the Alpha and the Omega, the First and the Last, the Beginning and the End."

THE REVELATION OF JESUS CHRIST REVEALS:

$^{6:15}$ And the kings of the earth, and the great men, and the rich men, and the chief captains, and the mighty men, and every bondman, and every free man, hid themselves in the dens and in the rocks of the mountains.

This verse reveals the universal terror that overtakes the world when the sixth seal is opened. From the most powerful rulers—"kings of the earth"—to the bondmen and commoners, no one is exempt from the fear and dread of God's wrath. The devastation from the great earthquake, cosmic disturbances, and environmental collapse causes a complete breakdown of human pride, social rank, and earthly power.

Those who once ruled nations, commanded armies, accumulated wealth, and stood in high positions are now reduced to hiding in fear. Their power, prestige, and possessions can't protect them from divine judgment. What's especially striking is that even the rich and mighty—those who are typically insulated from earthly disasters—are just as desperate as slaves and commoners, seeking shelter "in the dens and in the rocks of the mountains."

It's a picture of total collapse—social, political, economic, and military systems crumbling. All confidence in man is shaken. This verse sets the tone for the true Day of the Lord, when humanity is brought face to face with the reality that refuge is not found in caves or mountains, but in Christ alone.

OLD TESTAMENT FORESHADOWS REVELATION:

And they shall go into the holes of the rocks, and into the caves of the earth, for fear of the LORD, and for the glory of His majesty, when He arises to shake terribly the earth. (Isaiah 2:19)

This verse perfectly mirrors Revelation 16:15 in both imagery and context. Both describe a universal dread that falls upon humanity—from the high-ranking to the humble—when God's terrifying presence and judgment are made known.

THE REVELATION OF JESUS CHRIST REVEALS:

6:16 And said to the mountains and rocks, Fall on us, and hide us from the face of Him that sits on the throne, and from the wrath of the Lamb.

This verse marks one of the most dramatic moments in Scripture—humanity's direct confrontation with the reality of divine judgment. The people of the earth, from the most powerful kings to the lowest servants (as described in verse 15), now plead with nature itself to bury them—not to escape physical destruction, but to avoid facing the presence of God and the Lamb.

What is especially striking here is the fear not just of judgment, but of the very face of God. They're terrified by His unveiled presence—His holiness, His justice, His truth. This is not merely about global catastrophe, but about spiritual accountability. Their request for the rocks and mountains to fall on them is a desperate plea for annihilation over confrontation. They would rather be crushed to death than stand before the One they have rejected.

The phrase "wrath of the Lamb" is intentionally paradoxical. Lambs are symbolic of innocence, gentleness, and sacrifice—especially Christ, the Lamb of God who takes away the sin of the world (John 1:29). But here, the Lamb is not passive—He is the risen, glorified Christ who now executes righteous judgment. Those who once dismissed or mocked His mercy must now face His holy wrath.

This verse powerfully illustrates that no one can hide from the truth of God's existence or His authority forever. There will come a time when His patience ends, and those who refused His grace must face His justice.

OLD TESTAMENT FORESHADOWS REVELATION:

The high places also of Aven, the sin of Israel, shall be destroyed: the thorn and the thistle shall come up on their altars; and they shall say to the mountains, Cover us; and to the hills, Fall on us. (Hosea 10:8)

This verse from Hosea foretells the coming judgment upon Israel for its idolatry and rebellion. The cry to the mountains to "cover us" and to the hills to "fall on us" is a plea to escape the terror of divine judgment—just as it is in Revelation 6:16. It reflects the same dread of God's presence in His role as righteous Judge.

THE REVELATION OF JESUS CHRIST REVEALS:

6:17 For the great day of His wrath is come; and who will be able to stand?

This verse concludes the terrifying sequence of the sixth seal, marking a dramatic climax in the first wave of God's judgment during the Tribulation. It is not merely a question, but a rhetorical cry of desperation from those experiencing the unraveling of the natural world and the undeniable reality of divine wrath.

"For the great day of His wrath is come." This phrase refers to the long-prophesied Day of the Lord—a time of divine judgment foretold by many Old Testament prophets (for example, Joel, Zephaniah, Isaiah). It signals a shift from human control to God's direct intervention in the affairs of earth. Up until this point, many may have dismissed God's sovereignty. But now, even the kings, military leaders, and wealthy elites recognize that the events unfolding are from God Himself—and that they are powerless to stop it.

"And who shall be able to stand?" This echoes Malachi 3:2, which asks, "But who may abide the day of His coming? And who shall stand when He appears?" It is a solemn reminder that no human strength, status, or wealth will be sufficient to endure God's judgment. Only those who are sealed by God—redeemed by the blood of the Lamb—will stand in the day of His wrath.

This moment strips away all illusions of control or self-sufficiency. It forces the unrepentant to acknowledge God's throne and the Lamb's authority. The phrase is both a warning and a call: Only those in Christ will be able to stand.

OLD TESTAMENT FORESHADOWS REVELATION:

And the LORD shall utter His voice before His army: for His camp is very great: for He is strong that executes His word: for the Day of the Lord is great and very terrible; and who can abide it? (Joel 2:11)

Joel prophesies the terrifying Day of the Lord, matching the language and tone of Revelation 6:17. It emphasizes the inevitability and overwhelming power of God's coming judgment.

THE REVELATION OF JESUS CHRIST REVEALS:

8:1 And when He had opened the seventh seal, there was silence in heaven about the space of half an hour.

The Seventh Seal Judgment—A Holy Pause. This verse marks a dramatic pause in the unfolding of divine judgment. Up until this point, the breaking of each seal has brought increasingly intense scenes of judgment, suffering, and cosmic disruption. But now as the seventh and final seal is broken by the Lamb (Jesus Christ), an unexpected silence settles over heaven—for about half an hour.

What does this silence mean?

1. **A Holy Pause Before Judgment**—The silence is both reverent and ominous. Heaven, typically filled with praise, worship, and proclamation (Revelation 4–5), now grows completely still. It is as though all of heaven holds its breath, in awe and in sorrow, knowing what is about to

be unleashed. The judgments that follow the seventh seal—symbolized by the seven trumpets—will be even more devastating than those before.

2. **A Prelude to Divine Wrath**—This silence is not peaceful; it's foreboding. In the Old Testament, silence is often associated with awe before God's judgment:

But the LORD is in His holy temple: let all the earth keep silence before Him. (Habakkuk 2:20)

Be silent, O all flesh, before the LORD: for He is raised up out of His holy habitation. (Zechariah 2:13)

3. **The Calm Before the Storm**—Just as a storm is often preceded by an eerie stillness, this heavenly silence anticipates a surge of divine action. It's the final quiet before the terrifying trumpet judgments that begin in chapter 9 (Revelation 8–9).

4. **A Sign of Solemnity**—The silence underscores the seriousness and gravity of what is to come. It highlights that what follows is not random chaos, but measured, intentional judgment. Heaven is not detached from earth's suffering—this pause communicates divine compassion, sorrow, and the weight of justice.

OLD TESTAMENT FORESHADOWS REVELATION:

Hold your peace at the presence of the Lord GOD: for the Day of the Lord is at hand: for the LORD has prepared a sacrifice, He has invited His guests. (Zephaniah 1:7)

This silence is tied directly to the Day of the Lord, which is the same period of divine wrath described in Revelation. In Revelation 8:1, the half-hour of silence in heaven mirrors these prophetic pauses, amplifying the awe and gravity of the moment before God's wrath is fully poured out through the trumpet judgments.

THE REVELATION OF JESUS CHRIST REVEALS:

8:2 And I saw the seven angels which stood before God; and to them were given seven trumpets.

This verse marks a pivotal transition in the Book of Revelation. After the seventh seal is opened in verse 1, we are introduced to seven angels who stand in the presence of God. These are not just any angels; they appear to be a distinct group, possibly archangels or angels of high rank, designated for a specific and solemn task—sounding the seven trumpet judgments.

The phrase "which stood before God" indicates their readiness and authority, emphasizing their role as divine messengers and executors of God's will. In ancient Jewish tradition (such as found in the Book of Tobit 12:15), there is mention of seven archangels who stand before God, including names like Gabriel and Raphael—though only a few are named in the canonical Bible.

Trumpets in biblical times were instruments of warning, announcement, and war. In the Old Testament, trumpets were used to:

- Call people to gather (Numbers 10:2–10).
- Signal battle (Joshua 6:4–20).
- Announce the Day of the Lord (Joel 2:1).

So here in Revelation 8:2, the seven trumpets are given to these angels as instruments of divine judgment. Each trumpet will unleash a specific, escalating judgment upon the earth—far more severe than the seal judgments. This prepares the reader for what is to come in the next verses: the trumpet judgments (Revelation 8:6–9:21 and 11:15–19).

This verse reminds us of the perfect order of God's plan. Judgment is not random; it is executed with divine timing and through divine agents. The transition from the seals to the trumpets shows a progressive revelation of God's wrath upon unrepentant humanity—offering a clear warning and call to repentance before it is too late.

Revelation 8:2 introduces us to a new series of judgments, orchestrated by seven angelic beings in heaven, each entrusted with a trumpet. These trumpets symbolize both warning and judgment, continuing the unveiling of God's righteous plan during the Tribulation.

OLD TESTAMENT FORESHADOWS REVELATION:

And seven priests shall bear before the ark seven trumpets of rams' horns: and the seventh day you shall compass (circle) the city (of Jericho) seven times, and the priests shall blow with the trumpets. And it shall come to pass, that when they make a long blast with the ram's horn, and when you hear the sound of the trumpet, all the people shall shout with a great shout; and the wall of the city shall fall down flat, and the people shall go up every man straight before him. (Joshua 6:4–5)

The Old Testament parallel to Revelation 8:2 most clearly appears in Joshua 6:4–5, where seven priests blow seven trumpets, leading to the fall of Jericho—a symbol of judgment. This imagery carries forward into Revelation, where seven angels blow seven trumpets, unleashing God's end times judgments upon the rebellious world.

THE REVELATION OF JESUS CHRIST REVEALS:

^{8:3} And another angel came and stood at the altar, having a golden censer; and there was given to him much incense, that he should offer it with the prayers of all saints upon the golden altar which was before the throne.

This powerful scene unveils a moment of heavenly intercession. The "another angel" mentioned is likely a high-ranking angelic figure—not Christ Himself, as some earlier interpreters assumed—who performs priestly duties before the heavenly throne. He holds a golden censer, a vessel used to carry incense, symbolizing purity, holiness, and sacred worship.

The "much incense" given to the angel is symbolic of divine approval and amplification of the saints' prayers. In the Old Testament, incense was a fragrant offering that ascended to God as a pleasing aroma (Exodus 30:7–8; Psalm 141:2). Here, the incense represents the intercessory role of heaven, blending with the prayers of the saints—those who are crying out for justice, mercy, and the fulfillment of God's promises.

The "golden altar" refers to the heavenly counterpart of the altar of incense in the tabernacle and temple. This altar is "before the throne," emphasizing that the prayers of God's people have a direct audience with the King of kings. This moment comes just before the trumpet judgments begin, showing that divine wrath is preceded by divine attention to prayer—a holy pause where intercession and worship are heard and acknowledge.

Revelation 8:3 reminds us that prayer is not forgotten in heaven. Even in the midst of cosmic upheaval, the cries of God's people rise like incense and are treasured before His throne. Judgment may be imminent, but God first honors the prayers of the faithful.

OLD TESTAMENT FORESHADOWS REVELATION:

Let my prayer be set forth before You as incense; and the lifting up of my hands as the evening sacrifice. (Psalm 141:2)

Revelation 8:3 draws its symbolism directly from the tabernacle rituals and temple worship. The angel with the golden censer parallels the high priest, the golden altar matches the altar of incense, and the incense mingling with prayer finds its counterpart in Psalm 141:2. These Old Testament images are fulfilled in the heavenly realm, revealing that God values and honors the prayers of His people—even amid judgment.

THE REVELATION OF JESUS CHRIST REVEALS:

^{8:4} And the smoke of the incense, which came with the prayers of the saints, ascended up before God out of the angel's hand.

This verse powerfully reveals the sacred union of prayer and heavenly intercession. The image of incense rising with the prayers of the saints symbolizes how God receives the cries of His people as a sweet and acceptable offering. In biblical times, incense was burned continually in the temple as a sign of worship and communion with God. Here, in the heavenly realm, this earthly symbol takes on eternal significance.

The angel doesn't merely hold incense; he offers it with the prayers of the saints—showing that our prayers are not forgotten. They are gathered, honored, and presented before the throne of God. This visual reinforces that God hears every plea, every cry for justice, every whispered prayer during tribulation. Nothing escapes His notice.

This verse also builds anticipation. These prayers rise just before the trumpet judgments are released. That suggests the prayers are not only heard—but are instrumental in prompting divine action. The saints cry out, and God responds in power. Revelation 8:4 is a moment of divine intimacy and cosmic preparation—reminding us that prayer moves heaven, even in the midst of judgment.

OLD TESTAMENT FORESHADOWS REVELATION:

And Aaron shall burn thereon sweet incense every morning: when he dresses the lamps, he shall burn incense upon it. And when Aaron lights the lamps at evening, he shall burn incense upon it, a perpetual incense before the LORD throughout your generations. (Exodus 30:7–8)

This passage refers to the golden altar of incense in the tabernacle, also echoed in Revelation 8:3. The priest's role in offering incense daily is symbolic of continual intercession—fulfilled in Revelation as the angel presents the saints' prayers in heaven. Old Testament verses such as this together show the continuity from earthly temple worship to heavenly intercession, where God always values and receives the prayers of His people.

THE REVELATION OF JESUS CHRIST REVEALS:

8:5 And the angel took the censer, and filled it with fire of the altar, and cast it into the earth: and there were voices, and thunderings, and lightnings, and an earthquake.

Revelation 8:5 marks a dramatic transition from the silence of heaven (Revelation 8:1) to a sudden unleashing of divine judgment. The angel, having just offered the prayers of the saints with incense before God (Revelation 8:3–4), now takes the censer—an instrument of worship—and fills it with fire from the altar and hurls it to the earth. This act is deeply symbolic and powerful.

"And filled it with fire from the altar, and cast it into the earth" represents God's holy presence, justice, and purifying judgment. It is the same altar where the prayers of the saints had just ascended. In this way, God is responding to the prayers of the faithful—especially the martyrs crying out for justice (Revelation 6:10). Their prayers have been heard, and now judgment begins.

"And there were voices, and thunderings, and lightnings, and an earthquake" reflect the awe-inspiring manifestation of God's glory and wrath. This same pattern of supernatural phenomena is seen throughout Scripture when God appears in judgment or majesty (Exodus 19:16–18 at Mount Sinai, and Ezekiel 1:13–14). These signs announce the seriousness and terror of what is to follow: the sounding of the seven trumpets.

This verse introduces the beginning of the trumpet judgments and shows that heavenly worship and earthly judgment are deeply connected. The censer—an instrument of intercession—becomes an instrument of retribution. It reminds us that God's justice is not blind vengeance but is deeply tied to the cries of His people and the righteousness of His throne.

Revelation 8:5 is a divine answer to the long-standing question of the persecuted saints: "How long, O Lord?" Judgment is now about to begin in earnest.

OLD TESTAMENT FORESHADOWS REVELATION:

And it came to pass on the third day in the morning, that there were thunders and lightnings, and a thick cloud upon the mountain, and the voice of the trumpet exceedingly loud; so that all the people that was in the camp trembled. And Moses brought forth the people out of the camp to meet with God; and they stood at the bottom part of the mountain. And Mount Sinai was altogether on a smoke, because the LORD descended upon it in fire: and the smoke thereof ascended as the smoke of a furnace, and the whole mountain quaked greatly. And when the voice of the trumpet sounded long, and waxed louder and louder, Moses spoke, and God answered him by a voice. (Exodus 19:16–19)

This mirrors Revelation 8:5 with thunder, lightning, voices (trumpet), and an earthquake—all pointing to God's presence and impending covenant judgment. Revelation 8:5 draws imagery from Mount Sinai—blending divine majesty, judgment, and justice. This event shows that when God moves in response to sin or in answer to the cries of His people, heaven and earth are shaken.

THE REVELATION OF JESUS CHRIST REVEALS:

8:6 And the seven angels which had the seven trumpets prepared themselves to sound.

This brief but powerful verse marks a critical turning point in the Book of Revelation. After the silence in heaven (Revelation 8:1), and the intense moment when the censer is cast to earth (Revelation 8:5), this verse signals the transition from warning to judgment. The seven angels, who have been entrusted with trumpets, now stand ready to act. Their preparation is deliberate—there is a holy anticipation in heaven. Each trumpet blast will usher in divine judgments that grow in severity, affecting the earth, sea, rivers, heavens, and even humanity itself. The Tribulation is intensifying!

Trumpets in the Bible were traditionally used for proclamation, warning, war, and worship (Numbers 10:9–10; Joel 2:1). Here, the trumpets serve as harbingers of God's justice, preparing to shake the natural world and confront human rebellion.

This moment also reveals God's measured and sovereign control—the judgments do not happen all at once. The angels prepare, and the events unfold in a structured, God-ordained sequence. Nothing is random in God's plan; judgment follows divine timing and purpose.

OLD TESTAMENT FORESHADOWS REVELATION:

Blow you the trumpet in Zion (Jerusalem), and sound an alarm in My holy mountain: let all the inhabitants of the land tremble: for the Day of the Lord is coming, for it is close at hand. (Joel 2:1)

This verse in Joel directly connects trumpet blasts with the Day of the Lord, a time of divine judgment, upheaval, and awe. Like Revelation 8:6, Joel emphasizes:

- A heavenly warning to all the earth.
- The use of trumpets to declare impending divine intervention.
- A call for trembling and repentance, as God's judgment draws near.

In this verse, the trumpet is not just a musical instrument—it's a divine signal. It marks the transition into greater judgment and supernatural activity on the earth.

SUMMARY OF REVELATION 6, 8:1–6

Revelation 6 marks the dramatic opening of the seven seal judgments by the Lamb of God—Jesus Christ. Each seal unleashes a divine judgment upon the earth, progressively revealing the severity of the Tribulation. The chapter begins with the first seal, introducing the rider on a white horse—a deceiver symbolizing the Antichrist, who brings a temporary and false peace (Revelation 6:1–2).

The second seal breaks that peace with a rider on a red horse, symbolizing war and bloodshed (Revelation 6:3–4). The third seal releases a black horse representing famine, where economic collapse causes people to labor for a day's food with a day's wage (Revelation 6:5–6). The fourth seal follows with a pale horse–Death and Hades claiming one-fourth of the earth through sword, hunger, disease, and beasts (Revelation 6:7–8).

The fifth seal shifts to a heavenly scene where the souls of martyrs cry out for justice beneath the altar, having been slain for their faith and testimony (Revelation 6:9–11). They are given white robes and told to rest a little longer until the full number of martyrs is complete.

The sixth seal unleashes cataclysmic events—earthquakes, cosmic disturbances, and the receding of the sky like a scroll. The sun turns black, the moon like blood, and stars fall from heaven. Mountains and islands are shaken from their places (Revelation 6:12–14). All people, from kings to slaves, hide in fear, recognizing that the "great day of His wrath is come" and questioning who can stand before the Lamb (Revelation 6:15–17).

The seventh seal (Revelation 8:1) opens with a stunning pause—silence in heaven for about half an hour. This profound moment marks a dramatic interlude, emphasizing the weight and solemnity of what is to come. It signals a shift from the seal judgments to the more intense trumpet judgments, showing that the worst is yet to unfold. The stillness prepares both heaven and earth for what lies ahead— further manifestations of God's justice, wrath, and ultimate redemption.

KEY TAKEAWAYS

- The Lamb breaks the seals—Only Christ has authority to execute God's judgment.
- Four horsemen—Symbols of conquest, war, famine, and death sweep across the earth.
- Martyrdom foretold—Believers who come to Christ during the Tribulation will face intense persecution.
- Cosmic cataclysms—God shakes the heavens and the earth to signal the coming of His Kingdom.
- Wrath and restoration—The judgments serve both to punish evil and to prepare the earth for Christ's reign.

Revelation chapter 6 and part of chapter 8 portrays the beginning of the end— a solemn warning and a hopeful reminder that God's justice will prevail. While terrifying for the rebellious, it is a reassurance to the faithful: God is in control, the Lamb is worthy, and His Kingdom is on the horizon.

Chapter 8

Revelation 7:
Interlude—The
144,000 Sealed Servants

GOD'S PAUSE BEFORE THE STORM—Before the trumpet judgments thunder across the earth with unstoppable fury—Revelation 7 gives us a breathtaking pause in the action. It is a moment of divine intermission, a calm before the storm so intense that Jesus Himself said if those days weren't shortened, no flesh would survive (Matthew 24:22). This chapter is not a break in the story—it's a revelation within the Revelation. A strategic pause. A sovereign sealing.

As the earth reels from the terror of the first seven seals—deception, war, famine, death, martyrdom, cosmic cataclysm, and a deafening silence in heaven—Revelation 7 zooms in on God's supernatural intervention. While the world trembles, heaven holds its breath. Angels are dispatched not to destroy, but to delay. Not to strike, but to seal.

In this holy pause, we witness God marking 144,000 from the twelve tribes of Israel—an act of divine preservation and prophetic fulfillment. While the judgments of the Tribulation roar on the horizon, these individuals are sealed with the protection and purpose of God. Revelation 7 reminds us that even in wrath, God remembers mercy. In the chaos of global collapse, God is not absent—He is orchestrating. He is claiming His own, even as the earth groans beneath judgment.

This chapter stands as both a warning and a comfort. Judgment is coming—but so is deliverance. The sealed are not spared from the storm, but they are secured in it. Their presence is a bold declaration that God never loses track of His promises, His people, or His purpose—even in the darkest hour of human history.

JESUS' TEACHINGS AND REVELATION 6–7 PARALLELS

In Matthew 24, Jesus gives His disciples a prophetic overview of the end times. He outlines the signs of His coming and the end of the age. Later, in Revelation 6 and 7, we see these same events begin to unfold as the Lamb opens the seven seals. Each seal corresponds closely with what Jesus had already taught—revealing that He, now in heaven, is executing the very prophecy He once delivered on earth.

1. **First Seal Judgment—False Christs**. Matthew 24:5: "For many shall come in my name, saying, I am Christ; and shall deceive many." Revelation 6:2: "And I saw, and behold a white horse: and he that sat on him had a bow; and a crown was given unto him: and he went forth conquering, and to conquer." The rider on the white horse symbolizes the Antichrist, the ultimate false messiah, deceiving the world under the guise of peace.

2. **Second Seal Judgment—Wars and Rumors of Wars**. Matthew 24:6–7: "And you shall hear of wars and rumors of wars . . . for nation shall rise against nation, and kingdom against kingdom." Revelation 6:4: "And there went out another horse that was red . . . to take peace from the earth, and that they should kill one another." The red horse signifies global conflict and bloodshed, exactly as Jesus described.

3. **Third Seal Judgment—Famine**. Matthew 24:7: ". . . and there shall be famines . . ." Revelation 6:5–6: ". . . a black horse . . . a measure of wheat for a penny, and three measures of barley for a penny . . ." The black horse represents economic collapse and worldwide famine, mirroring Jesus' warning.

4. **Fourth Seal Judgment—Pestilences and Death**. Matthew 24:7: ". . . and pestilences . . ." Revelation 6:8: ". . . a pale horse: and his name that sat on him was Death, and Hell followed with him . . ." The pale green horse (from the Greek *chloros*) signals widespread death through plagues, famine, and violence.

5. **Fifth Seal Judgment—Persecution and Martyrdom**. Matthew 24:9–10: "Then shall they deliver you up to be afflicted, and shall kill you: and you shall be hated of all nations . . ." Revelation 6:9–11: ". . . I saw under the altar the souls of them that were slain for the Word of God . . ." Jesus foretold that His followers would face intense persecution, and the fifth seal reveals the martyrs crying out for justice.

6. **Sixth Seal Judgment—Natural Disasters and Cosmic Signs**. Matthew 24:7, 29: ". . . earthquakes in diverse places . . . the sun be darkened, and the moon shall not give her light . . ." Revelation 6:12–14: ". . . a great earthquake; and the sun became black . . . and the moon became as blood . . . the stars of heaven fell . . ." Earthquakes and celestial disturbances follow as the sixth seal is opened—just as Jesus predicted.

7. **Interlude—Worldwide Preaching of the Gospel**. Matthew 24:14: "And this gospel of the Kingdom shall be preached in all the world for a witness unto all nations . . ." Revelation 7:1–4: ". . . sealed a hundred and forty and four thousand . . ." Following the sixth seal, an interlude in chapter 7 reveals that 144,000 Jewish servants are sealed. Their mission is to evangelize the earth during the Tribulation, fulfilling Jesus' declaration that the gospel would be preached to all nations.

These parallels confirm that Jesus not only prophesied these end-time events—He brings them to pass. What He declared in Matthew 24, He initiates in Revelation 6 and 7. This prophetic alignment strengthens our understanding of the sequence and significance of end-time events, providing a clear, divine timeline from Jesus' mouth to the final judgment.

THE REVELATION OF JESUS CHRIST REVEALS:

7:1 And after these things I saw four angels standing on the four corners of the earth, holding the four winds of the earth, that the wind should not blow on the earth, nor on the sea, nor on any tree.

Revelation 7:1 opens a moment of divine suspension—what many scholars refer to as a *pause in judgment*. The phrase "after these things" signals a shift in scene, transitioning from the cataclysmic events of Revelation 6 and 8:1–6 to a heavenly perspective of preservation and mercy.

The "four angels" represent divine agents of control and authority. Their position on the "four corners of the earth" is a figurative way of describing the totality of the earth—the north, south, east, and west. This isn't a statement of geography but a symbolic representation of global reach. The "four winds" often symbolize judgment and chaos in biblical prophecy (Jeremiah 49:36; Daniel 7:2).

Here, they are restrained, indicating that God is temporarily holding back the coming destruction.

The command to hold back the wind "on the earth, the sea, and the trees" emphasizes total stillness—a supernatural pause in the natural order. Wind often brings movement, life, and change. To stop the wind is to halt the forward motion of judgment. It's a moment of divine suspense where even nature holds its breath.

This verse sets the stage for the sealing of the 144,000—God's servants who must be marked before the next wave of judgments begins. It highlights God's mercy in the midst of wrath. Before unleashing further devastation, God ensures the protection of those He has called. The message is clear: even during the Tribulation, God remains sovereign over creation and committed to preserving His remnant.

OLD TESTAMENT FORESHADOWS REVELATION:

And upon Elam (Khuzestan Province in modern Iran) will I bring the four winds from the four quarters of heaven, and will scatter them toward all those winds; and there shall be no nation where the outcasts of Elam shall not come. (Jeremiah 49:36)

This verse, like Revelation 7:1, refers to "four winds" coming from the four directions of the earth, symbolizing divine judgment or dispersion. The winds in Jeremiah represent God's instrument of scattering and upheaval, much like how the winds in Revelation symbolize the impending judgments being held back temporarily by the four angels.

THE REVELATION OF JESUS CHRIST REVEALS:

7:2 And I saw another angel ascending from the east, having the seal of the living God: and he cried with a loud voice to the four angels, to whom it was given to hurt the earth and the sea.

In this verse, John witnesses a fifth angel rising from the east—symbolically significant as the direction of light, hope, and divine intervention. Biblically, the east is often associated with the glory of God and His coming (Ezekiel 43:2), as well as the direction from which Christ will return (Matthew 24:27).

This angel bears the "seal of the living God," a mark of divine ownership and protection. Just as ancient kings used seals to signify authority, authenticity, and protection, so too does this seal mark those who belong to God. This seal is about to be placed on the foreheads of the 144,000 servants (Revelation 7:3), symbolizing spiritual preservation amid earthly judgment.

Importantly, the angel calls out to the four angels (from Revelation 7:1) who are ready to unleash devastating judgments on the earth and sea. But before the destruction begins, they are commanded to pause. This dramatic interlude underscores God's mercy—He delays judgment to protect His faithful servants.

This verse illustrated a powerful truth: even in the midst of divine wrath, God never forgets His remnant. Before judgment is poured out, He marks His own for protection and preservation.

OLD TESTAMENT FORESHADOWS REVELATION:

And the LORD said unto him, Go through the midst of the city, through the midst of Jerusalem, and set a mark upon the foreheads of the men that sigh and that cry for all the abominations that be done in the midst thereof. (Ezekiel 9:4)

In this passage, God commands an angelic figure to go through Jerusalem and mark the foreheads of those who mourn over the nation's sins. Those marked are spared from the coming judgment that the other angels will execute. This act of marking the faithful for protection mirrors the sealing of the 144,000 in Revelation 7:2–3.

Both scenes show a divine pause before judgment, during which God's faithful are sealed, marked, and protected—a demonstration of mercy amid wrath. The consistency between these two scriptures shows that God's pattern of sealing His people before judgment is a theme carried from the Old Testament into the Revelation of Jesus Christ.

THE REVELATION OF JESUS CHRIST REVEALS:

7:3 Saying, Hurt not the earth, neither the sea, nor the trees, till we have sealed the servants of our God on their foreheads.

This verse marks a divine pause in the unfolding judgments of the Tribulation. Before the next wave of catastrophic destruction is allowed to proceed, an angel issues a command to hold back judgment until a specific group of people—the servants of God—are sealed on their foreheads.

The seal is symbolic of ownership, protection, and divine commissioning. In ancient times, kings and rulers used seals to authenticate authority and secure protection over people or property. In this context, God places His seal on 144,000 Jewish believers (Revelation 7:4–8), setting them apart during the Tribulation. These are not apostles, prophets, pastors, or teachers, but evangelists—God's specially chosen witnesses—who will boldly proclaim the gospel in the midst of escalating chaos and wrath.

Their sealing ensures their divine protection, not just from physical harm, but also from spiritual deception. They are preserved by God to evangelize the lost and usher in a great harvest of souls, even as judgment falls around them. This sealing also echoes Ezekiel 9:4–6, where God's faithful are marked before judgment falls on Jerusalem.

Revelation 7:3 reveals God's mercy even amid wrath. Before destruction continues, He ensures that His mission and His messengers are in place, and His purposes of redemption are still active during the darkest hour of human history.

OLD TESTAMENT FORESHADOWS REVELATION:

And He said, It is a light thing that You should be My Servant to raise up the tribes of Jacob, and to restore the preserved ones of Israel: I will also give You for a light to the Gentiles, that You may be My salvation unto the end of the earth. (Isaiah 49:6)

Revelation 7:3 describes 144,000 sealed servants of God—Jewish evangelists who will proclaim the gospel during the Tribulation. This aligns with Isaiah 49:6, where God prophetically declares that His chosen ones (Israel) will be a light to the Gentiles (nations) and bring salvation to the ends of the earth.

While Isaiah's prophecy ultimately points to the Messiah, it also reflects God's broader purpose for Israel as a witnessing nation, which is partially fulfilled through the 144,000 in Revelation 7. These sealed servants carry the gospel globally at a time of great judgment, just as Isaiah foretold a mission that would reach beyond Israel to the nations.

THE REVELATION OF JESUS CHRIST REVEALS:

7:4 And I heard the number of them which were sealed: and there were sealed a hundred and forty and four thousand of all the tribes of the children of Israel.

In this verse, John, hears the angel announcing the sealing of the 144,000, a divine act of preservation and commissioning by God in the midst of the Tribulation. These 144,000 individuals are clearly identified as Jewish believers, with 12,000 sealed from each of the twelve tribes of Israel. This is a direct and literal reference, not symbolic, and ties into the broader biblical theme of God's faithfulness to Israel and His prophetic promises concerning their future.

The context shows that after the Church Age concludes—when the Church is no longer mentioned from Revelation 4 to 19—the narrative shifts entirely to Israel. Everything becomes unmistakably Jewish: the Lamb, the Lion of Judah, the tabernacle, the temple in heaven, and now, the 144,000 sealed Jewish servants. The Tribulation is also known as "the time of Jacob's trouble" (Jeremiah 30:7), signaling that God's redemptive focus has returned to His covenant people, Israel.

These 144,000 are not random believers—they are divinely chosen, sealed, and protected for a specific purpose during the most devastating time in human history. Their mission is evangelistic. In Revelation 14, we discover more about their characteristics: they are purchased by the blood of the Lamb, pure and undefiled, prepared and sealed, protected from harm, persistent in following the Lamb, and bold preachers of the gospel. These young Jewish men are set apart by God to bring in a great harvest of souls—millions from every nation, tribe, and language.

Their sealing ensures their survival through the chaos of the trumpet judgments, which will soon begin. This act of sealing is not merely symbolic; it is a divine guarantee of protection and commissioning. God is not finished with Israel. These sealed servants prove that His plan includes a remnant that will boldly proclaim salvation in the darkest days. In a world ruled by the Antichrist, when martyrdom is rampant and deception abounds, these 144,000 will shine as God's witnesses, proclaiming the eternal gospel and drawing multitudes to Christ.

In Revelation 7:9, we see the fruit of their ministry—a multitude no one could number, from every nation, standing before the throne and the Lamb. This reminds us that even amid wrath, God's mercy and desire for salvation remain. Revelation 7:4 is not just a record of numbers—it's a declaration of God's enduring promise to Israel and His unstoppable mission to redeem.

OLD TESTAMENT FORESHADOWS REVELATION:

And it shall come to pass afterward, that I will pour out My Spirit upon all flesh; and your sons and your daughters shall prophesy, your old men shall dream dreams, your young men shall see visions. And also upon the servants and upon the handmaids in those days will I pour out My Spirit. And I will show wonders in the heavens and in the earth, blood, and fire, and pillars of smoke. The sun shall be turned into darkness, and the moon into blood, before the great and terrible Day of the Lord come. And it shall come to pass, that whosoever shall call on the name of the LORD shall be delivered: for in Mount Zion and in Jerusalem shall be deliverance, as the LORD has said, and in the remnant whom the LORD shall call. (Joel 2:28–32)

Joel 2:28–32 speaks of a divinely chosen remnant who will be preserved and empowered in the end times. Like the 144,000 in Revelation 7, this remnant is chosen and protected by God in the midst of coming judgment. The prophetic empowerment of this group echoes the evangelistic calling of the 144,000.

THE REVELATION OF JESUS CHRIST REVEALS:

[7:5] Of the tribe of Judah were sealed twelve thousand. Of the tribe of Reuben were sealed twelve thousand. Of the tribe of Gad were sealed twelve thousand.

This verse begins the detailed listing of the twelve tribes of Israel, each contributing 12,000 individuals to make up the 144,000 who are sealed by God. These sealed individuals are ethnic Jews, descendants of Jacob, chosen and marked by God for a unique purpose during the Tribulation.

"Of the tribe of Judah were sealed twelve thousand." Interestingly, Judah is listed first, though Reuben was Jacob's firstborn son. This is no accident. Judah receives the preeminence because Jesus Christ, the Messiah, is the Lion of the Tribe of Judah (Revelation 5:5). Judah's ascendancy in the list emphasizes the Messianic lineage and the fulfillment of Old Testament prophecy.

"Of the tribe of Reuben were sealed twelve thousand." Reuben, the actual firstborn son of Jacob, comes next. He lost his place of prominence due to sin (Genesis 35:22), which is why Judah often takes the lead in tribal listings post-Exodus. Yet Reuben is not forgotten. He is still included in the sealing—God's grace restores even those with a blemished past.

"Of the tribe of Gad were sealed twelve thousand." Gad was one of the sons of Leah's maid Zilpah (Genesis 30:9–11). Though not born from Jacob's wife, Gad is still fully considered part of the covenantal tribes. The inclusion of Gad affirms that God's promises extend to all legitimate tribal descendants, regardless of birth order or maternal origin.

OLD TESTAMENT FORESHADOWS REVELATION:

Of Judah; Nahshon the son of Amminadab . . . Of Reuben; Elizur the son of Shedeur . . . Of Gad; Eliasaph the son of Deuel . . . (Numbers 1:7, 1:5, 1:11, respectively)

This passage records the census of the twelve tribes of Israel during the wilderness journey. Each tribe is named specifically, and leaders are appointed from among them. This census was for military organization and preparation, while Revelation 7 presents a spiritual sealing for divine protection and witness during the Tribulation. However, the structure and tribal order reflect continuity between the Old Testament people of God and God's prophetic purposes in the New Testament.

THE REVELATION OF JESUS CHRIST REVEALS:

7:6 Of the tribe of Aser were sealed twelve thousand. Of the tribe of Nepthalim were sealed twelve thousand. Of the tribe of Manasses were sealed twelve thousand.

This verse continues the list of the 144,000 individuals—12,000 from each of the twelve tribes of Israel—whom God seals for divine protection and service during the Tribulation. These three tribes—Asher (Aser), Naphtali (Nepthalim), and Manasseh (Manasses)—each contribute 12,000 faithful, set apart for a unique purpose in the unfolding of God's redemptive plan.

"Of the tribe of Aser were sealed twelve thousand." Asher was Jacob's eighth son, born to Zilpah, Leah's maidservant (Genesis 30:12–13). His name means "happy" or "blessed." Asher's inheritance was in the fertile northern part of Israel along the Mediterranean coast. Symbolically, Asher represents abundance and provision, qualities that may mirror the spiritual nourishment these sealed believers bring during a time of global famine, despair, and natural terrors.

"Of the tribe of Nepthalim were sealed twelve thousand." Naphtali was the sixth son of Jacob and the second of Bilhah, Rachel's handmaid (Genesis 30:7–8). His name means "wrestling," reflecting Rachel's struggle. Naphtali's tribe settled in the northern region of Galilee; an area later graced by Jesus' early ministry (Matthew 4:13–16). Naphtali often symbolizes spiritual tenacity and grace under pressure, fitting for a remnant who must endure tribulation yet remain faithful.

"Of the tribe of Manasses were sealed twelve thousand." Manasseh was the firstborn son of Joseph, adopted by Jacob as his own (Genesis 48:5). His name means "causing to forget," referring to Joseph's forgetfulness of past suffering. Manasseh received territory on both sides of the Jordan River, becoming a half-tribe with his brother Ephraim. Interestingly, Manasseh is listed in place of Dan in Revelation 7—a substitution that has drawn much speculation (for example, Dan's association with idolatry in Judges 18:30). Manasseh may represent those who have overcome past pain and idolatry to serve God faithfully.

OLD TESTAMENT FORESHADOWS REVELATION:

And of Asher he said, Let Asher be blessed with children; let him be acceptable to his brethren, and let him dip his foot in oil . . . And of Naphtali he said, O Naphtali, satisfied with favor, and full with the blessing of the LORD . . . Though this next verse focuses on Joseph as a whole, it includes Manasseh: . . . they are the ten thousands of Ephraim, and they are the thousands of Manasseh . . . (Deuteronomy 33:24, 33:23, 33:17, respectively)

These verses were part of Moses' blessing of the tribes. These verses also show that God had long-established prophetic purposes and blessings for these tribes, and Revelation 7 reveals the end-time fulfillment of those promises by sealing 12,000 faithful from each tribe.

THE REVELATION OF JESUS CHRIST REVEALS:

7:7 Of the tribe of Simeon were sealed twelve thousand. Of the tribe of Levi were sealed twelve thousand. Of the tribe of Issachar were sealed twelve thousand.

This verse continues the divine roll call of the 144,000 Jewish evangelists—12,000 sealed from each of the twelve tribes of Israel. The inclusion of Simeon, Levi, and Issachar here is both deeply significant and prophetically rich, especially when compared to earlier tribal listings in the Old Testament.

"Of the tribe of Simeon were sealed twelve thousand." The tribe of Simeon had historically diminished in influence and population, partially due to Jacob's rebuke of Simeon and Levi in Genesis 49:5–7 for their violence at Shechem. By the time of the kingdom division, Simeon had been largely absorbed into the territory of Judah. Yet here in Revelation, we see a full restoration, with 12,000 sealed from Simeon. This signifies that God never forgets a promise—even tribes once scattered are sovereignly remembered in His redemptive plan.

"Of the tribe of Levi were sealed twelve thousand." The inclusion of Levi is especially noteworthy. The tribe of Levi was originally set apart for priestly service and did not receive a territorial inheritance in the land of Israel (Numbers 18:20–24; Deuteronomy 10:9). In earlier tribal enumerations, Levi is often omitted to maintain the number twelve when Joseph's sons (Ephraim and Manasseh) are counted as separate tribes.

Yet here, Levi is counted—indicating that in this time of divine sealing, God is emphasizing spiritual calling over territorial inheritance. Levi's return to the list may also underscore a priestly role these 144,000 play, as spiritual intercessors during the Tribulation.

"Of the tribe of Issachar were sealed twelve thousand." Issachar, the ninth son of Jacob and Leah, was described in Genesis 49:14 as a strong donkey lying between burdens—symbolic of a tribe willing to serve in practical ways. In Judges 5:15, Issachar is seen as faithfully joining Deborah and Barak in battle. Their presence in Revelation 7 reaffirms their continued role in supporting God's purposes, even in the intense spiritual warfare of the end times.

OLD TESTAMENT FORESHADOWS REVELATION:

Take you (Levi) the sum of all the congregation of the children of Israel, after their families, by the house of their fathers . . . Simeon and Levi are brethren; instruments of cruelty are in their inhabitations . . . Issachar is a strong donkey couching down between two burdens . . . (Numbers 1:2, Genesis 49:5, Genesis 49:14, respectively)

While Levi is excluded from the military census in Numbers 1 (as they were set apart for priestly duties), Simeon and Issachar are included. This tribal listing is significant for understanding Israel's foundational structure, and the comparison with Revelation 7 shows how God rearranges and reclaims the tribes for His end-time purposes.

THE REVELATION OF JESUS CHRIST REVEALS:

[7:8] Of the tribe of Zabulon were sealed twelve thousand. Of the tribe of Joseph were sealed twelve thousand. Of the tribe of Benjamin were sealed twelve thousand.

This verse concludes the listing of the 144,000 sealed servants of God—12,000 from each of the twelve tribes of Israel. As with the previous verses, each of these tribes represents a remnant of Israel set apart by God for a special purpose during the Tribulation. The inclusion of these final three tribes—Zabulon (Zebulun), Joseph, and Benjamin—continues to reflect God's faithfulness to His covenant with the descendants of Jacob.

"Of the tribe of Zabulon were sealed twelve thousand." Zebulun was the tenth son of Jacob and the sixth born to Leah (Genesis 30:20). His tribe was located by the sea and known for commerce and ships (Genesis 49:13). Though not prominent in the Old Testament narrative, Zebulun's inclusion here shows that no tribe is forgotten in God's redemptive plan.

"Of the tribe of Joseph were sealed twelve thousand." Interestingly, Joseph is named here instead of his sons Ephraim and Manasseh. This is significant because in many tribal lists, Joseph's sons replace him to maintain the number twelve when Levi is omitted. In Revelation 7, Manasseh is mentioned (Revelation 7:6), but Ephraim is omitted, possibly due to idolatry associated with Ephraim in the Old Testament (Hosea 4:17). Naming Joseph instead may serve as a collective honor to his legacy and spiritual faithfulness.

"Of the tribe of Benjamin were sealed twelve thousand." The youngest son of Jacob and the only son born in the Promised Land (Genesis 35:18), Benjamin was deeply beloved. His tribe was known for its fierce warriors (Judges 20:16) and was the tribe of Israel's first king, Saul (1 Samuel 9:1–2). The apostle Paul was also from the tribe of Benjamin (Romans 11:1; Philippians 3:4). Their inclusion here reflects mercy and restoration, especially considering their turbulent Old Testament history.

Revelation 7:5–8 presents a remarkable listing of twelve tribes from which 144,000 Jewish men are sealed—12,000 from each tribe—demonstrating God's unwavering faithfulness to Israel. Though the Church has been raptured at this point (as many scholars believe), God's redemptive plan for His chosen people continues. This sealing signifies divine ownership, protection, and purpose, setting these men apart as fearless evangelists during the Tribulation.

Despite centuries of dispersion and lost genealogies, God knows precisely who belongs to each tribe, affirming His sovereign control. The unique tribal list, which includes Levi and Joseph but omits Dan and Ephraim, highlights that God's selection is not merely based on genealogy but on spiritual calling. Each tribe, regardless of past prominence or failure is honored in this end times mission—emphasizing that no obedience is forgotten, no heritage is lost, and no promise remains unfulfilled in God's ultimate plan of restoration and salvation.

OLD TESTAMENT FORESHADOWS REVELATION:

Rejoice, Zebulun, in your going out . . . Blessed of the LORD be his (Joseph) land . . . The beloved of the LORD shall dwell in safety by him (Benjamin) . . . (Deuteronomy 33:18, 33:13–17, 33:12, respectively)

These blessings by Moses reflect God's covenantal faithfulness and prophetic promises to each tribe, which are reactivated and emphasized in Revelation 7 as He seals these tribes for a special purpose during the Tribulation.

THE BOOK OF REVELATION

The 144,000 Sealed from the Tribes of Israel

 Judah "praise"

Symbol: Lion (Gen. 49:9-10)
Location: Jerusalem, Bethlehem, and Hebron
❖ The tribe of the monarchy; the Messianic bloodline

 Reuben "behold a son"

Symbol: Water (Gen. 49:3-4)
Location: Outside Israel, east of the Dead Sea (Num. 32:1)
❖ The tribe known for its huge number of herds and flocks

 Gad "fortune or luck"

Symbol: Troop (Gen. 49:19)
Location: Outside Israel along the Jordan River
❖ The tribe herders of cattle; fiercest warriors of Israel

 Aser "happy"

Symbol: Food (Gen. 49:20)
Location: Northern costal region
❖ The tribe known for its prosperity and good food

 Nepthalim "my struggle"

Symbol: Deer (Gen. 49:21)
Location: Upper Galilee, included the city of Hazor
❖ The tribe known for his eloquent speech; swiftness

 Manasses "forgetfulness"

Symbol: Branch (Gen. 49:22)
Location: Two large territories, east and west
❖ God made Joseph forget all his hardships (Gen. 41:51)

 Simeon "to hear"

Symbol: Gate (Gen. 34:24-25)
Location: Enclave of land within Judah's territory
❖ The tribe known for deceit and murder (Gen. 49:5-7)

 Levi "joined"

Symbol: Breastplate (Ex. 28:30)
Location: 48 cities scattered throughout the entire country
❖ The tribe for the religious leadership of the Jews

 Issachar "he will hire"

Symbol: Donkey (Gen. 49:14)
Location: Near Sea of Galilee, valley of Jezreel
❖ The tribe of scholars; created the Israelite calendar

 Zebulun "to dwell in"

Symbol: Ship (Gen. 49:13)
Location: Lower Galilee
❖ The tribe of seafaring, shipping, and trade; brave soldiers (Jud. 5:18)

 Joseph "he will add"

Symbol: Wheat (Gen. 37:7)
Location: Spanned the Jordan River; northernmost group
❖ The tribe split into two: Ephraim and Manasseh

 Benjamin "son of south"

Symbol: Wolf (Gen. 49:27)
Location: North of Jerusalem, in ancient Israel
❖ The tribe known for its warrior-like people

THE REVELATION OF JESUS CHRIST REVEALS:

^{7:9} After this I beheld, and, lo, a great multitude, which no man could number, of all nations, and kindreds, and people, and tongues, stood before the throne, and before the Lamb, clothed with white robes, and palms in their hands.

This verse reveals one of the most awe-inspiring scenes in the Book of Revelation—a great multitude standing before the throne and before the Lamb, clothed in white robes and waving palm branches. John emphasizes that this multitude is so vast that "no man could number" them, and they come from "all nations, and kindreds, and people, and tongues." This clearly indicates a global harvest of souls during the seven-year Tribulation, brought about through the fearless ministry of the 144,000 sealed Jewish evangelists described in the preceding verses.

Though the Church has been raptured at this point, God's work of salvation is far from finished. The 144,000 serve as anointed messengers—likely penetrating hard-to-reach regions like the Middle East, Asia, and areas where Christian evangelism has been restricted or persecuted. As conditions on earth grow desperate and judgments intensify, hearts that were once closed will open to the truth of the gospel. Many of these people—Gentiles and others who never heard or accepted the message during the Church Age—will respond to the call of salvation.

The white robes represent the righteousness of Christ granted to these believers, and the palm branches are symbols of victory, worship, and celebration. Even amid tribulation, redemption continues. These souls have been spiritually rescued out of the darkest hour in human history. However, as later verses confirm, most of them will suffer martyrdom for their faith.

This scene stands as a powerful reminder that God's grace reaches even into the most chaotic and terrifying times. The gospel will go forth, and the result will be a global, uncountable multitude who surrender to the Lamb—even at the cost of their lives.

OLD TESTAMENT FORESHADOWS REVELATION:

They shall not hunger nor thirst; neither shall the heat nor sun smite them: for He that has mercy on them shall lead them, even by the springs of water shall He guide them. And I will make all My mountains a way, and My highways shall be exalted. Behold, these shall come from far: and, lo, these from the north and from the west; and these from the land of Sinim. (Isaiah 49:10–12)

Isaiah 49:10–12 is not just a parallel—it is a prophetic foreshadowing of what is fulfilled in Revelation 7:9–17. Both passages speak of:

- Global inclusion of the redeemed.

- Divine protection and comfort.
- A shepherding Messiah guiding His people.
- A return or gathering from every direction.

This passage reveals God's redemptive plan reaching beyond Israel to embrace both Jew and Gentile—spanning time, space, and covenant. Isaiah's prophetic vision finds its ultimate fulfillment in Revelation 7:9, where the global worship of the Lamb reflects the promised salvation extending to all nations, tribes, peoples, and tongues.

Irene and I sat at a large glass coffee table, our Bibles and notes spread out between us. A soft lamp glowed overhead as evening set in outside the window.

Irene leaned forward, her brow furrowed. "Ann, I've been going over the sequence again—Daniel's 70th Week, the seals, the trumpets—and I keep running into the same issue."

I looked up. "What's troubling you?"

Irene exhaled slowly. "It's the first 3½ years of the Tribulation. We know that's when the Antichrist rises to power. But if God is already releasing the seal and trumpet judgments—judgments that seem to reorder the earth, pull the continents back together, and wipe out a third of the land, sea, drinking water, and even darken a third of the sun, moon, and stars—how does the Antichrist have time to deceive the world, consolidate control, and establish a global empire?"

I smiled softly, sensing Irene's heart for truth. "That's a really important observation. And you're right—it does look like there's a tension between what God is doing to judge and restore, and what Satan is doing to manipulate and destroy. But remember, both are happening under God's sovereign timing."

Irene nodded. "So you're saying they don't cancel each other out?"

I shook my head. "Not at all. In fact, I think they work in tandem—though in very different ways. Let's step back and walk through the timeline."

I opened my Bible to Daniel 9, and then flipped to Revelation. "We know Daniel's 70th Week is seven years, right? It's split into two halves—each 3½ years. The first half is when the Antichrist rises to power, and the second half—what Jesus called the 'Great Tribulation'—is when the full wrath and chaos unfold."

Irene tapped her pen against her notebook. "And the midpoint is the abomination of desolation?"

"Exactly." I pointed to Revelation 13. "That's when the Antichrist sets himself up in the rebuilt Third Temple, claiming to be God. That's when the masks come off. That's also when Satan is cast down to earth, and I believe, possesses or fully empowers both the Antichrist and the False Prophet."

Irene tilted her head. "So . . . are you saying the False Prophet doesn't show up until then?"

"Right." I nodded. "The False Prophet—this second beast who performs signs and enforces worship—rises in Revelation 13, after the first beast is fully revealed. His job is to promote the Antichrist and force people to worship him. But before that? The Antichrist's power is more political than supernatural. He comes with peace, flattery, false unity. He doesn't need fire from heaven yet— just promises and persuasion."

Irene leaned back in her chair, thinking. "So during the first half, God is already judging the earth—seals are broken, the trumpet blasts begin—but the Antichrist is still playing the part of a savior?"

"Yes. And that's the tension you're feeling." My voice softened. "God is shaking the world—through war, famine, death, and environmental upheaval. It's judgment, yes—but like the plagues of Egypt, it carries a redemptive thread. He's cleansing and reordering the earth. At the same time, Satan is positioning his pieces, biding his time—waiting for the world to grow desperate enough to embrace his deception."

Irene glanced down at her notes. "That explains the restoration theme—the landmass reforming, bitter waters, a third of the light gone. It's like God is dismantling man's systems while purifying the natural world."

"Exactly," I said. "The trumpet judgments do two things—they warn and they cleanse. They clear the way for Christ's Kingdom, but first, they set the stage for a false king to rise—briefly."

Irene was quiet for a moment. "So the Antichrist doesn't cause the destruction—he capitalizes on it. He steps into the chaos God allows, pretending to be the one who can fix it."

I smiled. "Exactly. He comes as a counterfeit Christ. The true King brings peace through righteousness. The Antichrist offers peace through deception— only to shatter it halfway through."

Irene jotted down three words: *False peace. Real judgment. Hidden chaos.*

"And the 144,000?" she asked. "They're sealed before the trumpet judgments begin, right?"

I nodded. "Yes—right between the sixth and seventh seals. God marks them to spread the gospel before judgment intensifies. They're His frontline witnesses. As the earth trembles and the skies darken, they shine like lights—offering hope in the midst of chaos."

Irene leaned forward, her voice softer. "So even in wrath, He remembers mercy."

I whispered, "Always."

THE REVELATION OF JESUS CHRIST REVEALS:

^{7:10} And cried with a loud voice, saying, Salvation to our God which sits upon the throne, and to the Lamb.

Revelation 7:10 is a powerful scene of triumphant worship, where the multitude of redeemed souls cries out in unison: "Salvation to our God which sits upon the throne, and to the Lamb." This declaration is both a praise and a proclamation. It acknowledges that salvation originates from God the Father, who sits sovereignly on the throne, and is made possible through the sacrificial work of Jesus Christ, the Lamb of God.

This scene follows the vision of a great multitude from every nation, tribe, people, and tongue (Revelation 7:9), emphasizing the global reach of the gospel message. These are individuals who have come out of the Tribulation—redeemed by grace, not through their own merit, but through the blood of the Lamb (Revelation 7:14). Their white robes symbolize purity and righteousness imputed to them through Christ.

The loud voice indicates unified, exuberant praise, reflecting both the joy of salvation and the recognition of divine authority. It also reinforces the central theme of the Book of Revelation: that Jesus is not only the Savior but also the rightful King. The use of "our God" signifies a personal relationship with the Almighty, and "the Lamb" highlights the cost of that salvation—Jesus' sacrificial death on the Cross.

In this moment, heaven echoes with the recognition that salvation belongs solely to God and the Lamb—not to human effort, religion, or works. It's a heavenly chorus that sets the tone for eternal worship and affirms that every saved soul, whether Jew or Gentile, owes their redemption entirely to the grace of God.

OLD TESTAMENT FORESHADOWS REVELATION:

Arise, shine; for your light is come, and the glory of the LORD is risen upon you. For, behold, the darkness shall cover the earth, and gross darkness the people: but the LORD shall arise upon you, and His glory shall be seen upon you. And the Gentiles shall come to your light, and kings to the brightness of your rising. (Isaiah 60:1–3)

Isaiah 60:1–3 prophetically anticipates that same global gathering in Revelation 7:10—a time when Gentiles (nations) are drawn to the light and salvation of the Lord. Darkness covers the earth in Isaiah, much like the Tribulation context of Revelation 7. Yet God's glory shines, and the nations respond. This parallel underscores the universal scope of redemption—Jew and Gentile alike, drawn to God's throne, worshiping the Lamb. The vision in Isaiah finds its ultimate fulfillment in Revelation, when that light is no longer just prophesied—it's gloriously seen.

THE REVELATION OF JESUS CHRIST REVEALS:

7:11 And all the angels stood round about the throne, and about the elders and the four beasts, and fell before the throne on their faces, and worshiped God.

This verse paints a breathtaking scene of worship in heaven, one that transcends human comprehension. It reveals the cosmic response to the multitudes of redeemed souls from (Revelation 7:9), who stand before the throne declaring salvation. Now, all of heaven—the angels, the elders, and the four living creatures—join in adoration and awe before God.

The angels, who have been ministering spirits throughout redemptive history (Hebrews 1:14), now surround the throne in reverent silence and submission. Their posture—falling on their faces—is a posture of deep humility, total surrender, and unreserved worship. This is not casual praise; it is intense, face-down worship, declaring the unmatched holiness and sovereignty of God.

The elders—often understood to represent the redeemed, symbolizing either the twenty-four divisions of the priesthood or the twelve tribes and twelve apostles—and the four living creatures, representing God's creation and His omniscience, join together in a heavenly chorus. Their united worship reveals divine order, where angelic beings and redeemed humanity glorify the Creator side by side.

Revelation 7:11 reminds us that worship is central in heaven. Everything in this verse points to the supremacy of God on the throne, the Lamb, and the awe-inspiring reality that salvation has brought both heaven and earth together in one song of eternal praise.

OLD TESTAMENT FORESHADOWS REVELATION:

Bless the LORD, you His angels, that excel in strength, that do His commandments, listening unto the voice of His word. Bless you the LORD, all you His hosts; you ministers of His, that do His pleasure. Bless the LORD, all His works in all places of His dominion: bless the LORD, O my soul. (Psalm 103:20–22)

Psalm 103:20–22 presents a powerful threefold call to worship that mirrors the heavenly scene in Revelation 7:11. It begins with the angels—mighty and obedient servants of God—then expands to include all of God's heavenly hosts,

His divine ministers, and finally, all of creation, culminating in the psalmist's personal praise. This progression parallels Revelation 7:11, where angels encircle the throne, the elders and living creatures (heavenly hosts) fall in worship, and a great multitude from every nation joins in adoration, reflecting God's all-encompassing plan for worship across heaven and earth.

————◆◆◆————

Irene stirred her coffee, deep in thought.

"Ann, I was reading through Revelation, and something struck me. People always say angels sing in heaven—but in Scripture, aren't they always speaking, no singing? Is that actually right?"

I nodded. "You're onto something, Irene. In Revelation 5:9, it's the elders and the four living creatures who *sing* a new song. But just a few verses later, in 5:11–12, the angels *say* with a loud voice, 'Worthy is the Lamb.' It doesn't say they sing."

Irene frowned. "What about when Jesus was born? Weren't the angels singing then?"

"Good question," I replied, flipping to Luke 2:13–14. "It says:"

And suddenly there was with the angel a multitude of the heavenly host praising God, and saying, Glory to God in the highest, and on earth peace, good will toward men. (Luke 2:13–14)

"Once again, *saying*, not singing."

Irene sat back. "That's so strange. Why wouldn't angels sing?"

I smiled. "Think about it—music is made of major and minor keys. Minor keys carry sorrow, longing, and pain. Even nature sings in them—the howl of the wind, the crash of the waves, the cry of a nightingale. All creation groans under the weight of the curse. But angels? They've never known suffering or redemption. They don't feel the minor keys."

Irene mused, "So they don't understand suffering the way we do."

"Exactly," I continued. "Major keys express triumph, victory, and joy. And humans sing because we've known both sorrow and redemption—lost and found, broken and healed, captive and set free. Angels haven't experienced that. They can speak of redemption, but they can't sing the song of the redeemed."

Irene's eyes widened. "That's why in Revelation 5:9, it's only the redeemed who sing—because we're the ones who've been bought by the blood of the Lamb!"

I nodded. "Exactly! Only a redeemed soul can sing the song of salvation. Angels proclaim God's glory, but they can't sing about redemption—they've never needed it."

Irene let out a breath. "Wow. That changes everything. Next time I hear a worship song about redemption, I'll remember—it's a melody only the redeemed can truly sing."

"Exactly. So sing loud, Irene—because it's a song even the angels can't sing."

Irene leaned back in her chair; eyebrows drawn in thought.

"Ann, this still has me thinking—if angels don't sing but still worship, then maybe worship isn't just about singing at all. I always thought of it as the songs we sing in church. But now I'm wondering . . . what *is* worship, really? What's the true definition?"

I smiled, Bible open in my lap.

"That's such an important question, Irene. A lot of people associate worship only with music—because it's emotional and stirring. But in Scripture, worship goes far deeper. In Revelation, it isn't a performance; it's a response. Worship is truth expressed through awe, reverence, gratitude, and surrender—because of who God is and what He's done."

Irene nodded, intrigued.

"So . . . what does worship actually look like in Revelation?"

I opened to Revelation. "Let me walk you through seven key themes of worship in this book. Each one reveals a different layer of what true worship looks like in heaven—and what it should look like here on earth too."

1. "Holy, holy, holy" (Revelation 4:8)

"This is worship rooted in God's character. The angels declare His holiness without ceasing. It starts with recognizing who God is—His purity, majesty, and perfection."

2. "Worthy are You" (Revelation 4:11; 5:8–10)

"This is worship in response to God as Creator and Redeemer. He is worthy because He made all things and redeemed us through the Lamb's sacrifice. It's about honoring His work and assigning Him ultimate value."

3. "To Him who sits on the throne" (Revelation 5:11–13)

"This is worship in its fullness. Countless angels, creatures, and elders join together, declaring that all power, riches, wisdom, strength, honor, glory, and blessing belong to Him. Nothing is withheld—it's total adoration."

4. "'Salvation to our God' and 'Amen: Blessing . . .'" (Revelation 7:9–12)

"A vast multitude from every nation cries out in praise, declaring that salvation belongs to God alone. This is worship marked by unity, gratitude, and awe across every tribe and tongue."

5. "The kingdoms of this world . . . we give You thanks" (Revelation 11:15–18)

"This moment of worship arises in response to God's justice and His eternal reign. It acknowledges His sovereign rule over all nations and history, giving thanks for the fulfillment of His kingdom."

6. "Great and marvelous are Your works" (Revelation 15:2–4)

"This worship celebrates God's righteous judgments. The redeemed proclaim His justice and truth, declaring that all nations will one day come and worship Him for His perfect ways."

7. The Four Hallelujahs (Revelation 19:1–8)

"This is the only time 'hallelujah' appears in the New Testament—shouted four times in triumphant praise. It celebrates God's final victory, His just judgments, and the joyous union of the Lamb and His Bride, the Church."

Irene sat in silence for a moment, wide-eyed. "So . . . true worship isn't just singing. It's declaring who God is, agreeing with His righteousness, celebrating His works, and surrendering everything in response to His worth."

I nodded. "Exactly. Worship is a lifestyle—it's not just about melody, but about majesty. When we truly grasp who God is and what He's done, worship becomes our natural response—whether we're singing, praying, falling on our faces, or simply standing in awe."

Irene smiled. "Wow. That changes everything. I want to worship like *that*."

I grinned. "Then you already are."

———◆◆◆———

THE REVELATION OF JESUS CHRIST REVEALS:

7:12 Saying, Amen: Blessing, and glory, and wisdom, and thanksgiving, and honor, and power, and might, be to our God forever and ever. Amen.

Revelation 7:12 is a stunning moment of pure, unfiltered worship in the heavenly realm. In response to the great multitude's proclamation of salvation (Revelation 7:10), all the angels, elders, and living creatures around the throne fall on their faces and echo back this powerful doxology. The verse begins and ends with the word *Amen*, a Hebrew term meaning "so be it," signifying total agreement and reverence for what is being declared.

This verse offers a sevenfold praise directed to God, reflecting the fullness and perfection of divine worship:

- Blessing—acknowledging God's generosity and favor.
- Glory—ascribing splendor and majesty to His name.
- Wisdom—honoring His divine insight and perfect judgment.
- Thanksgiving—expressing gratitude for His salvation and mercy.
- Honor—showing deep respect for His holiness and authority.
- Power—recognizing His supreme and sovereign rule.
- Might—praising His strength and ability to act and conquer.

Each attribute highlights a different aspect of God's nature, and together they form a complete circle of praise—emphasizing that He alone is worthy of worship for all eternity. This scene echoes Old Testament passages like 1 Chronicles 29:11 and Psalm 96:6, where similar themes of glory and strength are ascribed to the LORD.

Ultimately, Revelation 7:12 shows us that worship in heaven is not silent or passive—it is loud, unified, and eternal. It is the natural response of all creation— angelic and redeemed—to the greatness of God and the Lamb who sits on the throne.

OLD TESTAMENT FORESHADOWS REVELATION:

Honor and majesty are before Him: strength and beauty are in His sanctuary. (Psalm 96:6)

This verse, like Revelation 7:12, reflects a heavenly worship scene where divine attributes are being exalted. "Honor" and "majesty" in Psalm 96:6 parallel the "honor" and "glory" found in Revelation 7:12, while "strength" mirrors the "power" and "might" also present in the Revelation doxology. The word "beauty" resonates with the awe and splendor of God's sanctuary, aligning with the expressions of thanksgiving and wisdom voiced in the heavenly chorus. Together, these scriptures present a consistent and timeless theme of majestic, attribute-rich worship that transcends eras—from David's psalms to John's vision—reminding us that true worship is not merely emotional, but deeply theological, exalting the very nature and character of God.

THE REVELATION OF JESUS CHRIST REVEALS:

7:13 And one of the elders answered, saying to me, What are these which are arrayed in white robes? And where did they come from?

In Revelation 7:13 one of the elders—heavenly representatives of redeemed humanity—engages John with a profound question: "Who are these who are arrayed in white robes? And where did they come from?" This is not asked out of ignorance but serves as a rhetorical device meant to draw John—and the reader—into a deeper understanding of God's redemptive plan. The multitude dressed in white robes has just been introduced in verse 9 as those from every nation, tribe, people, and language, standing before the throne.

The elder's question points to both identity and origin—"Who are they?" and "Where did they come from?"—highlighting the mystery and significance of this group. The white robes symbolize righteousness and purification, suggesting they've been made clean, not by their own merit, but through divine means. John, overwhelmed and likely unsure, does not attempt to guess. Instead, he responds humbly in the next verse, acknowledging the elder's greater insight.

This interaction reflects John's role as a witness and messenger. He is present to observe and record, not necessarily to interpret. The elder's engagement prepares us for the divine explanation in verse 14—that this great multitude are those who have come out of the Tribulation, having washed their robes in the blood of the Lamb. This passage reminds us that even in the midst of judgment, God is bringing forth salvation on a global scale, fulfilling His promise that the gospel will reach all nations.

OLD TESTAMENT FORESHADOWS REVELATION:

Now Joshua was clothed with filthy garments, and stood before the Angel. And He answered and spoke unto those that stood before Him, saying, Take away the filthy garments from him. And unto him He said, Behold, I have caused your iniquity to pass from you, and I will clothe you with change of raiment (white robes). And I said, Let them set a clean turban upon his head. So they set a clean turban upon his head, and clothed him with garments. And the Angel of the Lord stood by. (Zechariah 3:3–5)

In both passages, we see heavenly figures discussing individuals who have undergone a change of garments, symbolizing spiritual cleansing and righteousness. The "white robes" in Revelation 7:13 represent purity and victory through the Lamb, just as the change of filthy garments for Joshua in Zechariah 3:3–5 represents forgiveness and restoration. Both scenes reflect a heavenly perspective on redemption and justification—key themes in God's plan.

This connection underscores the continuity between the Old and New Testament themes of atonement, righteousness, and divine transformation.

THE REVELATION OF JESUS CHRIST REVEALS:

^{7:14} And I said to him, Sir, you know. And he said to me, These are they which came out of great tribulation, and have washed their robes, and made them white in the blood of the Lamb.

In Revelation 7:14, one of the elders reveals to John the identity of the great multitude clothed in white robes. These are not ordinary saints from prior ages, nor are they the Church that was raptured before the Tribulation. Instead, these are *Tribulation saints*—those who came to faith in Christ during the most intense period of human suffering, known as the Tribulation Age. When the elder asks John who they are, John humbly replies, "Sir, you know," acknowledging that this is a heavenly mystery beyond his understanding. The elder then explains that these individuals "have washed their robes and made them white in the blood of the Lamb." This statement underscores the heart of the gospel—salvation and spiritual cleansing come only through the sacrificial blood of Jesus Christ.

Though they missed the Rapture, these converts responded to the preaching of the 144,000 Jewish evangelists and chose Christ, even in the face of persecution and death. Their white robes symbolize victory, righteousness, and purity—not earned by works, but granted through faith in the Lamb. They refused to take the mark of the beast, even at the cost of their lives. Now, they are eternally safe in the presence of God. This scene offers both comfort and warning: God's mercy extends even into the darkest days, but the cost of discipleship during the Tribulation will be unimaginably high.

OLD TESTAMENT FORESHADOWS REVELATION:

Come now, and let us reason together, says the LORD: though your sins be as scarlet, they shall be as white as snow; though they be red like crimson, they shall be as wool. (Isaiah 1:18)

Both verses emphasize cleansing and purification through divine intervention. Revelation 7:14 speaks of those who "made their robes white in the blood of the Lamb"—a symbolic reference to spiritual purification through Christ's sacrifice. Isaiah 1:18 conveys the same message of transformation: sin-stained garments becoming white, symbolizing forgiveness and righteousness, though written centuries earlier.

This beautifully ties together the redemptive thread running from the Old Testament into the New Testament—God's consistent promise of cleansing through His grace.

THE REVELATION OF JESUS CHRIST REVEALS:

^{7:15} Therefore are they before the throne of God, and serve Him day and night in His temple: and He that sits on the throne will dwell among them.

This verse shifts our attention to the blessed state of the Tribulation saints—those who endured unimaginable persecution during the seven-year Tribulation and ultimately gave their lives for their newfound faith in Christ. These believers are distinct from the Church Age saints who were raptured prior to this time and who appear earlier in Revelation adorned with crowns, having gone through the Bema Seat Judgment for reward. The Tribulation saints, in contrast, were saved during the period of intense wrath and deception. Their salvation was immediate, their devotion was costly, and their time on earth was short. As a result, they stand not crowned, but clothed in white robes—a sign of their righteousness, their victory in Christ, and the purity granted through the blood of the Lamb.

Their position "before the throne of God" reveals that they are honored and accepted into the very presence of God. They serve Him day and night in His temple, not as priests of the Old Covenant, but as redeemed worshipers whose lives became living sacrifices. Their service is continuous, unhindered by earthly limitations, suggesting both privilege and purpose in eternity. This picture is one of restoration and reward—not by merit, but by grace. Though they missed the Rapture and endured terrifying judgment, they were rescued in spirit and now take part in the heavenly worship scene.

The second part of this verse is particularly tender: "He that sits on the throne shall dwell among them." This echoes the theme of God's desire to dwell with His people, seen in the tabernacle in the wilderness, Solomon's Temple, and ultimately fulfilled in Christ's incarnation—"God with us." But here, in Revelation, it reaches its ultimate fulfillment. No longer mediated by tents or temples, the Lord Himself now abides directly with the redeemed. The word used here for "dwell" carries the sense of pitching one's tent—tabernacling with them—bringing to mind the Feast of Tabernacles and its significance.

This detail about palm branches—first seen in Revelation 7:9—connects back to the Feast of Tabernacles in passages like Nehemiah 8:15–17. In the Old Testament, palm branches were used to create temporary booths or shelters, reminding Israel of God's provision and presence during their wilderness journey. In heaven, these branches represent victory, deliverance, and joy. Though these saints had been massacred, martyred, and maligned on earth, in heaven they are given palm branches—a symbol of triumph. No longer weary wanderers or outcasts, they now celebrate under God's eternal covering.

Their robes, described as white, are not thin or symbolic garments. The language and context suggest something magnificent—robes like fine garments, rich and radiant, like an exquisite stole. These robes reflect not just purity but divine dignity, preparation for the marriage supper of the Lamb. While they may not wear golden crowns like the raptured saints, their white robes are heavenly garments of honor and beauty, signifying they belong to the King.

This scene reveals God's heart of mercy. Even during the most severe judgment in human history, God still extends salvation. These Tribulation saints are evidence that even in wrath, God remembers mercy (Habakkuk 3:2). They are a testimony that it's never too late to turn to Him—and though their earthly lives were short, their eternity is secured. Now, they serve not out of duty, but from overwhelming gratitude, in the very presence of the One who saved them.

OLD TESTAMENT FORESHADOWS REVELATION:

My tabernacle also shall be with them: yes, I will be their God, and they shall be My people. (Ezekiel 37:27)

This verse from Ezekiel is part of a prophetic vision of Israel's future restoration, pointing to a time when God Himself will dwell among His people—an idea fulfilled in Revelation 7:15 where the Lord "will dwell among them."

THE REVELATION OF JESUS CHRIST REVEALS:

7:16 They will hunger no more, neither thirst anymore; neither will the sun light on them, nor any heat.

This verse offers a tender glimpse into the compassion of God for those who have suffered during the Tribulation. The multitude standing before the throne in white robes—redeemed through the blood of the Lamb—have endured great affliction. Many of them likely faced deprivation, starvation, exposure to the elements, and brutal persecution for their refusal to take the mark of the beast or to worship the Antichrist. Revelation 7:16 is God's promise of comfort and reversal: the hardships they endured on earth will never touch them again.

The language used echoes God's care for His people in earlier Scripture. Hunger and thirst were often symbols of judgment or hardship (Lamentations 4:4–5; Amos 8:11), but in the presence of God, these former sufferings vanish. This promise also mirrors the messianic prophecy of Isaiah 49:10: "They shall not hunger nor thirst; neither shall the heat nor sun smite them: for He that has mercy on them shall lead them, even by the springs of water shall He guide them." In both passages, we see the gentle, nurturing nature of God's eternal care.

"Neither shall the sun light on them, nor any heat" reminds us not only of the physical torment that many martyrs faced, possibly including exposure or abandonment in desert-like conditions, but also of God's complete and encompassing protection in His eternal Kingdom. No environmental threat, no harsh climate, no earthly pressure can touch them now.

Revelation 7:16 marks the end of suffering and the beginning of eternal relief for those who persevered through the darkest time in history. It reminds us that God is not distant from our pain—He is the healer of it, and in His presence, every wound is mended and every sorrow turned to joy.

OLD TESTAMENT FORESHADOWS REVELATION:

The LORD is your keeper: the LORD is your shade upon your right hand. The sun shall not smite you by day, nor the moon by night. (Psalm 121:5–6)

This passage beautifully aligns with Revelation 7:16, emphasizing God's protective presence. In Psalm 121:5–6, the psalmist speaks of God as a vigilant guardian who shields His people from harm—both natural and supernatural. Likewise, In Revelation 7:16, those who have endured the Tribulation are now forever protected in the presence of God, free from hunger, thirst, and the harsh elements. This parallel highlights the continuity of God's promises from the Old Covenant to the New, offering comfort, rest, and restoration to His faithful.

THE REVELATION OF JESUS CHRIST REVEALS:

7:17 For the Lamb which is in the midst of the throne will feed them, and will lead them to living fountains of waters: and God will wipe away all tears from their eyes.

This verse offers one of the most tender and hopeful promises in all of Scripture. Revelation 7:17 presents a picture of divine comfort, care, and restoration. The Lamb, who is at the center of the throne, is not distant or removed from His people—He is in their midst. He is not only the object of worship, but also the Shepherd of His people. This is a beautiful reversal: the Lamb becomes the Shepherd, fulfilling the prophetic language of Psalm 23:1–2 and echoing the words of Jesus in John 10:11, "I am the good shepherd: the good shepherd gives His life for the sheep."

The phrase "will feed them" speaks of nourishment, provision, and spiritual satisfaction. These are not casual converts; they are the ones who came out of the Tribulation (Revelation 7:14), likely martyred for their faith. They were once hungry, thirsty, and persecuted on earth—but now they are comforted in the presence of the Lamb. He leads them to "living fountains of waters"—a reference that alights with Old Testament imagery like Isaiah 49:10 and Psalm 36:9, where God is the source of life and refreshment. Living water is symbolic of eternal life, renewal, and the indwelling of the Holy Spirit.

The final promise, "God will wipe away all tears from their eyes," underscores that this is more than physical restoration—it is emotional and spiritual healing. This intimate act of God Himself wiping away their tears reveals

His nearness and compassion. It anticipates the full fulfillment in Revelation 21:4, when death, mourning, and pain will be no more.

Though this multitude is distinct from the 144,000 (who are sealed Jewish evangelists), their connection is significant. The ministry of the 144,000 during the Tribulation results in this vast number of Gentile and Jewish believers being brought into the Kingdom. The 144,000 are described later in Revelation 14:1–5 as spiritually pure, blameless, and "following the Lamb wherever He goes"—a spiritual elite chosen for a unique mission. Yet both groups—those sealed for service and those saved through their witness—share in the ultimate comfort and care of the Lamb who reigns.

In this verse, we see a profound truth: those who suffer for Christ will be comforted by Christ. He will not only rescue them from wrath but will personally shepherd and heal them for all eternity.

OLD TESTAMENT FORESHADOWS REVELATION:

The LORD is my shepherd; I shall not want. He makes me to lie down in green pastures: He leads me beside the still waters. (Psalm 23:1–2)

Just as the Lamb in Revelation 7:17 leads the redeemed to "living fountains of waters," Psalm 23:1–2 presents the Shepherd leading His sheep to restful, nourishing places—green pastures and still waters. Both passages highlight God's tender provision, guidance, and care. The imagery of a shepherd caring for his flock shows the consistency of God's love from the Old to the New Testament, and reveals His desire to restore and refresh His people, especially after seasons of suffering.

SUMMARY OF REVELATION 7

Revelation 7 serves as an interlude before the trumpet judgments, offering a profound picture of God's mercy amid judgment. While Revelation 6 details the unfolding wrath of God on earth, Revelation 7 shifts the focus to heaven and a divine pause—showcasing God's protective and redemptive plan during the seven-year Tribulation.

The chapter opens with the sealing of 144,000 servants of God—12,000 from each of the twelve tribes of Israel (Revelation 7:1–8). This sealing marks God's preservation of a faithful remnant of Jewish believers who will serve as evangelists during the Tribulation. These men are protected supernaturally from the judgments to come and are set apart for a specific mission: to proclaim the gospel to the nations in a time of great distress.

Immediately after this, John sees a great multitude that no one could number, from every nation, tribe, people, and language, standing before the throne and before the Lamb (Revelation 7:9). They are clothed in white robes and hold palm branches, symbolizing victory and deliverance. One of the elders explains that these are those who came out of the Tribulation, having washed their robes in the blood of the Lamb (Revelation 7:13–14).

The chapter ends with a beautiful scene of eternal comfort: the redeemed serve God day and night in His Heavenly Temple, and He shelters them with His presence. No more hunger, thirst, or suffering will touch them. The Lamb will shepherd them, lead them to living waters, and God Himself will wipe away every tear from their eyes (Revelation 7:15–17).

KEY TAKEAWAYS

- God seals his servants—The 144,000 Jewish believers are protected and commissioned during the Tribulation.
- A multitude saved—The ministry of the 144,000 leads to a vast number of Jews and Gentiles coming to Christ.
- Tribulation converts—These are not raptured saints, but those who were saved during the Tribulation and martyred for their faith.
- Heavenly comfort—The redeemed find shelter, provision, and peace in the presence of God and the Lamb.
- Victory and worship—The palm branches and white robes declare the triumph of salvation, and the worship of God is central and eternal.

Revelation 7 is a divine pause between the seal judgment and trumpet judgment scenes—a breathtaking reminder that even in wrath, God remembers mercy. It highlights His faithfulness to Israel, His global plan of salvation, and His tender care for those who come to Him, even in the darkest times.

Chapter 9

Revelation 8–9:
Trumpet Judgments
The Tribulation Age—
Daniel's 70th Week: First 3½ Years

REVELATION'S RESET SETS THE STAGE—Irene and I regroup after several days apart—both refreshed, but with a deeper sense of urgency. As my publisher and spiritual confidante, Irene knows the gravity of the message I have been called to write. Our time apart has only fueled the fire, and now, sitting across from each other with open Bibles and marked-up notes, we prepare to tackle the next prophetic chapter—together. This isn't just editing a manuscript; it's stewarding a divine assignment.

"Ann, I've missed our talks. It's been a few days, but I can't stop thinking about what's coming next in Revelation. So here we are . . . the Lamb has opened the seals, and now we're on the edge of something huge—God is about to unleash the trumpet judgments."

"Yes, Irene. Everything's about to shift. But think about this: if God restores the earth to a single landmass—like it was in the beginning—*before* the trumpet judgments begin, that changes everything. It's like He's resetting the stage for His reign. The chaos of the seals ends, and now the world is unified, not just in judgment, but in geography."

"That's wild to think about—like in the days of the garden of Eden, or even before the continental divide after the Flood in the time of Peleg. God brings the land back together: one continent, one global arena for what's coming next."

I nodded. "Exactly. And don't forget—by this point, the Church has been raptured. Let's say that's around 2 billion people gone in an instant. That leaves about 6 billion on earth when the Antichrist steps onto the scene."

"Right. And during the first 3½ years of the Tribulation, he brings this false sense of peace . . . but behind the peace, death is marching."

"Yes. God allows war, famine, and death to sweep the globe—just like the seal judgments showed us. One-fourth of the population gone. That's 1.5 billion souls. We're down to 4.5 billion people on the planet."

"And then we see the martyrs in heaven, Ann—those who gave their lives rather than deny Christ. That scene confuses me. It shows martyrs crying out to God under the altar, asking how long until He avenges their blood."

Irene continued. "But I thought the Antichrist doesn't start persecuting believers until after the abomination of desolation. That's when the False Prophet comes onto the scene and everything escalates."

"So . . . who's killing these people?"

I nodded slowly, clearly encouraged by the question. "You're right—chronologically speaking, the Antichrist's brutal reign doesn't fully begin until the midpoint of the Tribulation. That's when he sets himself up in the rebuilt Third Temple as God and demands worship. But persecution doesn't wait for the False Prophet to arrive."

Irene tilted her head. "So then what? These aren't the people the Antichrist goes after?"

I turned a few pages in my Bible and pointed to Matthew 24:9. "Remember what Jesus said?"

> Then shall they deliver you up to be afflicted and shall kill you, and you shall be hated of all nations for My name's sake. (Matthew 24:9)

"That spirit of persecution is already alive in the world—and after the Rapture, it will only intensify. As of 2025, there are approximately 15.7 million Jews and over 2.4 billion professing Christians worldwide. When the Rapture occurs, millions will be taken—but millions more will be left behind."

I continued. "And then, amid the chaos and despair, others will be led to faith in Christ. Millions more will come to believe during the early years of the Tribulation. But a broken, terrified world won't take kindly to that. Just like we see today—the world's hostility toward Jews and Christians is escalating—and after the Rapture, it will explode. The hatred will deepen."

"This global revival will meet a global backlash."

Irene's eyes widened. "So this isn't something that begins with the Antichrist—it's a spiritual war that's been raging since the beginning. The world's been hostile to God's people all along. After the Rapture, it's like the restraint is lifted, and that ancient hatred finally unleashes without limit."

I turned and pointed to Ephesians 6:12:

> For we wrestle not against flesh and blood, but against principalities, against powers, against the rulers of the darkness of this world, against spiritual wickedness in high places. (Ephesians 6:12)

I looked back at her. "So, yes, Irene—what we're witnessing isn't just political collapse or global instability. It's spiritual warfare on a cosmic scale. Governments are falling. Economies are unraveling. The seal judgments are ripping the world apart. And in the midst of that chaos, people will be desperate—desperate to find someone to blame."

"Anyone who refuses to conform—especially those who cling to Christ—will become the target of that rage."

Irene looked down at the verses again. "That makes sense. These martyrs—Revelation says they died for the Word of God and for their testimony. So they weren't just casualties of war or famine like the fourth seal. They were targeted by their faith."

I nodded. "That's the key. The fourth seal—war, famine, disease—that takes out a quarter of the population, both believers and unbelievers. But the fifth seal shifts focus. It shows us those who were killed specifically because they followed Christ. They are true martyrs."

"And their prayer . . ." Irene said softly. "'How long, O Lord . . .' That means the suffering isn't over. More persecution is still to come."

"Yes," I said. "They're told to rest a little while longer—until the full number of martyrs is complete. That's looking ahead to the Great Tribulation, when the Antichrist's wrath fully erupts. But even now, in the first half of the Tribulation, the cost of following Christ is already deadly."

Irene leaned back slowly. "So this isn't just a moment of sorrow. It's a warning. And a glimpse of God's justice to come."

"And His mercy too," I added. "Because even in wrath, He still sees His people. Their blood isn't forgotten—it's precious. And He promises to make it right."

"It's powerful," I continued. "And it brings us to the sixth seal—when the earth quakes, the sky tears open like a scroll, and creation itself is shaken to the core. In that moment, there's no mistaking what's happening. This isn't natural. This isn't political. This is God!"

I shook my head. "No scientist can explain it away. No leader can take credit."

"The sixth seal is God's unmistakable signature—written across the sky and carved into the land. The land, unified. The people, terrified. And then . . . silence."

Irene sighed. "Thirty minutes of complete silence in heaven. That's not just a pause—it's like the entire universe is holding its breath."

"Yes. And right after, God seals the 144,000—Jewish evangelists marked by His hand. Untouchable. Unshakable. Sent out on a divine mission before the trumpet judgments begin."

Irene recapped, "So at this point, we've got one landmass, 4.5 billion people, silence in heaven, and 144,000 sealed warriors for the gospel. It's like the final pieces of the puzzle are falling into place."

I smiled. "But let's remember what Paul said—we only know in part. We see through a glass darkly. Only the Father and our Lord Jesus Christ know the full revelation. We're just catching glimpses . . . powerful, world-shaking glimpses."

> For now we see through a glass, darkly; but then face to face: now I know in part; but then shall I know even as also I am known. (1 Corinthians 13:12)

"Still, Ann . . . what a privilege to be searching these things out together. It makes me want to stay watchful, ready, and faithful to the end."

"Me too, Irene. Me too."

A HOLY HUSH BEFORE THE TRUMPETS

The opening of the seventh seal marks not just the end of the seal judgments, but the solemn transition into a new phase of God's unfolding wrath: the trumpet judgments. What follows isn't immediate destruction—but silence.

> And when He had opened the seventh seal, there was silence in heaven about the space of half an hour. (Revelation 8:1)

This silence isn't an afterthought. It is heaven's response to the gravity of what is coming. The praise halts. The thunderings cease. Even the angelic host falls quiet. It's a sacred pause—the kind that signals something world-altering is about to break loose.

The heavenly realm has been the backdrop of worship, prayer, and unfolding judgment since Revelation 4. But now, at the threshold of the trumpet judgments, we see Heaven's Temple take center stage. The golden altar. The incense. The fire. The prayers of the saints. This moment reminds us that judgment is never separated from intercession. The cry of the martyrs and the longing of every believer—*"Thy Kingdom come"*—are heard. And they are answered.

An angel, separate from the seven, steps forward—not to blow a trumpet, but to tend the altar. He offers incense with the prayers of the saints. Then, in a solemn shift, he fills the censer with fire and hurls it to earth. It is no longer intercession—it is the beginning of retribution. Heaven's liturgy has moved from worship to wrath.

This moment reveals that the tabernacle in heaven is not symbolic. It is active. The blueprint given to Moses wasn't just ceremonial; it was prophetic. What takes place in Revelation 8 is rooted in that ancient design—but its consequences are global. When heaven moves, the earth trembles.

And now, the seven angels stand ready. Each holds a trumpet—an instrument of divine declaration. In Scripture, trumpets announced war, summoned assemblies, and herald divine appearances. Here, they signal the next phase of God's judgment.

But before the first one sounds, we're invited to pause again.

Not in fear, but in reverence.

The silence reminds us that God's judgments are not impulsive. They are deliberate, preceded by grace, and saturated with purpose. The prayers of the saints have been heard. The world has been warned. The time has come.

Let the trumpets sound.

THE REVELATION OF JESUS CHRIST REVEALS:

^{8:7} The first angel sounded, and there followed hail and fire mingled with blood, and they were cast upon the earth: and the third part of trees was burnt up, and all green grass was burnt up.

The First Trumpet Judgment—One-Third Vegetation Scorched. This verse marks the sounding of the first trumpet, initiating a series of terrifying, divine judgments that devastate the earth's ecological systems. The imagery is stark and literal—hail and fire mingled with blood falling from the heavens. This is not poetic symbolism; it echoes the plagues of Egypt, especially the plague of hail and fire in Exodus 9:22–26, where the judgment struck Egypt's land, but spared the children of Israel in Goshen. In the same way, Revelation draws from that precedent to show God's ability to execute precise, supernatural judgment on rebellious humanity while preserving His faithful remnant.

The first trumpet judgment directly targets the plant life of earth: a third of the trees are burned up, and all green grass is scorched. This has catastrophic implications. Trees and vegetation are not just scenery—they are life support systems. They provide oxygen, food, and shade, and maintain the balance of the climate. When these are destroyed, mankind begins to suffer almost immediately.

- Oxygen levels drop, causing breathing difficulties.
- Cattle and grazing livestock perish due to the loss of grass, which affects global food supply.
- Mass death of domestic and wild animals causes an unbearable stench and the spread of disease.
- Smoke and ash from the massive fires pollute the air, creating a global crisis of unbreathable air and environmental collapse.

The addition of blood in this fiery storm reinforces the idea that these are not natural wildfires or atmospheric events. This is a supernatural judgment from God—not random, but specific and intentional. The blood may be symbolic of death or actual blood supernaturally manifested, much like the Nile turning to blood in Exodus 7. Either way, it signals death, destruction, and divine wrath.

Furthermore, this ecological judgment weakens the very structures of human survival. It affects every nation, regardless of borders. This is global devastation. And yet, it's only the beginning—the first of seven trumpet judgments.

This verse reminds us that God is reclaiming the earth. The environment, long corrupted by sin, idolatry, and demonic influence, is being purified by fire. Satan's grip on creation is being broken. Every tree, every blade of grass, and every breath we take has been sustained by God's mercy. But now, mercy gives way to judgment, and nature itself groans under the weight of sin (Romans 8:22). This trumpet blast is a wake-up call—God is not just judging individuals but the very systems of life that mankind depends on.

Revelation 8:7 is a literal judgment on the environment. It echoes the judgments of Egypt, foreshadowing greater plagues to come. It reveals the fragility of life without God, the seriousness of rebellion, and the urgency of repentance before God's wrath is fully unleashed.

OLD TESTAMENT FORESHADOWS REVELATION:

And the LORD said unto Moses, Stretch forth your hand toward heaven, and there may be hail in all the land of Egypt, upon man, and upon beast, and upon every herb of the field, throughout the land of Egypt. And Moses stretched forth his rod toward heaven: and the LORD sent thunder and hail, and the fire ran along upon the ground; and the LORD rained hail upon the land of Egypt. So there was hail, and fire mingled with the hail, very grievous, such as there was none like it in all the land of Egypt since it became a nation. And the hail smote throughout all the land of Egypt all that was in the field, both man and beast; and the hail smote every herb of the field, and broke every tree of the field. Only in the land of Goshen, where the children of Israel were, was there no hail. (Exodus 9:22–26)

Revelation 8:7 parallels the seventh plague in Exodus 9:22–26, where God sent hail and fire upon Egypt, destroying crops and trees. Just as He once judged Egypt to show His power and deliver His people, this global judgment during the Tribulation reflects God's wrath against a rebellious world. It is a literal and cataclysmic assault on the earth's natural systems, revealing the seriousness of divine judgment.

THE REVELATION OF JESUS CHRIST REVEALS:

[8:8] And the second angel sounded, and as it were a great mountain burning with fire was cast into the sea: and the third part of the sea became blood.

The Second Trumpet Judgment—One-Third Seas Devastated. Revelation 8:8 describes the second trumpet judgment, a catastrophic event that brings devastation to earth's oceans. John records that "as it were a great mountain burning with fire" was cast into the sea, turning a third of the sea into blood. The phrase "as it were" is key—it indicates that this fiery mass was not literally a mountain, but something resembling one in scale and appearance. This kind of apocalyptic language suggests a cosmic impact event, likely an asteroid or meteor, entering earth's atmosphere in a blaze of fiery destruction and plunging into the ocean.

This fiery object is not a natural disaster in the traditional sense; it is a direct act of divine judgment. The fact that it is not on NASA's radar speaks of its supernatural origin—dispatched not by space or science, but by one of the seven angels carrying out God's orders. When it strikes the sea, the result is catastrophic. A third of the ocean is transformed into blood, echoing the first plague in Egypt (Exodus 7:17–21), when the Nile was turned to blood and aquatic life perished. This imagery is meant to convey judgment, death, and pollution—life systems are collapsing.

The ecological impact is unimaginable. Marine life dies en masse, further disrupting the food chain and accelerating the global crisis. The seas, one of earth's primary sources of oxygen, become toxic. The stench from decaying sea life adds to the already unbearable atmosphere from the previous judgment of burning grass and trees. This judgment is not symbolic; it is real, physical, and deadly. It reveals that even earth's strongest natural systems—its oceans—are not immune to divine wrath. In this moment, the sea, often viewed as a place of mystery and power, becomes a graveyard, as God begins to dismantle the corrupted systems of the world one judgment at a time.

OLD TESTAMENT FORESHADOWS REVELATION:

And Moses and Aaron did so, as the LORD commanded; and he lifted up the rod, and smote the waters that were in the river, in the sight of Pharaoh, and in the sight of his servants; and all the waters that were in the river were turned to blood. And the fish that was in the river died; and the river stank, and the Egyptians could not drink of the water of the river; and there was blood throughout all the land of Egypt. (Exodus 7:20–21)

Revelation 8:8 parallels the first plague in Exodus 7:20–21, where the Nile turned to blood, and life within it perished. The judgment strikes not only the sea's appearance but its ability to sustain life and provide oxygen. The devastating event signals the unraveling of earth's natural systems, emphasizing that God's wrath is now touching creation itself in literal and catastrophic ways.

THE REVELATION OF JESUS CHRIST REVEALS:

8:9 And the third part of the creatures which were in the sea, and had life, died; and the third part of the ships were destroyed.

Revelation 8:9 reveals the catastrophic aftermath of the second trumpet judgment, where divine wrath directly impacts the sea. Following the fiery object—described by John as "a great mountain burning with fire"—crashing into the ocean, the results are devastating: one-third of all marine life perishes, and one-third of all ships are destroyed. The scale of this judgment is staggering. Imagine the unimaginable stench from dead sea creatures floating atop bloody, oxygen-depleted waters. The sea, often symbolic of nations and commerce, now becomes a place of death and decay.

The passage draws attention to three specific consequences:

- First, the death of a third of sea creatures points to an ecological disaster of massive proportions. Since the ocean plays a vital role in maintaining the planet's oxygen levels—particularly through phytoplankton—this judgment directly affects earth's atmosphere and habitability. Breathing becomes more difficult. Life on land suffers because the systems of the sea are unraveling.

- Second, the destruction of a third of oceanic vessels sends a ripple through global trade and economy. With over 50,000 merchants ships transporting goods at any given moment today, a one-third loss would disrupt global supply chains, leading to economic collapse, scarcity, and panic among surviving populations. The symbolic and literal blow to commerce strikes at the heart of civilization's infrastructure.

- Finally, the psychological and physical toll of this judgment cannot be overstated. The imagery of fiery impact, bloodied seas, decaying sea life, and wrecked fleets paints a grim picture of a world in chaos. The first trumpet scorched the earth's greenery; the second now poisons its oceans. And this is only the beginning. The first two trumpet judgments have radically altered life on earth, shaking both natural ecosystems and human institutions. The tribulation intensifies, and the world reels from the compounded weight of God's judgment.

OLD TESTAMENT FORESHADOWS REVELATION:

Son of man, take up a lamentation for Pharaoh king of Egypt, and say unto him, You are like a young lion of the nations, and you are as a whale in the seas: and you came forth with your rivers, and troubled the waters with your feet. And fouled their rivers. Thus says the Lord GOD; I will therefore spread out My net over you with a company of many people; and they shall bring you up in My net. I will also water with your blood the land wherein you swim even to the mountains; and the rivers shall be full of you. (Ezekiel 32:2–3, 6)

Revelation 8:9 also echoes Old Testament imagery, particularly Ezekiel 32:2–3, 6, where judgment is pronounced against Pharaoh, and blood pollutes the waters. The sea monster imagery and ecological ruin in Ezekiel serve as a prophetic parallel to the devastation seen in Revelation.

These judgments demonstrate God's sovereign authority over creation and the systems mankind depends on. Even in the earliest trumpet blasts, the earth is plunged into ecological, economic, and societal turmoil—reminding us of the cost of rebellion and the need to seek God's mercy while there is still time.

THE REVELATION OF JESUS CHRIST REVEALS:

[8:10] And the third angel sounded, and there fell a great star from heaven, burning as it were a lamp, and it fell upon the third part of the rivers, and upon the fountains of waters.

The Third Trumpet Judgment—One-Third Waters Poisoned. This third trumpet judgment unleashes devastation upon the earth's freshwater supply—rivers, springs, and underground sources. John describes seeing something "like a great star, burning as it were a lamp," falling from heaven. The language "as it were" signals that this isn't a literal star, but a celestial object of enormous scale and brilliance—possibly a comet, asteroid, or other heavenly body, ablaze as it penetrates earth's atmosphere.

The imagery strongly suggests a supernatural intervention—this is no random cosmic collision. The object is deliberately directed, likely by an angelic command under divine authority. Some scholars and prophecy teachers, like the late Tom Horn, have suggested that this "star" could align with known objects like the asteroid Apophis, scheduled for an extremely close flyby of Earth on April

13, 2029. Though NASA currently predicts no impact, the spiritual insight is this: God—not NASA—holds ultimate authority over the heavens. If God wills it, no scientific forecast can stop it.

Interestingly, the name given in verse 11—Wormwood—implies bitterness, poison, and judgment. It is striking that the Ukrainian word *Chernobyl* also means "wormwood," offering a chilling parallel to the 1986 nuclear disaster. Though Chernobyl is not the fulfillment of Revelation 8:10, it stands as a haunting foreshadowing—a real-world event that gives us a glimpse into what the coming judgment could look like: widespread contamination, mass casualties, and the poisoning of vital resources.

The third trumpet affects one-third of the world's freshwater, making it bitter and deadly. This judgment severely impacts drinking water—already a vulnerable global resource—and will result in massive death and suffering. Humanity, already reeling from the destruction of vegetation and marine ecosystems under the first two trumpets, now faces another blow—the poisoning of life's most basic necessity: water.

This is a sobering reminder that the earth is not under the control of man, but of Almighty God. He who spoke creation into existence also holds the authority to judge it. The third trumpet is both a literal catastrophe and a theological declaration: that sin brings consequences, and creation itself groans under the weight of human rebellion.

OLD TESTAMENT FORESHADOWS REVELATION:

Therefore thus says the LORD of hosts, the God of Israel; Behold, I will feed them, even this people, with wormwood, and give them water of gall to drink. (Jeremiah 9:15)

The reference to *wormwood* echoes Old Testament warnings, such as Jeremiah 9:15, where God declares He will give His people wormwood and bitter water as a form of judgment. This event illustrates God's control over creation and His righteous wrath poured out on a rebellious world. The judgment poisons a third of the world's freshwater, causing widespread suffering and death, and marks a dramatic escalation in the intensity of the Tribulation's plagues.

THE REVELATION OF JESUS CHRIST REVEALS:

[8:11] And the name of the star is called Wormwood: and the third part of the waters became wormwood; and many men died of the waters, because they were made bitter.

Revelation 8:11 brings a sobering detail to the third trumpet judgment—the star that falls from heaven is named *Wormwood*. The name itself carries deep biblical and symbolic meaning. In the Old Testament, *wormwood* refers to a bitter herb known for its toxicity, often symbolizing sorrow, calamity, or divine judgment (Jeremiah 9:15; Lamentations 3:15, 19). Here, it becomes literal, as this "star" poisons a third of the earth's freshwater sources—rivers and springs—making them bitter and deadly.

The use of the name *Wormwood* emphasizes not only the physical bitterness of the water, but also the bitter consequences of humanity's rebellion against God. This star may be interpreted by some as a comet or asteroid, others as a supernatural agent of judgment—but regardless of its form, the result is catastrophic. Many people die simply because they drink the contaminated water.

This verse reflects the escalating severity of the trumpet judgments. The first trumpet scorched vegetation, the second devastated the seas, and now the third strikes at the planet's drinking water. In this progression, life-sustaining systems—food, oxygen, and now water—are all under siege. It is a divine wake-up call, echoing the plagues of Egypt, but on a global scale.

Revelation 8:11 is not just about environmental disaster—it is about divine justice. The bitter waters serve as both judgment and a call to repentance, as God systematically dismantles the comforts and necessities that humanity takes for granted, urging them to turn back to Him before it is too late.

OLD TESTAMENT FORESHADOWS REVELATION:

Lest there should be among you man, or woman, or family, or tribe, whose heart turns away this day from the LORD our God, to go and serve the gods of these nations; lest there should be among you a root that bears gall and wormwood. (Deuteronomy 29:18)

This judgment is not just ecological, but profoundly symbolic: it reflects the bitterness of sin and the devastating consequences of rejecting God's truth. The imagery of *wormwood* draws from Old Testament language that connects bitterness with apostasy and divine retribution. This trumpet judgment serves as a stark warning to a world that has turned away from the Living Water, Jesus Christ, and now experiences the bitter taste of rebellion's consequences.

THE REVELATION OF JESUS CHRIST REVEALS:

8:12 And the fourth angel sounded, and the third part of the sun was smitten, and the third part of the moon, and the third part of the stars; so as the third part of them was darkened, and the day shone not for a third part of it, and the night likewise.

The Fourth Trumpet Judgment—One-Third Celestial Lights Darkened. Revelation 8:12 introduces the fourth trumpet judgment, marking a profound disruption in the celestial order. When the fourth angel sounds his

trumpet, one-third of the sun, moon, and stars are darkened. This partial darkening impacts both day and night, reducing the amount of natural light that the earth receives. For the first time in human history, the rhythm of sunlight and moonlight—so familiar and constant—is visibly shaken.

This judgment directly affects the earth's environment. With one-third less sunlight, global temperatures begin to drop. The world, already reeling from poisoned waters, diminished oxygen, and widespread death, now faces growing cold and increasing darkness. The natural balance is further destabilized, causing deep anxiety and confusion among the world's remaining population.

The prophetic words of Jesus in Luke 21:25 echo here:

> There will be signs in the sun, in the moon, and in the stars; and on the earth distress of nations, with perplexity. (Luke 21:25)

These cosmic signs serve as both warnings and judgments. The word "perplexity" in Luke's passage means to be trapped in an inescapable dilemma—an exact reflection of the Tribulation's escalating crises. The judgment of the fourth trumpet magnifies mankind's helplessness in the face of God's power and sets the stage for even greater upheaval.

This trumpet judgment affects not only the physical world but also the psychological state of humanity. The diminished light is a symbol of diminishing hope. God is stripping away creation's blessings—light, warmth, and clarity—to reveal the true darkness of a world that has rejected Him. Yet even in this, there is a divine purpose: to bring about repentance before the final judgments unfold.

OLD TESTAMENT FORESHADOWS REVELATION:

> The earth shall quake before them; the heavens shall tremble: the sun and the moon shall be dark, and the stars shall withdraw their shining. (Joel 2:10)

This prophetic verse in Joel 2:10 mirrors Revelation 8:12 in its vivid imagery of celestial disruption. Both passages depict cosmic signs involving the darkening of the sun, moon, and stars, signaling divine judgment and the nearness of the "Day of the Lord." These signs are not just symbolic—they reflect God's sovereign intervention in the natural world to get the attention of mankind and warn of coming wrath.

THE REVELATION OF JESUS CHRIST REVEALS:

> [8:13] And I beheld, and heard an angel flying through the midst of heaven, saying with a loud voice, Woe, woe, woe, to the inhabiters of the earth by reason of the other voices of the trumpet of the three angels, which are yet to sound!

This verse marks a dramatic turning point in the unfolding judgments of Revelation. Up to this point, the trumpet judgments have unleashed catastrophic ecological and cosmic disruptions: the earth, sea, fresh waters, and celestial lights have all been struck. But now, before the new trumpet sounds, a heavenly messenger interrupts the sequence with a solemn warning—an angel (some manuscripts say "eagle") flying through mid-heaven shouts a triple "Woe!" to all who dwell on the earth.

The repetition of "woe" three times isn't for dramatic flair—it signifies escalating severity. Each "woe" corresponds to the final three trumpet judgments (trumpets five, six, and seven), also referred to as the first, second, and third woes (Revelation 9:12, 11:14, 11:15). These final judgments will go beyond natural disasters—they will directly affect humanity with intense demonic torment, supernatural invasions, and cosmic upheaval. This angel is not simply announcing a warning: he is delivering a divine forecast of terror, calling attention to the spiritual and physical horrors about to descend.

The fact that this announcement is made from the midst of heaven ensures all creation hears it. It is universal in scope. The angel proclaims it with a loud voice, indicating urgency, authority, and intensity. God is still warning—still allowing space for repentance—even as judgments intensifies.

This verse also reveals God's mercy amid wrath. Before the most terrifying trumpet blasts unfold, He sends a messenger to alert humanity—underscoring the reality that God's justice is always paired with opportunity for repentance. Yet tragically, many will still refuse to turn.

Revelation 8:13 is a divine pause before a storm, a trumpet blast of its own kind. It signals that the worst is yet to come, and that the following three trumpet judgments (the "woes") will usher in unprecedented spiritual and earthly torment. The angel's warning stands as both a prophetic announcement and a merciful call for awareness in the final moments before intensified judgment.

OLD TESTAMENT FORESHADOWS REVELATION:

Son of man, prophesy and say, Thus says the Lord GOD; Wail you: Woe to the day! For the day is near, even the Day of the Lord is near, a cloudy day; it shall be the time of the nations. (Ezekiel 30:2–3)

Ezekiel 30:2–3 serves as a powerful Old Testament parallel to Revelation 8:13, both proclaiming a coming period of divine judgment. In Ezekiel, the prophet is commanded to issue a mournful cry: Woe for that day!—a signal that the Day of the Lord is imminent. This prophetic declaration highlights a time of great distress, described as a "a cloudy day" and a time of doom for the nations.

Similarly, Revelation 8:13 warns of three escalating "woes" that are about to unfold upon the earth, emphasizing the severity of what is to come. Both passages function as divine announcements that God's judgment will soon descend on a rebellious world. The tone is urgent, the imagery ominous, and the message clear: the time of mercy is closing, and the time of reckoning has arrived.

Irene and I sat beneath the old tree in her garden, our table cluttered with study materials, open Bibles, and ancient maps rustling in the breeze. Several days had passed since our last discussion, and now, a quiet urgency hung in the air—as if heaven itself were holding its breath.

"Ann, it's been too many days since we last sat down like this. I've missed it. And honestly, with everything we've been studying, my mind won't stop racing. We're now at the point where God unleashes the first four trumpet judgments—and I can't shake the thought: these echo the plagues Moses called down on Egypt."

"They absolutely do. The first trumpet—hail and fire mixed with blood—echoes the seventh plague in Egypt. But this time, it's global. One-third of all trees and all green grass burned—that's catastrophic. Yet, just like Goshen was spared during Egypt's judgment, I believe this may primarily strike the Gentile nations outside the biblical lands. Even in wrath, God shields His people."

"Yes! Ann . . . when the second trumpet sounds and a 'mountain burning with fire' crashes into the sea, it's the Nile all over again—waters turned to blood. But this time, it's the oceans. One-third becomes blood. Massive death. Still, just like Goshen was spared in Egypt, I believe Israel's land and waters may again be preserved."

"Especially now that the earth may have returned to its Genesis state—a single landmass, a restored Pangaea. If the sixth seal judgment reunified the continents, creating a shared geography for all nations, then the Antichrist's peace treaty with Israel and her regional neighbors could rapidly extend to a global agreement."

I continued. "He's likely sheltered in a preserved region, cloaked in silence while the rest of the earth groans in agony. He'll seize that moment—rising as a false savior, offering 'peace' even as he tightens his grip on a broken, desperate world."

"It makes eerie sense, Ann. Then comes the third trumpet—Wormwood. A blazing star falls from heaven, poisoning a third of the fresh water. Not the seas—our drinking water. No shade, no grass . . . and this is only the beginning."

"Then the fourth trumpet—one-third of the sun, moon, and stars go dark. The skies dim. Temperatures plunge. Food cycles falter. Time itself feels broken—both day and night cut short by a third. Survival turns to chaos. And yet, even in this darkness, God's judgments remain precise—deliberate and measured."

Irene nodded. "And where does all this center? The biblical lands—the inheritance of Shem, Ham, and Japheth. The ancient territories, mapped after the Flood, are the cradle of civilization. It's as if God is restoring the earth not just geographically, but prophetically—taking us back to the world of Genesis after the waters receded, and ultimately, to Eden itself in Revelation."

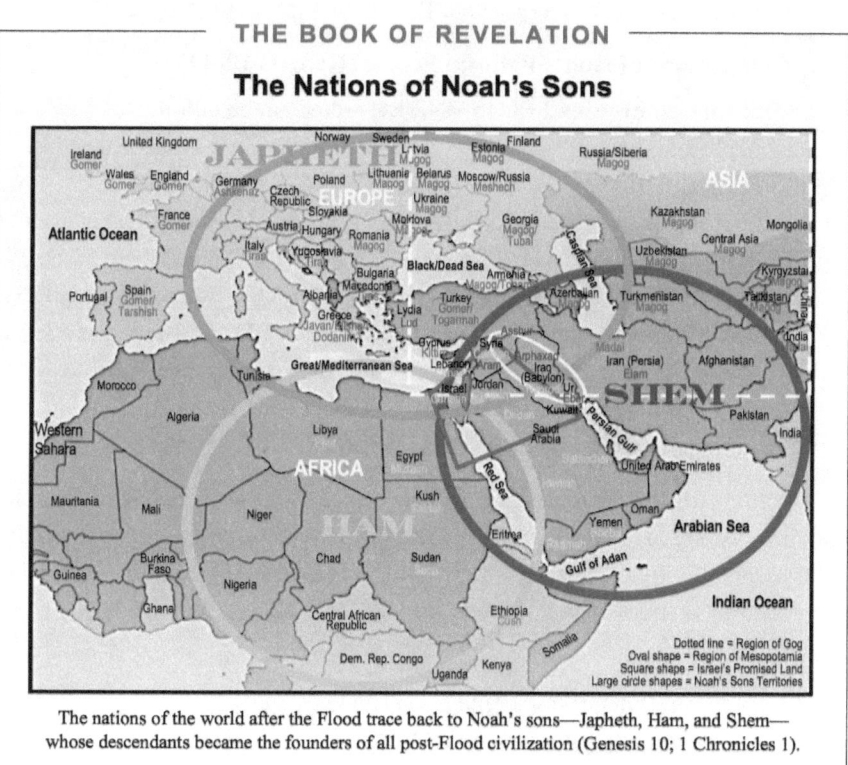

The nations of the world after the Flood trace back to Noah's sons—Japheth, Ham, and Shem—whose descendants became the founders of all post-Flood civilization (Genesis 10; 1 Chronicles 1).

"The genealogies are astounding. When you trace the Hebrew root meanings of the names from Adam to Noah in Genesis 5, a message emerges: 'Man is appointed mortal sorrow; but the Blessed God shall come down, teaching that His death shall bring the despairing comfort.' It's the gospel—hidden in plain sight, embedded within the very first book of the Bible."

Early Generations of God's Faithful People (Genesis 5)

1. Adam (man)—4000 BC to 3070 BC—born on day 6, died at age 930
2. Seth (is appointed)—3870 BC to 2958 BC—died at age 912
3. Enos (mortal)—3765 BC to 2860 BC—died at age 905

4. Cainan (Kenan) (sorrow)—3675 BC to 2765 BC—died at age 910
5. Mahalaleel (the blessed God)—3605 BC to 2710 BC—died at age 895
6. Jared (shall come down)—3540 BC to 2578 BC—died at age 962
7. Enoch (teaching)—3378 BC to 3013 BC—God took him at age 365
8. Methuselah (His death shall bring)—3313 BC to 2344 BC—died at 969
9. Lamech (the despairing)—3126 BC to 2349 BC—died at age 777
10. Noah (comfort or rest)—2944 BC to 1994 BC—died at age 950

Early Generations of God's Faithful People (Genesis 10–11)

11. Shem (fame)—2442 BC to 1842 BC—died at age 600
12. Arphaxad (healer; releaser)—2342 BC to 1904 BC—died at age 438
13. Salah (lift up; exalt)—2307 BC to 1874 BC—died at age 433
14. Eber (cross over; pass through)—2277 BC to 1813 BC—died at age 464
15. Peleg (to split or divide)—2243 BC to 2004 BC—died at age 239
16. Reu (his friend; his shepherd)—2213 BC to 1974 BC—died at age 239
17. Serug (shoot; branch; entwine)—2181 BC to 1951 BC—died at age 230
18. Nahor (light; lamp)—2151 BC to 2003 BC—died at age 148
19. Terah (wanderer)—2122 BC to 1917 BC—died at age 205
20. Abraham (exalted father)—2052 BC to 1877 BC—died at age 175

I continued. "As a result, the Bible's genealogies preserve the Messianic bloodline leading to the birth of Christ. The first twenty generations cover roughly 2,000 years of biblical and early world history. The next 2,000 years—marked by 42 generations—trace the unfolding of biblical, global, and Middle Eastern history."

- 14 generations from Abraham to David,
- 14 generations from David to the Babylonian exile, and
- 14 generations from the exile to Jesus Christ.

"It's wild to think about, Ann. Adam lived long enough to speak with Lamech—Noah's father. And Noah could have spoken to Abraham. This isn't mythology—we're talking about eyewitness history: passed down, protected, and preserved."

"And then there's Methuselah—Noah's grandfather. His name in Hebrew means 'his death shall bring.' And wouldn't you know it? The Flood came just seven days after he died."

"It's as if his life was a divine countdown—and his death, the very trigger for judgment. That's not just symbolism; it's prophetic precision."

"Exactly, Irene. The Flood changed everything—diet, environment, even government. Afterward, God permits the eating of meat, likely because the post-

Flood earth couldn't sustain human life as it once did. This marked the beginning of the Age of Human Government, instituted with the Noahide Laws—a divine framework meant to stabilize a drastically altered world."

The Seven Laws of Noah

1. Do not deny God.
2. Do not blaspheme God.
3. Do not murder.
4. Do not engage in illicit sexual relations.
5. Do not steal.
6. Do not eat flesh torn from a living animal.
7. Establish courts of justice to uphold these laws.

Irene nodded. "It's a pattern—God grants a fresh start, humanity rebels, and judgment follows. Over and over again. But the consistent thread? God's mercy—and His plan for redemption. Even now, in the midst of the trumpet judgments, He's not acting randomly. He's precise. Four trumpets in, and what do we see?"

"One-third of the land—burned. Trees gone. Grass incinerated. One-third of the oceans—turned to blood. Marine life—dead. One-third of the freshwater—made bitter. People dying of thirst. And now, one-third of the sun, moon, and stars—dimmed. Cold. Darkness. Confusion."

Irene nodded. "And your theory—that the southern third of the unified landmass is annihilated—Australia, Antarctica, India, South America, and southern Africa—makes eerie sense. That would leave North America and Eurasia: Europe, Asia, the Middle East, and northern Africa. It fits a pattern—a progressive narrowing of judgment. God is drawing the world's eyes back to the biblical lands, to the inheritance of Noah's sons. It's as if He's spotlighting the Messianic line, tracing it all the way back to the genealogies in Genesis 5 and 10–11."

"Yes, Irene. And maybe—just maybe—this is part of God's final reset. A divine restoration not only of land and nations, but of vision. We're witnessing the collapse of man's systems . . . and the unveiling of God's Kingdom."

"Because even in the midst of judgment, Ann, God extends mercy. His message still echoes: 'Return to Me.' *The Revelation Reset* isn't just about wrath—it's a final call to redemption before the King returns."

I nodded. "Now the stage is set. The judgments, the geography, the genealogies—they've all aligned. The Antichrist rises from the ashes, convinced he holds power. But we know the truth: his reign is temporary. God's plan is advancing—and it's glorious."

We sat in silence—the kind that speaks louder than words. The air felt heavy with all we had just uncovered: judgment and mercy, history and destiny, woven into a tapestry only God could design.

Neither of us moved. The weight of what was coming next settled over us in a holy stillness.

Then, softly, the wind stirred the pages of our Bibles—

as if heaven itself were turning to the next chapter.

THE REVELATION OF JESUS CHRIST REVEALS:

⁹:¹ And the fifth angel sounded, and I saw a star fall from heaven to the earth: and to him was given the key of the bottomless pit.

The Fifth Trumpet Judgment—First Woe. This verse opens the fifth trumpet judgment, also known as the first woe (Revelation 8:13). It introduces a terrifying shift in the Tribulation timeline—from judgments in the natural world (land, sea, freshwater, darkness) to direct demonic torment unleashed upon humanity.

John reports seeing "a star fall from heaven to the earth," and he makes it clear this is not a literal celestial body like an asteroid or comet. Instead, the language shifts as John refers to the star using masculine pronouns ("to him . . . he opened . . ."), indicating that this "star" is actually a person or being.

This being is understood to be Satan, or one acting under his authority. Cross-referencing this imagery with Luke 10:18, where Jesus says, "I beheld Satan as lightning fall from heaven," and Isaiah 14:12, "How are you fallen from heaven, O Lucifer, son of the morning," further affirms the identity of this fallen star. The name "Lucifer" comes from the Latin word meaning *light-bearer* or *morning star*, and Satan is often portrayed in Scripture as a once-glorious being who fell due to pride and rebellion.

This being is given a key—he does not take it by force. This shows that he only has authority because it is granted to him by God. Even in judgment, God remains sovereign. The key is to the bottomless pit, or the abyss (Greek: *abussos*), a prison for the most wicked and dangerous demonic beings. This is the same abyss the demons in Luke 8:30–31 begged Jesus not to send them to: "And they begged Him that He would not command them to go out into the abyss."

The abyss is a literal place—an underground, bottomless, supernatural prison where particularly vile demons have been bound since their rebellion. 2 Peter 2:4 and Jude 6 speak of angels who sinned, being bound in chains of darkness reserved for judgment. These references point to a class of fallen angels who left their God-given domains and committed grotesque acts in Noah's time (Genesis 6), resulting in their immediate imprisonment.

Revelation 9:1 begins the release of these imprisoned beings. With the key in hand, this fallen being (Satan or one acting on his behalf) opens the abyss, initiating a direct demonic assault on humanity. These are not just evil spirits but physical, grotesque entities that will torment the unsealed people on the earth. This judgment marks the beginning of supernatural horror during the Tribulation, signaling that the events on earth have transitioned from bad to unimaginable.

This trumpet judgment should stir a deep urgency in the heart of every believer—for the lost, for the lukewarm, for the distracted. Because when the Church is removed (Revelation 4:1), and this moment arrives, those left behind will face a hellish reality beyond anything the world has ever known.

OLD TESTAMENT FORESHADOWS REVELATION:

How are you fallen from heaven, O Lucifer, son of the morning! How are you cut down to the ground, which did weaken the nations! (Isaiah 14:12)

This verse prophetically addresses the fall of Lucifer (Satan), mirroring the imagery in Revelation 9:1 of a being (symbolized as a star) falling from heaven to earth. Both passages reflect the judgment and descent of Satan from his heavenly domain, aligning with the New Testament portrayal of his limited but catastrophic role during the Tribulation.

THE REVELATION OF JESUS CHRIST REVEALS:

9:2 And he opened the bottomless pit; and there arose a smoke out of the pit, as the smoke of a great furnace; and the sun and the air were darkened by reason of the smoke of the pit.

In this verse, the "star" (identified in verse 1 as a fallen being, most likely Satan) is given authority to open the bottomless pit—a place in Scripture associated with demonic imprisonment, darkness, and divine judgment. The term "bottomless pit" is not merely symbolic; it refers to a real and terrifying place in the spiritual realm—deep within the earth or outside of time and space—where the most vile of demonic beings are restrained.

Once opened, this pit releases an overwhelming cloud of smoke, described as being like a great furnace—emphasizing its intensity, heat, and the suffocating darkness it brings. The image strongly mirrors the destructive fires of Sodom and Gomorrah (Genesis 19:28), or the smoke from Egypt's furnaces during the plagues (Exodus 9:8–10). The smoke darkens the sun and the air, symbolizing both literal environmental impact and the growing spiritual oppression over the earth.

This is not a natural event—it is a supernatural infestation. The darkening of the sun and air is not just due to pollution or volcanic eruption. It is demonic in origin, signaling that a shift has occurred in the spiritual atmosphere of the earth. God's protective restraints are loosening, and demonic entities—until now locked away—are being unleashed.

This verse serves as a spiritual and physical turning point in the Tribulation. Not only is the natural world reeling from the first four trumpet judgments, but now the spiritual realm breaks into the physical. The demonic floodgate has opened. And what follows in the next verses is not only terrifying—but calculated. God is still in control, using even these unleashed forces for His sovereign purposes of judgment and, ultimately redemption.

OLD TESTAMENT FORESHADOWS REVELATION:

And he looked toward Sodom and Gomorrah, and toward all the land of the plain, and beheld, and, lo, the smoke of the country went up as the smoke of a furnace. (Genesis 19:28)

In Revelation 9:2, smoke rises from the bottomless pit "as the smoke of a great furnace," darkening the sun and air. In Genesis 19:28, smoke from divine judgment also rises "as the smoke of a furnace." Both passages depict judgment scenes where the atmosphere is polluted and obscured by smoke caused by supernatural or divine wrath. The imagery of a furnace-like smoke signals devastating destruction and sets the stage for what follows—whether it's the fall of Sodom or the unleashing of demonic forces.

This Genesis reference helps show that God's judgment in Revelation is consistent with His character and actions in earlier biblical history—measured, symbolic, and terrifying in purpose.

THE REVELATION OF JESUS CHRIST REVEALS:

9:3 And there came out of the smoke locusts upon the earth: and to them was given power, as the scorpions of the earth have power.

Revelation 9:3 marks a terrifying escalation in the judgments during the Tribulation: "And there came out of the smoke locusts upon the earth: and unto them was given power, as the scorpions of the earth have power." These are not ordinary locusts, but demonic entities released from the abyss. Their origin—emerging from the smoke of the bottomless pit—clearly reveals their supernatural and infernal nature. They are unleashed by divine permission to torment humanity, emphasizing that their power is not inherent but granted by God for a specific judgment purpose.

Unlike natural locusts that devour vegetation, these creatures have no interest in crops. Instead, they have power like that of earthly scorpions—to inflict pain. This torment is directed specifically at unrepentant humanity—those who do not bear the seal of God on their foreheads (verse 4), distinguishing the 144,000 sealed Jewish evangelists as protected from this judgment.

These demonic beings symbolize a horrifying preview of hell unleashed on earth. Their torment lasts five months, a time span that matches the natural life cycle of locusts, yet in this case, it represents prolonged, inescapable suffering. It is important to note that while these beings inflict agony, they are not permitted to kill. This highlights the judgment's purpose—not to destroy life but to lead people to repentance. God is granting a final opportunity for hardened hearts to turn to Him before it's too late.

The imagery of these locusts as scorpion-like beings, likely with tails that sting, echoes the tormenting power of demonic oppression. Their release signals that the restraint previously placed on the worst of fallen angels has been temporarily lifted. These beings had been so evil that even the demons in Jesus' day begged not to be sent to the abyss (Luke 8:31). Now, God allows them to rise and execute torment—serving as a severe wake-up call to the unrepentant world.

In this act of judgment, we still see God's mercy. As horrific as it seems, this torment is meant to bring about repentance. Death is withheld; the suffering is temporary but purposeful. God is not willing that any should perish (2 Peter 3:9), and even at this late stage of judgment, He is calling sinners to turn from their rebellion. The terrifying release of these demonic locusts is both a consequence of unrepentant sin and a merciful warning—an urgent call to repentance before final judgment falls.

OLD TESTAMENT FORESHADOWS REVELATION:

And the LORD said unto Moses, Stretch out your hand over the land of Egypt for the locusts, that they may come up upon the land of Egypt, and eat every herb of the land, even all that the hail has left. And Moses stretched forth his rod over the land of Egypt, and the LORD brought an east wind upon the land all that day, and all that night; and when it was morning, the east wind brought the locusts. And the locusts went up over all the land of Egypt, and rested in all the coasts of Egypt: very grievous were they; before them there were no such locusts as they, neither after them shall be such. For they covered the face of the whole earth, so that the land was darkened; and they did eat every herb of the land, and all the fruit of the trees which the hail had left; and their remained not any green thing in the trees, or in the herbs of the field, through all the land of Egypt. (Exodus 10:12–15)

In Exodus, the locusts are literal and cause massive ecological destruction as judgment on Egypt. In Revelation, the locusts are demonic, symbolic of a spiritual judgment, but still very real in their tormenting power—targeting humans instead of vegetation. The shared theme is clear: God uses locusts as instruments of judgment, though in Revelation, the scale, purpose, and nature of the judgment is far more severe and supernatural.

THE REVELATION OF JESUS CHRIST REVEALS:

9:4 And it was commanded them that they should not hurt the grass of the earth, neither any green thing, neither any tree; but only those men which have not the seal of God on their foreheads.

In Revelation 9:4, we see a striking shift in God's method of judgment. Unlike the natural destruction seen earlier—such as in the first trumpet where trees and grass are burned—this judgment is highly targeted and spiritual in nature. The demonic locusts released from the abyss are commanded not to harm the vegetation or natural environment, which is unusual for locusts. Instead, their sole target is human beings—specifically, those who do not have the seal of God on their foreheads.

This reveals divine restraint and precision. These creatures do not act out of instinct or chaos—they operate under direct command from God. Their torment is limited to unbelievers—those who have rejected Him and were not sealed. This sealing likely refers first to the 144,000 Jewish evangelists mentioned in Revelation 7, who are marked with God's seal on their foreheads. But it may also extend to the Tribulation saints—those who repent and come to faith in Christ after the Rapture but before death.

Paul affirms this concept of sealing in the Church Age. He teaches that the Holy Spirit is given to believers at the moment of faith as a seal and guarantee ("earnest") of their future inheritance.

In whom you also trusted, after that you heard the word of truth, the gospel of your salvation: in whom also after that you believed, you were sealed with that Holy Spirit of promise. Which is the earnest of our inheritance until the redemption of the purchased possession, unto the praise of His glory. (Ephesians 1:13–14)

Ephesians 4:30 further connects the seal of the Holy Spirit to sanctified living and warns believers not to grieve the Holy Spirit. The seal lasts until the "day of redemption"—the future glorification of believers. In both the Church Age and the Tribulation, God's seal represents ownership, identity, and protection. Just as He protected Israel from the plagues of Egypt (Exodus 8:22–23, 9:4, 11:7), He marks His own—even in the midst of judgment.

And grieve not the Holy Spirit of God, whereby you are sealed unto the day of redemption. (Ephesians 4:30)

The fact that these beings are instructed not to touch any green thing also underscores that their mission is not ecological, but spiritual and personal—to torment rebellious humanity, not destroy nature. It also contrasts their demonic nature with God's orderly sovereignty—even hellish forces cannot move beyond the boundaries God permits.

This verse serves as a terrifying but hopeful reminder: even in judgment, God knows who belongs to Him, and He protects His own. It's a foreshadowing of the final separation between those who follow the Lamb and those who follow the beast.

OLD TESTAMENT FORESHADOWS REVELATION:

For the LORD will pass through to smite the Egyptians; and when He sees the blood upon the lintel, and on the two doorposts, the LORD will pass over the door, and will not suffer the destroyer to come in unto your houses to smite you. (Exodus 12:23)

In Exodus 12:23, the Israelites are marked with the blood of the lamb on their doorposts for protection. In Revelation, God's people are sealed on their foreheads for protection. In both, a divine destroyer or judgment is commanded to spare those who bear God's sign. The theme of God distinguishing His people during judgment is central in both passages.

This pattern of divine protection for the obedient and faithful—amid chaos and wrath—is a recurring biblical principle that connects Old and New Testament prophecy.

THE REVELATION OF JESUS CHRIST REVEALS:

9:5 And to them it was given that they should not kill them, but that they should be tormented five months: and their torment was as the torment of a scorpion, when he strikes a man.

This verse unveils one of the most terrifying judgments of the Tribulation—the release of demonic torment from the abyss. The locust-like creatures are not permitted to kill, but to inflict excruciating pain upon humanity. Their assault is divinely limited to five months—the typical lifespan of a natural locust swarm, generally from May to September in the Middle East.

These demonic beings cause intense agony likened to the sting of a scorpion—known to cause burning pain, swelling, and sometimes even convulsions. The emphasis here is that death is withheld. People will long to die (as the next verse states), but they will not be able to. This divine limitation—inflicting pain but forbidding death—is a form of judgment mingled with mercy. It is severe, yet still provides an opportunity for repentance.

Interestingly, the five-month duration—150 days—mirrors the time the floodwaters prevailed during Noah's Flood (Genesis 7:24). This is more than a coincidence; it's a symbolic parallel. In Noah's day, the flood cleansed the earth physically. In Revelation, the torment warns the earth spiritually. Both mark seasons of divine judgment, and both carry a plea: Turn back to God.

This judgment, then, is not just punitive—it is also redemptive. God is shaking the world, calling out to those left behind to repent before it is eternally too late.

OLD TESTAMENT FORESHADOWS REVELATION:

And the waters prevailed upon the earth a hundred and fifty days. (Genesis 7:24)

Both Revelation 9:5 and Genesis 7:24 mention a five-month—150 day—period in which God's judgment is unleashed upon the earth. In Genesis, the judgment came in the form of a global Flood—a physical purging of wickedness. In Revelation, the judgment comes through demonic torment—spiritual and physical agony inflicted upon those who reject God. Both instances emphasize the intensity and duration of divine judgment, serving as both punishment and a stark call to repentance.

THE REVELATION OF JESUS CHRIST REVEALS:

9:6 And in those days will men seek death, and will not find it; and will desire to die, and death will flee from them.

This haunting verse describes the intense psychological and physical torment unleashed during the fifth trumpet judgment—so severe that people will long for death as an escape, but will be unable to attain it. Death, therefore, takes a divine leave of absence. For five agonizing months, the demonic locust-like creatures from the abyss will inflict unrelenting suffering on all those without the seal of God on their foreheads. Yet, they are forbidden from killing their victims.

The statement that "death shall flee from them" implies a supernatural restraint. This is not merely emotional despair or mental illness—it is literal, divine prevention of physical death. God allows the torment but withholds the release of death, perhaps to give people one final opportunity to repent. It is an act of both justice and mercy. Just as God withheld judgment in Noah's day for 120 years while Noah preached (Genesis 6:3); here, too, God withholds finality so that hearts might turn to Him.

This verse also exposes the depth of human despair during the Tribulation. After repeatedly rejecting God, humanity will face judgment so intense that even death offers no relief. In a complete reversal of the modern mindset—where death is often seen as the ultimate escape from suffering—even suicide will be impossible. In this divine moment, judgment reigns, and every exit is sealed. There will be no hiding, no fleeing—only the inescapable reality of God's justice.

Thus, Revelation 9:6 is a solemn warning: to resist God's grace now is to risk future torment where mercy is still offered—but under unimaginable pressure.

OLD TESTAMENT FORESHADOWS REVELATION:

And death shall be chosen rather than life by all the residue of them that remain of this evil family, which remain in all the places where I have driven them, says the LORD of hosts. (Jeremiah 8:3)

This verse captures the despair and agony of divine judgment—where people long for death, but it eludes them. This reflects the condition during the fifth trumpet, where torment is so intense that people seek death, but cannot find it.

THE REVELATION OF JESUS CHRIST REVEALS:

9:7 And the shapes of the locusts were like to horses prepared to battle; and on their heads were as it were crowns like gold, and their faces were as the faces of men.

This verse opens one of the most graphic and symbolic visions in all of Revelation. John, receiving this vision directly from Jesus Christ and writing under the Holy Spirit's inspiration, uses similes like "as it were" and "like" to express what words can barely contain. That's why Revelation 9 is filled with similes—phrases like "as it were" and "like"—because these beings are utterly beyond anything known to mankind. What he witnesses is so otherworldly, so terrifying, that language bends under the weight of the vision.

The "locusts" John sees are not natural insects; they are demonic creatures released from the bottomless pit. Their appearance "like to horses prepared to battle" implies they are powerful, fast, and war-ready—fierce like war horses charging into conflict. The image speaks of discipline, formation, and terrifying strength.

The "were as it were crowns like gold" suggest authority or invincibility—these creatures operate under divine allowance and cannot be easily stopped. They are conquerors in their own realm, assigned a task of tormenting humanity.

The "faces were as the faces of men" emphasize intelligence and intentionality. These are not mindless insects. They possess awareness, cunning, and perhaps even mock the image of man, whom they now torment. This mixture of human and beastly characteristics echoes prophetic descriptions in books like Joel and Nahum, where invading armies are described in similar beast-like terms.

Revelation 9:7 reveals the unnatural and horrifying nature of the demonic horde unleashed during the fifth trumpet judgment. Their terrifying appearance combines strength, authority, and intelligence—making them not only physically destructive but psychologically tormenting as well. John's repeated use of "like" and "as" highlights that what he saw defies the limits of human language.

OLD TESTAMENT FORESHADOWS REVELATION:

The appearance of them is as the appearance of horses; and as horsemen, so shall they run. Like the noise of chariots on the tops of mountains shall they leap, like the noise of a flame of fire that devours the stubble, as a strong people set in battle array. (Joel 2:4–5)

Just like Revelation 9:7, Joel uses similes to describe a terrifying, swift, and organized force that brings judgment. Many Bible scholars believe Joel's prophecy refers to a literal locust plague with future apocalyptic overtones, making it a prophetic foreshadowing of the demonic locust army John witnesses in Revelation.

THE REVELATION OF JESUS CHRIST REVEALS:

9:8 And they had hair as the hair of women, and their teeth were as the teeth of lions.

This verse continues the vivid and terrifying description of the demonic locusts unleashed from the abyss during the fifth trumpet judgment. The use of similes—"as the hair of women" and "as the teeth of lions"—emphasizes both their deceptive beauty and their brutal savagery.

"Hair as the hair of women" likely points to a certain seductive or deceptive appearance. In biblical times, long hair was often associated with beauty and allure (Song of Solomon 4:1). These demonic beings may appear strangely attractive or mesmerizing, giving a false sense of security or allure, only to bring great torment.

"Teeth as the teeth of lions" signifies raw ferocity, destructive force, and intimidation. In Scripture, lions symbolize both strength and devouring power—and here, they emphasize the terrifying nature of the locusts. Although they are not permitted to kill, their ability to inflict pain is fierce, targeted, and unrelenting.

These combined attributes form a horrific hybrid of seduction and savagery. At first glance, they seem almost regal or alluring—with crowns on their heads and long hair like women. But their true nature is violently deceptive: scorpion tails (Revelation 9:10), iron breastplates (Revelation 9:9), and lion's teeth.

It's a vivid illustration of Satan's strategy—to appear as an angel of light (2 Corinthians 11:14), while delivering only torment and ruin beneath the surface.

OLD TESTAMENT FORESHADOWS REVELATION:

For a nation is come up upon my land, strong, and without number, whose teeth are the teeth of a lion, and he has the cheek teeth of a great lion. (Joel 1:6)

This verse in Joel 1:6 describes a locust invasion as a destructive army with lion-like teeth, just as Revelation 9:8 describes the demonic locusts with "teeth as the teeth of lions." Joel's prophetic language uses imagery of natural locust plagues, which serves as a foreshadowing of the supernatural, apocalyptic plague seen in Revelation. This verse from Joel establishes a prophetic backdrop for Revelation's vivid, intensified fulfillment.

THE REVELATION OF JESUS CHRIST REVEALS:

[9:9] And they had breastplates, as it were breastplates of iron; and the sound of their wings was as the sound of chariots of many horses running to battle.

This verse continues the terrifying description of the demonic locusts unleashed from the bottomless pit. Again, John uses similes like "as it were" and "as the sound of" because the creatures he is seeing are unlike anything in the natural world. These are not literal insects or military machines such as helicopters, as some have speculated. These are supernatural beings—demonic in origin—released directly from the abyss (bottomless pit). Their "breastplates of iron" symbolize their invincibility and terrifying resilience. They are not easily harmed, and they press forward like warriors in an unstoppable army.

The "sound of their wings" is deafening, likened to "chariots of many horses running to battle," a phrase evoking the noise and terror of ancient warfare. This would have immediately resonated with first-century readers, who would associate such a sound with chaos, dread, and destruction. The imagery also mirrors prophetic language from the Book of Joel, where invading locusts are described in militaristic terms (Joel 2:5). John's emphasis is clear: these are not natural locusts, nor are they symbolic representations of man-made war machines. These are literal, terrifying, and hellish creatures with one purpose—tormenting unrepentant humanity for five long months. They are instruments of divine judgment, but their origin is demonic, emerging from a place reserved for the most wicked spiritual beings.

In all of this, the sovereignty of God remains evident. These creatures cannot act beyond what they are permitted. Their power, their duration of torment, and their targets are all determined by divine decree—highlighting both the severity of God's judgment and His measured restraint.

OLD TESTAMENT FORESHADOWS REVELATION:

The noise of a whip, and the noise of the rattling of the wheels, and of the prancing horses, and of the jumping chariots. The horseman lifts up both the bright sword and the glittering spear: and there is a multitude of slain, and a great number of carcasses; and there is none end of their corpses; they stumble upon their corpses. (Nahum 3:2–3)

The clattering, thundering sound of war in Revelation 9:9 is compared to the beating wings of the demonic locusts—"as the sound of chariots of many horses running to battle." The imagery is apocalyptic and overwhelming, evoking terror and chaos. Though Nahum's prophecy describes the fall of Nineveh, his symbolic language—war machines, noise, speed, and fear—mirrors the terrifying onslaught of Revelation 9. The thundering chariots and charging horses in both texts serve as vivid metaphors for unstoppable, divinely permitted destruction. Together, they emphasize the violence of judgment, the power of unseen forces, and the spiritual terror of rejecting God.

THE REVELATION OF JESUS CHRIST REVEALS:

9:10 And they had tails like to scorpions, and there were stings in their tails: and their power was to hurt men five months.

This verse reinforces and expands upon the torment described in verses 3 and 5. The creatures unleashed from the abyss are again said to possess tails like scorpions, emphasizing their supernatural design for pain, not death. The sting in their tails speaks to targeted, intelligent affliction rather than random destruction. This torment is not metaphorical—it's a divinely permitted, literal, physical agony meant to serve as a final wake-up call to the unrepentant.

The five-month duration, again, mirrors the 150 days of judgment during Noah's Flood (Genesis 7:24), symbolizing a measured judgment, set by God's authority. Just as God once cleansed the earth with water, here He shakes the earth with demonic torment. However, unlike the Flood, where the judgment resulted in mass death, this torment is designed to stop just short of death, prolonging suffering in hopes of leading people to repentance.

This verse is both a warning and a window into God's mercy: even in wrath, He always desires repentance over ruin (2 Peter 3:9). The torment serves as both judgment and opportunity—for as long as there is breath, there is still a chance to turn to Him.

OLD TESTAMENT FORESHADOWS REVELATION:

I will heap mischiefs upon them; I will spend My arrows upon them. They shall be burnt with hunger, and devoured with burning heat, and with bitter destruction: I will also send the teeth of beasts upon them, with the poison of serpents of the dust. (Deuteronomy 32:23–24)

This passage speaks of divine judgment through physical suffering, including "the poison of serpents"—which closely parallels the tormenting stings like scorpions in Revelation 9:10. Both passages portray painful affliction unleashed as a consequence of rebellion, as part of God's righteous judgment.

THE REVELATION OF JESUS CHRIST REVEALS:

9:11 And they had a king over them, which is the angel of the bottomless pit, whose name in the Hebrew tongue is Abaddon, but in the Greek tongue has his name Apollyon.

This verse introduces one of the most chilling figures in the Book of Revelation—the king of the demonic locusts unleashed from the bottomless pit. Unlike natural locusts, which are noted in Proverbs 30:27 as having *no king*, these are supernatural, demonic beings under the command of a powerful spiritual ruler. The fact that they have a king marks them as unnatural and organized, suggesting they are part of a coordinated assault against humanity under divine judgment.

The king's name is given in both Hebrew and Greek—Abaddon (Hebrew) and Apollyon (Greek)—both of which translate to "Destroyer." This name reflects not just a title, but a nature: one of destruction, death, and chaos. While some debate whether this being is Satan himself or a high-ranking fallen angel in his hierarchy, many scholars interpret this as a reference to Satan or a demonic general acting under his command, since it fits the broader pattern of Revelation's escalating spiritual warfare.

The use of dual languages—Hebrew and Greek—also underscores the universality of this terror. Whether from a Jewish or Gentile perspective, the destroyer's identity and mission are unmistakable: he is a being of destruction, empowered to torment, not simply destroy. This judgment isn't random chaos; it is directed and allowed by God as part of the unfolding wrath in the Tribulation.

Theologically, this moment serves as a stark contrast to Christ, who is called the Good Shepherd and King of kings. Christ leads His people to life, healing, and restoration. Abaddon or Apollyon leads his horde to death, torment, and ruin. This is a vivid display of the spiritual battle between the kingdom of light and the kingdom of darkness. As always in Revelation, even in judgment, God's ultimate goal remains: to lead people to repentance before the final wrath is complete.

OLD TESTAMENT FORESHADOWS REVELATION:

Hell is naked before him, and destruction (Abaddon) has no covering. (Job 26:6)

In Hebrew, the word translated *destruction* in this verse is Abaddon, the very same word used in Revelation 9:11. It's used poetically in the Old Testament to refer to the realm of the dead, destruction, or the underworld, and it is closely associated with Sheol—the grave or place of the dead.

THE REVELATION OF JESUS CHRIST REVEALS:

9:12 One woe is past; and, behold, there come two woes more hereafter.

Revelation 9:12 marks a sobering pause in the progression of judgments. The verse serves as a divine checkpoint—a moment of reflection after the first woe—the fifth trumpet judgment—has completed its course. For five months, the inhabitants of earth have endured a relentless, demonic torment from the locust-like creatures unleashed from the abyss—an agony so intense that people longed for death, but could not die (Revelation 9:5–6). Now, the Scripture declares: that torment is over . . . but not the judgment.

The phrase "one woe is past" confirms the conclusion of the fifth trumpet judgment and the first woe. Yet, rather than bringing relief, the warning immediately turns toward the future: "Behold, there come two woes more hereafter." This word "behold" (Greek: *idou*) grabs the reader's attention. It signals urgency. The worst is not over—it is only beginning.

These woes are not symbolic of minor misfortunes. In the prophetic context, "woes" are divine judgments of escalating severity. The next two trumpet blasts—the sixth and seventh—will unveil even more horrifying judgments. The second woe—sixth trumpet—brings an army that kills a third of mankind (Revelation 9:13–21), and the third woe—seventh trumpet—introduces the final bowl judgments and the climax of God's wrath.

The use of the word "woe" three times (Revelation 8:13) sets apart the last three trumpet judgments as distinct in magnitude and impact. These are not natural calamities or human wars. They are supernatural judgments, unveiling the wrath of God, and targeting the unrepentant inhabitants of the earth.

This verse acts as a divine warning signpost: The first judgment was a glimpse. The second and third will be even more catastrophic. It also reinforces the longsuffering of God, who—despite the horror of judgment—still delays full wrath in hopes of repentance (2 Peter 3:9). But for those who persist in rebellion, the next woes await.

OLD TESTAMENT FORESHADOWS REVELATION:

You, therefore, son of man, prophesy, and strike your hands together, and let the sword be doubled the third time, the sword of the slain: it is the sword of the great men that are slain, which enters into their privy chambers. (Ezekiel 21:14)

Ezekiel 21:14 foretells progressive waves of judgment—sword after sword after sword. Just as Revelation warns of three woes, Ezekiel speaks of a "third strike" of divine judgment, building in intensity. Both passages convey that each successive act of judgment is worse than the last, a warning to the unrepentant.

This connection underscores God's consistent pattern throughout Scripture: mercy first, warning second, and then increasingly severe consequences of continued rebellion.

THE REVELATION OF JESUS CHRIST REVEALS:

^{9:13} And the sixth angel sounded, and I heard a voice from the four horns of the golden altar, which is before God.

The Sixth Trumpet Judgment—Second Woe. This verse marks the beginning of the sixth trumpet judgment, also known as the second woe. The scene shifts back to the Heavenly Temple, specifically to the golden altar before God, where the four horns symbolize power, intercession, and judgment. This is the same altar referenced earlier in Revelation 8:3–5, where the prayers of the saints are mingled with incense and cast to earth.

The fact that a voice comes from the altar—not from the throne or an angel—emphasizes that this next judgment is directly connected to divine justice and the cries of the martyred saints. Their prayers have reached the altar, and now a response comes forth. The golden altar, originally a place of mercy and intercession in the Old Testament tabernacle (Exodus 30:1–10), now becomes the launch point for devastating judgment, showing that the time for mercy is closing and the time for reckoning has arrived.

The four horns could also symbolize God's complete sovereignty over the earth's four corners, suggesting this judgment will have global consequences. What follows is the release of four fallen angels bound at the Euphrates River, leading to the death of a third of mankind. This solemn moment underscores the terrifying seriousness of rejecting God's grace—judgment is no longer delayed.

OLD TESTAMENT FORESHADOWS REVELATION:

And you shalt make an altar to burn incense upon: of shittim wood shalt you make it. A cubit shall be the length thereof, and a cubit the breadth thereof; four-square shall it be: and two cubits shall be the height thereof: the horns thereof shall be of the same. And you shalt overlay it with pure gold, the top thereof, and the sides thereof round about, and the horns thereof; and you shalt make unto it a crown of gold round about. (Exodus 30:1–3)

This passage establishes the golden altar as a place of intercession and atonement in the Old Covenant. In Revelation 9:13, we see a shift: the same altar now becomes a launch point for judgment, not mercy. This transformation reflects the progression from God's patience to His righteous wrath during the Tribulation.

THE REVELATION OF JESUS CHRIST REVEALS:

9:14 Saying to the sixth angel which had the trumpet, Loose the four angels which are bound in the great river Euphrates.

This verse introduces a chilling moment in the sixth trumpet judgment: four specific angels, currently bound in the Euphrates River, are released. Their restraint suggests that these are not holy angels, but fallen ones—evil spiritual beings whose freedom is restricted until this precise moment in God's prophetic timeline. Their location is no accident. The Euphrates River, one of the four rivers that flowed from Eden (Genesis 2:14), also became a symbol of the cradle of civilization and rebellion—most notably, Babylon.

The mention of the Euphrates points to a region historically saturated with opposition to God's authority. Nimrod's ancient city of Babel (Genesis 10:8–10, 11:1–9) and later Babylon (Daniel 1–5), both sites of organized rebellion against God, were rooted in this region. Revelation 18:2 later refers to Babylon as the "dwelling place of demons," reinforcing the spiritual corruption tied to this geographical location. That the four angels are bound there suggests they have been divinely imprisoned, likely since their fall, awaiting this moment of unleashed judgment.

Their release is not random—it is a divine act of judgment. The command to "loose" them signifies that what follows will be part of God's sovereign plan to bring wrath upon an unrepentant world. The spiritual and historical weight of this location reminds us that rebellion has consequences, and God will one day confront it with justice.

OLD TESTAMENT FORESHADOWS REVELATION:

But the prince of the kingdom of Persia withstood me one and twenty days: but, lo, Michael, one of the chief princes, came to help me; and I remained there with the kings of Persia. (Daniel 10:13)

In Daniel 10:13, there is a glimpse into the spiritual warfare happening behind the scenes—involving angelic beings and demonic forces over geographic regions. The "prince of Persia" and "kings of Persia" are generally understood by Bible scholars to be demonic territorial spirits. Similarly, Revelation 9:14, four powerful fallen angels (demons) are bound in the Euphrates region, a literal and spiritual battleground.

THE REVELATION OF JESUS CHRIST REVEALS:

9:15 And the four angels were loosed, which were prepared for an hour, and a day, and a month, and a year, for to slay the third part of men.

This verse marks a terrifying escalation in the judgments of God during the Tribulation. While the earlier trumpet (the fifth) released demonic locusts that tormented but did not kill, the sixth trumpet unleashes four powerful fallen angels who do kill—specifically, one-third of humanity. These are not symbolic figures; they are literal beings, imprisoned until God's appointed time.

The precision of their release—an hour, a day, a month, and a year—emphasizes God's sovereignty and divine timing. This phrase reveals that this judgment was preordained and scheduled in God's eternal calendar. Nothing is accidental or random in the Book of Revelation. God is fully in control of even the darkest judgments.

The fact that a third of the population is killed is staggering. Considering the devastation already wrought by previous judgments, this implies a global death toll in the billions. These four angels are not general agents of destruction; they have a specific mission: mass execution on an unprecedented scale.

Unlike the demonic tormentors from the fifth trumpet who were forbidden from killing, these beings are permitted—and even assigned—to bring death. This is not just about physical destruction; it's a stark warning about spiritual consequences for those who continue to reject God even in the face of escalating judgment.

The Euphrates River, mentioned in the previous verse, is no random location. It holds deep biblical significance—identified in Genesis 2:14 as one of the rivers flowing from Eden, the cradle of early human civilization. It later became the heartland of empires hostile to God—Babylon, Assyria, and others waged war against His people. Now, in Revelation, it becomes the staging ground for a deadly judgment—as if history has come full circle. The very region where rebellion once rose now becomes the site where God's justice is poured out.

The famous Jewish sage Ramban (Nachmanides) once said, *"The deeds of the fathers are a sign for the children."* In other words, what happened to the patriarchs becomes a prophetic pattern for future generations. We often read the Bible with modern eyes—looking for isolated stories or moral lessons—but we miss the larger tapestry. The Bible isn't just recounting history—it's replaying it, showing us that humanity continues to rebel, and God continues to redeem. If we fail to recognize these repeating patterns, we risk repeating the same mistakes. The judgment at the Euphrates is not just about the future—it's a return to the very beginning.

This verse underscores both the justice and longsuffering of God. These angels were "prepared," which means their mission has been held back—delayed until this precise moment. God's mercy restrained them until now, but once released, they execute swift and lethal judgment. It's a sobering reminder that while God is patient, His justice will not be withheld forever.

OLD TESTAMENT FORESHADOWS REVELATION:

For this is the Day of the Lord GOD of hosts, a day of vengeance, that He may avenge Him of His adversaries: and the sword shall devour, and it shall be satiated and made drunk with their blood: for the Lord GOD of hosts has a sacrifice in the north country by the River Euphrates. (Jeremiah 46:10)

This verse refers to a time of divine judgment and vengeance by the LORD, tied geographically to the Euphrates River—the same location from which the four demonic angels are released in Revelation. The language of bloodshed, vengeance, and divine judgment is a strong thematic match.

THE REVELATION OF JESUS CHRIST REVEALS:

9:16 And the number of the army of the horsemen were two hundred thousand thousand: and I heard the number of them.

This verse describes an overwhelming and terrifying army unleashed upon the earth during the sixth trumpet judgment. The number "two hundred thousand thousand" translates to 200 million—an astonishing figure that emphasizes the sheer magnitude and scope of this demonic force. John does not estimate the number; he *hears* it, suggesting divine precision and certainty, not speculation.

This is no conventional military force. The "horsemen" described in the following verses possess grotesque, supernatural features—signs that this is a spiritual, possibly demonic army, empowered to carry out divine judgment. Their sheer number—200 million—underscores the severity of the sixth trumpet plague: a coordinated, unstoppable assault resulting in the death of one-third of humanity. The message is sobering and unmistakable: this is not human warfare—it is a divinely timed judgment designed to shake the earth to its core.

Yet even here, God's sovereignty is on full display. The exact number, the exact timing—"an hour, and a day, and a month, and a year"—reveal that this is no accident. It is not chaos, but calculated justice—a final, redemptive warning to a world that still has time to repent.

OLD TESTAMENT FORESHADOWS REVELATION:

A fiery stream issued and came forth from before Him: thousand thousands ministered unto Him, and ten thousand times ten thousand stood before Him: the judgment was set, and the books were opened. (Daniel 7:10)

"Thousand thousands" and "ten thousand times ten thousand" express vast, innumerable hosts, mirroring the astronomical number John heard—200 million horsemen. While Daniel 7:10 describes angelic beings or divine court attendants,

Revelation 9:16 speaks of a demonic apocalyptic army. Both passages emphasize overwhelming numbers tied to judgment. The symbolic use of huge numbers reinforces God's control over vast forces—both heavenly and, in judgment, even demonic ones.

THE REVELATION OF JESUS CHRIST REVEALS:

9:17 And thus I saw the horses in the vision, and them that sat on them, having breastplates of fire, and of jacinth, and brimstone: and the heads of the horses were as the heads of lions; and out of their mouths issued fire and smoke and brimstone.

This vivid description given by John is part of the terrifying sixth trumpet judgment. What he sees is not symbolic military equipment, but a literal, supernatural army of 200 million terrifying beings unleashed upon the earth. John describes the riders as having breastplates of fire (red), jacinth (deep blue), and brimstone (Sulfur-yellow)—colors associated with destruction, judgment, and hell itself.

The horses are not ordinary animals. Their lion-like heads symbolize ferocity and overwhelming power, while the fire, smoke, and brimstone issuing from their mouths indicate the means by which they execute judgment. These are not metaphors for human weapons but represent supernatural agents of death.

This is no ordinary army. These creatures are possibly demonic entities or a hybrid force specifically prepared for this moment of global judgment. The fact that their tails later are described like serpents (verse 19) shows that every part of their form is a weapon, leaving no escape for their victims. They are relentless in their mission to kill one-third of mankind.

The scene echoes God's sovereignty in judgment—His longsuffering patience has reached a limit. Even in the midst of wrath, the details emphasize that God controls even the instruments of judgment, down to their number and the hour of their release.

OLD TESTAMENT FORESHADOWS REVELATION:

They shall lay hold on bow and spear; they are cruel, and have no mercy; their voice roars like the sea; and they ride upon horses, set in array as men for war against you, O daughter of Zion. (Jeremiah 6:23)

Both passages describe forces characterized by their relentless and unforgiving nature. The overwhelming noise associated with these armies emphasizes their immense size and the terror they invoke. The imagery of warriors on horseback is prevalent in both descriptions, symbolizing swift and powerful agents of judgment. While Jeremiah 6:23 refers to an invading army as a form of divine judgment against Jerusalem, Revelation 9:17 portrays a supernatural force unleashed during the end times. Both serve as sobering reminders of the severity of divine judgment and the instruments through which it may be executed.

THE REVELATION OF JESUS CHRIST REVEALS:

9:18 By these three was the third part of men killed, by the fire, and by the smoke, and by the brimstone, which issued out of their mouths.

This verse marks one of the most catastrophic moments in the Tribulation period. It refers to the deadly power of the 200 million strong demonic cavalry described in the previous verse. These three elements—fire, smoke, and brimstone—are not just physical agents of destruction but are symbols of divine wrath and judgment throughout Scripture. Each one signifies overwhelming torment and chaos:

- Fire symbolizes consuming judgment.
- Smoke points to suffocating confusion and darkness.
- Brimstone (sulfur) evokes imagery of hell and eternal punishment.

These horrific forces—fire, smoke, and brimstone—erupt from the mouths of the monstrous beings, emphasizing that their destruction is not random, but deliberate, supernatural, and divinely permitted. Unlike the fifth trumpet, where victims were tormented but not killed, this sixth trumpet unleashes death on a staggering scale: one-third of humanity is wiped out. It's an astronomical loss of life, underscoring the escalating intensity of the trumpet judgments—and the urgency of God's final warnings to a rebellious world.

This verse underscores the lethality of this army and shows that mankind's continued rebellion against God invites deeper judgment. The previous opportunities for repentance are now followed by irreversible consequences. Still, the goal behind such devastation remains redemptive in nature—God is trying to shake the unrepentant to recognize their need for salvation before it is eternally too late.

OLD TESTAMENT FORESHADOWS REVELATION:

Then the LORD rained upon Sodom and upon Gomorrah brimstone and fire from the LORD out of heaven. (Genesis 19:24)

This verse reflects divine judgment through fire and brimstone—the same destructive elements mentioned in Revelation 9:18. Just as Sodom and Gomorrah were judged for their unrepentant wickedness, so too will a third of mankind be judged through similar fiery elements during the sixth trumpet judgment. Both portray God's righteous wrath poured out through catastrophic means.

THE REVELATION OF JESUS CHRIST REVEALS:

^{9:19} For their power is in their mouth, and in their tails: for their tails were like to serpents, and had heads, and with them they do hurt.

This verse continues John's vivid description of the terrifying demonic cavalry unleashed during the sixth trumpet judgment. These creatures are no ordinary beings—they are supernatural agents of destruction, unlike anything in the natural world. Their power is said to reside both in their mouths, from which fire, smoke, and brimstone emerge (verse 18), and in their tails, which are compared to serpents with heads that inflict pain.

This dual source of torment—mouths that kill and tails that wound—suggests that these creatures are fully equipped to cause maximum suffering and devastation. The imagery of serpents also evokes satanic symbolism and deception (Genesis 3), reinforcing the idea that these beings are satanically inspired or controlled. Their grotesque form and function emphasize that this judgment is both supernatural and severe, part of God's measured response to persistent rebellion and unrepentance during the Tribulation.

Revelation 9:19 portrays a fearsome demonic army whose entire design is to hurt and kill, fulfilling God's righteous judgment while urging the remaining inhabitants of the earth to repent before it is too late.

OLD TESTAMENT FORESHADOWS REVELATION:

The elder and honorable, he is the head; and the prophet that teaches lies, he is the tail. (Isaiah 9:15)

While Isaiah 9:15 is metaphorical, it sheds light on the symbolic use of the "tail" as an instrument of deception and harm, much like the serpent-like tails of the demonic horsemen in Revelation 9:19 that "do hurt." Both passages deal with spiritual corruption and affliction, driven by deceitful or destructive forces.

THE REVELATION OF JESUS CHRIST REVEALS:

^{9:20} And the rest of the men which were not killed by these plagues yet repented not of the works of their hands, that they should not worship devils, and idols of gold, and silver, and brass, and stone, and of wood: which neither can see, nor hear, nor walk.

Revelation 9:20 presents one of the most sobering realities in all of Scripture—the hardness of the human heart even in the face of overwhelming divine judgment. Despite the unimaginable terror and devastation unleashed through the trumpet judgments—including demonic torment and the death of a third of humanity—those who survive still refuse to repent.

The verse highlights the root cause of their rebellion: the "works of their hands," a direct reference to idolatry and the worship of manmade things. Gold, silver, brass, stone, and wood—these materials were often used in ancient times to fashion idols. The description mirrors Old Testament condemnations of idolatry, such as in Psalm 115:4–7 and Jeremiah 10:3–5, where idols are described as blind, deaf, and lifeless—utterly powerless to help or save. Yet, mankind clings to them.

Even more disturbing is the association with the worship of devils (demons). This reveals that idolatry is not just a misguided religious act, but often a form of demonic influence or allegiance (1 Corinthians 10:20). The refusal to repent shows a deliberate, hardened resistance against God's mercy and truth.

This verse serves as a warning that judgment alone does not guarantee repentance. Without humility and the conviction of the Holy Spirit, people can witness the worst of divine wrath and still cling to their sin. It underscores the importance of genuine repentance and how stubbornness can seal one's fate even when mercy is still within reach.

OLD TESTAMENT FORESHADOWS REVELATION:

Their idols are silver and gold, the work of men's hands. They have mouths, but they speak not: eyes have they, but they see not: They have ears, but they hear not: noses have they, but they smell not: They have hands, but they handle not: feet have they, but they walk not: neither speak they through their throat. They that make them are like unto them; so is every one that trusts in them. (Psalm 115:4–8)

Psalm 115:4–8 mocks the helplessness and worthlessness of idols. It reveals the absurdity of bowing to lifeless objects made by man—objects that resemble life but lack any true power or divinity. Revelation 9:20 picks up that same idea in the final days: despite God's judgments, many will cling to dead religion and demonic worship, refusing to repent. It's as if history repeats—humanity again worships lifeless idols, turning from the living God.

THE REVELATION OF JESUS CHRIST REVEALS:

9:21 Neither repented they of their murders, nor of their sorceries, nor of their fornication, nor of their thefts.

This sobering verse reveals the spiritual condition of those who survive the devastating trumpet judgments. Despite the terrifying plagues and destruction unleashed upon the earth, the remaining people still refuse to repent. Their hearts are hardened, and their sin has such a grip on them that even divine judgment does not bring them to their knees.

This verse lists four specific sins:

1. **Murders**—Murders, which reflect a total disregard for the sanctity of life. In a time when lawlessness increases and violence becomes normalized, the shedding of innocent blood—whether through crime, war, or hatred—goes unrepented.

2. **Sorceries**—Sorceries is translated from the Greek word *pharmakeia*, a term that refers not only to occult practices and witchcraft but also to drug use and mind-altering substances that were often associated with pagan worship. It speaks of deception, demonic influence, and humanity's pursuit of spiritual power apart from God.

3. **Fornication**—Fornication, from the Greek *porneia*, refers to all forms of sexual immorality. In the final days, sexual sin will be rampant and celebrated as a form of liberation, even though it stands in direct opposition to God's design for purity and covenant love. Still, even after judgment, people will cling to this rebellion.

4. **Thefts**—Thefts reflects a world dominated by greed, dishonesty, and exploitation. Whether through direct stealing, corruption, or unjust systems, the desire for gain at any cost remains unrepented.

What's most striking in this verse is not just the depth of sin listed, but the refusal to repent despite overwhelming evidence of God's wrath and mercy. These judgments are not simply punitive—they are warnings, opportunities to turn back to God. Yet the people in Revelation are so spiritually blind and morally calloused that even suffering does not awaken their conscience. This verse serves as a prophetic warning to every generation. It is a call to examine our hearts and remember the words of Jesus: "Repent, for the Kingdom of Heaven is at hand" (Matthew 4:17). Now is the time to turn—before it's too late.

OLD TESTAMENT FORESHADOWS REVELATION:

Will you steal, murder, and commit adultery, and swear falsely, and burn incense unto Baal, and walk after other gods whom you know not; And come and stand before Me in this house, which is called by My name, and say, We are delivered to do all these abominations? (Jeremiah 7:9–10)

Both passages emphasize not just the presence of these sins—but the arrogance and spiritual delusion of those committing them. In Jeremiah's day, the people still showed up to the temple as if they were righteous, just as Revelation shows end times people experiencing judgment yet still refusing to repent.

Both verses underscore a timeless truth: God calls for repentance, but people often cling to sin—even in the face of judgment.

A quiet stillness settled over Irene's study. Open Bibles lay across the table, notebooks filled with scribbled insights, and maps—ancient and modern—sprawled like pieces of a prophetic puzzle. She drew a slow breath and gently closed her Bible, her eyes thoughtful and distant, still tracing the thread of prophecy through time.

"Before we step into the next interlude . . . Ann, pause with me," she said softly. "Just consider where we are. The sixth trumpet has sounded. Billions are gone. The very landscape of the earth has shifted. And through every judgment, God's voice has thundered—loud, clear, undeniable."

"Yes, Irene. And with that judgment, another third of humanity is gone. We started with 4.5 billion before the trumpet judgments began. Now, after the sixth trumpet . . . we're at 3 billion."

She nodded. "And don't forget the estimated 1.5 billion Tribulation saints who will be saved during those seven years. That means we could be looking at just 1.5 billion people left on earth."

I drew in a slow breath, the weight of it all pressing down. "And the bowl judgments haven't even begun."

The weight of it all was almost unbearable—and yet, it was so precise. Ordered. Just like in the beginning.

Irene nodded slowly. "That's exactly what He's doing again—dividing, separating, restoring order."

"Exactly. Even in judgment, He's laying the foundation for something holy. Just like in creation—first He forms, then He fills. Judgment removes the chaos; restoration follows."

"So . . . what comes next?"

I exhaled. "The second interlude. But this one isn't like Revelation 7. That was about sealing—about protection. This one feels different. Heavier. Like the quiet before the final breath of mercy is withdrawn. The world's been warned, judged, refined . . . and still, they refuse to repent."

Irene's shoulders sank. "It's chilling. Even with demonic armies unleashed, the skies darkened, the seas turned to blood . . . they still cling to their idols, their sorceries, their immorality, their thefts. Their hearts—hardened like stone."

I lowered my gaze. "That's what burdens me most, Irene. Not the judgments . . . but the pride. The stubbornness. I see it already—today. In homes, churches, marriages, even pulpits. People unwilling to bow. Even when the truth is staring them in the face."

Irene nodded, her voice steady. "It's sobering, yes. But maybe that's why we're writing this—not just to explain the Book of Revelation, but to warn. To wake the Church."

"Yes. To remind them that God is not chaotic—He is perfectly precise. And His Word—every word—is unfolding with divine purpose."

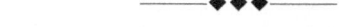

SUMMARY OF REVELATION 8–9

Revelation 8 and 9 mark the sounding of the first six trumpet judgments—God's escalating response to a rebellious world during the first half of the Tribulation. These judgments, released after the breaking of the seventh seal, reflect both divine justice and God's continued call to repentance.

The scene opens in Revelation 8:1 with a striking silence in heaven for about half an hour—a moment of solemn anticipation before the storm of judgment. Seven angels are given seven trumpets, and another angel offers incense at the golden altar, symbolizing the prayers of the saints. The fire from the altar is cast to the earth, triggering thunder, lightning, and an earthquake—heralding the beginning of the trumpet blasts.

The first four trumpets—judgment on creation:

1. **First Trumpet—Environmental Destruction**. Hail and fire mixed with blood strike the earth, burning a third of the trees and the green grass (Revelation 8:7).

2. **Second Trumpet—Sea Turned to Blood**. A blazing mountain falls into the sea, turning a third of it to blood, killing sea life and destroying ships (Revelation 8:8–9).

3. **Third Trumpet—Star Called Wormwood**. A star named Wormwood poisons a third of the rivers and springs, causing many to die (Revelation 8:10–11)

4. **Fourth Trumpet—Cosmic Darkness**. A third of the sun, moon, and stars are darkened, disrupting the rhythm of day and night (Revelation 8:12).

An eagle then cries out, "Woe, woe, woe . . ."—a warning that the next three trumpet judgments will be even more devastating (Revelation 8:13).

5. **Fifth Trumpet—First Woe—Demonic Torment**. A fallen star opens the abyss, releasing demonic locusts to torment humanity for five months. Their king is Apollyon, the Destroyer. They are forbidden to kill, but their sting brings unbearable pain (Revelation 9:1–11).

6. **Sixth Trumpet—Second Woe—Demonic Army of Death**. Four fallen angels at the Euphrates River are released to lead a demonic cavalry of 200 million, killing one-third of humanity with fire, smoke, and sulfur (Revelation 9:13–19).

Despite these terrifying judgments, the world refuses to repent. The chapter ends with a sobering indictment:

Neither repented they of their murders, nor of their sorceries, nor of their fornication, nor of their thefts. (Revelation 9:21)

KEY TAKEAWAYS

- The trumpet judgments intensify in scope and severity, moving from ecological disaster to supernatural torment.
- God's wrath is measured and deliberate, rooted in justice and mercy, not chaos.
- Despite overwhelming signs, humanity remains unrepentant, clinging to rebellion.
- The judgments are deeply tied to the prayers of the saints, showing God's active response to intercession.
- These are not merely acts of punishment—they are divine wake-up calls to a world on the brink.

Revelation 8–9 gives a sobering glimpse of the first six trumpet judgments—judgments that strike the land, sea, skies, and the human soul. With each trumpet, the warning grows louder, and yet the hearts of many grow harder. Still, God's actions remain precise, purposeful, and patient.

But the final trumpet—the seventh trumpet—has not yet sounded.

In the next chapter, we will enter a powerful interlude in Revelation 10 and 11 filled with mystery, prophecy, and a shift in heavenly authority. There we will encounter the little book, the sealing of the seven thunders, the measuring of the temple, and the bold testimony of the Two Witnesses.

And then, in Revelation 11:15, the seventh trumpet will sound.

That trumpet changes everything.

Chapter 10

Revelation 10–11: Interlude—Little Book, Seven Thunders, Temple, Two Witnesses

WHEN HEAVEN SPEAKS AND EARTH TREMBLES—
Revelation 10 and 11 form the longest interlude in the Book of Revelation, a dramatic pause between the sixth and seventh trumpet judgments. These chapters shift the focus from the sweeping judgments on the earth to specific prophetic moments that highlight God's sovereignty and the role of His witnesses during the Tribulation.

In Revelation 10, John sees a mighty angel descending from heaven with a little book in hand, symbolizing divine message yet to be fully revealed. As John prepares to write what the seven thunders utter, he is commanded to seal them— reminding us that some elements of God's plan remain hidden. John is then told to eat the little book, which is sweet in his mouth but bitter in his stomach, representing the joy of receiving God's Word and the sorrow of the coming judgment it contains.

Revelation 11 shifts to the earthly realm, where John is instructed to measure the temple of God, signaling divine ownership and protection. This chapter also introduces the Two Witnesses, powerful prophetic figures who will minister in Jerusalem for 1,260 days. Clothed in sackcloth, they are empowered to perform miracles and proclaim truth in the face of opposition. Their ministry, death, and miraculous resurrection serve as a bold testimony to God's authority even in the darkest days.

Together, these chapters remind us that in the midst of chaos and judgment, God is still speaking, still calling, and still empowering His servants to bear witness to the truth.

THE REVELATION OF JESUS CHRIST REVEALS:

[10:1] And I saw another mighty angel come down from heaven, clothed with a cloud: and a rainbow was upon his head, and his face was as it were the sun, and his feet as pillars of fire.

As the apocalyptic judgments momentarily pause between the sixth and seven trumpets, John introduces a new and awe-inspiring figure: a mighty angel descending from heaven. The words "And I saw" mark a fresh vision—one that carries unique weight, especially since John doesn't use this phrase again until Revelation 13:1. That gap signals a significant interlude. What John sees here is not another cycle of destruction, but a divine declaration wrapped in mystery and majesty.

This angel isn't ordinary. His appearance is extraordinary—so glorious, in fact, that many scholars and prophecy teachers have pondered whether this could be Christophany, a pre-incarnate or symbolic appearance of Christ. Let's break down what John describes:

- "Clothed with a cloud"—In Scripture, clouds often signify divine presence (Exodus 13:21; Matthew 17:5). This evokes majesty and glory, a heavenly aura that sets this figure apart.
- "And a rainbow was upon his head"—A striking crown, echoing the rainbow around God's throne (Revelation 4:3), symbolizing mercy, covenant, and divine promise. This isn't merely decoration; it's a visual echo of God's faithfulness.
- "And his face was as it were the sun"—Radiating pure light, this mirrors the description of Jesus in Revelation 1:16, whose face shines with divine brilliance.
- "And his feet as pillars of fire"—A reference to judgment and purity. Fire refines and consumes; this angel stands as one ready to tread holy ground with authority.

His stance is global—one foot on the sea, and the other on the land (verse 2)—declaring universal dominion. His voice like a lion's roar (verse 3) reverberates with the authority of God Himself (compare with Amos 3:8 and Revelation 5:5). And he will soon lift his hand to heaven and swear an oath by

Him who lives forever, proclaiming that there will be no more delay (verses 5–6)—a powerful shift in heaven's timeline.

While debate remains whether this mighty angel is Jesus or a high-ranking archangel bearing His authority, one thing is clear: this is a divine messenger of immense power and glory, ushering in a final series of judgments and announcing that God's redemptive plan is reaching its climax.

OLD TESTAMENT FORESHADOWS REVELATION:

> Then I lifted up my eyes, and looked, and behold a certain man clothed in linen, whose waist was girded with fine gold of Uphaz: His body also was like the beryl, and his face as the appearance of lightning, and his eyes as lamps of fire, and his arms and his feet like in color to polished brass, and the voice of his words like the voice of a multitude. (Daniel 10:5–6)

Revelation 10:1 "his face was as it were the sun." Daniel 10:6 "his face as the appearance of lightning." Both express radiance, glory, and divine brilliance. Revelation 10:1 "his feet as pillars of fire." Daniel 10:6 "his arms and his feet like polished brass." The imagery suggests purity through fire, strength, and heavenly authority. Both passages portray a glorious heavenly being, so radiant and fearsome that human strength collapses in their presence (Daniel 10:8–9). This reinforces the idea that the angel is Revelation 10 is no ordinary angel, but a messenger of divine authority—possibly Christ Himself or one bearing His likeness and power.

Irene and I sat in a cozy library, its walls lined with well-worn books and ancient commentaries. A gentle rain tapped against the windowpanes with a steady, soothing rhythm. Cradling steaming mugs of tea, we sat in thoughtful silence—surrounded by the wisdom of the ages—reflecting on the prophetic threads woven through Revelation and Daniel.

"Ann, I've been reading and rereading that passage in Revelation about the mighty angel . . . and I keep wondering—is Michael the only archangel? His name comes up a lot, but is he really the only one with that title? Could there be others?"

"That's a great question, Irene. In all of Scripture, Michael is the only angel who's specifically called an *archangel*. We see that in Jude 1:9, where it says:"

> Yet Michael the archangel, when contending with the devil, when he disputed about the body of Moses, dared not bring against him a railing accusation, but said, The Lord rebuke you! (Jude 1:9)

"So if we're going strictly by what Scripture says, Michael is the only one actually given that title."

"So . . . just one archangel?"

"Possibly. 'Archangel' means 'chief' or 'ruling angel,' so it's reasonable to think there might be others with similar rank or authority. But Scripture only refers to Michael with that specific title."

"Take Gabriel, for example," I continued. "He clearly holds a high-ranking role—delivering messages to Daniel, Zechariah, and Mary. Yet, Scripture never refers to him as an archangel. That title is given only to Michael."

"That's interesting . . . Michael always seems to appear when something major is unfolding. So what exactly is his role?"

"That's because Michael is heaven's warrior. His name—'Who is like God?'—isn't just a question; it's a declaration. A challenge to any who oppose God's authority. In Daniel 10:21, he's called the 'prince' of Israel, which means he's been given a divine assignment: to guard and intervene on Israel's behalf. Michael stands as both defender and enforcer of God's rule."

"So . . . he's Israel's angelic commander?"

"Exactly, Irene. In Daniel 10, the prophet had been fasting and praying for three weeks. Gabriel finally arrived, explaining that he was delayed by the 'prince of the kingdom of Persia'—a demonic principality—until Michael came to his aid. Michael stepped in as the spiritual reinforcements."

"That moment reveals something powerful," I continued. "Even angels face resistance in the unseen realm. There's a spiritual war raging behind the scenes—and Michael stands at the heart of it."

Irene nodded. "So Gabriel's delay was due to spiritual warfare—and it was Michael who stepped in to break through?"

"Yes. Michael is like God's general. In moments of spiritual conflict—especially those involving nations or prophetic turning points—he shows up. And then in Revelation 12:7–8, we see him again, this time leading a heaven's army against the dragon, Satan. It says:"

> And there was war in heaven: Michael and his angels fought against the dragon; and the dragon fought and his angels, And prevailed not; neither was there place found any more in heaven. (Revelation 12:7–8)

"This marks the moment when Satan is finally cast out of heaven—permanently."

"Wait—so Michael is the one who actually casts Satan out of heaven?"

"Yes! It's one of the most dramatic moments in all of Scripture. Satan loses access to the heavenly realm—no more accusing the brethren before God day and night. And it's Michael who leads the charge."

"This moment ties directly to Michael's role as the defender of God's people," I continued. "When Satan is finally cast down, it marks a turning point in the heavenly courtroom—judgment is being executed, and the Kingdom is moving forward."

"I never realized Michael was so central. I always thought he was just one of many angels . . . but now I see—his role is far more significant."

"He's absolutely central to the spiritual battle of the end times. Michael doesn't just defend Israel—he clears the way for the final stages of God's redemptive plan. Every time he appears in Scripture, it marks a major turning point in prophetic history."

"So it seems Michael and Gabriel each have distinct roles—Michael for spiritual warfare, Gabriel for delivering divine messages?"

"That's right, Irene. Gabriel is the messenger of revelation—he delivers God's Word. Michael is the guardian of righteousness—he fights to defend it. When both appear in Scripture, especially in Daniel and Revelation, you can be sure something monumental is unfolding—both on earth and in heaven."

THE REVELATION OF JESUS CHRIST REVEALS:

10:2 And he had in his hand a little book open: and he set his right foot upon the sea, and his left foot on the earth.

In this verse, the mighty angel introduced in verse 1 takes a commanding stance—one foot on the sea and one on the land—while holding a little book already open in his hand. Every element of the scene conveys authority, divine intention, and sovereign order. Nothing is accidental; this is a deliberate act within God's unfolding plan.

The angel holds a "little book open"—not sealed, not hidden, but fully revealed. This stands in deliberate contrast to the sealed scroll in Revelation 5, which only the Lamb—Jesus—was worthy to open. The "little book" may contain a specific prophetic message, possibly signaling the next phase of judgment or John's personal commission to continue prophesying, as clarified in verse 11.

Its small size compared to the grand scroll of Revelation 5 suggests that it holds a portion of divine revelation, focused and urgent, meant to be consumed and internalized by John in the verses that follow.

This angel's posture is as profound as his message. One foot on the sea, the other on the land—it's a stance of dominion, signaling that the message he brings applies to the entire earth. The sea and land symbolize the whole recreated order, encompassing all nations, peoples, and realms—both settled and untamed.

It's also symbolic of judgment reaching every corner of the globe. This angel doesn't hover or observe—he plants himself firmly, as if to declare: heaven's authority is now grounded on earth.

The angel's attitude or posture suggests that he is immense in stature, possibly towering in appearance, with the earth and the sea serving as pedestals beneath his feet. This imagery echoes Old Testament appearances of divine beings or heavenly messengers, such as in Daniel 10, where a mighty figure stands radiant and awe-inspiring.

Is this angel Jesus?

While the description of this angel in Revelation 10:1–2 bears striking resemblance to descriptions of Jesus (such as in Revelation 1 and Daniel 10), there are compelling reasons many scholars believe this angel is not Jesus:

1. Jesus is giving the vision to John in this chapter. It would be odd for Him to appear in the middle of a vision He is narrating.

2. Jesus does not return to earth until Revelation 19. This event occurs between the sixth and seventh trumpet judgments—before His Second Coming.

3. The Greek word used in Revelation 10:1 is "*allos*" (another of the same kind), not "*heteros*" (another of a different kind). This suggests the angel is of the same category as others previously mentioned—not divine, but mighty.

4. In Revelation, Jesus is never referred to as "the Angel of the Lord"—a title associated with His pre-incarnate appearances in the Old Testament Christophanies. Instead, He is called "the Lion of the Tribe of Judah," "the Lamb," "the Alpha and Omega," and "King of kings."

If not Jesus, then who is this mighty angel? A strong case can be made that it could be Michael the archangel:

- Michael is the only angel called an "archangel" in Scripture (Jude 1:9).
- He is portrayed as mighty, authoritative, and warrior-like, especially in defending Israel (Daniel 10:13, 21, 12:1).
- In Revelation 12:7, Michael leads the heavenly army in casting out Satan—a pivotal role in end-time events.
- His name means "Who is like God?"—emphasizing his resemblance to divine majesty without being divine Himself.

Michael is a powerful representative of God's authority and presence. His posture in Revelation 10:2—one foot on the sea, one on the land—echoes the kind of territorial authority and divine commission we see associated with him throughout Scripture.

Revelation 10:2 presents a mighty and majestic angel—possibly Michael—who holds an open book and takes a dominant stance over land and sea. His appearance signals global authority, a shift in prophetic tone, and an urgent revelation about to unfold.

While the description may resemble Christ in some ways, the textual evidence more strongly supports this figure as a high-ranking messenger, not the Messiah Himself. This moment sets the stage for what follows: a solemn oath, a sealed message, and a renewed prophetic calling for John.

OLD TESTAMENT FORESHADOWS REVELATION:

Every place where on the soles of your feet shall tread shall be yours: from the wilderness and Lebanon, from the river, the River Euphrates, even unto the uttermost sea shall your coast be. (Deuteronomy 11:24)

This verse from Deuteronomy speaks of God granting Israel authority over every place their feet touch—a covenant promise tied to their obedience and inheritance. In Revelation 10:2, the mighty angel standing with one foot on the sea and the other on the earth echoes this imagery. It is a symbolic act that conveys universal dominion and divine ownership of all creation. Just as God gave Israel authority over physical territory, this angel—perhaps representing Michael—stands as heaven's emissary, declaring that God's sovereign plan is now taking hold across the whole earth and sea.

This visual posture isn't just geographical—it's theological. It reminds us that nothing is outside God's jurisdiction. As the end-time judgments unfold, the whole earth is being brought under His final authority.

THE REVELATION OF JESUS CHRIST REVEALS:

^{10:3} And cried with a loud voice, as when a lion roars: and when he had cried, seven thunders uttered their voices.

As the mighty angel takes his divine stance—one foot on the sea and one on the land—he lifts his voice. But this is no ordinary cry. John compares it to the roar of a lion, a symbol of raw, unmatched authority, echoing the prophetic strength of the Lion of the tribe of Judah. The angel's voice is meant to arrest attention—not just of the earth, but of the heavens and principalities as well.

The lion's roar is often symbolic in Scripture of royal power, judgment, and divine authority. Amos 3:8 says:

The lion has roared, who will not fear? The Lord GOD has spoken, who can but prophesy? (Amos 3:8)

This parallel affirms that the angel's roar is not just a heavenly announcement—it is a prophetic war cry, signaling that heaven is preparing to retake possession of the earth.

Many believe this angel is none other than Michael the archangel, heaven's warrior. If that's the case, then this is not only a declaration—it's a battle cry announcing that Satan's dominion over the earth is nearly over. The time of reclaiming what was lost in Eden has come.

Immediately following the roar, seven thunders utter their voices. This phrase is mysterious and unique to Revelation 10, prompting speculation and deep study throughout Church history. But Scripture may offer us a clue.

Psalm 29:3–9 repeatedly describes "the voice of the LORD" in powerful, thunderous terms—seven times, in fact:

1. "The voice of the LORD is upon the waters . . ."
2. "The voice of the LORD is powerful . . ."
3. "The voice of the LORD breaks the cedars . . ."
4. "The voice of the LORD divides the flames of fire . . ."
5. "The voice of the LORD shakes the wilderness . . ."
6. "The voice of the LORD makes the hinds to calve . . ."
7. "In His temple everyone speaks of His glory."

Many scholars and preachers agree: the seven thunders may very well represent the sevenfold voice of God—complete, majestic, irresistible. When the angel roars, it is as if God Himself answers, echoing through the heavens and shaking creation with His thunder.

This would not be the first time God's voice sounded like thunder. In John 12:28–29, when the Father speaks audibly about glorifying His name, the crowd says, "It thundered." Also, in Exodus 19:16, thunder accompanies God's descent on Mount Sinai.

In prophetic terms, this moment is monumental. The roar and the seven thunders are not merely for drama—they serve as a heavenly declaration of authority. The world has been under a lease of rebellion since the fall of Adam. But this roar and thunder signal that the deed of the earth is being reclaimed.

The little book in the angel's hand, the breaking of the seals, and now the thunders of God's voice—all point to this truth: Satan's dominion is ending. God's Kingdom is rising. The King is preparing to return.

Revelation 10:3 gives us a breathtaking moment where heaven's might and mystery meet. A mighty angel—likely Michael—roars like a lion, and the voice of God responds with seven thunders, signaling divine authority, judgment, and a reclamation of creation. The stage is set. The earth is on notice. And the spiritual realm trembles, knowing that God is about to complete what He started.

OLD TESTAMENT FORESHADOWS REVELATION:

The LORD also shall roar out of Zion, and utter His voice from Jerusalem; and the heavens and the earth shall shake: but the LORD will be the hope of His people, and the strength of the children of Israel. (Joel 3:16)

The roar of the mighty angel in Revelation 10:3 mirrors the roar of the LORD in Joel 3:16, symbolizing prophetic judgment, cosmic authority, and divine intervention. This is an ideal parallel when studying God's voice in the context of end-times prophecy, as Joel also speaks of nations gathered for judgment, aligning perfectly with the Revelation 10 interlude.

THE REVELATION OF JESUS CHRIST REVEALS:

10:4 And when the seven thunders had uttered their voices, I was about to write: and I heard a voice from heaven saying to me, Seal up those things which the seven thunders uttered, and write them not.

This verse is one of the most mysterious moments in the entire Book of Revelation. John, the faithful recorder of heavenly visions, hears the powerful utterance of the seven thunders—which many scholars associate with the voice of God Himself (Psalm 29)—and he prepares to do what he's always done: write it down. But something unexpected happens.

"Seal up those things which the seven thunders uttered, and write them not." This is the only time in Revelation where John is explicitly told not to reveal what he hears. Everywhere else in the book, even when describing unspeakable horror or astonishing glory, he is instructed to write. But here, there is intentional divine silence—a concealment.

This is deeply significant. It tells us that not everything in God's plan has been revealed. There are aspects of end times events, heavenly decrees, or divine judgments that are too holy, too terrifying, or too strategically reserved for public record. Even in this most revealing of books—the Revelation of Jesus Christ— there are still secrets only heaven knows.

Why the secrecy? Possible interpretations:

1. **A Sovereign Mystery**—God reserves the right to hold back part of His plan. It reminds us that He is sovereign, and we are to walk by faith, not by full knowledge—Deuteronomy 29:29, says:

The secret things belong unto the LORD our God: but those things which are revealed belong unto us and to our children forever, that we may do all the words of this law. (Deuteronomy 29:29)

2. **Divine Timing**—Perhaps these thunderous declarations are meant for another time—possibly during the Great Tribulation, when they will be understood by those who live through them.

3. **A Judgment Too Great to Bear**—Some believe the content of the seven thunders could involve a level of judgment so severe, or so targeted, that it would overwhelm even the faithful reader. Like Paul in 2 Corinthians 12:4, who heard "unspeakable words" in paradise, John is shown that some things are not meant for earthly disclosure—yet.

This moment reminds us that Revelation is not merely a puzzle to be solved, but a holy unveiling that still leaves space for awe, reverence, and wonder. God shows us much—but not all. We are given enough to be watchful, enough to be ready, but not so much that we ever forget who's truly in control of the timeline: the Lamb on the throne.

As curious readers, we echo John's impulse—we want to know what the seven thunders said! But the command to seal it up calls us to trust. Whatever those thunders declared, they are part of God's righteous plan, and in His perfect time, we will know fully, even as we are fully known (1 Corinthians 13:12).

Until then, we watch, we worship, and we wait.

OLD TESTAMENT FORESHADOWS REVELATION:

And he said, Go your way, Daniel: for the words are closed up and sealed till the time of the end. (Daniel 12:9)

Daniel is told to seal up prophetic words for a later time. Like Daniel, John is forbidden to reveal what he hears, reminding us that even in prophetic revelation, God retains divine secrets, to be disclosed in His perfect timing.

THE REVELATION OF JESUS CHRIST REVEALS:

10:5 And the angel which I saw stand upon the sea and upon the earth lifted up his hand to heaven.

In this verse, we return to the striking image of the mighty angel, whose posture—one foot on the sea and one on the land—already symbolizes divine authority over all creation (Revelation 10:2). But now the angel adds another solemn gesture: he lifts up his hand to heaven.

This action signifies something profound: the angel is preparing to swear a divine oath. Lifting the hand to heaven is an ancient biblical gesture that symbolizes making a solemn vow before God—a declaration that invokes the authority and witness of heaven itself.

This is not a casual act. In fact, swearing by heaven or lifting one's hand toward heaven is found in multiple significant biblical moments:

- Genesis 14:22—Abram lifts his hand to the LORD when making a vow to the Most High God.
- Deuteronomy 32:40—God Himself says, "For I lift up my hand to heaven, and say, I live forever," when proclaiming judgment.
- Daniel 12:7—A man clothed in linen lifts both hands to heaven and swears by Him who lives forever, just like in Revelation 10:6.

This parallel is especially important, as Daniel 12:7 and Revelation 10:5–6 are strikingly similar—both describe heavenly messengers raising a hand (or hands) to heaven and making declarations tied to the end of time.

By standing on both land and sea and lifting his hand to heaven, the angel spans all domains of creation:

- Sea represents the untamed and unknown.
- Land represents the inhabited and known world.
- Heaven represents divine authority and eternal witness.

This angel is effectively bridging heaven and earth, indicating that the words he is about to speak carry the full authority of God's throne. He stands as a mediator of judgment, not on his own behalf, but as a commissioned messenger of the Almighty.

This act of lifting the hand is the prelude to the proclamation in verse 6—a bold declaration that there will be no more delay, time is nearly up. The mysteries of God are about to be fulfilled. What was once held back will now be unleashed.

Revelation 10:5 is not just a physical gesture—it's a heavenly announcement. The angel's lifted hand signals a turning point in prophetic history. The events that follow will be executed with the full backing of heaven, and the divine plan will no longer be delayed.

OLD TESTAMENT FORESHADOWS REVELATION:

And say unto them, Thus says the Lord GOD; In the day when I chose Israel, and lifted up My hand unto the seed of the house of Jacob, and made Myself known unto them in the land of Egypt, when I lifted up My hand unto them, saying, I am the LORD your God. In the day that I lifted up My hand unto them, to bring them forth of the land of Egypt into a land that I had searched out for them, flowing with milk and honey, which is the glory of all lands. (Ezekiel 20:5–6)

God lifts His hand in an oath when making a covenant promise to Israel. The angel in Revelation 10:5 imitates this gesture—lifting his hand to heaven—

representing a divine oath, a moment of profound heavenly authority, and the certainty of God's unfolding plan on earth.

THE REVELATION OF JESUS CHRIST REVEALS:

[10:6] And swore by Him that lives forever and ever, who created heaven, and the things that therein are, and the earth, and the things that therein are, and the sea, and the things which are therein, that there should be time no longer.

This verse marks a climactic turning point in the Book of Revelation. The mighty angel, who stands with one foot on the sea and one on the land, now takes an oath of divine authority. He lifts his hand to heaven (verse 5) and swears by the eternal Creator—the One who made heaven, earth, and sea, and everything in them. This is the highest form of oath, invoking God as the eternal, sovereign Maker of all.

The angel's oath—swearing by Him who lives forever and ever—emphasizes the eternal, unchanging nature of God. Unlike earthly kingdoms that rise and fall, God's reign is everlasting (Psalm 90:2; Deuteronomy 32:40). This is no ordinary vow. The angel calls upon the Creator—not just as witness, but as the One who authored time, space, and all creation. What is about to unfold carries the full weight of divine authority—and once declared, it cannot be undone.

This moment parallels Daniel 12:7, where a heavenly being also swears by Him who lives forever, signaling the end of a prophetic timeline.

"Time no longer." What does that mean? The phrase in Revelation 10:6— "that there should be time no longer"—is better translated as "there will be no more delay." This doesn't mean that time itself ceases to exist. Instead, it signals that the period of divine waiting and restraint has come to an end. God's timeline is now moving forward without pause. The moment for patience is over—the final phase of judgment is about to begin. Throughout the earlier chapters of Revelation, God's judgment has been strategically restrained, unfolding in measured phases (seals, trumpets, etc.). But now, the angel announces that the delay is over—God's plan is moving into its final and unrestrained phase.

The declaration that there will be "no more delay" indicates that the mystery of God (verse 7) is about to be completed. Everything the prophets foretold, everything John has seen so far—is culminating. The moment for final judgments and Christ's return is rapidly approaching. This is heaven's formal announcement that history is converging with eternity.

OLD TESTAMENT FORESHADOWS REVELATION:

For in six days the LORD made heaven and earth, the sea, and all that in them is, and rested the seventh day: wherefore the LORD blessed the sabbath day, and hallowed it. (Exodus 20:11)

In Exodus, God is identified as the Creator of heaven, earth, and sea, and of all things within them. In both Revelation 10:6 and Exodus 20:11, God's identity as Creator affirms His authority and ownership over all creation. The angel in Revelation swears by the same Creator, signaling the end of delay and the beginning of God's final acts of justice and redemption.

THE REVELATION OF JESUS CHRIST REVEALS:

10:7 But in the days of the voice of the seventh angel, when he will begin to sound, the mystery of God should be finished, as He has declared to His servants the prophets.

This verse is a pivotal declaration in the Book of Revelation, marking a transition from divine restraint to prophetic fulfillment. The mighty angel who has just sworn by the eternal Creator (verse 6) now connects the sounding of the seventh trumpet with the completion of God's mystery—a mystery long foretold by the prophets.

The reference to "the days of the voice of the seventh angel" points forward to Revelation 11:15, when the seventh trumpet sounds and loud voices in heaven proclaim, "The kingdoms of this world are become the kingdoms of our LORD, and of His Christ."

Unlike the previous trumpets, which brought waves of judgment, the seventh trumpet ushers in the final phase of God's plan. It is the transition point from the Tribulation's judgments to the unveiling of Christ's visible reign on earth.

The phrase "mystery of God" refers to God's redemptive plan that has been unfolding throughout history—but which remained partially hidden until its final revelation in Christ. It includes:

- The full inclusion of the Gentiles in salvation (Ephesian 3:4–6).
- The establishment of God's Kingdom on earth (Daniel 2:44; Isaiah 9:6).
- The final defeat of evil and restoration of creation (Romans 8:18–23).
- The revealing of Jesus Christ as King of kings and Lord of lords.

Now, at the seventh trumpet, this mystery—once whispered through the prophets and revealed in part through Christ's First Coming—will be completed in power and glory.

"As He has declared to His servants the prophets." This line roots Revelation in the continuity of biblical prophecy. The events John sees are not disconnected from the Old Testament—they are the culmination of it. Isaiah, Jeremiah, Daniel, Ezekiel, Zechariah—all spoke of a day when God would fully restore His Kingdom, judge wickedness, and reign forever. This verse affirms that Revelation is not a new story, but the completion of what was long foretold.

OLD TESTAMENT FORESHADOWS REVELATION:

The anger of the LORD shall not return, until He have executed, and till He have performed the thoughts of His heart: in the latter days you shall consider it perfectly. (Jeremiah 23:20)

God's judgment and purposes will be fully realized and understood in the latter days. Revelation 10:7 echoes Jeremiah's theme: that what God spoke long ago through the prophets will now be perfectly fulfilled, and the time for completion has arrived with the sounding of the seventh trumpet.

THE REVELATION OF JESUS CHRIST REVEALS:

10:8 And the voice which I heard from heaven spoke to me again, and said, Go and take the little book which is open in the hand of the angel which stands upon the sea and upon the earth.

This verse marks a turning point for the apostle John—not just in vision, but in calling. Until now, he has been a witness: observing judgments, hearing heavenly declarations, and faithfully recording what he sees. But now, he is commanded to act—to physically engage with the vision by taking the open scroll from the hand of the mighty angel. The scroll is no longer sealed. John is invited to receive its contents—not just to understand them, but to embody them. What he takes in, he will soon proclaim. What he swallows, he will soon prophesy.

The "little book" refers to an open scroll held by the mighty angel introduced earlier in this chapter. This is not the same scroll as the sealed book in Revelation 5, which only the Lamb was worthy to open. The fact that this scroll is already open suggests its contents are ready to be revealed and digested—literally and symbolically—by John. Its description as "little" may imply that it contains a specific prophetic assignment, possibly related to the next phase of judgment or the second half of the Tribulation—the Great Tribulation. This moment marks a personal shift for John, as he moves from observer to active participant in proclaiming God's message.

The angel standing with one foot on the sea and one on the earth symbolizes universal authority. This imagery echoes language from Deuteronomy 11:24 and Joshua 1:3, where God promises His people dominion over the land wherever their feet tread. Here, the covenantal symbolism is expanded to a cosmic scale. By placing one foot on the sea and one on the land, the angel is declaring God's authority over the entire created order. This posture reinforces the idea that he has been commissioned to reclaim the earth for God's Kingdom and to carry out His final judgments on a global scale.

The voice from heaven speaks again, this time addressing John directly: "Go and take the little book." This moment is significant. John is no longer just a witness to divine revelation—he is now an active participant in the prophetic drama. In the following verses (9–10), John is not only instructed to take the book but to consume it—a powerful symbol that the Word of God must be internalized before it can be proclaimed. This act echoes the calling of earlier prophets like Ezekiel and Jeremiah, who were also commanded to "eat" God's Words before delivering His message.

Ezekiel was told, "Eat this scroll, and go speak to the house of Israel" (Ezekiel 2:8–3:3), and Jeremiah declared, "Your words were found, and I did eat them; and your word was unto me the joy and rejoicing of my heart" (Jeremiah 15:16). In both cases, the consumption of the Word signified not just understanding—but embodiment. Likewise, John's act of taking and eating the scroll marks a divine commissioning—a transition from witness to prophet—as he prepares to speak forth the final revelations and judgments of God.

Revelation 10:8 signals a crucial moment in the unfolding apocalypse. The heavenly voice commissions John to receive the open scroll from the mighty angel—symbolizing readiness for prophetic fulfillment. This act of taking the scroll represents both the authority of God's judgment and the responsibility of His servants to proclaim it. As the scroll moves from the hand of the angel to the heart of the prophet, the stage is set for deeper revelations and intensified judgments in the chapters ahead.

OLD TESTAMENT FORESHADOWS REVELATION:

But you, son of man, hear what I say unto you; Be not you rebellious like that rebellious house: open your mouth, and eat that I give you. And when I looked, behold, a hand was sent unto me; and, lo, a roll of a book was therein. And He spread it before me; and it was written within and without: and there was written herein lamentations, and mourning, and woe. Moreover He said unto me, Son of man, eat that you find; eat this scroll, and go speak unto the house of Israel. So I opened my mouth, and He caused me to eat that scroll. And He said unto me, Son of man, cause your belly to eat, and fill your bowels with this scroll that I give you. Then did I eat it; and it was in my mouth as honey for sweetness. (Ezekiel 2:8–3:3)

Ezekiel receives and consumes a scroll, signifying his prophetic call. Just as Ezekiel is told to eat the scroll and then speak to Israel, John in Revelation 10:8 is told to take the open book, symbolizing his commission to prophesy again to the many peoples, nations, tongues, and kings (Revelation 10:11).

THE REVELATION OF JESUS CHRIST REVEALS:

[10:9] And I went to the angel, and said to him, Give me the little book. And he said to me, Take it, and eat it up; and it will make your belly bitter, but it will be in your mouth sweet as honey.

This verse continues the dramatic interaction between the apostle John and the mighty angel who holds a now-open scroll—distinct from the sealed scroll of Revelation 5. Unlike that scroll, which only the Lamb was worthy to open, this "little book" is already unsealed and ready to be received. John is not merely told to take it, but to eat it—a deeply symbolic act rooted in Old Testament prophetic tradition. This imagery draws from the visions of Ezekiel (Ezekiel 3:1–3) and Jeremiah (Jeremiah 15:16), where the prophets are commanded to "eat" God's Word before proclaiming it. Again, the message must be internalized before it can be faithfully declared.

The initial sweetness of the scroll represents the joy and awe of receiving divine revelation. God's Word is often described as sweet:

- Psalm 119:103: "How sweet are your words unto my taste! Yea, sweeter than honey to my mouth!"
- Jeremiah 15:16: "Your words were found, and I did eat them; and Your word was unto me the joy and rejoicing of my heart."

For John, receiving prophecy directly from heaven would have been an exhilarating, sacred honor—the sweetness of divine intimacy and truth.

But the bitterness comes in internalizing the reality of what the prophecy contains: judgment, destruction, rebellion, and the pain of those who refuse to repent. This is the weight of prophetic responsibility—knowing that the truth you deliver will not always bring peace but often division, sorrow, or resistance.

It parallels what Ezekiel experienced: after tasting the scroll, his mission became one of lamentation, mourning, and woe (Ezekiel 2:10). This dual response—sweetness and bitterness—underscores that the Word of God is both grace and truth, life and judgment, hope and warning.

The Bible consistently likens God's Word to spiritual food:

- Bread—"Man shall not live by bread alone . . ." (Matthew 4:4).
- Milk—"Desire the sincere milk of the Word . . ." (1 Peter 2:2).
- Meat—"I have fed you with milk, and not with meat . . ." (1 Corinthians 3:2).
- Honey—"Sweeter also than honey and the honeycomb" (Psalm 19:10).

Taking in the scroll represents digesting God's Word, making it part of one's being—not just knowing it intellectually, but allowing it to transform you internally. Only then can John be qualified to "prophesy again before many peoples, and nations, and tongues, and kings" (Revelation 10:11).

Revelation 10:9 presents a profound moment of prophetic commissioning. John is told to eat the scroll—symbolizing the internalization of God's Word. It is sweet in his mouth, reflecting the joy of revelation, but bitter in his stomach, showing the anguish of judgment and the heavy cost of prophetic obedience. This verse reminds us that true ministry is not just about receiving divine insight, but also about bearing its weight with humility and boldness.

OLD TESTAMENT FORESHADOWS REVELATION:

Your words were found, and I did eat them; and Your word was unto me the joy and rejoicing of my heart: for I am called by Your name, O Lord GOD of hosts. I sat not in the assembly of the mockers, nor rejoiced; I sat alone because of Your hand: for You have filled me with indignation. (Jeremiah 15:16–17)

Jeremiah's experience reflects the emotional weight of prophetic calling—God's Word brings joy, but also deep burden, isolation, and holy indignation. Just like John in Revelation 10:9, Jeremiah found the initial sweetness of communion with God followed by the bitterness of carrying a heavy message to a rebellious people.

THE REVELATION OF JESUS CHRIST REVEALS:

10:10 And I took the little book out of the angel's hand, and ate it up; and it was in my mouth sweet as honey: and as soon as I had eaten it, my belly was bitter.

This moment is deeply symbolic. Just as Ezekiel and Jeremiah had to eat the Word of God before delivering their prophetic messages, here John is told to consume the "little book" from the angel's hand. The act of eating the scroll signifies more than just learning or understanding—it means fully absorbing the message, letting it become part of the prophet's very being. Before John can proclaim, he must first experience the Word of God in his own soul.

Spiritual and practical application:

- The Word of God brings both sweetness and sorrow. It is a joy to receive and a heavy task to deliver.
- For anyone proclaiming—pastors, teachers, prophets, or believers—the message may be glorious, but its impact can be painful.
- God's ultimate plan includes judgment not because He delights in destruction, but because He is just, and sin must be addressed.
- Even in prophecy, there is mercy—a delay that allows more people to repent. But eventually, judgment must come.

By eating the scroll, John is commissioned again to proclaim God's message—not only to Israel or the Church, but to "many peoples, nations, tongues, and kings" (verse 11). His internalizing of the Word marks the beginning of a deeper ministry during the most intense time of human history—the last half of the Tribulation called the Great Tribulation.

Revelation 10:10 is a powerful picture of prophetic obedience. John receives and eats the little scroll, tasting its sweet truth but also experiencing its bitter consequences. This reflects the heart of biblical prophecy: God's Word is both joy and judgment, and those called to declare it must embrace both. John's experience reminds us that the message of Christ must be fully internalized—even when it's difficult—so that we may faithfully speak truth in a world that desperately needs it.

OLD TESTAMENT FORESHADOWS REVELATION:

My son, eat your honey, because it is good; and the honeycomb, which is sweet to your taste: So shall the knowledge of wisdom be unto your soul: when you have found it, then there shall be a reward, and your expectation shall not be cut off. (Proverbs 24:13–14)

Wisdom—in this Proverb—is compared to honey: sweet, desirable, and nourishing to the soul. But true wisdom also carries weight. It brings understanding of divine truth, human rebellion, and coming judgment—just as John's experience does in Revelation 10:10. Both passages reflect the idea that divine revelation is not just information—it's transformational. You take it in like food. It nourishes, but it also awakens your responsibility to act.

Whereas honey is sweet to the taste, wisdom is sweet to the soul. But that wisdom—once digested—comes with expectation, reward, and sobering understanding. John experiences this same dynamic: sweetness in receiving God's message, but bitterness in realizing its gravity and consequences.

THE REVELATION OF JESUS CHRIST REVEALS:

10:11 And he said to me. You must prophesy again before many peoples, and nations, and tongues, and kings.

This verse marks a turning point in John's prophetic calling. After eating the little scroll—sweet in the mouth, bitter in the belly—John is recommissioned to continue declaring God's Word. The phrase "You must prophesy again" indicates that John's mission is not over; in fact, it's just entering a new phase. He must now prophesy again, but this time, with even more clarity, weight, and global impact.

The message of Revelation, as given to John, is not a private vision—it is a universal declaration. It is meant to go out to many peoples, nations, tongues, and kings—a phrase that echoes Revelation 7:9, emphasizing the global reach of God's message and judgment.

The scroll he consumed was sweet in his mouth because God's Word is always good and true. But it turned bitter in his belly because it contained visions of terrifying judgment, human rebellion, and mass suffering during the Great Tribulation.

The bittersweet nature of prophecy is at the core of Revelation 10:11:

- It is sweet to declare that Christ is coming to rule and reign.
- But it is bitter to witness the devastating events that must unfold beforehand—plagues, wars, apostasy, persecution, and the rise of the Antichrist.

True prophetic ministry is never just about excitement—it also comes with a burden. John, like Ezekiel and Jeremiah before him, must bear the weight of delivering truth, no matter how difficult.

This verse also underscores the worldwide audience for Revelation:

- "Peoples"—ethnic groups.
- "Nations"—sovereign powers.
- "Tongues"—language groups.
- "Kings"—political rulers.

In other words, no one is exempt. The prophecy is for everyone. The coming judgments will touch every corner of the globe, and every leader, nation, and culture will be held accountable before God.

This prophecy will circulate—and has circulated—around the world, just as Jesus said in Matthew 24:14:

> And this gospel of the Kingdom shall be preached in all the world for a witness unto all nations; and then shall the end come. (Matthew 24:14)

This verse also reminds us that as human civilization builds its towers—political, economic, and religious systems—they often drift into rebellion and apostasy. The "achievements" of mankind apart from God are ultimately empty and corrupt. God will bring them to account. He will be vindicated. And only Christ will remain as the righteous King. This is a warning, but also a comfort: The Lord will not let injustice stand. His Word will go out to all, and in the end, His name will be glorified in all the earth.

Revelation 10:11 is John's renewed call to prophetic duty—this time with global scope and intensified urgency. After internalizing the bittersweet message, John is told to speak again, declaring God's truth to every people, nation, language, and ruler. This final stage of prophecy will unveil the fullness of God's judgment and redemption. The future belongs to Christ, and His Word will not return void.

OLD TESTAMENT FORESHADOWS REVELATION:

Then the word of the LORD came unto me, saying, Before I formed you in the belly I knew you; and before you came forth out of the womb I sanctified you, and I ordained you a prophet unto the nations. Then said I, Ah, LORD GOD! Behold, I cannot speak: for I am a child. But the LORD said unto me, Say not, I am a child: for you shalt go to all that I shall send you, and whatsoever I command you, you shalt speak. Be not afraid of their faces: for I am with you to deliver you, says the LORD. Then the LORD put forth His hand, and touched my mouth. And the LORD said unto me, Behold, I have put My words in your mouth. See, I have this day set you over the nations and over the kingdoms, to root out, and to pull down, and to destroy, and to throw down, to build, and to plant. (Jeremiah 1:4–10)

Both John and Jeremiah are reluctant yet obedient prophets, tasked with delivering messages of judgment and redemption to a wide audience. The prophetic Word is not limited to Israel—it goes out to the whole world, targeting nations, rulers, and all people groups. In Revelation 10:11, John is recommissioned during a time of intense judgment. Similarly, Jeremiah was called during a time of national crisis and spiritual decline in Judah. Both are voices in the wilderness, crying out with God's truth even when it is bitter to deliver and difficult to hear.

Like John, Jeremiah was called by God to be a prophet to many nations and kingdoms. His message, like Revelation's, was a mix of warning and hope—rooting out evil and preparing for restoration. Both prophets were handpicked by God, commissioned to speak His truth, and entrusted with a global reach.

———◆◆◆———

"Ann, can I just be honest for a minute? I'm getting overwhelmed with all these so-called prophets on YouTube. Everyone's 'prophesying,' but it's like a circus of visions and timelines and Rapture dates—and I just can't tell anymore who's real and who's not. Doesn't the Bible give us a way to discern this?"

"Yes, Irene. And thank you for saying that out loud—so many believers feel the same way but stay silent. God absolutely gave us a spiritual litmus test, and you're right to be cautious. There are eternal ramifications to following someone who says, 'Thus says the Lord' when God hasn't spoken."

"Exactly. And sometimes they *sound* so anointed. They use Scripture, they pray eloquently, they even seem humble. But something still doesn't sit right in my spirit."

"That check in your spirit is discernment, and we need more of it in these last days. Let's go back to Jeremiah 1:4–10—the calling of a true prophet. God said: 'Before I formed you in the womb I knew you; before you were born I sanctified you; I ordained you a prophet to the nations.' That's not a self-appointed role. That's not someone uploading a video because they had a dream after too much pizza."

Irene laughed. "True! So, what sets Jeremiah apart?"

"A few things. First, his calling came from God, not man. Second, his message was often unpopular, not motivational. And third, he was sent to uproot and tear down, to build and to plant—not to entertain or gain followers. The true prophet's job is to speak truth even when it hurts. And it often comes at a personal cost."

"That's so different from today's Instagram-style prophets who say, 'You're about to be blessed beyond measure!' every twenty-four hours."

"Exactly, Irene. Now, for the biblical test—it's twofold. Everyone talks about Deuteronomy 18:22:"

> When a prophet speaks in the name of the LORD, if the thing follow not, nor come to pass, that is the thing which the LORD has not spoken, but the prophet has spoken it presumptuously: you shalt not be afraid of him. (Deuteronomy 18:22)

"So yes," I continued, "if their prophecy doesn't come true, they're false. That's Test One."

"But there's more?"

"Yes. Deuteronomy 13:1–5 gives Test Two. Even if their signs and wonders come true, if they lead you away from God's law—His commandments and character—they are still a false prophet. That's the part we often miss."

"So even a miracle-working, prediction-accurate person can be a false prophet if they lead us into lawlessness?"

"Exactly. Satan masquerades as an angel of light. He's subtle. Look at the Garden—he didn't come with horns and a pitchfork. He came with a question: 'Did God really say . . .?' False prophets today do the same. They bend Scripture just enough to tickle ears but not convict hearts."

Irene shuttered. "That's terrifying—and sobering. Because I see how quickly people will follow someone just because they sound deep or mystical."

"And that's why discernment isn't optional—it's spiritual armor. We must ask: Does this message align with the full counsel of God's Word? Does it exalt Christ and His righteousness, or does it lead me to idolize a person or seek emotional highs without true repentance?"

"Ann, you're really helping me see the bigger picture. Sometimes we get so caught up in decoding the symbols—like 666—that we lose sight of the person behind the number. Or worse, we forget why it matters in the first place."

"Exactly. Revelation isn't just about deciphering symbols. It's about revealing Christ—and exposing the counterfeit. Every prophecy, every vision, every interpretation must draw us closer to the heart of Jesus. If it doesn't then it's noise—maybe even dangerous noise."

"So, let me get this straight: a true prophet has a divine call, speaks hard truth, lives righteously, and always glorifies God—not themselves?"

"That's right. And their words will line up with Scripture, not just emotionally resonate. We're not called to follow feelings—we're called to follow truth."

"I needed this. Thank you for reminding me that God hasn't left us in the dark. He gave us the Word, the Holy Spirit, and wisdom. We just have to use them."

"Amen, Irene. Because in a time when false prophets multiply, the true remnant must discern—and stand."

THE TURNING POINT OF THE TRIBULATION

Revelation 11 marks a pivotal moment in the unfolding drama of the end times. The setting is Jerusalem, and the timing corresponds to the first half of Daniel's 70th Week—the prophesied seven-year period outlined in Daniel 9:27.

By this point in the Tribulation, Israel has rebuilt the Third Temple, signaling a return to Old Testament-style worship, including sacrifices. The presence of a measurable temple—along with a renewed distinction between Jews and Gentiles—marks a temporary dispensational shift, echoing the patterns of the Old Covenant. This moment signifies more than just ritual revival; it reveals that God's prophetic focus has returned to Israel, setting the stage for the dramatic events that will unfold in the final 3½ years—known as the Great Tribulation.

This chapter opens with John being instructed to measure the temple of God, but notably to exclude the outer court, which has been given over to the Gentiles. This act of measuring is not about architecture—it is deeply symbolic, representing God's ownership, protection, and divine authority over His people and His sacred space. Even in the midst of global chaos and rising opposition, this measuring act declares that God is still in control, marking out what belongs to Him and drawing clear boundaries between the holy and the profane.

In Revelation 10:11, John is told that he must prophesy again concerning many peoples, nations, tongues, and kings. Revelation chapters 11 through 14 serve as a direct extension of that commission, offering a parenthetical interlude within the broader prophetic timeline. Rather than advancing the chronology, these chapters amplify the narrative—zooming in on key figures, unfolding events, and spiritual dynamics that define the midpoint of the Tribulation. This section provides critical context, revealing the identities, conflicts, and divinely orchestrated events that shape the final 3½ years.

At the heart of Revelation 11 are the mysterious Two Witnesses, appointed by God to prophesy for 1,260 days, clothed in sackcloth. Their ministry—marked by miraculous power, prophetic judgment, martyrdom, and resurrection—unfolds on earth even as the conflict between heaven and hell escalates. The chapter culminates with the sounding of the seventh trumpet, a prophetic declaration that the time is drawing near for God's redemptive plan to be completed. This trumpet sets the stage for the final outpouring of wrath, which will be fully revealed in Revelation 15–16 through the seven bowl judgments.

Notably, this chapter begins on earth—with measuring rods and prophetic ministry—and ends in heaven, in verse 19, with the opening of the Heavenly Temple and the revealing of the Ark of the Covenant. This dramatic shift reminds us that, even amid earthly upheaval, the sovereignty of God remains unshaken and His covenantal promises remain in view.

Revelation 11 is more than just narrative—it is a divine transition point. A prophetic hinge between the first and second halves of the Tribulation, it calls us to discern the times, to understand God's enduring covenants, and to behold His grace and justice in perfect balance. What unfolds in this chapter prepares us not only for what's coming, but for the unshakable truth that God's sovereignty governs both heaven and earth.

THE REVELATION OF JESUS CHRIST REVEALS:

[11:1] And there was given me a reed like to a rod: and the angel stood, saying, Rise, and measure the temple of God, and the altar, and them that worship therein.

This verse opens with a symbolic yet striking command—John is given a measuring reed, much like a surveyor's rod, and instructed to measure the temple of God, the altar, and the worshipers within. Measuring in Scripture often represents ownership, protection, and judgment. It's God saying, "This is Mine. I'm watching closely. I will preserve what belongs to Me."

But here's the prophetic tension: there was no Jewish temple standing in John's day. When he received this vision (around AD 95), the Second Temple had already been destroyed by the Romans in AD 70—more than 20 years earlier. And yet, John sees a temple standing. This isn't allegorical; it's prophecy. This passage clearly points to a future, literal rebuilding of the Jewish temple in Jerusalem—something that has not happened even to this day.

Modern developments have made this prophecy more relevant than ever. With today's technology and preparations already underway in Israel—including the Temple Institute's readiness with priestly garments, sacred instruments, and architectural blueprints—a Third Temple could be rebuilt quickly once the right conditions are met. Revelation 11:1 thus stands as a critical marker for readers of prophecy: the Tribulation temple is coming.

John is also told to measure not just the physical structure, but "them that worship therein." This speaks to the spiritual condition of the worshipers, not just the ritual or space. God isn't only interested in the structure—but in those who approach Him there. The measuring rod becomes both a symbol of divine evaluation and covenantal intimacy. It's a reminder that God is still watching over His people—even amid global chaos.

This verse sets the stage for what follows in Revelation 11, especially the shocking contrast with the outer court, which is not to be measured. Why? Because it has been handed over to the Gentiles, who will trample the Holy City for 42 months—the first half of the Tribulation (three and a half years). It's a glimpse of coming desecration, echoing Daniel 9:27 and Jesus' warning in Matthew 24:15 about the "abomination of desolation."

In short, Revelation 11:1 is loaded with meaning:

- It confirms a future Third Temple in Jerusalem.
- It affirms God's authority and judgment over what is His.
- And it signals that even during Tribulation, true worship and true worshipers are still central to God's redemptive plan.

OLD TESTAMENT FORESHADOWS REVELATION:

And He brought me there, and, behold, there was a man, whose appearance was like the appearance of brass, with a line of flax in His hand, and a measuring reed; and He stood in the gate. And the maid said unto me, Son of man, behold with your eyes, and hear with your ears, and set your heart upon all that I shall show you; for to the intent that I might show them unto you are you brought here: declare all that you see to the house of Israel. (Ezekiel 40:3-4)

In both passages, a prophet is given a measuring reed and is told to observe and record details about the temple. In Ezekiel, the measuring is tied to a future prophetic temple—often referred to as the Millennial Temple. In Revelation 11:1, John is similarly instructed to measure the temple of God, the altar, and the worshipers, symbolizing divine ownership, assessment, and coming judgment.

This parallel underscores the continuity between Old and New Testament prophetic visions regarding God's house and His people—and highlights how measuring often represents God's sovereign authority, readiness to judge, and intent to restore what belongs to Him.

THE REVELATION OF JESUS CHRIST REVEALS:

11:2 But the court, which is without the temple leave out, and measure it not; for it is given unto the Gentiles: and the Holy City will they tread underfoot for forty and two months.

John is commanded not to measure the outer court of the temple—a significant prophetic detail. The act of measuring symbolizes divine ownership, protection, and favor. The omission of the outer court represents that this area, and symbolically Jerusalem itself, will be overrun and desecrated by Gentile powers during the final phase of Daniel's 70th Week—the Great Tribulation.

The phrase "given unto the Gentiles" refers to the foreign domination and spiritual desecration of Jerusalem. This aligns with Jesus' prophecy in Luke 21:24:

And they shall fall by the edge of the sword, and shall be led away captive into all nations: and Jerusalem shall be trodden down of the Gentiles, until the times of the Gentiles be fulfilled. (Luke 21:24)

The 42 months (or 1,260 days) signify a literal 3½-year period—half of the seven-year Tribulation. Many Bible scholars interpret this as the second half, when the Antichrist breaks his covenant with Israel (Daniel 9:27), enters the rebuilt Jewish temple, halts sacrificial worship, and declares himself to be God (2 Thessalonians 2:4). This act triggers the greatest persecution Israel has ever faced—a time so severe that Jesus warned, if those days were not shortened, no flesh would survive (Matthew 24:22).

The distinction between the inner court (measured) and the outer court (excluded) represents the division between God's preserved remnant and the world under judgment. While God secures His covenant people, the outer court and the Holy City are left to the trampling feet of unholy nations, setting the stage for final judgment.

Additionally, this verse serves as a preamble to judgment. In prophetic Scripture, measuring often precedes either construction or destruction. In this context, the temple must be rebuilt—necessary for this prophecy to be fulfilled— but judgment is imminent. As 1 Peter 4:17 reminds us, judgment begins at the house of God and then ripples outward through the nations.

OLD TESTAMENT FORESHADOWS REVELATION:

Then I heard a holy one speaking; and another holy one said to that certain one who was speaking, 'How long will the vision be, concerning the daily sacrifices and the transgression of desolation, the giving of both the sanctuary and the host to be trampled underfoot?' (Daniel 8:13)

Trampling the sanctuary parallels the phrase "tread underfoot" in Revelation 11:2. The sanctuary being given over in Daniel 8:13 mirrors the outer court left to the Gentiles in Revelation. Together, these verses point to a prophetic timeline of Gentile dominance and desecration that must run its course before Israel's redemption is fulfilled.

"Ann, I've been watching all these prophetic updates, and I keep hearing talk about the rebuilding of the Jewish temple. But I'm confused—where would they even build it? Isn't the Temple Mount already occupied by the Dome of the Rock?"

"That's such a great question, Irene—and one that's fascinated Bible scholars, archaeologists, and even world leaders for centuries. You're right: the traditional view places both the First and Second Temples exactly where the Dome of the Rock stands today. But more recent research is starting to challenge that assumption."

"Really? I always thought the golden dome marked the exact spot of the Holy of Holies."

"That's what most people believed for a long time. But now, many experts are starting to question it. In fact, there are three major theories about the true location of the Jewish temple—and any one of them could reshape how we understand end-time prophecy."

"Okay, Ann, now you've got me hooked. What are the three theories?"

"Let's start with the northern conjecture, proposed by Dr. Asher Kaufman. He studied the alignment of ancient gates, rock formations, and historical maps. Kaufman believes the original Holy of Holies stood at a site now known as the Dome of the Tablets—or Dome of the Spirits—just north of the Dome of the Rock."

"So if that's true, then the Dome of the Rock wouldn't even be in the way?"

"Exactly. Revelation 11 says the outer court is given to the Gentiles and is not to be measured. If Kaufman is right, then the Dome of the Rock might actually sit within that outer court area—fulfilling Revelation 11:2 in a startlingly literal way."

"That's incredibly specific. So what are the other theories?"

"There's also the southern conjecture, supported by Tuvia Sagiv. He argues that the temple stood south of the Dome of the Rock, near the Hulda Gates. Ancient sources like the Mishnah suggest that the height and slope leading up to the temple don't match the Dome of the Rock's current location—but do align with a more southern site. Sagiv also points out that no ancient texts mention the underground tunnel systems that would be required for the traditional location to fit."

"So, either north or south—but not directly under the Dome of the Rock?"

"That's the idea. Then there's the historical overlay. In AD 70, the Romans destroyed the temple. By AD 135, after the Bar Kokhba Revolt, Emperor Hadrian rebuilt Jerusalem as Aelia Capitolina and reportedly placed an equestrian statue of himself over what they believed was the Holy of Holies. Interestingly, that spot lines up with where the Al-Kas fountain stands today—not the Dome of the Rock."

"So we might already know the true location—but politics and restricted access are keeping us from confirming it archaeologically?"

"Exactly. The Waqf—which means 'endowment' in Arabic and refers to the Islamic custodians of the Temple Mount—has been known to bulldoze artifacts by the truckload, often in an attempt to erase Jewish ties to the site. It's tragic."

"So . . . do you think the Third Temple will be rebuilt before the Tribulation begins?"

"Like I mentioned earlier, the Bible doesn't specifically say when the Third Temple will be rebuilt. But based on Jesus' words in Matthew 24:15, Paul's warning in 2 Thessalonians 2:4, and John's vision in Revelation 11:1–2, it strongly suggests that a physical temple will exist during the Tribulation. The Antichrist will enter that temple, exalt himself, and desecrate it. So yes, a Third Temple will be standing—likely at some point during the first 3½ years of the Tribulation. The exact timing and location are still debated, but one thing is clear: everything is aligning faster than many people realize."

"I have chills. It's incredible how archaeology and prophecy intersect so precisely."

"It is. The location might still be uncertain to us—but not to God. And as believers, we're not just looking at blueprints—we're looking for the Blessed Hope: our soon coming King."

————◆◆◆————

THE REVELATION OF JESUS CHRIST REVEALS:

[11:3] And I will give power to My Two Witnesses, and they will prophesy a thousand two hundred and threescore days, clothed in sackcloth.

This verse introduces one of the most compelling and mysterious elements of the Tribulation: God's Two Witnesses, empowered to prophesy for 1,260 days—

equivalent to 3½ years on the 360-day prophetic calendar. Their presence is unmistakably divine, deeply rooted in both Old Testament prophecy and New Testament fulfillment.

The phrase "Two Witnesses" carries profound legal and spiritual significance. Under Mosaic Law, a matter was confirmed by the testimony of two or more witnesses (Deuteronomy 17:6, 19:15). Jesus affirms this principle in Matthew 18:16. These Two Witnesses are described as prophets (verse 6), operating under Old Testament prophetic authority, not just foretelling future events, but also calling people to repentance and speaking judgment.

They are clothed in sackcloth, a symbol of mourning, repentance, and national lamentation (Jonah 3:5–6; Joel 1:13; Daniel 9:3). Their message will not be one of comfort, but of urgent warning—a final call to repentance before the full outpouring of God's wrath.

Their ministry takes place in Jerusalem—"where also our Lord was crucified" (Revelation 11:8)—reinforcing their connection to both judgment and redemption. While some interpret their mission as occurring during the second half of the Tribulation, many scholars persuasively argue that their 1,260 day ministry unfolds during the first half, setting the stage for the dramatic midpoint betrayal by the Antichrist.

Why is this important? Because if the Two Witnesses were ministering during the second half of the Tribulation, it would seem unnecessary for them to be called up into heaven just before Christ's return. But if their ministry takes place during the first half, they may very well be the instruments God uses to awaken Israel's 144,000—who then carry the gospel to the nations (Revelation 7:4–8; Romans 11:25).

Everything about the Two Witnesses mirrors Old Testament figures:

- Their dress (sackcloth).
- Their miracles (plagues, shutting the sky, turning water to blood).
- Their bold confrontation of evil—recalling Elijah, Moses, Jeremiah, and others.

They seem out of place in a modern world, like men dropped in from a different age—because they are. God, in His perfect sovereignty, brings them forth to do in modern times what they did in ancient times.

God gives them power to protect themselves—fire proceeds from their mouths to destroy their enemies (verse 5)—and power to strike the earth with plagues (verse 6). This is not vengeance but righteous judgment, designed to turn hearts to repentance before it's too late. Their mission is redemptive, even as it is severe.

Revelation 11:3 marks a divine intermission in the judgments to spotlight God's mercy and justice. These two prophets are God's legal witnesses—His final summons to a rebellious world. Their presence proves that even in wrath, God remembers mercy (Habakkuk 3:2). They call the world to repentance, but they also declare God's ownership of the earth, preparing the way for the rightful King—Jesus Christ—to return and reign.

OLD TESTAMENT FORESHADOWS REVELATION:

Then answered I, and said unto him, What are these two olive trees upon the right side of the candlestick and upon the left side thereof? And I answered again, and said unto him, What be these two olive branches which through the two golden pipes empty the golden oil out of themselves? And he answered me and said, Know you not what these be? And I said, No my lord. Then said he, These are the two anointed ones, that stand by the LORD of the whole earth. (Zechariah 4:11–14)

Both passages mention two individuals with a divine mission. Zechariah's two olive trees—later interpreted as Zerubbabel and Joshua the high priest—represent anointed witnesses, just like the Two Witnesses in Revelation 11:3. Zechariah 4:11–14 describes them as standing "by the LORD of the whole earth," which is echoed in Revelation 11:4, calling the witnesses "the two olive trees . . . standing before the God of the earth." These prophetic roles, symbols, and imagery closely link the two passages—showing that Revelation builds upon and amplifies the prophetic vision given to Zechariah.

THE REVELATION OF JESUS CHRIST REVEALS:

11:4 These are the two olive trees, and the two candlesticks standing before the God of the earth.

This verse directly echoes the imagery found in Zechariah 4:11–14, where the prophet Zechariah sees a vision of two olive trees flanking a golden lampstand. In Zechariah's vision, these two olive trees are described as "the two anointed ones who stand beside the LORD of the whole earth." Revelation 11:4 draws on that prophetic symbol and identifies the Two Witnesses as fulfilling this ancient vision—they are not only empowered by God but also divinely appointed to stand as representatives of truth and judgment during a time of global deception.

Symbolism of the olive trees and candlesticks:

- Olive Trees symbolize anointing and the Spirit of God (Zechariah 4:6: "Not by might nor by power, but by My Spirit . . ."). These witnesses are God's anointed vessels, operating under divine authority and spiritual empowerment.

- Candlesticks (lampstands) represent witness-bearing and illumination (as in Revelation 1:20). These Two Witnesses shine the light of God's truth into the darkness of the Tribulation period, much like the churches are meant to do.

The description "standing before the God of the earth" emphasizes their heavenly authority and commission. They are not rogue prophets—they are God's official representatives, sent to prophesy and confront the Antichrist's reign and the rebellion of the world.

While the verse does not name them, much speculation surrounds their identity. Some interpret them as symbolic, others believe they are literal historical figures. The strongest candidates based on biblical precedent are:

- Moses and Elijah—who appeared together at the Mount of Transfiguration (Matthew 17:1–3), represent the Law and the Prophets. Moses symbolizes the Torah (the Law), and Elijah represents the Prophets—together embodying the entire Old Testament witness. Their miracles also parallel those in Revelation 11:6: Moses brought plagues upon Egypt, and Elijah shut the heavens so that it did not rain.
- Enoch and Elijah—also considered possible candidates, since neither experienced death (Genesis 5:24; 2 Kings 2:11). This view draws support from Hebrews 9:27: "And as it is appointed unto men once to die, but after this the judgment."

Revelation 11:4 identifies the Two Witnesses as divinely anointed prophetic figures who will shine as God's light during a time of great darkness. They stand before God, marked by spiritual authority, empowered by His Spirit, and entrusted with a mission that mirrors the great prophetic ministers of old. They are both symbols and individuals, bridging the prophetic hope of the Old Testament with the eschatological fulfillment of the New Testament.

OLD TESTAMENT FORESHADOWS REVELATION:

But I am like a green olive tree in the house of God: I trust in the mercy of God forever and ever. (Psalm 52:8)

The olive tree in this Psalm is a symbol of righteousness, anointing, and steadfast witness in the house of God. In Revelation 11:4, the Two Witnesses are described as olive trees standing before God—just like the psalmist in Psalm 52:8 who identifies with the olive tree in God's house. This verse reinforces the idea of the Two Witnesses being faithful, divinely empowered servants rooted in God's presence and purpose—just like the imagery of a flourishing, spiritually steadfast olive tree.

————◆◆◆————

"Ann, I've been thinking . . . Could John—either the Apostle or even John the Baptist—be one of the Two Witnesses in Revelation 11?"

"That's an intriguing thought, Irene—and one that many people have wondered about. Let's unpack it together."

Irene nodded. "I mean, in Revelation 10:11, John is told, 'You must prophesy again before many peoples, nations, tongues, and kings.' That sure sounds like a mission still ahead of him, doesn't it?"

"It really does sound like it! But here's the key: John's prophetic role wasn't about walking the earth again—it was about delivering a message that would outlive him. That calling was fulfilled through the rest of the Book of Revelation, especially chapters 12 through 22. Through his writing, John *has* prophesied to the nations and kings. His vision has gone global—and it's still speaking, centuries later."

"Ahh, so it's not necessarily about him physically standing in front of the nations?"

"Exactly, Irene. Think about it—his words have reached billions of people, translated into hundreds of languages over the past two thousand years. That's a powerful fulfillment of Revelation 10:11. John didn't need to be one of the Two Witnesses to complete that calling."

"Okay, that makes sense. But what about John the Baptist? Didn't the Book of Malachi say he would return?"

"Great question—and this one has layers. Malachi 4:5 says, 'Behold, I will send you Elijah the prophet before the coming of the great and dreadful Day of the Lord.' It doesn't mention John the Baptist by name, but here's where it gets interesting."

"Go on . . ."

"When John the Baptist came, Jesus said something remarkable in Matthew 11:14: 'If you are willing to receive it, he is Elijah who is to come.' And in Luke 1:17, the angel told Zechariah that John would go 'before the Lord in the spirit and power of Elijah.'"

Irene leaned in, curious. "So . . . John the Baptist was kind of a 'type' of Elijah?"

"Exactly. John wasn't literally Elijah, but he fulfilled the prophecy spiritually—preparing the way for Jesus' First Coming. But the literal return of Elijah, as spoken of in Malachi, is believed by many scholars to refer to someone—possibly Elijah himself—who will appear before Christ's Second Coming. That's why many believe Revelation 11:4 is pointing to him as one of the Two Witnesses."

"So John the Baptist did fulfill the prophecy—but not the one tied to the Tribulation?"

"Right. He fulfilled the First Coming aspect of that prophecy. But the 'great and dreadful Day of the Lord' that Malachi speaks of—that's still future. It refers to the Tribulation period. That's when the Two Witnesses rise up in Jerusalem. And while their exact identity is debated, it's unlikely to be John the Revelator or John the Baptist."

"Thanks for walking me through that, Ann. It's incredible how the Bible weaves it all together—Old Testament prophecy, New Testament fulfillment, and Revelation's end-time forecast."

"It truly is, Irene. It shows just how sovereign and intentional God is— nothing in His Word is random."

THE REVELATION OF JESUS CHRIST REVEALS:

11:5 And if any man will hurt them, fire proceeds out of their mouth, and devours their enemies: and if any man will hurt them, he must in this manner be killed.

This verse reveals the divine protection and supernatural authority granted to the Two Witnesses during their prophetic ministry. For 1,260 days, they are empowered by God to carry out their mission in the midst of chaos and hostility, and anyone who attempts to harm them faces immediate and fiery judgment.

The fire proceeding from their mouths is both literal and symbolic. In the Old Testament, fire often represented God's judgment (Jeremiah 5:14; 2 Kings 1:10). Here, it demonstrates that these witnesses are not just preaching repentance—they are also executing divine judgment upon those who oppose God's message. Their mouths are instruments of both prophetic truth and righteous retribution.

The phrase "he must in this manner be killed" underscores that this is not an act of personal vengeance but a divine decree. Their enemies are consumed not because the witnesses choose violence, but because God has appointed them as instruments of justice during a time of unparalleled spiritual darkness.

This moment echoes the prophetic ministries of Elijah and Jeremiah, who were given authority to shut the heavens, call down fire, and speak words of judgment. Whether symbolic or literal, the fire confirms their heavenly backing and frightens many into recognizing that these are not ordinary men—they are God's emissaries, proclaiming His truth during the Tribulation.

At its core, Revelation 11:5 serves as a sobering reminder: God protects His messengers until their assignment is complete, and those who stand against God's truth do so at their own peril.

OLD TESTAMENT FORESHADOWS REVELATION:

And Elijah answered and said to the captain of fifty, 'If I am a man of God, then let fire come down from heaven and consume you and your fifty men.' And fire came down from heaven and consumed him and his fifty. (2 Kings 1:10)

Elijah's fiery judgment was an unmistakable sign of divine authority—and a warning not to oppose the messenger of God. In a strikingly similar manner, the Two Witnesses of Revelation 11:5 are granted power to call down fire and protect themselves supernaturally. This direct intervention signifies not only their authority but also the urgency of their message and the seriousness of the rebellion on earth during the Tribulation.

THE REVELATION OF JESUS CHRIST REVEALS:

[11:6] These have power to shut heaven, that it rain not in the days of their prophecy: and have power over waters to turn them to blood, and to smite the earth with all plagues, as often as they will.

This verse reveals the extraordinary authority given to the Two Witnesses during their prophetic ministry. Their power is both miraculous and judgmental, echoing some of the most dramatic demonstrations of divine authority seen in the Old Testament.

The phrase "shut heaven, that it rain not" immediately recalls the ministry of Elijah, who declared a drought in Israel that lasted for three and a half years (1 Kings 17:1; James 5:17). This drought was not merely a meteorological phenomenon—it was a prophetic act of judgment meant to turn the hearts of a rebellious nation back to God. In the same way, the Two Witnesses will bring about drought as a sign of divine disapproval and a call to repentance.

This recalls Moses before Pharaoh, when the Nile River was turned to blood (Exodus 7:17–20). Water is essential for life, and when it is corrupted, it signifies judgment, death, and disruption to human survival. This plague mirrors one of the judgments that will reappear later during the bowl judgments (Revelation 16:4–6), showing the overlap and intensification of God's wrath in the Tribulation.

The phrase "as often as they will" emphasizes the sovereign discretion given to these prophets. They will not act arbitrarily, but they are clearly operating with divine endorsement and empowerment. These plagues could include disease, darkness, famine, hail, and other supernatural afflictions—similar to the ten plagues on Egypt (Exodus 7–12). Their repetition in Revelation shows us that God's judgment in the end times is consistent with His past acts of justice.

- These acts are not just punitive—they are redemptive. God is still reaching out to a rebellious world through dramatic signs, calling people to repentance before it's too late.

- The authority of the Two Witnesses demonstrates that God has not abdicated His throne, even as the Antichrist rises. His messengers are empowered, bold, and unmistakable.
- Their ability to wield judgment at will shows us the severity of the times—we are not in the age of passive warnings anymore, but of decisive actions.

OLD TESTAMENT FORESHADOWS REVELATION:

For I will at this time send all My plagues upon your heart, and upon your servants, and upon your people; that you may know that there is none like Me in all the earth. (Exodus 9:14)

In the days of Moses, God used plagues to confront Pharaoh's hardened heart and demonstrate His unmatched sovereignty. Similarly, in Revelation 11:6, the Two Witnesses are granted the authority to smite the earth with plagues "as often as they will." This mirrors the divine power shown through Moses and reflects God's unchanging strategy: to awaken repentance and reveal His supremacy in the midst of rebellion.

THE REVELATION OF JESUS CHRIST REVEALS:

11:7 And when they will have finished their testimony, the beast that ascends out of the bottomless pit will make war against them, and will overcome them, and kill them.

This verse marks a sobering turning point in the ministry of the Two Witnesses. After 1,260 days of bold, miraculous testimony, clothed in sackcloth and calling the world to repentance, their mission comes to its divinely appointed end—but not in the way many would expect.

"And when they will have finished their testimony." God is completely sovereign over their assignment. Not one moment of their mission is cut short. The Two Witnesses are invincible until their task is done—a reminder that no enemy can thwart God's timing for His servants. "Their testimony" refers to the prophetic message they proclaimed, likely centered on repentance, judgment, and the coming Kingdom.

"The beast that ascends out of the bottomless pit." This marks the first mention of "the beast" in Revelation—a figure who becomes increasingly prominent in later chapters, especially Revelation 13. Emerging from the abyss (Greek: *abussos*), this beast represents a demonic, anti-Christ power energized by hell itself. The imagery highlights its satanic origin and signals the intensifying spiritual warfare unfolding on earth.

"Will make war against them, and will overcome them, and kill them." Though empowered by God, the Two Witnesses are not exempt from suffering or death. God permits the beast to temporarily overcome them, not due to weakness or failure, but as part of His greater prophetic plan. Their deaths will shock the world—but also set the stage for a divine demonstration of resurrection and judgment.

This verse shows us a deeper truth: Victory in God's eyes is not always survival—it is faithful completion of the mission. The world's apparent triumph over the Two Witnesses is short-lived, as we'll see in the verses that follow.

OLD TESTAMENT FORESHADOWS REVELATION:

And his power shall be mighty, but not by his own power: and he shall destroy wonderfully, and shall prosper, and practice, and shall destroy the mighty and the holy people. And through his policy also he shall cause craft to prosper in his hand; and he shall magnify himself in his heart, and by peace shall destroy many: he shall also stand up against the Prince of princes; but he shall be broken without hand. (Daniel 8:24–25)

Daniel 8:24–25 prophesies of a fierce king, empowered supernaturally, who destroys the holy people—much like the beast in Revelation 11:7 who makes war with and kills the Two Witnesses. The phrase "not by his own power" matches the satanic origin of the beast "ascending out of the bottomless pit." Both texts speak of deception, war, and temporary victory over God's chosen ones, highlighting the spiritual war leading up to final judgment.

"Ann, I'm a little confused. In Revelation 11:7, it says the beast comes out of the bottomless pit. But then in Revelation 13:1, the beast rises out of the sea. Are those two different beasts?"

"Great question, Irene! At first, it might seem like they're different figures, but both are actually describing the same person—the Antichrist—just from two different angles."

"Really? Then why the different origins? One's from the bottomless pit, and the other from the sea? That sounds like two different places."

"It's symbolic. The bottomless pit—or abyss—represents the Antichrist's spiritual origin. His power comes directly from Satan, possibly even through demonic possession. That's why Revelation 11:7 highlights the pit—it's emphasizing the spiritual warfare side of the story, especially coming right after the Two Witnesses."

"So when it says the beast rises from the sea, that's not literal—it means something else?"

"Exactly. In prophetic language, the sea often represents the Gentile nations or the broader geopolitical world. So when the beast rises from the sea, it suggests he emerges from the global system—likely as a political leader who appears to be just another figure on the world stage."

"Wow . . . so Revelation is revealing both his demonic origin and his global rise to power?"

"Yes! Revelation 11:7 highlights his demonic empowerment, while Revelation 13 reveals his rise among the nations. One is his spiritual source; and the other, his political platform."

"That's actually really powerful. I always thought maybe it was two different beasts."

"You're not alone. But when you look at the big picture, it's just showing two dimensions of the same evil figure—a world leader energized by the forces of darkness."

"Thanks, Ann. That makes the whole thing much clearer now!"

THE REVELATION OF JESUS CHRIST REVEALS:

^{11:8} And their dead bodies will lie in the street of the great city, which spiritually is called Sodom and Egypt, where also our Lord was crucified.

There's no doubt this is Jerusalem, the city where Jesus Christ was crucified. Yet in this prophetic context, it's not referred to by name, but rather by its spiritual condition: "spiritually is called Sodom and Egypt."

- Sodom represents moral depravity—perversity, pride, and defiance of God's order (Genesis 19).
- Egypt represents bondage and idolatry—a nation that held God's people captive and hardened its heart against His wonders (Exodus 1–14).

By using these terms, the Holy Spirit reveals that Jerusalem, in the end times, will mirror the corruption and rebellion of both ancient Sodom and Egypt. This is a spiritual indictment, not just of a city, but of an entire system of resistance to God's messengers and His truth.

In ancient Jewish tradition, denying burial was a deep disgrace. Here, the world celebrates their deaths and leaves their corpses exposed—a symbol of contempt and triumph. This gruesome display is broadcast to the world, which celebrates their silence. But heaven is not done with them yet (as we'll see in verses 11–12).

- This verse reminds us that God's prophets are never honored by the world (Matthew 23:37).
- Though Moses and Elijah—or whomever the Two Witnesses may be— were honored in their own time by God's people, in the end, their anointing makes them enemies of the world.
- And yet, their mission will not be interrupted. They are invulnerable until their assignment is fulfilled (verse 7). Their death isn't a defeat—it's a transition toward a greater demonstration of God's power.

OLD TESTAMENT FORESHADOWS REVELATION:

Hear the word of the LORD, you rulers of Sodom; give ear to the law of our God, you people of Gomorrah! (Isaiah 1:10)

In this verse, God calls Jerusalem "Sodom"—not literally, but to rebuke their moral and spiritual corruption. Just like in Revelation 11:8, this prophetic language exposes the city's deep rebellion against God. The people had kept religious rituals but had lost righteousness, justice, and mercy—thus spiritually becoming like Sodom.

THE REVELATION OF JESUS CHRIST REVEALS:

11:9 And they of the people and kindreds and tongues and nations will see their dead bodies three days and a half, and will not suffer their dead bodies to be put in graves.

This verse presents a grim and sobering moment in the prophetic timeline: the bodies of God's two mighty witnesses lie lifeless in the streets of Jerusalem. Their assassination by the Antichrist (Revelation 11:7) sparks a global spectacle and reveals the hardened heart of the world during the Tribulation.

John writes that "people and kindreds and tongues and nations" will gaze upon their dead bodies for three and a half days—a precise timeframe, underscoring the prophetic nature of this event. In John's day, such global viewing would seem impossible, but modern technology (satellites, news media, internet, smartphones) now makes it entirely plausible for the entire world to witness an event unfolding in real-time.

This global spectacle intensifies the world's mockery and hatred toward God's prophets. These two men—who boldly proclaimed truth, performed miracles, and called for repentance—are now publicly shamed as the world watches. In ancient Jewish tradition, denying someone burial was a profound insult, symbolizing curse and disgrace. To leave a body unburied was to strip it of even the most basic dignity. This reaction exposes the depth of spiritual hostility the world had developed toward God's witnesses.

This act fulfills Psalm 79:1–3, where Jerusalem's downfall is described, and God's servants are left without burial:

> The dead bodies of Your servants have they given to be meat unto the fowls of the heaven, the flesh of Your saints unto the beasts of the earth. Their blood have they shed like water round about Jerusalem; and there was none to bury them. (Psalm 79:1–3)

The world's refusal to bury the witnesses further reflects its rejection of God's message. Their deaths become a public "celebration" (verse 10), revealing the full depravity of a society under strong delusion and global deception.

But the three and a half day period is divinely ordained. Just as Jesus rose after three days, these Two Witnesses—though despised and discarded—are destined for resurrection and vindication. Their unburied state sets the stage for God to publicly glorify them in front of those who once mocked them (Revelation 11:11–12).

OLD TESTAMENT FORESHADOWS REVELATION:

> And they shall go forth, and look upon the carcasses of the men that have transgressed against Me: for their worm shall not die, neither shall their fire be quenched; and they shall be an abhorrence unto all flesh. (Isaiah 66:24)

This verse paints a vivid prophetic picture of public spectacle and shame, where the unburied corpses of the rebellious become a visible sign of judgment. Similarly, in Revelation 11:9, the dead bodies of the Two Witnesses are exposed for three and a half days, seen by people of every nation and language, reinforcing the idea of global defiance and hardened hearts even in the face of God's power.

THE REVELATION OF JESUS CHRIST REVEALS:

> 11:10 And they that dwell upon the earth will rejoice over them, and make merry, and will send gifts one to another; because these two prophets tormented them that dwelt on the earth.

This verse reveals the shocking moral inversion of the world during the Tribulation. Instead of mourning the death of God's holy prophets, the world celebrates it—like a twisted global holiday. People will rejoice, throw parties, and exchange gifts, not because a war ended or peace was restored, but because the voices of truth and righteousness have been silenced.

These Two Witnesses had tormented the earth—not through evil, but through truth, righteous judgment, and miraculous signs that exposed sin and called people to repent. The word "tormented" here reflects how the conviction of sin can feel like torment to those who refuse to turn to God.

This reaction reflects Romans 1 in action—people have exchanged the truth of God for a lie, and now they celebrate darkness instead of light. The world is so hardened that the death of God's messengers becomes a cause for joy.

This scene also foreshadows how the Antichrist's rule will be applauded by a spiritually blind world. Yet, this celebration will be short-lived. As the next verses will show, God is not finished with His Two Witnesses—and neither is He finished with His plan for redemption and justice.

OLD TESTAMENT FORESHADOWS REVELATION:

And it came to pass, when Ahab saw Elijah, that Ahab said unto him, are you he that troubles Israel? (1 Kings 18:17)

And the king of Israel said unto Jehoshaphat, There is yet one man, Micaiah the son of Imlah, by whom we may inquire of the LORD: but I hate him; for he does not prophesy good concerning me, but evil. (1 Kings 22:8)

Just like the Two Witnesses in Revelation 11:10 are hated because they "tormented" those on the earth with their truth-telling and judgments, Elijah was considered a *troubler of Israel* by King Ahab. Similarly, Micaiah was despised by King Ahab because he only prophesied judgment and not smooth words. In both the Old Testament and New Testament examples, the world hates the messenger because it hates the message—a message of repentance, judgment, and God's uncompromising truth.

THE REVELATION OF JESUS CHRIST REVEALS:

[11:11] And after three days and a half the Spirit of life from God entered into them, and they stood upon their feet; and great fear fell upon them which saw them.

This verse describes one of the most stunning moments in the entire Book of Revelation—a divine resurrection, visible to the world.

Just when the world believed the Two Witnesses were defeated—left dead, dishonored, and unburied for three and a half days—God breathes life back into them. The phrase "Spirit of life from God" echoes Genesis 2:7, where God breathed life into Adam. This is no metaphor. It's a literal, public resurrection—undeniable and divine. Their rising mirrors Christ's resurrection on the third day, reinforcing a redemptive pattern: vindication follows apparent defeat.

As their bodies lay in full view, broadcast across the globe, the world celebrated. But their sudden resurrection flips triumph to terror. "Great fear fell upon them" isn't mere dread—it's paralyzing awe. These weren't misguided zealots. They were God's prophets—and now, the world knows it. God always has the final word.

This moment reminds us that God's servants are invincible until their mission is complete. Even in death, they are not abandoned. What man tries to silence, God raises up. The resurrection of the witnesses foreshadows a future global reckoning: God will not be mocked, and truth—no matter how fiercely opposed—will rise again.

OLD TESTAMENT FORESHADOWS REVELATION:

So I prophesied as He commanded me, and breath came into them, and they lived, and stood upon their feet, an exceedingly great army. (Ezekiel 37:10)

Just as God breathed life into the dry bones of Israel in Ezekiel's vision—reviving them and causing them to stand upon their feet—so too does God breathe life into the Two Witnesses after three and half days of lying dead in the street. Both passages demonstrate God's sovereign power to resurrect, restore, and vindicate His servants—whether it be a nation (Israel) or two prophetic witnesses.

THE REVELATION OF JESUS CHRIST REVEALS:

11:12 And they heard a great voice from heaven saying unto them, Come up here. And they ascended up to heaven in a cloud; and their enemies beheld them.

After three and a half days of worldwide shame and humiliation—where the dead bodies of the Two Witnesses lay in the streets of Jerusalem while the world celebrated their death—God steps in with dramatic power. A "great voice from heaven" breaks the silence and commands: "Come up here." This same divine phrase was spoken to John in Revelation 4:1 when he was called into the heavenly realm to witness things to come. Here, it is a command of resurrection, vindication, and ascension—a personal rapture for the Two Witnesses.

"They ascended up to heaven in a cloud" echoing:

- Jesus' own ascension in Acts 1:9—"He was taken up, and a cloud received Him out of their sight."
- And likely connecting to 1 Thessalonians 4:17, where the righteous are caught up in the clouds to meet the Lord.

This cloud signifies divine presence and glory, often seen in Scripture when God shows up in power (Exodus 13:21; Matthew 17:5).

Perhaps the most sobering detail: "And their enemies beheld them." This is not a private ascension. It's public, undeniable, and deeply unsettling to those who rejoiced in their death. Their resurrection and rapture are visible to the very ones who despised them. What had once been global mockery now becomes global awe and terror.

This verse is a vivid reminder that:

- God always has the final word.
- His servants may suffer persecution, rejection, even death—but their story doesn't end there.
- Resurrection is real. Reward is real. And vindication is guaranteed.

OLD TESTAMENT FORESHADOWS REVELATION:

Then it happened, as they continued on and talked, that suddenly a chariot of fire appeared with horses of fire, and separated the two of them; and Elijah went up by a whirlwind into heaven. (2 Kings 2:11)

Just as the Two Witnesses in Revelation 11:12 are called up to heaven and ascend in a cloud, so too did Elijah ascend visibly into heaven in the Old Testament. His departure was supernatural, public, and marked the completion of his prophetic mission—just like the Two Witnesses. Both scenes signify God's approval, divine authority, and vindication before onlookers—enemies and followers alike.

THE REVELATION OF JESUS CHRIST REVEALS:

[11:13] And the same hour was there a great earthquake, and the tenth part of the city fell, and in the earthquake were slain of men seven thousand: and the remnant were affrighted, and gave glory to the God of Heaven.

This verse captures heaven's immediate response to the resurrection and ascension of the Two Witnesses. At the very moment of their vindication, a massive earthquake strikes Jerusalem—not as a random disaster, but as a deliberate, divine wake-up call to a defiant world.

- "The same hour" highlights the precision of God's judgment. There is no delay between the Witnesses' ascension and the earthquake—it is synchronized and intentional.
- A tenth of the city falls, signaling severe yet restrained judgment. God targets rather than obliterates, offering correction with mercy.
- 7,000 people perish—possibly symbolizing completeness or prominent figures, intensifying public shock and fear.

The most unexpected response comes from "the remnant"—survivors who had likely mocked the witnesses just days before. Now, overcome with fear, they "give glory to the God of Heaven." This doesn't necessarily signify full repentance or widespread salvation, but it does mark a sobering shift in perspective. What was once contempt turns to awe. It's a window of grace, a final opportunity to recognize God's hand before the final judgments fall.

This moment stands as a testimony: even in judgment, God offers mercy. The Two Witnesses' ministry, rejected and ridiculed in life, bears fruit in death. Their resurrection and ascension affirm their divine calling. The world saw their humiliation—but also their victory. Heaven responded. Earth trembled. And hearts, even if briefly, turned toward glory.

OLD TESTAMENT FORESHADOWS REVELATION:

And His feet shall stand in that day upon the Mount of Olives, which is before Jerusalem on the east, and the Mount of Olives shall cleave (split) in the midst thereof toward the east and toward the west, and there shall be a very great valley; and half of the mountain shall remove toward the north, and half of it toward the south. And you shall flee to the valley of the mountains; for the valley of the mountains shall reach unto Azal: yes, you shall flee, like as you fled from before the earthquake in the days of Uzziah king of Judah: and the LORD my God shall come, and all the saints with you. (Zechariah 14:4–5)

In Revelation 11:13, a great earthquake shakes Jerusalem immediately after the ascension of the Two Witnesses. This is a divine response—shocking the world and resulting in the death of 7,000 people, causing the remnant to give glory to God. In Zechariah 14:4–5, we also see a massive earthquake that reshapes Jerusalem geographically at the Lord's return, triggering people to flee in fear, acknowledging the Lord's divine power.

Both passages involve: A great earthquake in Jerusalem. Mass casualties or panic. A reaction of fear or recognition of God's glory. Events closely connected to the end times and the Lord's intervention.

THE REVELATION OF JESUS CHRIST REVEALS:

11:14 The second woe is past; and, behold, the third woe comes quickly.

This short but crucial verse marks a transition point in the Book of Revelation. It brings closure to the sixth trumpet judgment—which included the second "woe"—and signals the imminent arrival of the seventh trumpet, which is also called the third woe.

"The second woe is past." The second woe encompasses the terrifying events unleashed by the sixth trumpet (Revelation 9:13–21), including:

- The release of the four bound angels at the River Euphrates.
- The slaughter of one-third of mankind by a demonic army numbering 200 million.
- The ministry, death, resurrection, and ascension of the Two Witnesses (Revelation 11:3–13).
- A devastating earthquake that killed 7,000 people in Jerusalem (Revelation 11:14).

All these horrors fall under the second "woe," which signifies a particularly severe judgment.

"The third woe comes quickly." With this declaration, John warns that the third woe is imminent—and it's no less terrifying. It is tied to the seventh trumpet (Revelation 11:15), which sets into motion the bowl judgments of God's final wrath (detailed in Revelation 15–16). This verse thus acts like a drumbeat of dread, alerting the reader that the final phase of God's judgment is about to begin.

This passage serves as a divine pause—a moment to catch one's breath before the full outpouring of wrath. The second woe demonstrated both judgment and mercy—as seen in the resurrection of the Two Witnesses and some giving glory to God. But now, the pace quickens. The final judgments will unfold rapidly.

It reminds us: God is not slow in judgment, but merciful—yet His justice will not delay forever.

OLD TESTAMENT FORESHADOWS REVELATION:

Blow you the trumpet in Zion, and sound an alarm in My holy mountain: let all the inhabitants of the land tremble: for the Day of the Lord comes, for it is near at hand; A day of darkness and of gloominess, a day of clouds and of thick darkness, as the morning spreads upon the mountains: a people great and strong; there has not been ever the like, neither shall be any more after it, even to the years of many generations. (Joel 2:1–2)

"Blow you the trumpet" corresponds with the trumpet judgments in Revelation 8–9, 11:15, particularly the final ones. The urgency and terror of the coming Day of the Lord mirrors the phrase "the third woe comes quickly" in Revelation 11:14. Joel 2:1–2, like Revelation 11:14, speaks of escalating judgment and calls people to repent before the final outpouring of wrath.

THE REVELATION OF JESUS CHRIST REVEALS:

[11:15] And the seventh angel sounded; and there were great voices in heaven, saying, The kingdoms of this world are become the kingdoms of our LORD, and of His Christ; and He will reign forever and ever.

The Seventh Trumpet Judgment—Third Woe. This verse marks a major turning point in Revelation. The sounding of the seventh trumpet is the beginning of the third woe (as announced in Revelation 11:14)—a climactic and final stage of God's judgment that will unfold in the seven bowl judgments (Revelation 15–16).

"The kingdoms of this world are become the kingdoms of our LORD, and of His Christ; and He will reign forever and ever." The declaration from heaven proclaims that all the kingdoms of the world—long under the influence of Satan (Matthew 4:8–9; John 12:31)—now rightfully belong to the LORD and His

Christ. This is not yet the visible establishment of Christ's earthly Kingdom (that comes in Revelation 19), but it is the legal proclamation of His rule. The seventh trumpet signals that the consummation of all things is underway.

Note that this trumpet is not the "last trump" mentioned in 1 Thessalonians 4:16 and 1 Corinthians 15:52, which is associated with the Rapture. This is the seventh trumpet blown by an angel, not by God. It introduces the final wave of judgments that will lead directly to Christ's return.

Heaven rejoices because Satan's reign is nearing its end. The proclamation of eternal reign reminds us that no earthly ruler, system, or power will stand against Christ. From this point forward, the remaining judgments will systematically dismantle every kingdom opposed to God's authority, preparing the way for the return of the King of kings.

- The seventh trumpet signals the formal announcement of Christ's impending visible rule on earth.
- This is declaration of conquest—Christ is reclaiming what is His.
- This marks the beginning of the second 3½ years of the Tribulation—when judgments intensify, but the path to ultimate victory begins.
- The kingdoms of this world—now under Satan's sway—will fall under the dominion of Jesus Christ, who will reign forever.

OLD TESTAMENT FORESHADOWS REVELATION:

I will declare the decree: the LORD has said unto Me, You are My Son: this day have I begotten You. Ask of Me, and I shall give You the nations for Your inheritance, and the uttermost parts of the earth for Your possession. You shalt break them with a rod of iron; You shalt dash them in pieces like a potter's vessel. (Psalm 2:7–9)

Psalm 2:7–9 prophetically anticipates the Messianic reign of Christ over all the nations—a dominion that becomes reality in Revelation 11:15, where the heavenly declaration proclaims: "The kingdoms of this world have become the kingdoms of our LORD and of His Christ." The "inheritance of the nations" in Psalm 2 is now fulfilled, ushering in the rule of Christ with absolute authority and eternal dominion.

THE REVELATION OF JESUS CHRIST REVEALS:

11:16 And the four and twenty elders, which sat before God on their seats, fell upon their faces, and worshiped God.

This verse captures a powerful moment of heavenly worship and awe in response to the sounding of the seventh trumpet—the third woe, which signals the transition toward the final judgments and the return of Christ.

The twenty-four elders represent the redeemed people of God—often interpreted as a symbolic union of the twelve tribes of Israel and the twelve apostles, signifying the totality of God's covenant people. These elders, who are seated in positions of authority and intimacy before God, now leave their thrones, fall on their faces, and worship. Their posture is one of absolute humility and reverence, acknowledging the sovereignty of God and the fulfillment of His eternal plan.

This act of worship signals a turning point in the heavenly narrative. The declaration in verse 15—that "the kingdoms of this world are become the kingdoms of our LORD"—evokes such overwhelming awe that those who have been sitting in glory now prostrate themselves before the LORD in anticipation of Christ's reign. It underscores that all power, authority, and dominion rightfully belong to God alone.

OLD TESTAMENT FORESHADOWS REVELATION:

And David said to all the congregation, Now bless the LORD your God. And all the congregation blessed the Lord GOD of their fathers, and bowed down their heads, and worshiped the LORD, and the king. (1 Chronicles 29:20)

Just as the twenty-four elders fall on their faces and worship God in heaven, the people of Israel in 1 Chronicles bowed and worshiped the LORD in a moment of national and spiritual significance—the crowning of Solomon and the acknowledgment of God's sovereignty over the kingdom. In both cases, there is a recognition of divine kingship, a transition of rule, and a corporate act of worship expressing submission to God's authority.

In Revelation 11:16, the heavenly elders respond to the announcement of Christ's eternal reign. In 1 Chronicles 29:20, the people of Israel respond to the establishment of a divinely appointed king. Both scenes reflect the convergence of heaven and earth under God's rule.

THE REVELATION OF JESUS CHRIST REVEALS:

[11:17] Saying, We give You thanks, O LORD God Almighty, which are, and was, and are to come; because You have taken to You Your great power, and have reigned.

This verse captures a powerful shift in heavenly worship. The twenty-four elders, representing redeemed humanity, fall on their faces to give thanks to God—not only for what He has done, but for what He is now actively doing. This marks a major turning point in redemptive history: God is no longer restraining His rule but is actively taking possession of His Kingdom on earth.

The phrase "LORD God Almighty" emphasizes God's absolute sovereignty and omnipotence. This title, used frequently in the Old Testament, reminds us that

He alone holds dominion over heaven and earth. The reference to God as the One "which are, and was, and are to come" echoes earlier language in Revelation (1:4, 1:8), signifying His eternality and faithfulness.

The phrase "You have taken to You Your great power, and have reigned" speaks of a decisive act—God asserting His rule after allowing Satan temporary dominion. The Greek verb *basileuo* translated "to reign" is in the aorist tense, indicating a completed action in the past—implying decisive, sovereign intervention has already taken place. God is no longer permitting evil to rule unchecked; He is now actively enforcing His rightful reign.

This moment forms part of a threefold acclamation by the elders (verses 16–18): Christ reigns supremely (verse 17); He judges righteously (verse 18); and He rewards graciously (verse 18).

This is also the third major worship scene involving the elders:

- In Revelation 4:10–11, they worship God as Creator.
- In Revelation 5:9–14, they worship the Redeemer.
- And here, in Revelation 11:17, they worship Him as Conqueror and King.

The focus has now shifted to the climactic moment of divine intervention—a heavenly acknowledgment that God is finally about to bring justice, judgment, and restoration to the earth. The long-anticipated reign of Christ is no longer future; it is breaking into the present.

OLD TESTAMENT FORESHADOWS REVELATION:

And there was given Him dominion, and glory, and a Kingdom, that all people, nations, and languages, should serve Him: His dominion is an everlasting dominion, which shall not pass away, and His Kingdom that which shall not be destroyed. (Daniel 7:14)

Both Revelation 11:17 and Daniel 7:14 describe God's final assumption of sovereign rule over the earth. The elders in Revelation are praising God for taking His great power and beginning to reign—just as Daniel prophesied of the Son of Man receiving an everlasting dominion. In both passages, the reign is not symbolic or spiritual only—it is literal, global, and eternal.

THE REVELATION OF JESUS CHRIST REVEALS:

[11:18] And the nations were angry, and Your wrath is come, and the time of the dead, that they should be judged, and that You should give reward to Your servants the prophets, and to the saints, and them that fear Your name, small and great; and should destroy them which destroy the earth.

Revelation 11:18 is a theological and prophetic turning point. It unveils the divine response to a rebellious world and presents a sweeping overview of final judgment and eternal reward.

"The nations were angry" echoes Psalm 2:1–2, where the nations rage against the LORD and His Anointed. Despite the fury and rebellion of humanity, God's wrath has now come, signaling the end of tolerance for sin and the beginning of righteous judgment. The verse marks God's full intervention in global affairs. The age-long patience of God has reached its divine limit, and the world now faces its Creator and Judge.

"And the time of the dead, that they should be judged." This is a reference to future resurrection and judgment, with two primary outcomes:

- Judgment of the wicked—the dead who rejected God.
- Reward for the righteous—His servants, prophets, and those who fear His name.

This dual outcome aligns with Daniel 12:2, where some awaken to everlasting life and others to shame and everlasting contempt. It also anticipates Revelation 20, where the Great White Throne Judgment occurs.

"And that you should give reward to your servants the prophets, and to the saints." God never forgets the faithfulness of His people. Prophets, saints, and all who fear His name—whether small or great—receive their eternal reward. This includes martyrs, intercessors, everyday believers, and those unknown to the world but honored in heaven. Jesus promised in Matthew 10:41–42 that even a cup of cold water given in His name would not go unrewarded.

"And should destroy them which destroy the earth." This final phrase is significant—it confirms that God holds humanity accountable not only for spiritual rebellion but also for physical corruption. Those who devastate creation—through idolatry, war, moral collapse, or environmental ruin—will be judged. This is a fulfillment of God's original mandate to steward the earth (Genesis 1:28) and a warning to those who desecrate what God called "good."

OLD TESTAMENT FORESHADOWS REVELATION:

Come, my people, enter you into your chambers, and shut your doors about you: hide yourself as it were for a little moment, until the indignation be over past. For, behold, the LORD comes out of His place to punish the inhabitants of the earth for their iniquity: the earth also shall disclose her blood, and shall no more cover her slain. (Isaiah 26:20–21)

Both passages speak of a climactic divine judgment on the nations, a moment when God moves from delay to action, revealing His justice against corruption, violence, and rebellion.

THE REVELATION OF JESUS CHRIST REVEALS:

[11:19] And the temple of God was opened in heaven, and there was seen in His temple the ark of His testament: and there were lightnings, and voices, and thunderings, and an earthquake, and great hail.

This verse brings Revelation 11 to a dramatic and climactic close. The imagery shifts suddenly from the praises of the twenty-four elders in heaven to the unveiling of the Heavenly Temple—a stunning declaration that God is about to dwell and act in a new, visible, and judgmental way on behalf of His people.

"The temple of God was opened in heaven." This opening is highly symbolic. It's not just about access—it's about revelation and readiness. The temple in heaven being opened implies that God's divine presence, justice, and holiness are now fully manifest. This may also indicate that just as heaven is revealing its temple, an earthly temple is also being prepared or opened—especially significant in light of the prior temple measurements in Revelation 11:1–2.

"And there was seen in His temple the ark of His testament." The Ark of the Covenant, or Ark of His Testimony, was the most sacred object in the Old Testament temple—the throne of God on earth and a symbol of His covenant with Israel. Its appearance in heaven reaffirms God's faithfulness to His promises, His sovereign rule, and the unbreakable covenant with His people. Though lost on earth, the "original" Ark has always been in heaven: the one on the earth was but a replica (Hebrews 9:23). God is showing that He remembers the covenant, and He is preparing to fulfill it completely.

This visible Ark represents intimacy, mercy, and judgment—because it was also the place where blood was sprinkled on the Day of Atonement, symbolizing both mercy and wrath. Its reappearance signals that God is now moving from intercession to intervention.

"And there were lightnings, and voices, and thunderings, and an earthquake, and great hail." These dramatic signs appear repeatedly in Revelation, marking moments of God's direct intervention in human history. Similar phenomena are seen in Revelation 4:5 and 8:5. Here, they function as a divine exclamation point—heralding the awesome power and impending judgment about to unfold through the bowl judgments introduced in *The Trumpet II*. This vivid display signals that the final phase of the Tribulation is imminent.

OLD TESTAMENT FORESHADOWS REVELATION:

You shall put the mercy seat on top of the ark, and in the ark you shall put the Testimony that I will give you. And there I will meet with you, and I will speak with you from above the mercy seat, from between the two cherubim which are on the ark of the Testimony, about everything which I will give you in commandment to the children of Israel. (Exodus 25:21–22)

This Old Testament verse describes the original Ark of the Covenant—the very object seen in heaven in Revelation 11:19. The ark in Exodus 25:21–22 was a visible symbol of God's presence, mercy, and covenant. It was where God would meet and commune with His people.

Just as God's glory and voice once filled the tabernacle and later the temple in the Old Testament, Revelation 11:19 shows His Heavenly Temple now fully opened with lightning, thunder, and hail—signs of His holiness, judgment, and power. This reinforces the idea that God is now revealing Himself not only as Savior but also as Judge, fulfilling His promises and preparing for the final judgments to come.

SUMMARY OF REVELATION 10–11

Revelation 10 and 11 form an interlude between the sixth and seventh trumpet judgments, offering a behind-the-scenes look at divine authority, prophetic mission, and God's faithful witness during judgment.

In chapter 10, a mighty angel appears holding a "little book," symbolizing God's Word—sweet to the faithful, yet bitter in its judgments. John is instructed to eat it and then commissioned to prophesy to all peoples, nations, tongues, and kings (Revelation 10:1–11).

Chapter 11 shifts to Jerusalem. John is given a reed to measure the temple—signifying God's ownership and protection—while the outer court is left to the Gentiles, who will trample the Holy City for 42 months (Revelation 11:1–2). During this time, Two Witnesses are appointed to prophesy for 1,260 days. Performing miracles reminiscent of Moses and Elijah, they call the world to repentance (Revelation 11:3–6). When their mission ends, the Antichrist kills them. Their bodies lie unburied in the streets for 3½ days as the world rejoices (Revelation 11:7–10).

But God intervenes. The breath of life enters them, and they rise and ascend to heaven before the watching world (Revelation 11:11–12). A great earthquake follows, killing 7,000 people and prompting the survivors to give glory to the God of Heaven (Revelation 11:13).

The chapter concludes with the sounding of the seventh trumpet: loud voices in heaven proclaim, "The kingdoms of this world are become the kingdoms of our LORD, and of His Christ; and He shall reign forever and ever." As the Heavenly Temple opens, the Ark of the Covenant is seen—symbolizing God's unshakable presence, promises, and power. This sets the stage for the climactic judgments to come (Revelation 11:15–19).

KEY TAKEAWAYS

- A divine interlude—Revelation 10–11 offer a holy pause, underscoring God's sovereignty amid chaos.
- John's renewed commission—The call to prophesy affirms the global relevance of Revelation's message.
- The Two Witnesses—Empowered By God, they boldly preach for 3½ years, calling the world to repent.
- Martyrdom and vindication—Their death is not the end. Their resurrection and ascension shake the earth and awaken fear and reverence.
- The seventh trumpet—The trumpet sounds the triumph of Christ, the joy of heaven, and the prelude to the final judgments.

Revelation 10–11 remind us that even in the darkest moments of Tribulation, God remains in control, His witnesses stand strong, and His Kingdom will prevail. These chapters anchor us in the certainty that every judgment is purposeful, every prophecy precise, and every promise sure—for the glory of God and the redemption of those who turn to Him.

But the story does not end here.

The prophetic narrative continues in *The Trumpet II*, which picks up where *The Trumpet I* ends—unfolding Revelation chapters 12 through 22. In this volume, the seven bowl judgments trigger a swift and sweeping series of climatic events, culminating in the final confrontation between good and evil—and the ultimate triumph of Christ's kingdom.

Key prophetic moments include:

- The war in heaven and Satan's expulsion to earth.
- The rise of the Antichrist and the False Prophet.
- The final outpouring of God's wrath through the seven bowl judgments.
- The unveiling and fall of Mystery Babylon—America exposed.
- The glorious return of Jesus Christ as King of kings.
- The dawn of the Millennial Kingdom.
- The unveiling of the Eternal State: a new heaven, new earth, and the radiant descent of New Jerusalem.

This is more than prophecy—it's destiny. The journey moves forward—toward justice, redemption, and the eternal reign of Christ.

Afterword:
The Invitation

BEFORE THE DOOR CLOSES—Irene sat quietly across from me, her eyes lingering on the final page of *The Trumpet I: The Ancient Prophecy That Reveals America's Final Hour*. Her hands rested on the worn edges, as if she didn't want to let it go.

She looked up, her voice low.

"Ann . . . this book—it's not just a wake-up call, is it?"

I met her gaze. "No. And what's even more important—it's only the beginning. This is just Volume One."

Her brows lifted slightly. "And the end?"

I nodded.

"Yes. *Trumpet I* takes us through Revelation chapters 1 through 11. But the rest—the rise of the beast, America's fate, the Battle of Armageddon, and the glorious return of Christ—that's all in *The Trumpet II: The Prophecy Continues—America's Final Hour Unveiled*, covering chapters 12 to 22."

She paused. "So Volume One is a warning?"

Again, I met her gaze.

"No. It's an invitation."

She leaned in.

"An invitation to what?"

Softly, I answered, "To choose. Not just where we stand in history . . . but where we'll stand in eternity."

A MOMENT OF DECISION

Irene exhaled. "We've just walked through chapters of prophecy—signs in the heavens, global unrest, deception running wild. You've made it clear we're closer to the edge than most realize."

"That's right. But none of it matters if people don't respond. Prophecy isn't a history lesson—it's a personal call to transformation."

I opened my Bible and pointed to Revelation 3:20:

> Behold, I stand at the door, and knock: if any man hears My voice, and opens the door, I will come in to him, and will dine with him, and he with Me. (Revelation 3:20)

Irene whispered, reading aloud, "Jesus is knocking."

"Yes," I said, looking at her. "But only we can open the door."

THE URGENCY OF SALVATION

Her voice was thoughtful now. "If time really is short, if prophecy is unfolding all around us—why do people hesitate?"

"Because deception is strong. And comfort . . . is addictive. Most people believe they have more time. But Scripture is clear—later might never come."

I turned to Isaiah 55:6:

> Seek the LORD while He may be found, call upon Him while He is near. (Isaiah 55:6)

I looked at Irene intently. "There will come a moment when the window of grace closes. Just like the ark in Noah's day. Once it's shut . . . it's shut."

She nodded, solemn. "Then the time is now."

"Yes, Irene," I whispered. "The time is now."

THE INVITATION

I opened the Bible again to a familiar place—John 3:16—and turned it toward her.

> For God so loved the world, that He gave His only begotten Son, that whosoever believes in Him should not perish, but have everlasting life. (John 3:16)

Irene's voice cracked slightly.

"So it's not about being good enough?"

"No. It's about faith. Surrender. Believing in Jesus and receiving the gift of salvation."

She blinked away the emotion.

"Then tell them, Ann. Tell them how."

How To Receive the Lord Jesus Christ as Your Lord and Savior

I nodded; heart full.

If you're reading this—dear reader—and feel the Holy Spirit nudging you—don't turn away. This is your moment.

1. **Acknowledge your need for salvation.**

For all have sinned and fall short of the glory of God. (Romans 3:23)

2. **Believe that Jesus is the only way.**

I am the way, the truth, and the life: no man comes unto the Father, but by Me. (John 14:6)

3. **Repent and turn to God.**

Repent, then, and turn to God, so that your sins may be wiped out. (Acts 3:19)

4. **Confess Jesus as your Lord and Savior.**

If you declare with your mouth, 'Jesus is Lord,' and believe in your heart that God raised Him from the dead, you will be saved. (Romans 10:9)

A Simple Prayer of Salvation

Simply pray this out loud:

"Heavenly Father, I come to You today. I confess that I am a sinner and I need Your forgiveness. I believe Jesus Christ died for me, and that He rose again. I receive Him as my Lord and Savior. Come into my life, fill me with Your Holy Spirit, and help me to follow You all my days. In Jesus' name, Amen."

Irene smiled, tears in her eyes.

"That's it?"

I nodded, returning the smile.

"That's it. Salvation is simple. It's a gift."

A NEW BEGINNING

Irene gently closed the manuscript, then spoke softly. "So . . . what happens next?"

I glanced out the window. The world outside looked the same—but we both knew everything had changed.

"I believe this is more than the end of a book," I said. "It's the beginning of a new chapter in human history."

She tilted her head.

"What do you mean?"

"When you view prophecy through a Hebrew lens, you begin to see patterns—cycles. Every year, when the last chapter of the Torah is read, the scroll is immediately rolled back to Genesis. There's no ending—just a new beginning. Fresh understanding, fresh insight."

She nodded slowly, intrigued. "That reminds me of Isaiah 34:4:"

And all the host of heaven shall be dissolved, and the heavens shall be rolled together as a scroll: and all falls off from the vine, and as a falling fig from the fig tree. (Isaiah 34:4)

She continued. "Both a warning and a promise—warning to the wicked that their world will collapse, and a promise to the faithful that God will remake all things new."

Nodding. "I believe He'll then unroll something new—new heavens, a new earth. Just like autumn leaves signal a change of season, we're stepping into a time of divine transition."

"And yet," I added, turning to Jeremiah 8:7, "God says the stork, the swallow, the turtledove all know their appointed times . . . but His people do not."

Yea, the stork in the heaven knows her appointed times; and the turtle and the crane and the swallow observe the time of their coming; but My people know not the judgment of the LORD. (Jeremiah 8:7)

I continued. "Even in Jesus' day, the religious leaders didn't recognize the hour they were in."

FINAL WORDS

Irene looked down at the closed manuscript, holding it close.

"Ann . . . they need to hear this."

I met her eyes, steady and full of hope.

"Yes, Irene. And they need to be ready—because the story isn't over."

I smiled softly. "Volume Two is coming. And with it, the rest of the Revelation of Jesus Christ. The next chapter will not only shake the world—but also reveal the victory of the Lamb in full."

He who has ears to hear, let him hear what the Spirit says to the churches. (Revelation 2:7)

The door is still open—but not for long.

Will you enter—dear reader—before it closes?

Acknowledgments

THANK YOU, GOD, OUR HEAVENLY FATHER. It is because of You that I have become a passionate student of Your Holy Scriptures.

I have always longed for a deeper understanding of the Bible and a more intimate knowledge of You. But it wasn't until I began studying the Holy Bible—King James Version, translated out of the original languages (Hebrew and Greek), with the previous translations diligently compared and revised, conformable to the edition of 1611, commonly known as the Authorized or King James Version—given to me over fifty years ago by my parents for my ninth birthday, that I truly found the fulfillment of those desires. Through the use of various study aids, and by reading and journaling through the Bible cover to cover, year after year, my longing was finally satisfied.

I am immediately grateful to my husband, Eric, for the opportunity to take on this task, which has shaped my life profoundly over these past few years. Thank you, Eric, for your honest feedback—despite the pain and frustration it sometimes caused us both. Your acceptance and partnership have made this book a serious contribution toward a life lived reflecting God's will.

Our intellectual comradeship has been unlike anything I have ever known. Our conversations about God have continually challenge and refined my work, making this book much stronger because of your encouragement.

To my parents, Charles and JoAnn: Words can never fully express how deeply I love and appreciate you both. Through every trial and triumph, you stood by Michael, Daniel, Joseph, and me with unwavering love and selfless sacrifice. I am forever grateful. I love you both—eternally.

To my sons: Matthew, John, and Jared:

To Matthew—you were the beginning of my true life journey, and for that, I am forever grateful.

To John and his beautiful extended family—your love and laughter brings light and ease into our lives.

To Jared—your honesty, your challenges, and your pursuit of truth continually inspire me to be better, purer, and more awake.

You, my sons, are the precious jewels of my life. Your very existence illuminates every breath I take.

To my Pastors John Kilpatrick and Brenda Kilpatrick: When I told God I needed more, He led me to you. Pastor John, your wisdom and leadership have guided my journey. And Brenda, your steadfast grace has deeply impacted me. Thank you both for walking in obedience and faithfully pouring into others—my life is forever changed.

To Evangelist Tiff and Judy Shuttlesworth: Thank you both for your unwavering devotion to God's Word. Tiff, your clear and powerful preaching and teaching on Bible prophecy ignited my passion for the end times. Judy, your steadfast support alongside him have deeply inspired me. I'm truly grateful for the influence you've both had on my spiritual journey.

And finally, to my Heavenly Father and my Lord Jesus Christ—thank You for placing within me the desire, energy, determination, and joy to pursue this calling. I am fully devoted and surrendered to You because You have always been fully devoted to me.

The Trumpet I: The Ancient Prophecy That Reveals America's Final Hour and *The Trumpet II: The Prophecy Continues—America's Final Hour Unveiled* are the outpouring of that devotion—a call to see, to understand, and to prepare. It is my prayer that these words stir every soul with urgency, awaken hope, and point to the promise and possibility found only in Christ.

If you have longed to truly understand God's Word . . .

If you have yearned for deeper insight into the Bible—and especially the Book of Revelation . . .

If you hunger for meaning, purpose, and direction in these final days . . .

Then this book is written for you.

Thank you for accepting the invitation.

May the journey you are about to begin draw you ever closer to the heart of God.

Author Photo © 2023 Edwin Wolfe

ABOUT THE AUTHOR—Lori Ann Moeszinger, affectionately known as "L," is the founder and creative force behind The Ridge Publishing Group and its family of imprints. A prolific American author, blogger, and publisher, Lori brings a passion for clarity, truth, and inspiration to everything she writes. Nestled in the lakeside beauty of Coeur d'Alene, Idaho, she draws daily inspiration from God's creation, her husbands' unwavering support, and the quiet companionship of their two beloved dogs.

Holding a Juris Doctorate in Law, along with an Associate's degree in Paralegal Studies, and a Bachelor's degree in Business Administration, Lori transitioned from a legal career to full-time authorship and publishing, embracing the freedom to pursue her calling. Since 2016, she has devoted her life to the study of biblical prophecy and Scripture, bringing both depth and urgency to her writing.

Under the byline L. A. Moeszinger, she writes extensively on business, law, and the publishing industry, helping authors bring their dreams to life. Under her full name, Lori Ann Moeszinger, she explores biblical truths, prophetic insights, and personal reflections rooted in faith. Her New Youniversity Chronicles and The Manhattan Diaries series showcase her versatile storytelling gifts across multiple genres and voices.

At the heart of all she writes is a deep conviction: that faith is the foundation for life, that blessings are to be shared, and that diligence is a divine calling. Her books are more than words—they are invitations to prepare, to believe, and to live with eternal purpose.

LATEST RELEASES

For More Information . . .

If you would like to explore more of what you've read in *The Trumpet*—or dive deeper into related teachings, prophetic studies, biblical insights, and the call to prepare for Christ's return—or if you're seeking salvation, discipleship, or a deeper understanding of God's end-time purposes, you are warmly invited to connect further. Write to:

The Ridge Publishing Group
P.O. Box 549
Coeur d'Alene, Idaho 83816

You can also discover the multifaceted worlds Lori Ann Moeszinger has woven through her books, blogs, and ministries. Each platform is designed to equip, inspire, and walk alongside you in your journey of faith, purpose, and readiness.

Parent Platforms:

RidgePublishingGroup.com—Home base for all Lori's imprints, books, publishing updates, and new releases.

PublisherAndHerWorld.com—Blog site offering publishing insights, author tools, and faith-based reflections for Christian writers.

Ministry Platforms:
GuardiansofBiblicalTruth.com—Focused on Bible teaching, prophecy, and end-time preparation.

Jesus-Says.com—Home of *Coffee with God*, featuring daily inspiration, personal testimonies, and Scripture-rooted teachings.

Author Platforms:
LAMoeszinger.com—Lori's personal author site with theological writings, spiritual reflections, and upcoming projects.

NewYouniversityChronicles.com—A movement for faith-driven personal growth through the *New Youniversity Chronicles* and *The Manhattan Diaries* book series.

ManhattanChronicles.com—Where urban life, cultural reflection, and spiritual depth meet.

Publishing and Writer Support Platforms:
AuthorsDoor.com—Tools, training, and encouragement for indie authors.

AuthorsRedDoor.com—A blog site for writers pursuing excellence in publishing, marketing and writing—offering wisdom, strategies, and encouragement.

Children, Young Adult, and Family Adventures:
EthanFoxBooks.com—Enter the world of Ethan Fox, where wonder meets character-building adventure.

KidsStagram.com—Creative content and blog posts for young readers and families.

STAY CONNECTED

We invite you to join our online communities and become part of a growing network of watchmen, believers, writers, seekers, and young adventurers preparing for what lies ahead. Explore, engage, and grow deeper through our private Facebook groups and social spaces:

- Ethan Fox KidsStagram Fan Zone—A creative and inspiring space for young readers, families, and fans of Ethan Fox's adventures.
- Publisher and Her World Forum—A supportive community for writers and publishing entrepreneurs seeking guidance, encouragement, and industry insights.

- Guardians of Biblical Truth Forum—A gathering place for believers to study Scripture, explore prophecy, share testimonies, and strengthen their walk with Christ.
- AuthorsDoor Strategy Forum—A mastermind group for authors and independent publishers dedicated to writing, marketing, and publishing strategies that make an impact.

You can find links to our social media spaces, as well as *free* newsletter subscriptions, resources, and more across our websites.

EXPLORE OUR YOUTUBE CHANNELS

Discover a rich library of content across nine unique YouTube channels under The Ridge Publishing Group umbrella. From biblical teaching and prophetic insight to author features and publishing resources, our channels include:

- Publisher Website
  - Publisher and Her World at Ridge Publishing Group
- Author Website
  - Live with LAM #Shorts
- Guardians of Biblical Truth
  - Guardians of Biblical Truths
  - Coffee with God! Jesus-Says #Shorts
- AuthorsDoor Group
  - AuthorsDoor Group
  - Authors Red Door #Shorts
- Ethan Fox Books
  - Ethan Fox Live
  - Ethan Fox KidsStagram Book Club Circle
  - KidsStagram Ethan Fox Books #Shorts

Each channel offers curated videos designed to inform, encourage, and equip viewers for deeper spiritual understanding and creative inspiration. Subscribe and journey with us through truth, storytelling, and timeless wisdom.

Stay watchful. Stay ready. Stay connected.

www.ingramcontent.com/pod-product-compliance
Lightning Source LLC
Chambersburg PA
CBHW020916140626
46545CB00015B/74